Praise for *Xcode 4 Unleashed*

"There are many great resources out there for learning iOS and Mac development that cover Objective-C and Cocoa. Xcode is an extremely important part of iOS and Mac development that often gets overlooked. You owe it to yourself to understand Xcode and all of its quirks and power user features to achieve maximum efficiency as a developer. *Xcode 4 Unleashed* can help you do just that."

—Tony Hillerson,
Member and Software Architect, Tackmobile.com

"Fritz Anderson's *Xcode Unleashed* series is the definitive guide to using Xcode. *Xcode 4 Unleashed* has been rewritten to cover the sweeping changes in recent versions of the product. I highly recommend this book to anyone who uses Xcode—newbies and grizzled veterans alike."

—Duncan Champney,
Director of Software Development, WareTo

Praise for *Xcode 3 Unleashed*

"I would recommend this book to anyone that is serious about programming on the Mac. It is an excellent resource; I plan to refer to it often."

—*Cortis Clark*

"I've been doing Mac OS X development for seven years, so I was surprised at how much new information I learned in this book. The details on building and the overview of Instruments were invaluable."

—*Dan Wood, Karelia Software*

"There isn't a better book on the market to understand Apple's powerful—yet free integrated development environment, Xcode. Fritz Anderson stands among the most literate programmers I know, simultaneously able to provide a high-level development narrative while delving into the countless crucial details that make up modern development. I recommend *Xcode 3 Unleashed* to both novices as an introduction and professionals as a reference."

—*Jonathan 'Wolf' Rentzsch, http://rentzsch.com*

"Whether you are new to programming on Mac OS X or a seasoned veteran, *Xcode 3 Unleashed* has something for you. The book is full of examples and practical information. I recommend this book for anyone doing serious development on Mac OS X 10.5."

—*Dave Dribin*

Fritz Anderson

Xcode® 4

UNLEASHED

 800 East 96th Street, Indianapolis, Indiana 46240 USA

Xcode® 4 Unleashed

ISBN-13: 978-0-672-33327-9
ISBN-10: 0-672-33327-9

The Library of Congress cataloging-in-publication data is on file.

Printed in the United States of America

First Printing May 2012

Trademarks

Warning and Disclaimer

Bulk Sales

Sams Publishing offers excellent discounts on this book when ordered in quantity for bulk purchases or special sales. For more information, please contact

U.S. Corporate and Government Sales
1-800-382-3419
corpsales@pearsontechgroup.com

For sales outside of the U.S., please contact

International Sales
international@pearson.com

Editor-in-Chief
Mark Taub

Acquisitions Editors
Trina MacDonald
Chuck Toporek

Managing Editor
Kristy Hart

Project Editor
Jovana San Nicolas-Shirley

Copy Editor
Apostrophe Editing Services

Indexer
Erika Millen

Proofreaders
Jess DeGabriele
Chrissy White

Technical Editors
Duncan Champney
Tony Hillerson
George Sealy
Rob Wittner

Publishing Coordinator
Olivia Basegio

Cover Designer
Gary Adair

Senior Compositor
Gloria Schurick

Contents at a Glance

Table of Contents

About the Author

Fritz Anderson has been writing software, books, and articles for Apple platforms since 1984. He has worked for research and development firms, consulting practices, and freelance. He was admitted to the Indiana bar, but thought better of it. He is now an iOS and Mac programmer for the Scholarly Technology department at the University of Chicago. He has two daughters.

Dedication

For Steve Jobs, who made my life's work possible,

and

for Kate and Bess, who made my life.

Acknowledgments

Only part of the effort that went into putting *Xcode 4 Unleashed* into your hands was spent at a text editor. I owe a debt of thanks to those without whom this book could not have been made.

Chuck Toporek, my editor, showed patience, good humor, and good sense in support of our second effort together. *Xcode 3.2 Unleashed* had reached nearly 400 pages when Apple announced Xcode 4, which would not see its first release for 8 months; major revisions spanned another 8. He encouraged a dispirited author through the long process of dumping everything, waiting, and starting again.

Chuck's assistant, Olivia Basegio, made sure the contracts, correspondence, (and advance payments!) all got through.

Trina MacDonald took over after Chuck left for Apple. She, and Jovana San Nicolas-Shirley, who oversaw production, were extremely accommodating with an author whose opinions on how to write a book are... exacting.

I'm especially grateful for the advice of the technical reviewers Chuck found for me. You did yeoman service in the face of a subject in rapid flux and saved me many embarrassments. Of course, any errors that remain are my own.

Quinn Dombrowski, boss and friend, took a kind interest in my book. She was generous with vacation time so I could get it done and patient when I began to fray under the strain of 60-hour weeks.

Bess and Kate bore more than daughters should of my doubts and frustrations, and were simply confident that I would do fine—which was all they needed to do.

We Want to Hear from You!

As the reader of this book, *you* are our most important critic and commentator. We value your opinion and want to know what we're doing right, what we could do better, what areas you'd like to see us publish in, and any other words of wisdom you're willing to pass our way.

You can email or write me directly to let me know what you did or didn't like about this book—as well as what we can do to make our books stronger.

Please note that I cannot help you with technical problems related to the topic of this book, and that due to the high volume of mail I receive, I might not be able to reply to every message.

When you write, please be sure to include this book's title and author as well as your name and phone number or email address. I will carefully review your comments and share them with the author and editors who worked on the book.

Email: feedback@samspublishing.com

Mail: Sams Publishing

         800 East 96th Street

         Indianapolis, IN 46240 USA

Reader Services

Visit our website and register this book at informit.com/register for convenient access to any updates, downloads, or errata that might be available for this book.

Introduction

IN THIS CHAPTER

▶ Introducing Xcode

▶ Understanding the goals of *Xcode 4 Unleashed*

▶ Considering organization

▶ Typographic conventions

Welcome to *Xcode 4 Unleashed*! This book shows you how to use Apple's integrated development environment to make great products with the least effort.

Xcode 4 is the descendant of a family of development tools dating back nearly 20 years to NeXT's ProjectBuilder. It started as a text editor, a user-interface designer, and a front end for UNIX development tools. It has become a sophisticated system for building applications and system software, with a multitude of features that leverage a comprehensive indexing system and subtle incremental parser to help you assemble the right code for your project—and get it right the first time.

That much power can be intimidating. My aim in *Xcode 4 Unleashed* is to demystify Xcode, giving you a gradual tour through examples that show you how you can use it day to day. If you come to Xcode 4 from previous versions, the changes may be overwhelming; Chapter 24, "Xcode 4 for Xcode 3 Veterans," is just for you, an introduction to where you can find the facilities you're accustomed to—even newcomers wanting a quick overview may find it useful.

How This Book Is Organized

First, a word on my overall plan for *Xcode 4 Unleashed*. This is a book about developer tools. If it teaches you something about how to use the Cocoa frameworks, or something about programming, that's fine, but that's incidental to showing you what Xcode can do.

Every tour needs a pathway, and every lesson needs a story. The first three parts of this book demonstrate Xcode through three applications—a command-line tool, an iOS app, and a Mac OS X application—that calculate and display some statistics in American football. None of the apps are useful; the graphical apps run almost entirely on sample data, but they demand enough of the development tools to give you a solid insight into how to use them.

The full code for the example programs is available online from www.informit.com/title/9780672333279. In the interest of space, I'll be showing only excerpts.

I'm using applications for iOS and a Mac OS X as examples, but read both Part II, "The Life Cycle of an iOS Application," and Part III, "Xcode for Mac OS X," even if you're interested only in one platform. The applications are only *stories*; the techniques apply to both platforms.

First Steps

In Part I, I'll take you from installing Xcode and running your first project, through basic debugging skills. You'll work through a small command-line application. The application may be simple, but you'll learn foundational skills you'll need before adding the complexity of graphical apps.

▶ **Chapter 1, "Getting Xcode"**: Some things to consider before you download Xcode 4; two ways to download and install it.

▶ **Chapter 2, "Kicking the Tires"**: Your first look at Xcode, setting a trivial project up and running it.

▶ **Chapter 3, "Simple Workflow and Passive Debugging"**: You'll write, build, and run a simple application and respond to a crash.

▶ **Chapter 4, "Active Debugging"**: You'll take charge of debugging by setting breakpoints and tracing through the program. I'll show you how to organize your workspace.

▶ **Chapter 5, "Compilation"**: A pause for a description of the process of building an application.

▶ **Chapter 6, "Adding a Library Target"**: Add a library target to a project and learn how to build a product from multiple targets.

▶ **Chapter 7, "Version Control"**: Why source control is important and how to take advantage of Xcode's built-in support for versioning through Git and Subversion.

The Life Cycle of an iOS Application

Part II tells the story of a small iPhone app and how to use Apple's developer tools to build it. It introduces you to the graphical editor for user interfaces and shows how to profile an app to optimize its speed and memory burden.

- Chapter 8, "**Starting an iOS Application**": You'll start by creating an iOS project and learn the Model/View/Controller design at the core of Cocoa on iOS and Mac OS X alike.

- Chapter 9, "**An iOS Application: Model**": Design a Core Data schema and supplement it with your own code.

- Chapter 10, "**An iOS Controller**": Create a controller to link your model to the on-screen views. On the way, I'll tell you about refactoring and Xcode's continual error-checking.

- Chapter 11, "**Building a New View**": You'll design the user-interface views for your app with the integrated Interface Builder and take advantage of source-code completion.

- Chapter 12, "**Adding Table Cells**": While adding an onscreen component to your app, you debug memory management and control how Xcode builds, runs, and tests your apps through the Scheme editor.

- Chapter 13, "**Unit Testing**": Unit testing can speed development and make your apps more reliable. I'll show you how Xcode supports it as a first-class part of the development process.

- Chapter 14, "**Measurement and Analysis**": Use Instruments to track down performance and memory bugs.

- Chapter 15, "**Storyboard**": Simplifying iOS development with Storyboard, which enables you to specify the whole structure of your app in just one file.

- Chapter 16, "**Provisioning**": The three things you must understand to put your app on a device, from testing to the App Store.

Xcode for Mac OS X

Part III shifts focus to Mac OS X development. Some concepts are more important to Mac OS X than iOS, but you'll be learning techniques you can use whatever your platform.

- Chapter 17, "**Starting a Mac OS X Application**": Carrying iOS components over to Mac OS X, Automatic Reference Counting (ARC), and menus and how to link them to the responder chain.

- Chapter 18, "**Wiring a Mac Application with Bindings**": As you build a popover window, you'll use Mac OS X bindings to simplify the link between your data and the screen. With autoresizing, you can set up views to resize themselves.

- Chapter 19, "**A Custom View for Mac OS X**": Add a custom view to your app to see how Interface Builder can lay it out and configure it, even though it's not a standard Cocoa component.

▶ **Chapter 20, "Localization and Autolayout"**: How you can translate your Mac and iOS apps into other languages. I'll show you how to use Lion's autolayout feature to give your views the right size and layout no matter how their contents change.

▶ **Chapter 21, "Bundles and Packages"**: You'll master the fundamental structure of most Mac and iOS products and how both platforms use the Info.plist file to fit apps into the operating system.

▶ **Chapter 22, "Frameworks"**: Package and share a complete subprogram you can incorporate into any Mac OS X application.

▶ **Chapter 23, "Property Lists"**: Learn the basic JSON-like file type for storing data in both Mac OS X and iOS.

Xcode Tasks

Part IV moves on to topics that deserve a more concentrated treatment than Parts II and III.

▶ **Chapter 24, "Xcode 4 for Xcode 3 Veterans"**: Written from the point of view of developers moving from Xcode 3's document-based approach to development to Xcode 4's "browser" model, this chapter can help you find what you need from Apple's developer tools.

▶ **Chapter 25, "Documentation in Xcode"**: How Xcode gives you both immediate help on API and browsable details on the concepts of Cocoa development. Find out how you can add your own documentation to the system.

▶ **Chapter 26, "The Xcode Build System"**: I'll show you the fundamental rules and tools behind how Xcode goes from source files to executable products.

▶ **Chapter 27, "Instruments"**: Using Apple's timeline profiler, you can go beyond basic performance and memory diagnostics to a comprehensive look at how your program uses its resources.

▶ **Chapter 28, "Snippets"**: A roundup of tips, traps, and features to help you get the most from the developer tools.

Appendixes

The appendixes contain references to help you get your bearings on Objective-C, master the build system, choose the right starting points for your project, and find help and support.

▶ **Appendix A, "Objective-C"**: A summary of the core programming language for development on Apple platforms, progressing from the simple additions it makes to C, to the specialized features that support Apple frameworks.

▶ **Appendix B, "Some Build Variables"**: The most important configuration and environment variables from Xcode's build system.

▶ **Appendix C, "Project and Target Templates"**: Where to start your new projects and files.

▶ **Appendix D, "Resources"**: A compendium of books, tools, and Internet resources to support your development efforts.

About Versions

This book was written over most of a year, through the Fall of 2011. In that period Apple issued three major revisions of Xcode, as well as major revisions to both iOS and Mac OS X. *Xcode 4 Unleashed* covers Xcode 4.2, the first version with full support for iOS 5 and Mac OS X 10.7 Lion.

To demonstrate legacy techniques, Part II targets iOS 4.3, with an excursion into iOS 5 for Storyboard. Part III covers a Lion application. Where possible, I've noted changes introduced in Xcode 4.3.

Conventions

This book observes a number of typographic and verbal conventions.

▶ Human-interface elements, such as menu items and button labels, are shown **like this**.

▶ Filenames and programming constructs are shown `like this`. This will sometimes get tricky, as when I refer to the product of the "Hello World" *project* (plain text, because it's just a noun) as the *file* `Hello World`.

▶ Text that you type in will be shown **`like this`**.

▶ A new term is called out *like this*.

You'll do some command-line work in the terminal. Some of the content is wider than this page, so input lines break with backslashes (\) at the ends. Long output lines break simply by splitting them and indenting the continuations. When that output includes long file paths, ellipses (...) replace components, leaving the significant parts.

About the sample code in this book: A significant portion of the code I'll have you write is wrong. As an experienced programmer, you will be in pain and want to correct it. Leave it alone; the errors are intentional.

I'll refer to the location of various development resources as the `/Developer` directory. Xcode 4.3 moved that directory into the Xcode app itself. You can find the additional developer applications in the **Xcode** menu.

For many, many years the Macintosh had a one-button mouse (don't laugh—most purchasers didn't know what a mouse was; try pushing the wrong button on an old Mac mouse). Now it has four ways to effect an alternative mouse click: You can use the right button on an actual mouse; you can hold down the Control key and make an ordinary click; you can hold down two fingers while clicking a multitouch trackpad (increasingly common even on desktop Macs); or you can tap at a designated corner of a multitouch trackpad. And there are more variations as you run through the configurations. Unless the distinction actually matters, the text simply calls for a "right-click," and you can sort it out.

PART I

First Steps

IN THIS PART

Getting Xcode

Before You Do Anything

Xcode 4 is a tool for building applications that use features from the most recent operating systems (OS) for the Mac and iPhone/iPad. To the first readers of this book, that means Mac OS X 10.6 and 10.7; and iOS 5.1. Xcode 4 doesn't support earlier software-development kits (SDKs) or PowerPC. (And you cannot test PowerPC apps on a Lion machine.)

If you need to use earlier SDKs, you must use Xcode 3.2 on a Mac booted from a 10.6 partition. Users have reported that Xcode 3.2.6 seems not to crash on Lion, but it won't install on a Lion system, so you must install Xcode 3 before you upgrade to Lion. Apple doesn't support it, and nobody has done exhaustive quality assurance on the 10.7/3.2.6 combination, so nobody recommends it.

Apple's position is that its operating systems are backward compatible, so you can always build against the SDK for the latest OS; if you don't use any API that's newer than your target OS supports, you won't have any trouble. This is true, unless you need to use `libcrypto`, which was replaced with an incompatible version in the 10.6 SDK, making it impossible to run a 10.6-linked application on 10.5 if it relies on that library. If you can't use the alternative APIs, you're stuck with Xcode 3.2.6.

People have asked whether they can pluck earlier SDKs from Xcode 3 installations and drop them into Xcode 4. Again, it appears to work but ultimately doesn't: The older SDKs rely on compilers and runtime libraries that are simply not available in Xcode 4.

Requirements

Apple is cagey about what the operating requirements are for Xcode, and that's understandable because it depends entirely on your usage and preferences.

▶ If you want the simple installer you can get from the App Store, you must be running Mac OS X 10.7 Lion. Apple strongly recommends using Lion for Xcode 4.2.

   If you run Snow Leopard (10.6), you must get the installer package from the Mac or iOS Dev Center web sites reachable from http://developer.apple.com/. The Snow Leopard installation does not include the 10.7 SDK, so you cannot develop for Lion-only features nor use Automatic Reference Counting.

▶ The Xcode application you download from the App Store is just under 2GB in size (at the time of this writing).

▶ How much disk space the installed Xcode takes up depends on what SDKs you have and what documentation sets you download. Allow 9GB.

▶ Xcode can be run in 1GB of memory, but don't expect to do much more than look at it. For the examples in this book, 2GB should be enough, but for medium-sized projects, a rule of thumb is that you need approximately 2GB, plus another 500MB for each processor core in your machine. Get more RAM if you can; most people haven't reached the point of diminishing returns.

▶ Xcode can run on a 32-bit processor, but a processor of that generation would probably be too slow to perform satisfactorily. The minima for this book are 64-bit, dual-core, and 1.8 GHz. More is better.

▶ Bigger—particularly, wider—displays are better. This book was written using a MacBook Air with 1440 pixels' horizontal resolution. With the display-management techniques you'll learn in this book, it's comfortable most of the time. A MacBook Pro (1920 x 1200) also works well.

The bottom-of-the-line Mac mini ($599 in the United States) is fine for the purposes of *Xcode 4 Unleashed*.

Installing Xcode

If you run Lion, obtaining Xcode is easy: Find it in the Mac App Store, enter your Apple ID and password, and download it. It's free. If you run Snow Leopard or simply want more options, see the "Through an Installer Package" section later in this chapter.

The download is just under 2GB. When the download finishes, you have the Xcode application file in your /Applications directory. Double-click it, and let Xcode complete its installation. You need to provide an administrator's credentials.

Unlike other installer packages you may have run, there are no options. Prior to Xcode 4.1, the installer offered customizations such as the directory that would receive the installation and what components would be included. No more; Xcode and the accompanying tools go into /Developer on your boot drive. All available SDKs and platforms are installed, along with command-line versions of the developer tools.

If a /Developer directory exists from an earlier Xcode, Xcode will offer to move it to the trash. This is optional. If you don't trust an upgrade install, you can get a fresh one by uninstalling Xcode and putting /Developer in the trash. You learn how to uninstall Xcode later in this chapter.

If you need to reinstall or install the developer tools on another computer, you can go to the Mac App Store again, and download Xcode to that computer.

After you install Xcode, you can rename the /Developer directory or even move it to another volume. However, throughout this book I'll assume that Xcode is installed in /Developer.

> **NOTE**
>
> With Xcode 4.3, Apple abolished the /Developer directory and the separate installer altogether. I'll direct you to some files in the /Developer that will be folded into the Xcode package, to be accessed through Xcode's menus. Read the Xcode release notes for the latest instructions.

What You Get

What did the installer do? The most obvious thing is the /Developer directory. It contains applications such as Xcode and Instruments; platform and SDK directories for headers, libraries, and tools specific to the various supported versions of iOS and Mac OS X; a private /usr/bin directory containing the command-line tools that Xcode uses internally; and some of the documentation for Xcode and the platforms it supports.

You got some system tools, including the Git version-control suite and primitive, kernel-level software to support the Instruments application's access to the internals of running applications.

There is also a UNIX development suite. The compilers and development tools that Xcode uses for its own purposes are installed in the /Developer tree. However, you may want to do command-line builds of other UNIX software. The installer puts compilers, linkers, and the like into /usr/bin and headers and libraries into /usr/include and /usr/lib.

> **NOTE**
>
> Xcode and its predecessor, Project Builder, have been evolving for more than 10 years, which means that while the subdirectory names are evocative, they are mostly historical. The SDKs directory contains software-development kits for Mac OS X, except for specialty tools for Mac development, which are inside the Platforms directory. The SDKs for iOS are also inside Platforms. The Documentation directory contains documentation on Xcode and the rudiments of Mac OS X, but the meat of it is in /Library/Developer/Documentation.

Most of the documentation isn't installed. Xcode downloads it the first time you run it. There are gigabytes of it; it changes more frequently than the developer tools—and you may not want it all—so it's not practical to bundle it into the Xcode installer. If you need anything beyond the basics (such as for older SDKs), see the **Documentation** tab in the **Downloads** panel of the Preferences window. Chapter 25, "Documentation in Xcode," covers documentation in depth.

Similarly, the installer doesn't include tools, such as a version of the iOS Simulator, for targeting devices that predate the current iOS SDK or debugging support for connected devices back to iOS 3. Together, these add up to more than a gigabyte, and Apple saw no point in bloating disk space and download times for facilities that not everyone uses. See the **Downloads** panel of the Preferences window, **Components** tab, to browse and fetch the available components.

Removing Xcode

Your life has changed. The honeymoon is over. You've had your look, and you're done. You've decided to edit a theatrical feature and you need the space. You're giving your Mac to your daughter in art school. For whatever reason, you're done with Xcode. How do you get rid of it?

If this were a normal Mac application, uninstallation would be simple: Drag it into the Trash. (In fact, with Xcode 4.3, that's what you do.) Xcode is not a normal Mac application. It installs tools, resources, and configuration files all through your hard drive. Throwing the Developer folder away will get rid of most of it but not all.

Apple has provided for this. Look in /Developer/Library. There you'll find a UNIX executable file named uninstall-devtools. If you have administrative privileges, open a Terminal window, type **sudo** and a space, and drag the file in. (Don't set the working directory in the /Developer tree; uninstall-devtools will refuse to run.) The Perl script in the file will crawl through your hard drive removing (almost) everything Xcode installed. This will still leave a skeleton of the Developer directory.

> **NOTE**
>
> You can also find a file named uninstall-developer-folder. That is not the file you are looking for. It supports the working of uninstall-devtools.

Now drag Developer into the Trash, and empty it.

Apple Developer Programs

If you run Lion, you can pick up Xcode 4 for free and start developing Mac OS X and iOS software. If your interest is in distributing Mac software on your own, your preparation is done: Build your apps, burn them to CDs, put them on the Internet, and good luck.

However, if you want to distribute your work on the Mac or iOS App Store—or if you want to test your iOS app on a device—you must go further. You need to pay for a membership in the Mac or iOS Developer Program. (If you need to, you can join both.)

Apple's policies and methods for joining developer programs are subject to change, so the following is an overview. Start by browsing to `http://developer.apple.com/`. Prominently featured are links to join the iOS and Mac developer programs. The programs will give you:

- ▶ Access to prerelease software, including operating systems and developer tools.

- ▶ Access to the parts of the developer forums (`http://devforums.apple.com/`) that cover nondisclosed topics.

- ▶ Two incidents with Developer Technical Support (DTS), Apple engineers who can advise you on development strategies and help you with troubleshooting. This is the only official, guaranteed way to get help from Apple. If you have the time, by all means go to a developer forum or mailing list first (you can find lots of leads in Appendix D, "Resources"), but if that fails, DTS is the best choice.

- ▶ The right to submit your applications for sale in the Mac or iOS App Store.

- ▶ In the case of iOS, the right to load your app into a device for debugging purposes (see Chapter 16, "Provisioning," for details).

Make your choice (whichever you choose, you'll be offered both programs), and you will be taken to a page with an **Enroll Now** button, citing the cost of a year's membership ($99 in the United States as of this writing).

The next step is to establish your status as a "registered Apple developer." Registered developers have few privileges beyond having a persistent record with Apple that can be used to sign up for developer programs. (There are a limited number of resources that your assent to terms and conditions entitles you to, most notably a free copy of Xcode 3.) If you're already registered, say so, and skip to the sign-up process. If you're not, present your Apple ID (such as you might use with iTunes)—or get one—fill out marketing and demographic questionnaires, and agree to the terms and conditions of Apple programs. They'll send you an email you can use to verify your contact information.

When you finish, you have your choice of programs. Select all you are interested in and can afford; the iOS and Mac programs are separate charges, and there's no discount. There's also a free Safari program, which enables you to develop and sign extensions for the desktop Safari web browser.

Next you have program-specific licenses to agree to. When that's done, you're a member.

Through an Installer Package

Before Xcode 4.1, Apple distributed Xcode only through a downloadable Installer package. Depending on whether a beta Xcode is available, or it seems, upon Apple's mood, you can get your hands on an Xcode installer package. As I write this, Apple provides Xcode 4.2 installer packages for Snow Leopard and Lion through the iOS and Mac Dev Centers.

The installer gives you more options. As you progress through the installation sequence, you will come to a page of options, as shown in Figure 1.1.

▶ **Essentials** aren't optional—they consist of Xcode, the build tools it needs to work, and the associated applications such as the Instruments profiler. You do have a choice of where to install it. Ordinarily, Xcode is installed in the /Applications directory on your boot volume. Click the pop-up menu under the **Location** column to see other choices or to use a save-file sheet to select another name and place. The location can be on any volume you choose. One reason to designate a different location would be if you had a previous installation of Xcode that you wanted to preserve. It's okay to have more than one developer-tools folder. They won't interfere.

▶ **System Tools** are auxiliary UNIX commands that must be installed on your boot volume. This includes the Git suite of version-control commands and the underpinnings of Instruments. You can choose not to install them if you have already installed them all (perhaps from a later version of the Xcode installer) and have reason not to replace them.

▶ **UNIX Development** includes compilers, linkers, and other development tools for the command line. These are substantially identical to the ones installed in the Essentials package, so why this separate option? The tools Xcode uses are all contained in the /Developer/usr directory, so they get put wherever the Xcode directory is. The Unix Development tools go into /usr/bin and related directories, where you can find them if you need to build software from the command line without resorting to Xcode—such as if you check out an open-source project and build it with the make command.

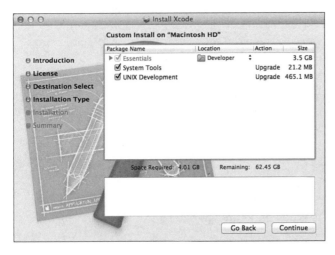

FIGURE 1.1   If you obtain Xcode through an installer package, you have some options on what components you can install and the placement of the Xcode directory.

▶ **Documentation** doesn't install any documentation. If you choose this option, the installer will set up Xcode so that after you install it, it will download the documentation for the SDKs you have. This can run up to 3 or 4 gigabytes, so you may choose to rely on online resources instead and uncheck this option. The documentation system will still work; it will just be slower and rely on your having an Internet connection.

Summary

This is a shorter chapter than it would have been if it discussed Xcode 3 or even 4.0. For most people, the best way to get and install Xcode is through the Mac App Store. It's relatively quick (it cut a lot of volatile and non-essential packages from the initial download), it's easy, and it's completely free.

Developing for Apple platforms is a little more complicated if you want to install an iOS app, even for testing, or to distribute your work through an App Store. That requires a program membership, and you saw what the options are and how to proceed.

Now that you have a usable installation of Xcode, it's time to see what you have.

Kicking the Tires

Now you have Xcode. It's time to start it up to see what it looks like.

Starting Xcode

The developer tools are all in the /Developer directory at the root of your boot drive. Go there in the Finder, and select the Applications directory. You see a few applications and a few folders. You're interested in two of them: Xcode, which is what this book is about; and Instruments, a sophisticated memory and performance profiler that you'll be seeing a lot of.

You'll be using both constantly, so you need both in the Dock at the bottom of your main screen. Drag Xcode and Instruments to the Dock—take care to drop them *between* icons, and not *on* them. You can now close that Finder window: It will be a long, long time before you need to return to it.

Now click the Xcode icon. It bounces to show Xcode is being launched, and soon you'll see the Welcome to Xcode window (see Figure 2.1).

If this is the first time you've ever run Xcode, the table on the right will be empty (No Recents); as you accumulate projects, the table will contain references to them, so you have a quick way to get back to your work.

On the left are other options:

▶ **Create a new Xcode project:** This is obvious enough; it's how you start work on a new product. You're about to do this, but hold off for the moment. You could also select **File→New→Project...** (⇧⌘N).

▶ **Connect to a repository:** Xcode recognizes that source control management is now essential to even the most trivial of projects. Your development effort might not start with your own work but with collaborative work pulled in from a source repository. Use this link to start.

▶ **Learn about using Xcode:** This links to Apple's documentation for Xcode. Apple's documentation is generally good, and for iOS and Mac OS X subjects, it's essential.

▶ **Go to Apple's developer portal:** This launches your browser and takes you to `http://developer.apple.com/`, the portal you followed if you signed up for a developer program. You'll be going back: If you want to sell through Apple's Mac App Store, or do any development on an actual iOS device, you must pass through the gateways Apple has set up.

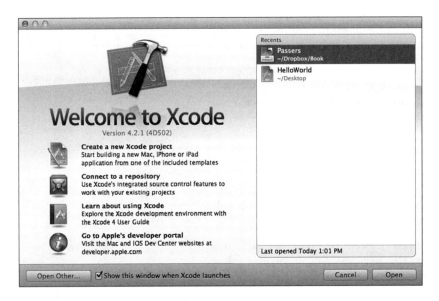

FIGURE 2.1   The Welcome to Xcode window lists the projects you most recently worked on and offers links to tutorials and documentation to get you started.

If you have an Xcode project that isn't listed in the Recents list, you can locate it through the get-file sheet offered by the **Open Other...** button. You can do the same thing with the **File→Open...** (⌘O) command. And if you tire of seeing this window, uncheck **Show this window when Xcode launches**; you can always get it back with **Window→Welcome to Xcode** (⇧⌘1).

> **NOTE**
>
> "Show this window when Xcode launches" is not quite accurate. If you had a project open when you last quit Xcode, it reopens automatically when you start it up again, and the welcome window won't appear.

Hello World

Just to get oriented, start with the simplest imaginable example project—so simple, you won't have to do any coding.

A New Project

Click the **Create a new Xcode project** link. Xcode opens an empty Workspace window and drops the New Project Assistant sheet in front of it (see Figure 2.2). Select **Mac OS X→Application** from the list on the left, and then select the **Command Line Tool** template from the icons that appear on the right. Click **Next**.

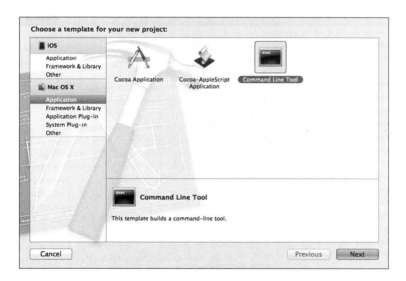

FIGURE 2.2   The New Project Assistant leads you through the creation of an Xcode project. First, you specify the kind of product you want to produce.

The next panel asks for the name of the project and the kind of command-line tool you want. Type **Hello World** in the **Product Name** field, and set the **Type** pop-up to C. Click **Next**. Finally, a put-file sheet appears, so you can select a directory to put the project into. For this example, select your Desktop. One more thing—*uncheck* the box labeled **Create local git repository for this project**. Source control (Chapter 7, "Version Control") is a good thing, but let's not deal with it in this trivial example. Click **Create**.

If you look on your Desktop, you can see that Xcode has created a folder named Hello World. The project name you specified is used in several places.

▶ It's the name of the project *directory* that contains your project files.

▶ It's the name of the project *document* (`Hello World.xcodeproj`) itself.

▶ It's the name of the *product*—in this case a command-line tool named `Hello World`.

▶ It's the name of the *target* that builds the product. I'll get into the concept of a target later; for now, think of it as the set of files that go into a product and a specification of how it is built.

▶ It's the name of the *target's* directory inside the *project's* directory.

▶ Suitably modified, it's the name of the `man`-file template for the tool (`Hello World.1`).

After you make your choices, Xcode unmasks the workspace for the Hello World project. (Figure 2.3). Don't look at it too closely just yet. Xcode starts you off with a view of the settings that control how `Hello World` is to be built. This is useful information, but for now, it's just details.

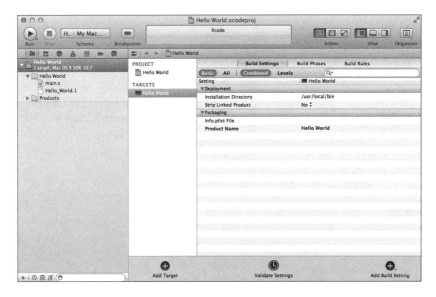

FIGURE 2.3   After you make your choices for the new project, Xcode reveals the Workspace window.

More interesting is the program code itself. The left column of the window is called the *Navigator area*. Find main.c in the list, and click it (see Figure 2.4). The Editor area, which fills most of the window, now displays the contents of `main.c`. This is the code for the canonical simplest-example program, known as "Hello, World."

The Navigator area displays many different things in the course of development—it's not just a file listing. It can display analyses and searches and build logs. Which list you see often depends on what Xcode wants to show you; you can choose for yourself by clicking the tiny icons in the bar at the top of the Navigator area. Hovering the mouse pointer over them shows you the names of the various views.

In this book, you'll meet all of them. For now, you care only about the Project navigator, the file list Xcode starts you with. Feel free to click the other icons, but to keep up with this example, be sure to return to the Project navigator, as shown in Figure 2.4.

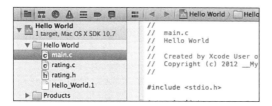

FIGURE 2.4   Clicking the name of an editable file in the Project navigator displays its contents in the Editor area.

Quieting Xcode Down

Xcode is a tool set that contains everything its creators could think of to provide a powerful, helpful environment for writing iOS and Mac OS X applications. Often, you barely need to begin a task, and Xcode offers to finish it for you. It will usually be right. I use these features all the time. I recommend them.

You're going to turn all of it off.

Automatic completions and indentations and code decorations and code fixes are great, once you know what's going on, but an automaton that snatches your work out of your hands, however helpfully, is straight out of *The Sorcerer's Apprentice*.

Better to start with what *you* want to do; when you're confident of what that is, then you have the discretion and control to direct Xcode as it helps you.

So you need to damp Xcode down a bit. You do all of this in Xcode's Preferences window, which you can summon with **Xcode→Preferences** (⌘**comma**). The Preferences window divides into panels, which you select with the icons at the top of the window.

To start, make sure the **General** panel is visible. Under **Issues**, uncheck **Show live issues**.

Next, select the **Text Editing** panel, which has two tabs. Select the **Editing** tab, and uncheck **Show: Code folding ribbon** and all the options under **Code completion:**.

In the **Indentation** tab, turn off **Line wrapping: Wrap lines to editor width** and the **Syntax-aware indenting** section.

Now Xcode mostly stays out of your way as you explore.

Building and Running

The program in main.c is correct and runnable. To prove it, select **Product→Run** (⌘**R**). Almost instantly, a heads-up window ("bezel") appears to tell you Build Succeeded. Xcode proceeds to run your program.

THE DEVELOPER TOOLS GROUP

If you're not an admin user for your Mac, the first time you debug or profile an application after logging in, you'll see a Security dialog, asking for the username and password for "a user in the 'Developer Tools' group." The reason is that developer tools are privileged to inspect the inner state of the programs they produce, and technically, that's a security breach. You have to authorize it. Enter an administrator's credentials; the privilege lasts until you log out.

You can shut the dialog up for good (and keep a nonadmin user from knowing an administrator's password) by adding your user account to the Developer Tools group. Open the Terminal application (at /Applications/Utilities/Terminal) and use the dscl (Directory Service command-line) utility:

```
sudo dscl . append /Groups/_developer GroupMembership username
```

where *username* is the short name of the account you want to authorize. You must be logged in to an account authorized to use sudo.

Things happen rapidly from here. A new area, the *Debug area*, appears at the bottom of your Workspace window. It has two panels—see Chapter 3, "Simple Workflow and Passive Debugging," for more details. For now, look at the panel on the right. It contains a lot of legal prose, but at the bottom you see the following:

Hello, World!
Program ended with exit code: 0

See Figure 2.5. The line in bold is the output of the printf() statement in main.c. Success.

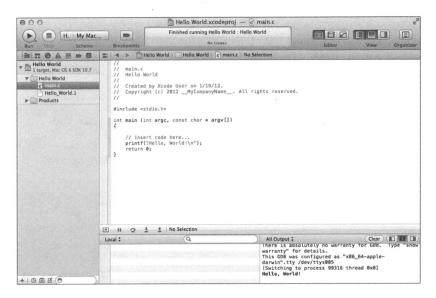

FIGURE 2.5   When you run Hello World, the Debug area appears, showing some legal language and the output of the program.

NOTE

The Debug area takes up space, and a good program doesn't crowd your work—whatever's in the Editor area—out of the window. In the toolbar at the top of the Workspace window, you will find a segmented control labeled **View** (see Figure 2.6). Each segment shows a schematic of the areas that might impinge on the Workspace window. Click the middle segment, which indicates an area at the bottom of the window, and the Debug area goes away.

FIGURE 2.6   The **View** control in the Workspace window's toolbar controls what areas are visible—in this case, the Navigation and Debug areas. To dismiss or recall the Debug area, click the middle segment.

The Real Thing

What Xcode just produced for you is an actual, executable application, not a simulation. To prove it, open the Terminal application. (You can find it at /Applications/Utilities/ Terminal, and you'd be well advised to add Terminal to your Dock.)

In Xcode, find the Hello World product in the Project navigator by clicking the disclosure triangle next to the Products folder icon. Drag the Hello World icon into the Terminal window, switch to Terminal, and press the Return key. (The path, to a file deep in a directory for build products, is remarkably long, but Terminal takes care of the necessary escaping.) "Hello, World!" appears.

If you want access to the executable file, select it in the Project navigator; then select **File→Show in Finder**—also available in the contextual menu shown when you right-click the Hello World icon. A window opens in the Finder showing you the file.

You're done! You can close the Workspace window (**File→Close Project** [⌥⌘W]) or quit Xcode entirely (**Xcode→Quit Xcode** [⌘Q]).

Getting Rid of It

There is nothing magical about an Xcode project. It's just a directory on your hard drive. If you don't want it any more, drag it to the trash. It's gone. It won't even show up in the Recents list in the Welcome to Xcode window or in the **File→Open Recent** menu.

That's it.

Okay, yes, the build products of the project still stick around, in a warren of directories inside ~/Library/Developer/Xcode. They aren't many or large in this case, but there's a principle involved. If you want them gone, the best way is to have Xcode remove them for you. With your Workspace window frontmost, select **Product→Clean** (⇧⌘K), and it will be done.

Summary

In this chapter, you had your first look at Xcode and discovered that it doesn't bite. You saw how to create a simple project—one you didn't even have to edit. You saw what happens when you run a project in Xcode, how to close a project and quit Xcode, and at last you got rid of the project entirely.

Next, we'll start doing some real work.

CHAPTER 3

Simple Workflow and Passive Debugging

This chapter begins your use of Xcode in earnest. Here's where I introduce the problem that is the basis for all the example code in this book.

The problem is the calculation of *passer ratings*. In American/Canadian football, quarterbacks advance the ball by throwing (passing) it to other players. The ball may be caught (received, a good thing) by someone on his own team, in which case the ball is advanced (yardage, more is better), possibly to beyond the goal line (a touchdown, the object of the game); or it may be caught by a member of the opposing team (intercepted, a bad thing).

Statistics are kept of all these things, over the course of a game, a season, or a career. But those are four numbers, and everybody wants a figure-of-merit, a single scale that says (accurately or not) who is the better passer. The National Football League and the Canadian Football League have a formula for passer ratings, yielding a scale running from 0 to (oddly) 158.3. A quarterback who rates 100 has had a good day.

As in Chapter 2, "Kicking the Tires," you start with a command-line project. Start Xcode and click **Create a new Xcode project**, or select **File→New→Project...** (⇧⌘N). In the New Project Assistant sheet, select a Mac OS X Command Line Tool, and name the tool `passer-rating`. For **Type:** again choose C.

Another difference: When you see the get-file sheet to select the location for the new project, check the box labeled **Create local git repository for this project**. Git is a *version-control system*, an essential part of modern development. You'll learn all about it in Chapter 7, "Version Control," but now is the time to start.

Again, you see target settings, which you can ignore for now. Instead, mouse over to the Project navigator on the left side of the Workspace window, and select `main.c`.

As you type closing parentheses, brackets, and braces, the corresponding opening character is briefly highlighted in yellow.

```
#import <stdio.h>
#import "rating.h"    // to be written soon

int main (int argc, const char * argv[])
{
    int         nArgs;
    do {
        int     comps, atts, yards, TDs;
        printf("comps, atts, yards, TDs: ");
        nArgs = scanf("%d %d %d %d %d",
                      &comps, &atts, &yards, &TDs);
        if (nArgs == 5) {
            float rating = passer_rating(comps, atts, yards, TDs);
            printf("Rating = %.1f\n", rating);
        }
    } while (nArgs == 5);

    return 0;
}
```

The rating calculation itself is simple. Put it into a file of its own: Select **File→New→ File...** (⌘N). The New File assistant sheet drops down; see Figure 3.1. Navigate the source list on the left and the icon array on the right thus: **Mac OS X→C and C++→C File**. Click **Next** and use the save-file sheet that appears to name the file **rating** (Xcode appends `.c` automatically). Click **Create**.

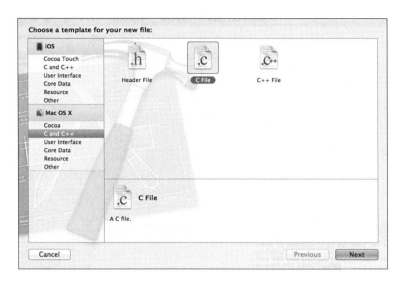

FIGURE 3.1   The New File assistant sheet offers many templates you can use to start a new file. Select the category from the source list on the left, and pick the template from the array of icons on the right.

This is what goes into `rating.c`:

```c
#import "rating.h"
static
double pinPassingComponent(double component)
{
    if (component < 0.0)
        return 0.0;
    else if (component > 2.375)
        return 2.375;
    else
        return component;
}
float
passer_rating(int comps, int atts, int yds, int tds, int ints)
{
    // See http://en.wikipedia.org/wiki/Quarterback_Rating

    double    completionComponent =
                 (((double) comps / atts) * 100.0 -30.0) / 20.0;
    completionComponent = pinPassingComponent(completionComponent);

    double    yardageComponent =
                 (((double) yds / atts) -0.3) / 4.0;
    yardageComponent = pinPassingComponent(yardageComponent);
```

```
double      touchdownComponent =
                20.0 * (double) tds / atts;
touchdownComponent = pinPassingComponent(touchdownComponent);

double      pickComponent =
                2.375 -(25.0 * (double) ints / atts);
pickComponent = pinPassingComponent(pickComponent);

double retval = 100.0 * (completionComponent +
                    yardageComponent +
                    touchdownComponent +
                    pickComponent) / 6.0;
    return retval;
}
```

> **NOTE**
>
> You see a few bugs in this code. Well spotted! Throughout this book, I'm going to give you some buggy code to illustrate debugging techniques. Just play along, okay?

By now, you've missed a couple of braces and are tired of tabbing to get the extra level of indenting. Xcode can do this for you—it's among the features you turned off in the last chapter.

Open the Preferences window (**Xcode→Preferences [⌘Comma]**) and select the **Text Editing** panel. In the **Editing** tab, check **Code completion: Automatically insert closing "}"**. In the **Indentation** tab, check **Syntax-aware indenting**.

Now type an open brace in your code at the end of a line. So what, it's a brace. Now press Return. Xcode adds two lines: Your cursor is now at the next line, indented one level, and a matching closing brace appears on the line after that.

Finally, you've noticed that both main.c and rating.c refer to a rating.h, which you'd use to notify main() of the existence of the passer_rating function. Press ⌘N again, and choose **Header File** from the available C and C++ files. Name it **rating** (Xcode will supply the .h for you), and put this into it:

```
float passer_rating(int comps, int atts, int yds,
                int tds, int ints);
```

Building

That's enough to start. Now try to run it. It's easy: Click the **Run** button on the toolbar, or select **Product→Run** (⌘R). It doesn't matter if you haven't saved your work; by default Xcode saves everything before it attempts a build. Xcode chugs away at your code for a bit...and stops:

▶ A heads-up placard flashes, saying "Build Failed."

▶ The Navigator area switches to the Issue navigator (fourth tab), which shows two items under main.c. One is tagged with a yellow triangle (a warning) and the other with a red octagon (an error). These include descriptions of the errors, which will be truncated; hover the mouse over them to see the full text in a tooltip (Figure 3.2, top).

▶ The editor highlights two lines in main.c. (Click a line in the Issue navigator if main.c isn't visible.) The line that triggered the warning is tagged in yellow, with a banner describing the warning and the error line in red, with a banner of its own (Figure 3.2, bottom).

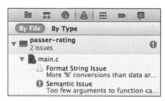

FIGURE 3.2   When Xcode detects build errors, it opens the Issue navigator to display them (top). Clicking an issue focuses the editor on the file and line at which the issue was detected (bottom).

It seems that the only place where I remembered about interceptions was the format string of the scanf call. The compiler was smart enough to match the number of format specifiers to the number of arguments of the scanf and complain. Similarly, I left off the last parameter to passer_rating, which is an outright error.

NOTE

For a compiler, an *error* is a flaw in your source that makes it impossible to translate your code into executable form. The presence of even one error prevents Xcode from producing a program. A *warning* indicates something in your source that can be translated but will probably result in a bug or a crash when you run it. Experienced developers do not tolerate warnings; a compiler option can make a build fail upon a warning just as though it were an error. Don't ever ignore a warning.

> **NOTE**
>
> Need a reminder of what `passer_rating` does with its parameters? Try this: With main visible in the Editor area, hold down the Command key and point the mouse at the symbol `passer_rating`. You'll see it turns blue and acquires an underline, as if it were a link on a standard web page. Click it: The editor jumps to the definition of `passer_rating`. You can jump back by clicking the back arrow button in the upper-left corner of the editor; by pressing ⌃⌘←; or by swiping to the right across the editor area with two fingers, if you've enabled the gesture in System Preferences.

You can dash off a fix fast:

```
do {
    int     comps, atts, yards, TDs, INTs;
    printf("comps, atts, yards, TDs, INTs: ");
    nArgs = scanf("%d %d %d %d %d",
                    &comps, &atts, &yards, &TDs, INTs);
    if (nArgs == 5) }
        float rating = passer_rating(comps, atts, yards, TDs, INTs);
        printf("Rating = %.1f\n", rating);
    }
} while (nArgs == 5);
```

To be conservative (you don't want Xcode to run the program if a warning remains), **Product→Build** (⌘B) will compile and link passer-rating without running it. You needn't have worried: It compiles without error, displaying a "Build Succeeded" placard.

Running

So now you have something runnable. Run it.

A few transformations take place: The Navigator area at the left switches to the Debug navigator (the fifth tab); a new view, the Debug area, appears at the bottom of the window; and the **View** control in the toolbar highlights its middle button to match the appearance of the Debug area (Figure 3.3).

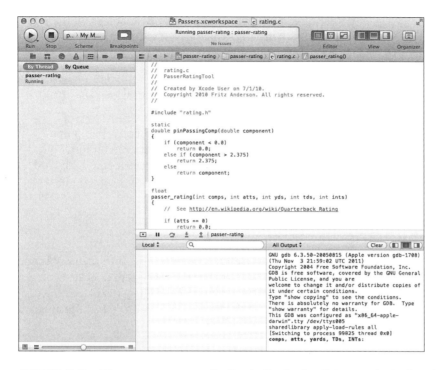

FIGURE 3.3   When you run an application in Xcode, the Debug navigator is selected, and the Debug area appears at the bottom of the screen.

The right half of the debug area is a console for communicating with the `passer-rating` tool. If all has gone well, it should show something like this:

```
comps, atts, yards, TDs, INTs:
```

which is just what the `printf()` was supposed to do. `passer-rating` waits for input, so click in the console area and type the following:

10 20 85 1 0 <return>

Something went wrong. `passer-rating` crashed. `gdb`, the debugging engine, hesitates for a moment as it takes control, and then the debugging displays fill up.

1. In the Debug navigator, a *stack trace* appears, showing what functions were executing at the time of the crash. The top line, labeled 0, is the name of the function, `_svfscanf_l`, that crashed; if you click it, you can see the assembly code (you don't have the source) focused on the instruction that went wrong. The next line is `scanf`, which you recognize as the function you called from `main`, the function on the next line.

   Xcode identifies `main` as your work by flagging it with a blue head-and-shoulders icon, and it automatically selects it.

2. In the Debug area, the left-hand pane fills with the names of variables and their values. You see, for instance, "**atts** = (int) 20," which is just what you entered. Chapter 4, "Active Debugging," discusses this more.

3. The Editor area has the most interesting change: A green flag at the left margin and a green banner at the right margin of the call to scanf. The banner says, "Thread 1: Program Received Signal: 'EXC_BAD_ACCESS'."

Xcode has a lot of these banners; often they are the only way it will convey important messages. You probably set your editor fonts to the smallest size you can comfortably read, so you can see more of your work at one time. The banners are one-line high, and their frames take up some space, so the text in them is smaller than you can comfortably read. The only solution is to select larger fonts for everyday use.

Simple Debugging

EXC_BAD_ACCESS signals the use of a bad pointer, perhaps one pointing into memory that isn't legal for you to read or write to. (Mac OS X's virtual-memory system allocates addresses so that any address that might be derived from a 32-bit integer is illegal, making it harder to cross ints and pointers.) Re-examine the line in main that crashed the application and allow a scale to fall from your eyes:

```
nArgs = scanf("%d %d %d %d %d",
              &comps, &atts, &yards, &TDs, INTs);
```

scanf collects values through pointers to the variables that will hold them. This call does that for all values except INTs, which is passed by value, not by reference. Simply inserting an &

```
nArgs = scanf("%d %d %d %d %d",
              &comps, &atts, &yards, &TDs, &INTs);
```

should cure the problem. Sure enough, running passer-rating again shows the crasher is gone:

```
passer-rating on 2011-12-03 18:45:13 -0500
comps, atts, yards, TDs, INTs: 10 20 85 1 0
Rating = 78.1
comps, atts, yards, TDs, INTs: <control-D>
Program ended with exit code: 0
```

NOTE

You ordinarily wouldn't want to run or debug a program under Xcode if another is running. Instead, you'd like the incumbent app to clear out. There are three ways to do this. You can click the **Stop** button in the toolbar; select **Product→Stop (⌘Period)**; or simply tell Xcode to run the new version. No matter how you do it, Xcode shows an alert sheet to verify that you want to stop the existing run, and you can click **Stop**. See Figure 3.4. You also have the option to **Add** the new version to the old one. Xcode will start a new execution context: You can switch between them in the Debug navigator, and the **Stop** button becomes a menu from which you can select which instance to stop.

FIGURE 3.4   When you tell Xcode to run an application while it already has an application running, it displays a sheet asking what you want to do with the existing app. Normally, you'd click **Stop**, but there is also the option to **Add** the new instance to run concurrently with the old one.

For the moment, you're done: The scanf call returns fewer than five inputs if the standard input stream ends. You end it as you would in a terminal shell, by pressing ^D. Xcode hesitates for a few seconds and then reports that the program ended.

NOTE

M and **A** badges are accumulating in the Project navigator. These have to do with version control. Nothing is wrong. Patience!

Summary

This chapter stepped you up to writing and running a program of your own. It introduced the first level of debugging: What to do when your program crashes. It turns out that Xcode offers good facilities to help you analyze a crash without your having to do much. You accepted Xcode's guidance, quickly traced the problem, and verified that your fix worked.

But you're not done with passer_rating. There are still bugs in it, and this time you must hunt for them.

## CHAPTER 4

Active Debugging

In passer-rating, you have a program that runs without crashing. This is an achievement, but a small one. Let's explore it a little more and see if we can't turn it into a program that works. This entails a small test and maybe some probing of the inner workings.

A Simple Test Case

Run passer-rating again. Give it the old data set if you like, for a short, mediocre game; but also try a rating for a quarterback who didn't play at all:

```
passer-rating on 2011-12-03 18:45:13 -0500
comps, atts, yards, TDs, INTs: 10 20 85 1 0
Rating = 78.1
comps, atts, yards, TDs, INTs: 0 0 0 0 0
Rating = nan
```

Hmm. Not what you expected. It doesn't crash, but it's wrong. A performance in which a passer never passed should be rated zero. passer-rating gave a rating of nan, which is a code for "not a number." That indicates a logical error in how the math was done.

Going Active

In your previous encounter with the debugger, it took control over passer-rating when a fatal error occurred. This time, you want the debugger to take control at a time of your choosing. By setting a *breakpoint* at a particular line in passer-rating, you tell the debugger to halt execution of the application at that line so that the contents of variables can be examined and execution resumed under your control.

Setting a Breakpoint

The easiest way to set a breakpoint is to click in the broad gutter area at the left margin of the application source code in one of Xcode's editors. Select rating.c in the Project navigator to bring that file into the editor. Scroll to the first line of the passer_rating function if it isn't visible, and click in the gutter next to the line that initializes completionComponent (see Figure 4.1, top). A dark-blue arrowhead appears in the gutter to show that a breakpoint is set there. You can remove the breakpoint by dragging the arrowhead to the side, out of the gutter; you can move the breakpoint by dragging it up or down the gutter.

> **NOTE**
>
> If you're keyboard-oriented, you can select among the navigators by pressing ⌘*n*, where *n* is the number of a tab in the Navigator area. Of course, then you must click something to use the navigator.

Something else happens. If this is the first time you've set a breakpoint in your project, the **Breakpoints** button in the toolbar will highlight. Because you've set a breakpoint, Xcode infers you want to stop at breakpoints, so it turns on the feature that does so.

You can avoid a breakpoint in three ways. The first is simply to drag it out of the gutter, but if you'll want to restore it, you won't have a marker for the line you were interested in. If you just want to turn a breakpoint off, click the dark-blue arrow; it will turn pale, and the debugger will ignore it (see Figure 4.1, bottom). Finally, clicking the **Breakpoints** button will cause the debugger to ignore all your breakpoints.

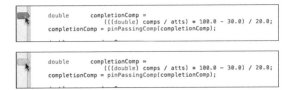

```
double     completionComp =
                 (((double) comps / atts) * 100.0 - 30.0) / 20.0;
completionComp = pinPassingComp(completionComp);


double     completionComp =
                 (((double) comps / atts) * 100.0 - 30.0) / 20.0;
completionComp = pinPassingComp(completionComp);
```

FIGURE 4.1   (top) Clicking the gutter at the left edge of the editor sets a breakpoint at that line of code. When the application reaches that line, execution will pause, and the debugger will display the state of the program. (bottom) Clicking an active breakpoint will preserve its place in your code, but the debugger will ignore it. The breakpoint arrow dims to show it is inactive.

The *only* difference between "running" and "debugging" in Xcode is whether that **Breakpoints** button is highlighted. If it's on, running the application will first launch the debugging engine (gdb or lldb as the case may be), which will in turn launch your application under its supervision. If it's off, you app will be run directly, and no debugger will be involved *unless* it crashes; then the debugger attaches itself to your app so you can (you hope) see what went wrong.

You don't need to stop and relaunch a program to start debugging it actively: Setting a breakpoint doesn't change your code, and it doesn't change the executable that was compiled from it. Now that the breakpoint is set, return to the debugger console, where `passer-rating` still awaits your input, and enter that line of five zeroes again.

> **NOTE**
>
> The Breakpoint navigator (the sixth tab in the Navigator area) lists all the breakpoints in your project. You can disable or delete breakpoints or navigate to the corresponding code.

Xcode hits the breakpoint and responds much as it did for that `EXC_BAD_ACCESS` error: The Debug navigator shows a stack trace from `main` to `passer_rating`, the variables pane in the left half of the Debug area displays the variables in their current state, and a green banner appears in the editor with the label "Thread 1: Stopped at Breakpoint 1." At the left margin, just outside the gutter, is a green arrowhead; as you go along, the arrowhead marks the line currently being executed.

> **NOTE**
>
> The Debug area consists of two panes: variables on the left and console on the right. The bar at the top of the Debug area contains a control at the right end that shows either or both panes. Sometimes Xcode takes the liberty of hiding one or the other. Use the pane control to restore your setup.

The Variables Pane

Turn your attention to the variables pane. You will see five lines flagged with a purple **A**, to designate function arguments, and five flagged with a blue **L**, for local variables (Figure 4.2, top). The arguments are all shown as "(int) 0," as you'd expect from the numbers you supplied. The local variables, such as `completionComponent`, are all shown as "(double) -nan(0x8000...)."

> **NOTE**
>
> Filter the variables pane with the pop-up menu at top-left. You can restrict it to local variables and arguments; open it up to include globals and statics; or leave it to Xcode to choose them automatically.

These would be garbage values left over from previous calls to `passer_rating` or other functions. Change the values of these variables to something that will make it easier to see when they change: Double-click each value so an editing field appears, type **-1**, and then press Return (Figure 4.2, bottom).

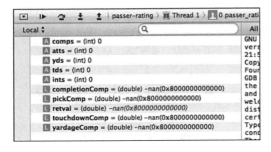

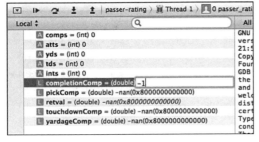

FIGURE 4.2   (top) The variables pane of the Debug area shows all the variables in the current scope and their values. Because passer-rating has been running, local variables are already filled with "garbage" values. (bottom) Double-clicking a value lets you edit a value for testing or convenience.

NOTE

There's another way to examine the values of variables: Hover the mouse pointer over any occurrence of a variable in your code. A tooltip shows the variable's name, type, and value. This is a handy way to browse the state of your program, particularly if you've hidden the body of the Debug area, but it has some limitations: You can't change values; you can't see all your variables at once; you can't examine variables (such as global or static variables) that don't appear in the immediate scope; and you don't get any sign that a value has changed.

Stepping Through

You're ready to watch passer_rating execute. Just above the variables pane is a bar containing a series of controls (Figure 4.3).

▶ **Hide/Show:** Reduces the Debug area to just the debugging bar and expands it again.

▶ **Continue:** Enables the program to run until it hits another breakpoint or crashes (**Product→Debug→Continue [^⌘Y]**).

▶ **Step Over:** Executes the current line and stops at the next one (**Product→Debug→Step Over [F6]**).

▶ **Step In:** Proceeds with execution until it enters the next function called on this line; you can resume control on the first line of that function (**Product→Debug→Step Into [F7]**).

▶ **Step Out:** Proceeds with execution until it leaves the current function; you can resume control in the caller (**Product→Debug→Step Out [F8]**).

▶ A jump bar traces the state of the program from the process to the thread to the current location in the stack trace. Each step lets you to examine a different process, thread, or function, and each step presents a submenu so that you can set all three levels with one mouse gesture.

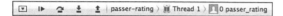

FIGURE 4.3   The bar at the top of the Debug area provides controls for advancing the execution of the program and navigating through its state.

> **NOTE**
>
> Your Mac may be set up so that the F~ keys are overridden by hardware-control functions such as volume and screen brightness or intercepted at the system level for other functions. Review the settings in the **Keyboard** panel of System Preferences if you want to clear these keys for Xcode's use. Holding down the fn key switches the function keys between the two uses.

You're interested in seeing what `passer_rating` does, line-by-line. The green arrowhead jumps to the next line, and something changes in the variables pane: `completionComponent`'s value changes to –nan(0x8000). This is a new value, so Xcode highlights it by italicizing it and coloring it blue. So now you know: The result is poisoned from the first calculation. Even if the other values are good, a nan in any part of a calculation makes the result a nan, too.

The next line calls `pinPassingComponent`; does that cure the error? Click **Step In** (the arrow pointing down into an underscore). The arrowhead jumps up the page to the first line of `pinPassingComponent`. Step through. You find that as `component` fails each of the tests in the `if` statements (nan doesn't compare to anything), the arrow follows execution, jumping over the lines that don't get executed. Stepping through the final `return` jumps execution to the exit point of the function and then to the next line of the caller.

Well, the disaster is clear, but there's one more thing you might be curious about: You terminated `passer-rating` by pressing ^D at the prompt. Does that kill the program itself, or does it just make `scanf` fail? What happens if you enter fewer than five numbers on an input line? What about non-numeric characters?

So while you're in `passer_rating`, click **Step Out**. For the five zeroes, nArgs is 5, just as you'd expect. Set a breakpoint just after the `scanf` call. Click **Continue**, so `passer-rating` prints the result and the prompt, and then awaits your input.

Experiment 1: Enter **10**, and press Return. The debugger doesn't break in. Apparently scanf waits until all its format specifiers are consumed. Okay; enter four more numbers. scanf returns, and nArgs is 5. Step through to watch control pass through the loop, and click **Continue** to execute scanf. (If you find the breakpoint is still set in passer_rating, click it to deactivate it, and click **Continue**.)

Experiment 2: Enter **R** and press Return. Ah! scanf returns immediately, with nArgs set to **0**. Step through, watch the loop test fail, *but don't let the program exit*. Before you execute return **0**, drag the green arrowhead back to the scanf call in the loop. This does exactly what it seems to: The next line that executes will be the line you dragged to. This makes it convenient to perform what-if tests without needing to reset your test case every time.

Experiment 3: But clicking **Continue** in this case doesn't work. scanf returns **0** immediately. Maybe getting the bad value closed out standard I/O. Stop the program with the button in the toolbar, and then run it again for…

Experiment 4: Enter **10**, press Return, and then press ^D. This doesn't kill the program; scanf reports through nArgs that one value was read. This time, if you drag the green arrowhead up to run scanf again, it returns −1, to indicate an I/O error. That's not enough for the program to work with, so the loop falls through, and passer-rating exits.

Well. That was fun. The point is that if you take active charge of the debugger, you can learn a lot about how your application works. A word of caution about resetting the program counter by dragging that arrowhead: Your code and the functions you call often have side-effects, changing the state of execution. Moving the program counter backward does not give you an undo facility: As you saw when you tried to re-execute scanf, what happened when the scan broke remains a fact of your code's environment, and retrying it was just another run—this time in a broken state.

Fixing the Problem

The problem in passer_rating was obvious: I never accounted for the possibility of zero attempts. Time to get back to rating.c and make the fix.

Behaviors

If you've been following along, you'll have found some annoyances:

▶ The Navigator area still shows the Debug navigator. You'll have to bring the Project navigator up so you can get to rating.c.

▶ The Debug area is still visible. It takes up room.

And this will be the case every time you run your program.

Xcode provides a solution. By default, it treats changes of build state passively: Whatever happens to the display stays there. But it allows for *behaviors* for you to reset what Xcode does at a few major events.

Examine the **Behaviors** panel of the Preferences window (Figure 4.4). You can see the available events listed on the left, divided into building, testing, running, searching, device restores, and file unlocking. You're interested in the **Run completes** event—what happens when your application exits.

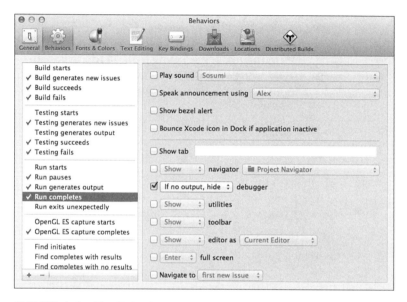

FIGURE 4.4   The **Behaviors** panel of the Preferences window. Here you can instruct Xcode to do any number of useful things when a major event occurs.

What you'd like is for the Debug area to go away and the Project navigator to come back when passer-rating exits. Clicking **Run completes**, you see that one action is already checked: The pop-up for the Debug area shows the **If no output, hide** debugger. This is a reasonable choice because you may want to refer to a program's printouts when you return to editing. The way it's set, exiting passer-rating would close the Debug area but doesn't because passer-rating prints prompts and results.

You can always show the Debug area again if you need it. So the first thing to do is to change the pop-up to **Hide**.

Above the Debug-area pop-up is a check box labeled **Show navigator** and a pop-up giving you a choice of navigators to show when this event happens. Check it, and select **Project Navigator**.

Try it: Run passer-rating one more time, enter some data, get a result, and then press ^D to terminate it. The window automatically changes to an editing state. Success.

TABS

You also see an option in the **Behaviors** panel labeled **Show Tab**, and it's tempting. True to the notion that Xcode is a browser for your project, you can add tabs to the window, each of which provides a different perspective on your work. Other editors can put separate files in each tab, but that misconceives Xcode's model. The feature is much more powerful but, in a way, also fragile.

Select **File→New→Tab** (⌘T) to switch to a new tab. It starts with the same content you had when you issued the command. Try selecting a different file in the project navigator, and use the toolbar's **View** control to expose the Utility area (on the right). Now switch back to the original tab: Not only does it show the original file, but the Utility area is closed.

Imagine another use. You might have tabs for three different purposes:

▶ One for straight text-editing: Nothing but the editor view and the Project navigator.

▶ One for Interface Builder, which takes up a lot of horizontal space: Navigator hidden (you'd use the jump bar to navigate); assistant view (the middle button of the **Editor** control) to show the header for the view's controller; and the Utility area shown for access to the component library.

▶ One for debugging, with the Debug navigator and Debug area displayed.

You can name tabs: Double-click the tab's label. (By default it shows the name of the file displayed.) It becomes editable, so you can name the tabs **Edit**, **Interface Builder**, and **Debugger**, respectively.

With that, you can open the **Behaviors** panel to set the **Run completes** action to **Show tab**, with the name of your **Edit** tab. Just remember to uncheck the **Show navigator** and **debugger** actions. The effect is that you can set changes in the window's appearance and function that are much more complex than the simpler options in the **Behaviors** panel.

This is great, as far as it goes. But it's unstable. The same freedom that lets you set each tab as you like doesn't prevent your changing that tab, losing the effort you put into arranging it and focusing it on the right type of file. If you have any behaviors lingering (such as exposing build issues or showing the Debug area), a simple build-and-go could ruin your carefully constructed Interface Builder tab, unless your system of tabs and behaviors changes to a separate context at every event.

The Fix

At last, you can repair `passer_rating`. After all this business with behaviors and tabs, fixing `passer_rating` is an anticlimax. Just add this to the start of the function:

```
if (atts == 0)
    return 0.0;
```

⌘R runs `passer-rating` one more time. Enter **0 0 0 0 0** at the prompt, and sure enough, you are rewarded with `Rating = 0.0`. Press ^D; the Debug area goes away, and the Navigator area returns to the Project navigator. Just what you want.

Summary

In this chapter, you used Xcode's debugger to take charge of `passer-rating` to track down a bug. You set a breakpoint, stepped through, into, and out of functions, examining and changing variables as you went.

You also picked up a couple of skills—setting behaviors and tabs—that make it easier to control Xcode's habit of changing its windows on its own initiative.

On the way, you came to a crucial insight: Xcode isn't meant to be just a source editor; it is a browser on the whole flow of your development effort.

Now you can take a break from that flow to have your first, focused view on what the Xcode tools are doing.

Compilation

Before continuing, let's review how computer programs are made. If you come to Xcode from long experience with GNU Make or another development environment, this discussion will be familiar to you.

Programmers use *source code* to specify what a program does; source code files contain a notation that, although technical and sometimes cryptic, is recognizably the product of a human, intended in part for humans to read. Even the most precise human communication leaves to allusion and implication things that a computer needs spelled out. If a passer-rating tool were to refer to the local variable yardageComp, for example, you'd care only that the name yardageComp should consistently refer to the result of a particular calculation. The central processor of a computer running an application, however, cares about the amount of memory allocated to yardageComp, the format by which it is interpreted, how memory is reserved for the use of yardageComp and later released, that the memory should be aligned on the proper address boundary, that no conflicting use be made of that memory, and, finally, how the address of yardageComp is to be determined when data is to be stored or retrieved there. The same issues must be resolved for each and every named thing in a program.

Compiling

Fortunately, you have a computer to keep track of such things. A *compiler* is a program that takes source files and generates the corresponding streams of machine-level instructions. Consider the following lines:

```
n = 0;
sum_X = sum_Y = sum_X2 = sum_Y2 = sum_XY = 0.0;
do {
    double      x, y;
    nScanned = scanf("%lg %lg", &x, &y);
    if (nScanned == 2) {
        n++;
        sum_X  += x;
        sum_X2 += x * x;
        sum_Y  += y;
        sum_Y2 += y * y;
        sum_XY += x * y;
    }
} while (nScanned == 2);
```

These 14 lines translate into some 60 lines of *assembly code,* a notation in which each line is a separate instruction to the processor:

```
LC1:    # The scanf format string:
    .ascii "%lg %lg\0"
    ### (A whole lot of assembly instructions omitted)


doRegression:                        # The doRegression function
    ### (Some setup omitted)

    xorl    %ebx, %ebx               # n = 0
    xorpd   %xmm4, %xmm4             # sum_Y = 0.0
    movapd  %xmm4, %xmm6             # sum_X = sum_Y
    movsd   %xmm4, -64(%rbp)         # sum_X2 = sum_Y
    movapd  %xmm4, %xmm5             # sum_Y2 = sum_Y
    movsd   %xmm4, -56(%rbp)         # sum_XY = sum_Y
    leaq    -48(%rbp), %r13          # r13 = address of y
    leaq    -40(%rbp), %r12          # r12 = address of x
    jmp L2                           # Jump to middle of loop

L7:
    incl    %ebx                     # Add 1 to n
    movsd   -40(%rbp), %xmm2         # Fetch x...
    addsd   %xmm2, %xmm6             # ... add it to sum_X
    movsd   -48(%rbp), %xmm0         # Fetch y...
    addsd   %xmm0, %xmm4             # ... add it to sum_Y
```

```
        movapd    %xmm2, %xmm0              # x...
        mulsd     %xmm2, %xmm0             # ... multiplied by x...
        addsd     -64(%rbp), %xmm0         # ... add sum_X2 to it...
        movsd     %xmm0, -64(%rbp)         # ... saved in sum_X2

        movsd     -48(%rbp), %xmm0         # Fetch y...
        addsd     %xmm0, %xmm4             # ... add it to sum_Y

        movapd    %xmm0, %xmm1             # y...
        mulsd     %xmm0, %xmm1             # ... multiplied by y...
        addsd     %xmm1, %xmm5             # ... add to sum_Y2

        mulsd     %xmm0, %xmm2             # Multiply x by y...
        addsd     -56(%rbp), %xmm2         # ... add sum_XY to it...
        movsd     %xmm2, -56(%rbp)         # ... saved in sum_XY
L2:
        # Prepare the arguments for scanf:
        movq      %r13, %rdx               # address of y
        movq      %r12, %rsi               # address of x
        leaq      LC1(%rip), %rdi          # address of the format string
        xorl      %eax, %eax               # clear scanf's return value

        # Save registers scanf might use:
        movsd     %xmm4, -80(%rbp)
        movsd     %xmm5, -96(%rbp)
        movsd     %xmm6, -112(%rbp)

        # Call scanf
        call      _scanf
        cmpl      $2, %eax                 # Did scanf return 2?

        # Restore the saved registers
        movsd     -80(%rbp), %xmm4
        movsd     -96(%rbp), %xmm5
        movsd     -112(%rbp), %xmm6
        je        L7                       # scanf returned 2; jump to top of loop
LBE2:
        # scanf returned not-2; continue.
```

> **NOTE**
>
> You don't need to understand this code deeply. The points to carry away are (1) source code becomes machine instructions; and (2) managing symbols is much of what a compiler does.

When imagining the tasks a compiler must perform to produce executable machine instructions from human-readable source, the first thing that comes to mind is the choice of machine instructions: the translation of floating-point add operations into addsd instructions or expressing the do/while loop in terms of cmpl, je, and jmp. Another important task is the management of *symbols*.

Even with that apparently straightforward task of translation, there are surprises: The code from doRegression() starts the loop by getting x and y from scanf(). If the two variables are filled, the loop next does the sums, but if the variables aren't filled, the loop exits: A straightforward progression of what-happens-next, top to bottom.

The compiler didn't see it that way. It had the insight that the tests for whether to do the sums and for whether to continue the loop are one and the same. So in the loop it generated—very different from the loop as written—the scanf() comes *at the bottom of the loop*. If the loop continues, control goes back to the top (L7:) where the sums are done. The nScanned variable is no longer even necessary: it was used only for the separate do-sums and continue-loop tests; with only one test, the variable goes away. If you trace this code in the debugger, the nScanned variable won't even show up; it simply isn't there.

The compiler preserves the correct behavior for the first run of the loop by entering the loop from the middle. The jmp L2 instruction goes straight to the setup for the scanf() call.

> **NOTE**
>
> The assembly code you're looking at was produced by telling the compiler to produce the fastest code it could. (It was passed the -03 optimization flag.) When you first write and debug a program, you don't want the compiler to optimize. One reason is that it simply takes longer. But as you see here, one of the variables you might want to monitor disappeared. In many cases, the compiler, and not the processor, is responsible for "scheduling" instructions so that all parts of the processor are being used as fully and efficiently as possible. Such optimized code can often execute lines of source out of order or even part by part simultaneously. The effect in the debugger is that the highlight for the line being executed jumps back and forth when you try to step through it, and variables change seemingly at random.

Each C function and every variable must be expressed in machine code in terms of regions of memory, with addresses and extents. A compiler must keep strict account of every symbol, assigning an address—or at least a way to get an address—for it and making sure that no two symbols get overlapping sections of memory.

In its analysis of doRegression(), the compiler budgeted a certain amount of memory in random access memory (RAM) for local variables and assigned general-purpose register rbp to keep track of the end of that block. The 8-byte floating-point number x was assigned to the memory beginning 40 bytes before the end of that block (rbp –40, or -40(%rbp) in the assembler's address notation); y was assigned to the 8 bytes beginning at -48(%rbp). The compiler made sure not to use that memory for any other purpose. Most of the sums for the regression don't even get stored in memory but are computed in the processor's floating-point registers and used from there. Register xmm6, for instance, holds the value of the sum_X variable. Again, the compiler makes sure that each symbol is associated with a particular piece of storage.

In an Xcode project, files that are to be compiled are found in the Target editor (get it by selecting the project icon in the Project navigator), under the **Build Phases** tab, in the "Compile Sources" build phase (see Figure 5.1).

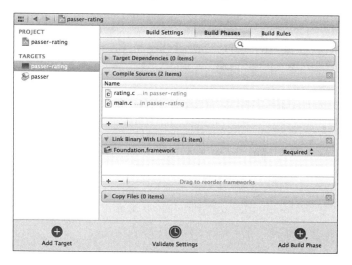

FIGURE 5.1   Selecting the project icon in the Project navigator displays an editor for the project and its targets. The **Build Phases** tab of the Target editor is a table showing the steps in building the target. Click the disclosure triangle in a phase's header to display the files that go into that phase. Even a simple build has a Compile Sources phase (upper) containing every file to be transformed into object files and a Link Binary with Libraries phase (lower) to designate precompiled system and private code to bind into a finished product.

Linking

The accounting task does not end there. Just before the bottom of the loop comes the instruction:

```
call _scanf
```

This line is the translation of the call to the scanf() function. What sort of symbol is _scanf? Examining a full disassembly of an application containing this routine won't tell you much: _scanf appears only once—when it is called. The compiled application does not contain any code or any memory allocated for _scanf.

And a good thing, too, as scanf() is a component of the standard C library. You don't want to define it yourself: You want to use the code that comes in the library. But the compiler, which works with only one .c or .m file at a time, doesn't have any way to refer directly to the starting address of scanf(). The compiler has to leave that address as a blank to be filled in later; therefore, in building a program, there has to be an additional step for filling in such blanks.

The product of the compiler, an *object file*, contains the machine code generated from a source file, along with directories detailing which symbols are defined in that file and which symbols still need definitions filled in. Under Xcode's compilers, Objective-C source files have the suffix .m; object files have the same name, with the .m removed and .o (for object) substituted. Libraries are single files that collect object files supplying useful definitions for commonly used symbols. In the simplest case, a library has a name beginning with lib and suffixed with .a.

The process of back-filling unresolved addresses in compiled code is called *linkage editing*, or simply *linking*. You present the linker with a set of object files and libraries, and, you hope, the linker finds among them a definition for every unresolved symbol your application uses. Every address that had been left blank for later is then filled in. The result is an executable file containing all the code that gets used in the application. See Figure 5.2.

This process corresponds to the "Link Binary With Libraries" build phase in the application's target listing. This phase lists all the libraries and frameworks against which the application is to be linked.

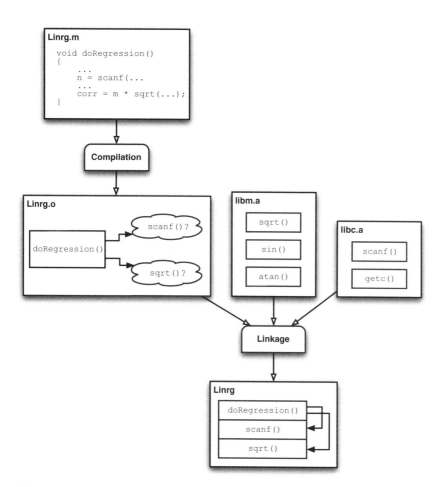

FIGURE 5.2   The process of turning source code into an executable binary, ruthlessly simpli-fied. You provide source code in `Linrg.m` (top left); compiling it produces an object file, `Linrg.o`, that contains your translated code, plus unresolved references to functions that weren't defined in `Linrg.m`. Other libraries (the notional `libm.a` and `libc.a`) contain machine code for those functions. It's the job of the linker to merge your code and the other functions you requested into a complete executable program (bottom).

Dynamic Loading

The process is one step more complicated than that. Standard routines, such as `scanf()`, will be used by many—probably hundreds—of applications at a time. Copying the machine code that implements `scanf()` into each application is a pointless waste of disk space. The solution is *dynamic loading*: The application leaves the addresses of common library functions unresolved even in the final executable file, providing the partial executable code along with a dictionary of symbols to be resolved and the system libraries to find them in. The operating system then fetches the missing code from a library that is shared systemwide and links it into the executable when the application runs.

Dynamic loading not only saves disk space, but can also save RAM and execution time. Dynamic libraries—collections of object files set up for dynamic linking and having the prefix lib and the suffix .dylib—load as read-only memory-mapped files. If two or more applications load the same dynamic library, the OS kernel will share the same in-RAM copy of the file between them. The second and subsequent users of a dynamic library therefore don't incur memory or load-time costs.

Also, dynamic libraries can be updated to fix bugs and improve performance. Installing a new version of a library can improve all the applications that use it, without any need to change the application code.

> **NOTE**
>
> You can't produce your own dynamic libraries for iOS. Dynamic linking still happens— everything the OS does for you is provided through dynamic libraries—but Apple does not support loading and executing anything but the main application code in iOS. On Mac OS X, third-party dynamic libraries are common. See Chapter 22, "Frameworks," for the most common scenario.

If dynamic libraries don't get linked with the application's executable code until run time, why do they figure in the linkage phase of the build process at all? There are two reasons. First, the linker can verify that all the unresolved symbols in your application are defined somewhere, and it can issue an error message if you specified a misspelled or absent function. Second, the linker-built tables in the dynamically linked code specify not only the symbols that need resolving, but also which libraries the needed definitions are to be found in. With files specified, the dynamic loader does not need to search all the system's libraries for each symbol, and the application can specify private dynamic libraries (in Mac OS X) that would not be in any general search path.

Xcode's Refinements

A traditional compiler sticks to what I've just described: It's a command-line tool that starts, reads your source code, writes some object code, and then stops. That's what gcc, the Free Software Foundation's widely used compiler, which Xcode used from the beginning, does. In Xcode 3.2, Apple began moving to a new compiler technology called llvm, which is a library that reads and analyzes source code. The code analyzers in traditional compilers "know" about your code on a line-by-line basis: If you make an error, they identify only the line in which the error happened. If you want to know where a symbol is defined or used, gcc can tell you what lines; llvm can tell you what *words*.

The specific version of `llvm` that incorporates Apple's analytic parser for the C family, including Cocoa memory-management semantics, is called `clang`. That's the name of the command-line tool Xcode's build system invokes. Apple's human-readable interface refers to the compiler as `llvm`, and I'll use that name unless I'm talking about the tool.

Xcode uses `llvm` as a conventional code-in code-out compiler, but because it is a library and can be bound into Xcode itself, it can do much, much more, even when you aren't building a product. Consider **Edit All in Scope**. When you click in the name of a local variable, you've seen that all instances of the variable in the same lexical scope acquire a dotted gray underline. If you hover the mouse pointer in that same variable, a badge appears that produces a pop-up menu if you click it. Select **Edit All in Scope**, and edit the variable you selected; all instances of the variable change in unison. See Figure 5.3.

```
+ (NSDictionary *) defaultDictionary
{
    static NSDictionary *       sDict = nil;
    static dispatch_once_t      onceToken;
    dispatch_once(&onceToken, ^{
        NSMutableDictionary *   temp = [NSMutableDictionary dictionary];
        for (NSString * key in [self numericAttributes])
            [temp setObject: @"0" forKey: key];
        //  FIXME: This is a candidate for string localization,
        //  though it's problematic, because I never use this method.
        [temp setObject: @"Opponents" forKey: @"theirTeam"];
        [temp setObject: @"Our Team" forKey: @"ourTeam"];
        [temp setObject: [sShortDate stringFromDate: [NSDate date]]
                forKey: @"whenPlayed"];
        sDict = [temp copy];
    });
    return sDict;
}
```

```
+ (NSDictionary *) defaultDictionary
{
    static NSDictionary *       sDict = nil;
    static dispatch_once_t      onceToken;
    dispatch_once(&onceToken, ^{
        NSMutableDictionary *   aDi = [NSMutableDictionary  dictionary];
        for (NSString * key in [self numericAttributes])
            [aDi setObject: @"0" forKey: key];
        //  FIXME: This is a candidate for string localization,
        //  though it's problematic, because I never use this method.
        [aDi setObject: @"Opponents" forKey: @"theirTeam"];
        [aDi setObject: @"Our Team" forKey: @"ourTeam"];
        [aDi setObject: [sShortDate stringFromDate: [NSDate date]]
                forKey: @"whenPlayed"];
        sDict = [aDi copy];
    });
    return sDict;
}
```

FIGURE 5.3   (top) The continuous `llvm` parser can track all instances of a symbol in a function and highlights them all when the insertion point is in one of them; the selected variable offers a pop-up menu. (bottom) Selecting **Edit All in Scope** from the pop-up echoes your edits to all instances of the variable.

The editor can identify those uses because the `llvm` library continually parses your code to inform it of what parts of the code refer to what objects. This is only one example of the services Apple calls Code Sense, centered on a continuously updated analytical index of your code.

You can build a compiler around `llvm`, as a tool that takes the `llvm` library's analyzed product and translates it into machine code. The upshot is that you have two choices for a compiler in Cocoa development:

▶ `llvm` is a compiler built with the `llvm` library. It is much faster than `gcc`, which earlier versions of Xcode used, and generates better code. Its error and warning messages are subtler and more accurate. It's the default compiler for all new projects, and unless you have compatibility needs, there's no reason not to use it.

▶ llvm-gcc is a hybrid: Its front end is the gcc parser, so the parsing behavior is compatible with the needs of older projects; its back end is the superior llvm code generator.

As of Xcode 4.2, pure gcc is no longer an option.

Additionally, llvm is the basis of Xcode's **Analyze** action (**Product→Analyze** [⇧⌘B]), which uses llvm as a static-analysis tool with a deep understanding of the requirements of correct code for iOS and Mac OS X applications. For instance, it's a common pattern that a method accepts a parameter that is a pointer to an NSError pointer. The caller is free to pass NULL for that parameter if it's not interested in the value. If the analyzer sees such a parameter, and you don't check for a NULL pointer before assigning through it, it will warn you. See Figure 5.4.

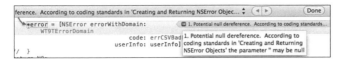

FIGURE 5.4   llvm combines insight into your code with Apple's coding conventions. Here, a method sets a returned NSError pointer without checking to see whether it might be NULL. When you issue **Product→Analyze (⇧⌘B)**, the compiler warns of the potential crash.

Could all this be done with code from the gcc compiler? In principle, yes, but two factors work against it. First, the gcc code is…mature. It's hard to repurpose code that has been through so many hands for so long. Second, gcc is subject to the Free Software Foundation's General Public License (GPL), which broadly prohibits the use of its software internally in other projects, unless those projects are made "free" themselves. Apple does not want to open-source Xcode, or other system software that uses the llvm library to compile code on-the-fly, which rules out using GPL code.

Incorporating a compiler into a code editor brings you one big feature that you can see right away: Xcode compiles your code continually, highlights errors as it finds them, and even offers suggestions on how to correct actual and potential errors. This also serves *predictive compilation*. A naïve approach—the traditional approach—to building a program is to make compilation a discrete step in the development process: It happens when you say it happens and goes on until it's done. Editing source code is (by computing standards) slow, and llvm can work at interactive speeds. While you are editing source, Xcode compiles it "on spec," in the hope you won't change it before you request a build. If it's right, most of the compiling will be done before you ask.

Compiler Products

Object files are the principal products of the compilation process: You're most often interested only in building something you can run and test. But sometimes, the compiler will identify issues or produce results that, with all diligence, you can't make sense of. In such cases, it's useful to see what the compiler did on the way to translating your code.

Also, the build process will produce files that encapsulate repetitive tasks, like compiling common header files. These, too, are compiler products.

Intermediate Products

C-family compilers were originally run in three stages, each feeding the next. Modern compilers merge the steps to gain a better understanding of how to generate the best code, but notionally the steps are still there, and you can get the products of each:

1. The *preprocessor* takes your code and outputs the "real" source after making simple string substitutions. When it finds #include and #import directives, it inserts the contents of the included files into the output stream. Macros from #define directives are expanded and substituted into the stream. Conditional directives admit or block sections of code in the input file.

   You can see the results of the preprocessor by clicking the related items menu (at the left end of the jump bar above the editor) and selecting **Preprocess**. The editor shows the full interpreted stream of the current source file. This can be long, but you can track down bugs by making sure that the code you thought you were compiling and the symbols you thought you were using are actually there.

   Choosing **Preprocess** from the root item in the jump bar of the assistant editor displays a preprocessed version alongside of the file you are editing. Also, you can issue **Product→Generate Output→Preprocessed File**.

2. The parser/generator takes the "simplified" preprocessed code, reduces it to logical constructs (parsing), and produces the assembly source for a machine-language program that does what the original source directs (code generation).

   Selecting **Assembly** from the related items menu, or the Assembly action in the jump bar of the assistant editor, shows you the assembly-language representation of a file. **Product→Generate Output→Assembly File** works as well.

3. An assembler reads the assembly source and reduces it to executable bytes in an object file, with references to be filled in by the linker. The otool command-line tool has a plethora of options for examining object files and libraries, with disassemblies and file layouts and limited options for editing. The nm tool is useful for examining the symbol tables in a library. See man otool and man nm for details.

Precompiled Headers

Mac and iOS applications draw on *frameworks*, packages of dynamic libraries, headers, and resources that define and link to the operating systems, human interface services, and more. Frameworks entail huge numbers of large header files. In early days, it made sense for programmers to speed up builds by carefully choosing the system headers they included, but the Cocoa frameworks are so interdependent that that isn't possible. Apple *strongly* warns against trying to pull pieces out of frameworks.

Framework headers are the first thing an implementation file imports, either directly or through headers of its own. You can set a *prefix file* to be injected automatically into the source stream of all your files; when you instantiate an iOS or Mac OS X project, Xcode automatically generates a .pch file and sets up the build settings to inject it. A typical prefix file looks like this:

```
#ifdef __OBJC__
    #import <Cocoa/Cocoa.h>
#endif
```

That's convenient, but it doesn't solve the problem of speed if the prefix is to be read and converted every time you compile a file. The .pch extension gives a clue to the solution: The file's intended purpose is as a source file for a *precompiled header*; if you opt for precompilation, llvm will read the .pch and save its parsing state. All subsequent uses of the prefix header will reload that saved state, saving you the time that repeating the compilation would have taken. There is another build setting for precompilation, and by default, it is on.

Summary

This chapter was a short but essential review of what happens when you compile and link a program. You saw how compilation not only translates your code into machine-executable code, but also it transforms it. The big task in building an executable is not translation, but the bookkeeping involved in allocating space to data and code and how it culminates in the linkage phase. Linkage can be done all at once, as in a static linker, but Mac OS X relies heavily on dynamic linkage, where much of the heavy work is done as the program starts running.

Now you have the background, and let's do something with it.

## CHAPTER 6

Adding a Library Target

The passer_rating function is a tremendous achievement—and hard-won. It plainly has applications beyond that simple command-line tool, so let's encapsulate its services for use in other programs.

All right, no, you won't, but doing so will introduce some important skills. So you can create a static library (an archive of reusable code) for passer_rating. You can move its code from the passer-rating tool into the new library and link it back into the tool.

Adding a Target

You don't need to start a new project to create a library— it's better if you don't. Open the passer-rating project in Xcode, and click the top entry, representing the project, in the Project navigator. This brings up the Project/Target editor. There is a big circled **+** button at the lower left of the Editor area labeled **Add Target**. Click it.

This produces a New Target assistant sheet, which organizes the available templates in the way you've already seen for projects and files.

1. In the column on the left, select **Mac OS X→Framework & Library**.

2. Xcode presents a choice of linkable targets. Pick **C/C++ Library** (passer_rating doesn't involve anything more than standard C), and click **Next**.

3. Name the product. You may be aware that UNIX static libraries have names of the form lib*name*.a. Don't worry about that; just provide the base name **passer**, and the build system can take care of naming the file.

4. Leave **Use Automatic Reference Counting** unchecked.

5. Select **Type: Static**, and accept **Project: passer-rating**.

6. Click **Finish**.

> **NOTE**
>
> You can find a comprehensive list of project, target, and file templates in Appendix C, "Project and Target Templates."

The Editor area is filled with a Target editor for the new "passer" target. In particular, look at the **Build Settings** tab, detailing options controlling how the compiler and linker build the library. You still don't need to worry about these; the defaults that come in the target templates are almost always good enough.

Targets

What have you done? What is a target?

A *target* describes a single build process in Xcode: It has a specific product, a specific set of files that go into the product, and a specific set of parameters for the build process.

Targets are organized into *build phases*. A build phase accepts files that are members of its target and processes them in a particular way. Source files (`.c`, `.m`, and `.cpp` files, most commonly, but other files for other compilers, as well) go into a "Compile Sources" phase; libraries, into a "Link Binary With Libraries" phase; and so on.

> **NOTE**
>
> Chapter 26, "The Xcode Build System," covers build phases and their role in the Xcode build system in detail.

You can change the files and settings as much as you like, but the type of the product, which determines what build process is used, can't change. If you start a static library, for instance, and then decide you need a dynamic library instead, you're out of luck. You must create a new target for a dynamic library and add the source files again.

Target Membership

Targets consist of a product (which you specified), build settings (which you've accepted), and member files, of which passer has none. You need to add something—specifically `rating.c`.

Adding Files to a Target

There are three ways to do this.

▶ Click the project in the Project navigator, and select `passer`, the library target, from the Targets list. Select the **Build Phases** tab. Find `rating.c` in the Project navigator, and drag it into the "Compile Sources" phase. The label shows that there is one item in the phase, and if you click the triangular disclosure button, you can see that `rating.c` is in the list (Figure 6.1).

▶ Undo that, so you will try the other way, by selecting `rating.c` in the Compile Sources table, and clicking the – button at the bottom of the table.

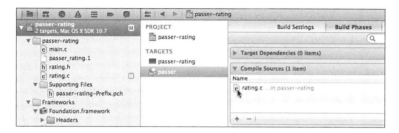

FIGURE 6.1   You can add a source file to a target by dragging it from the Project navigator into the "Compile Sources" phase. This gives you the most control of the role the file plays in the build process.

NOTE

Removing a file from a build phase won't delete the file or remove it from your project.

Now click the **+** button. A sheet containing the project outline drops down. Click `rating.c` and then the **Add** button. If you click **Add Other...** , you can add files to the build phase and the project in one step.

▶ The third way is to come at it from the other end: Click `rating.c` in the Project navigator. Then expose the Utility area by clicking the right-hand segment of the toolbar's **View** control. Make sure the first tab, the File inspector, is selected. The File inspector lets you control the way Xcode treats the selected file. (Or files; if you select multiple files in the Project navigator, the settings will affect all of them.) One of the sections is **Target Membership**, listing all the targets in the project. For `rating.c`, click the check box for the `passer` target (Figure 6.2).

FIGURE 6.2   The File inspector in the Utility area has a section for target membership, listing all the targets in the project. Check the targets you want the file to be a member of. Xcode can guess the build phase from the type of the file.

The advantage to working from the build-phase end is that you have control over which phase a file goes into. Yes, .c files will almost always be compiled, but suppose you were creating a programmer's editor for Mac OS X that has file templates embedded in it. Your TemplateFile.c file *looks* like C source—it is—but you want it bundled as a text file, not compiled as source. The phase you want is "Copy Bundle Resources" (available only for application and bundle targets), not "Compile Sources." If you start from the build phase, there's no ambiguity.

Working from the file's end of the chain has an advantage of its own: If your project has many targets, the check boxes enable you to add or remove files in all of them at once, without having to visit the Target editors and hunt the files up. Xcode can guess which build phases they should go into, and its guesses are usually correct.

NOTE

When you create a new file, using **File→New→File...** (⌘N), you get a shortcut to assigning targets from the file end: The save-file dialog for the new file includes a picker for the targets you want to add it to. Similarly, when you add files, **File→Add Files to...** (⌥⌘A), you're given a target picker. Again, Xcode will guess at the build phases (Figure 6.3).

FIGURE 6.3   When you create or add a file to a project, Xcode lets you select the targets the file is to contribute to.

However you added `rating.c` to the `passer` library, remember to *remove* it from the `passer-rating` target. The whole point of having a library is that clients don't need to include the source for the services it provides.

Headers in Targets

What about `rating.h`? You can't add it to an application target from the file end: Headers aren't compiled—they merely contribute to implementation files. If you want them inside an application bundle for some reason, you can drag them into the "Copy Bundle Resources" phase.

`rating.h` *can* be added to a *library* target. You can choose the role the header plays in your product:

- ▶ **Project**, if it's to be visible only inside your project, as an element in a build.
- ▶ **Public**, if it's to be installed somewhere such as `/usr/local/include`, or the `Headers` directory of a framework.
- ▶ **Private**, if it's to be installed in the `PrivateHeaders` directory of a framework.

Select `rating.h` in the Project navigator, and open the Utility area to expose the File inspector (first tab). There you'll find the by-now-familiar Target Membership panel. Check the `passer` target, and select the role from the pop-up menu in that row of the table.

If you're serious about `passer` being a public utility, `rating.h` should be installed in a globally visible location. Set its visibility to **Public**.

A Dependent Target

In the toolbar's **Scheme** menu, select **passer -My Mac 64-bit**; then click **Run**. (If the left-most button in the toolbar doesn't say **Run**, hold down on that button and select **Run** from the list that drops down.) passer is a library, so it doesn't run anything, but the library builds, and the build succeeds.

Switch the **Scheme** to **passer-rating -My Mac 64-bit**. Click **Run**. The build fails. Let's see why. Select the Issue navigator (fourth tab at the top of the Navigator area), where you'll see a table with one item carrying a red **!** icon. Click that line, and the Editor area fills with a description of the problem:

```
Undefined symbols for architecture x86_64:
  "_passer_rating", referenced from:
      _main in main.o
ld: symbol(s) not found for architecture x86_64
clang: error: linker command failed with exit code 1 (use -v to see invocation)
```

In other words, **main** called passer_rating, but the linker couldn't find that function. See Figure 6.4.

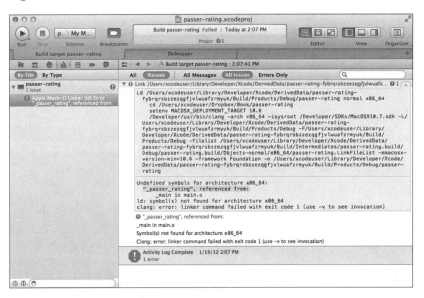

FIGURE 6.4   The Issue navigator lists all the problems that arose in your build. Clicking an issue presents an editor displaying the location of the problem. In this case, the error came at the link phase, so the editor displays the link command and the error messages it printed.

This makes sense: You removed rating.c, and therefore passer_rating, from the passer-rating target, and you haven't told that target where to find it. Yes, the file and the library product are still in the project, but it's the passer-rating target, not the project, that determines what files go into the passer-rating tool.

Adding a Library

So you need to correct the `passer-rating` target, which means going to the Target editor. You know the drill: In the Project navigator, select the passer-rating item at the top of the list. In the targets list, select `passer-rating` and then the **Build Phases** tab.

You want to link `libpasser.a`, the product of the `passer` target, into `passer-rating`. It's straightforward: Open the "Link Binary With Libraries" build phase, and click the **+** button. A sheet appears with a two-section list. The first section, titled "Passer-Rating Project," lists the libraries the project produces—in this case, only `libpasser.a`. Select it and click **Add**.

Now click **Run**. The build succeeds, `passer-rating` runs, and when you enter some test data, it works. Everything is great.

IMPLICIT DEPENDENCIES

If you were running Xcode 3, your work would not be done. It would not have been enough that you told the target to link `libpasser.a`. You would also have had to tell it that to build correctly, it must bring `libpasser.a` current with any changes you had made to it: You would have had to declare a dependency on the `passer` target.

For example: Say you changed `passer_rating` to add a logging `printf` statement. You make the change and run `passer-rating`.

In Xcode 3, you wouldn't see the log message because without an explicit directive to rebuild `libpasser.a` whenever its constituent files changed, `passer-rating` would have accepted the library as it was. This isn't a problem unique to the old Xcode; if you want a dependency in a `make` project, you have to declare it explicitly in the makefile.

Xcode 4 is different: You added `libpasser.a` from a sheet in which you picked it from the products of the current project. Xcode 4 is smart enough to figure out that if you need the library, you need it in its up-to-date form. It rebuilds the library when it has to.

The **Build Phases** tab maintains a "Target Dependencies" phase to share projects with Xcode 3, which needs it.

You can turn automatic building of dependencies off by unchecking **Find Implicit Dependencies** in the Scheme editor sheet (**Product→Edit Scheme...** [⌘<]); pick the **Build** panel from the list on the left. Without implicit dependencies, you're back to setting them in the "Target Dependencies" build phase.

Debugging a Dependent Target

One more thing: Suppose you develop a new interest in `passer_rating` and want to debug it as the command-line tool calls it. The tool and the function are produced by different targets; does that matter?

See for yourself: Set a breakpoint at the assignment to `completionComponent`. Run `passer-rating`.

Sure enough, the debugger stops the application at the breakpoint. Xcode can consolidate the debugging information across the targets that go into the current executable.

Summary

You've divided the `passer-rating` application into a main executable and a static library. It hardly deserves it, but it's just an example.

On the way, you created a target to assemble and build the files needed for the new library and distributed files between the library and the main program. You added the `libpasser.a` library product to the main `passer-rating` target.

You saw that Xcode does right by you in two important ways: Adding the library to the application target not only linked the library into the application, but also ensured that the library is always brought up to date when the application is built. And it incorporated the debugging information from the library, so you can examine the working of the library while the application is running.

Next, a chapter about hygiene.

CHAPTER 7

Version Control

There isn't much to the passer-rating project—about 120 lines of source, plus the contents of the project file—but you have already invested a lot of time and trouble in it. So far, you've simply created some source code, but soon you will be moving on from *creation* to *change*. If you're like most programmers, you are conservative of the code you've written. An old function may no longer be required, but it may still embody a valuable understanding of the underlying problem.

One solution might be simply to keep all the obsolete code in your active source files, possibly commented-out or guarded by #if 0 blocks, but this bloats the file and obscures code that actually does something. When the revisions get more than one layer deep, it can be difficult to track which blocked-out stretch of code goes with which.

A *source-control* (or *version-control*) system is a database that keeps track of all the files in a project and allows you to register changes to those files as you go. Version control frees you to make extensive changes, secure in the knowledge that all the previous versions of each file are still available if you need to roll your changes back.

You may have heard of version control and concluded that it's only for large projects with many developers. It is true that it makes it much easier to manage large code bases and to coordinate the efforts of large teams. But even if you work alone:

▶ You will still make extensive changes to your source.

▶ You will still need to refer to previous versions.

▶ You will still need to revert to previous versions to dig yourself out of the holes you dug with those extensive changes.

▶ You will find it easier if you can make changes cleanly, rather than trying to make sure you caught all the obsolete code in comments and `#if 0` blocks.

▶ You will likely need to work on more than one computer, each of which may contribute different changes to your code base.

As I said in Chapter 3, "Simple Workflow and Passive Debugging," if you are going to change your code, *ever*—if you save a file more than once—you ought to put it under version control. Xcode 4 makes it easy.

Taking Control

So I've convinced you. You want to get your project under source control. How do you start?

If you took my advice in Chapter 3, you've started. When you place a new project on disk, Xcode offers a check box, **Create local git repository for this project**. You checked it. The `passer-rating/` directory contains a hidden `.git/` directory that indexes the project, and Xcode tracks the files you add and edit.

Creating a Git Repository by Hand

Didn't do that? You'll have to visit the Terminal application (`/Applications/Utilities/Terminal`), but it's easy to tell Git to set up a local repository:

1. Focus the shell on the project directory using the `cd` command:

   ```
   $ cd ~/Desktop/MyProject
   ```

2. This step is optional: Git ordinarily treats any file in your working directory as fair game for archiving. But if you share your repository (even with yourself, on another machine), you don't want to include settings particular to your sessions with Xcode—things such as window positions or what areas are visible. Those things change all the time, and you wouldn't want your version-control system complaining that you have to commit them before you can do anything else. The `.gitignore` file, in the root directory of your project, contains patterns for files and directories you don't want to be sucked up by Git.

   You can create the `.gitignore` file with a text editor, but the simplest way to do it is just to type it in on the command line:

   ```
   $ cat > .gitignore
   xcuserdata/
   <control-D>
   ```

If you have other files you don't want to track, add patterns of your own to the list. It's a bad idea to track files such as `.o` object files or other build products because there's no point: Anyone who updates or pulls from the repository has the source files that produce the build products; the product files take up a lot of room for no advantage. The patterns are in the common "glob" format: *.o. Exclude directories by appending a "/" to their names, as shown in this example.

> **NOTE**
>
> A full list of suggested .gitignore items for Objective-C projects can be found at https://github.com/github/gitignore/blob/master/Objective-C.gitignore.

3. Now set up a Git repository. Ridiculously easy:

```
$ git init
Initialized empty Git repository in
    /Users/xcodeuser/Desktop/MyProject/.git/
```

With this, Git adds a .git/ directory that holds an empty repository.

> **NOTE**
>
> You may have installed a version of Git on your own, either before you switched to Xcode 4 or because you want some additional feature or bug fix. If you did, your copy is probably in the /usr/local/ tree, and you put that directory into your search path. Xcode doesn't see your search path; when it uses Git, it is hard-coded to use the tool at /usr/bin/git.

4. You don't want an empty repository; you want your files in it. Git calls any file it doesn't have in the repository "untracked." The add subcommand adds them to the tracking list (though not yet to the repository):

```
$ git add .
```

The "." designates the current directory, and Git adds everything in that directory that it hasn't been told to ignore. The files are now in the "staging area," where their existence and contents are registered, but not yet in the repository itself.

5. Finally, copy the files into the repository. Only when you do this will they show up in the project's history, and in the copies of the files your collaborators can get from your repository:

```
$ git commit -m 'Initial checkin'
master (root-commit) 5295b15] Initial checkin
Committer: Xcode User <xcodeuser@Macintosh-304.local>
.
.
.
6 files changed, 341 insertions(+), 0 deletions(-)
create mode 100644 .gitignore
create mode 100644 MyProject.xcodeproj/project.pbxproj
```

```
.
. adding other files
.
```

Git attaches your name and email address to every commit. If you don't tell Git what those are, it will infer them from your UNIX-registered username (which is probably right) and the name of your computer (which is probably wrong for your email address). The first time you commit, Git prints instructions on how to set those things properly.

6. If your project was open all this time, Xcode will probably notice it's now under control. If not, just use **File→Source Control→Refresh Status**.

The State of Your Files

Xcode presents a model of source control that unifies the different models of the two systems it supports. Git and Subversion treat files as being in various states relative to their repositories. Let's review them.

How Subversion Views Files

Subversion recognizes six kinds of files:

- ▶ **Not Controlled:** The file is not part of the Subversion repository for this working directory.

- ▶ **Scheduled for Addition:** The file is new to the project. You've scheduled it with svn add, and the next commit will ship it off to the repository.

- ▶ **Scheduled for Deletion:** You've used svn delete or one of its aliases to tell Subversion to delete the file and end the file's history at the next commit.

- ▶ **Modified:** The file has been changed and will go into the repository at the next commit.

- ▶ **Conflicted:** When you pulled updates in from the repository, some of the changes you pulled in couldn't be reconciled with changes you made. Subversion will balk at any attempt to check changes in until you correct the conflict. You must tell Subversion when you have resolved the conflict.

- ▶ **Unmodified:** The file is in the repository and hasn't changed since your last checkin.

How Git Views Files

In Git's world, a file can be in one of six states:

- ▶ **Ignored:** The file's name matches a pattern in the .gitignore file. Git never attempts to manage it unless you explicitly add it to the repository.

▸ **Untracked:** Git sees the file, but it's neither in the repository nor staged for adding to the repository. There is no history of its previous contents. The `git add` command *stages* it for entry into the repository.

▸ **Modified:** In a way, this isn't much different from an untracked file: Its contents won't go into the repository until it is staged. However, its previous contents *are* in the repository and can be compared against the current version or restored. It, too, can be readied to commit its contents with the `git add` command.

▸ **Staged:** The file has been designated (with `git add`) for inclusion in the next commit. Why doesn't the `add` command simply put the modified/new contents into the repository? Because you usually make logical changes to your code in more than one file—a method in a `.m` file, its declaration in a header, and its use in other `.m` files—and it doesn't make sense to register or roll back changes that are only partway made. When you stage a file, you assemble it into a logical group that will be committed all at once.

▸ **Unmerged:** You changed the file and attempted to pull in changes from another repository, and the two sets of changes couldn't be reconciled. Git marks the file to highlight the conflicts, and warns you if you attempt a commit without resolving the conflict. When you modify and restage the file, Git takes it that the conflicts are resolved and stops complaining.

▸ **Unmodified:** The file's current state, as registered with `git commit`, is what's in the repository. So far as Git is concerned, there's nothing more to be done with it unless you want to inspect or restore an earlier state. When you edit and save the file, it becomes "modified," and the `add`/`commit` cycle begins again.

If you delete a file, that counts as a modification. `git rm` will stage the deletion for the repository. `git rm` can do the deletion and staging in one step.

If you move or rename a file, that's equivalent to a `git rm` of the file at its old location or name and `git add` at the new one. `git mv` does it all in one step. However you do it, Git notices that the "old" and "new" files are identical, and the file's track in the history will be unbroken.

How Xcode Views Files

Xcode's view is different because its demands as an IDE require another layer of abstraction. When dealing with a version-controlled project, files have five states:

▸ **Unmodified**, with no badge on the file's entry in the Project navigator: The file's history is in the repository, and you haven't saved any changes.

▸ **Modified**, with an "M" badge: The file is in a repository, but you've changed it since it was last committed. Git sees these files in the "modified" but not "staged," state; in Subversion they're just "modified." If you withhold a modified file from a commit, Xcode will do what is necessary to prevent the underlying system from committing it. Xcode's commit process folds the add-and-commit dance into one step.

▶ **Added**, with an "A" badge: You've created a new file in the project
(**File→New→File...**, [⌘N]) or added an existing one and copied it to the project
directory (**File→Add Files to...**, ⌥⌘A). Xcode automatically stages the added file
with Git or Subversion.

▶ **Conflicted**, with a red "C" added to any other status indicator: When you merge
changes from another repository into your own, it may not be possible to determine
which lines from which files are to survive the merge—more on this soon. Xcode
flags these with a C and refuses further commits until you use **File→Source
Control→Mark as Resolved** to clear the conflicted state. This reflects Subversion's
model of conflicts, which you have to mark as resolved; Git tracks conflicted files
but clears them automatically when you edit and stage them.

▶ **Unknown**, marked "?": The file is in the project directory but not in the repository.
This is equivalent to Git's "untracked" state.

Your First Commit

Before you go any further, set up for the next steps by making sure all that work is in the
local repository. Nearly every file in the Project navigator is marked "M," and you must
clear those out.

In the simplest case, checking your changes in is easy. Select **File→Source
Control→Commit...**(⌥⌘C). A sheet appears (Figure 7.1) showing your changes and offering a text-editing area for your notes on what you changed.

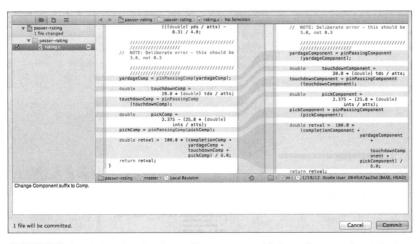

FIGURE 7.1   Selecting the **Commit**... command brings down a sheet that compares your
most recent changes against the last commit to the local repository. The text area at the
bottom receives your notes on what was changed.

Always enter a commit message. Always. The whole idea of version control is that you should know what you did, when, and why. The benefit is lost if you don't commit at every logical point in your progress, or if you don't record what you did. It doesn't have to be elaborate; in this case, "First version with libpasser.a" will do fine. If you do have more to say, bear in mind the convention that the message should begin with a brief sentence summarizing the change, a blank line, and then the details. Many tools rely on this format to provide at-a-glance logs.

The Commit sheet includes a navigator of its own, listing the files in the project that have source-control status. If you want to exclude a file from a commit (maybe its changes don't relate to the subject of this particular commit), or add a file to the repository, you can check or uncheck them in the navigator. If there was a previous version of a file in the repository, the Commit sheet will show how you changed it since then, with your work in the left pane, the old version in the right. That's a real editor: If you want to clean up a file before checking it in, you can edit it right in the Commit sheet.

Click **Commit**. Your work goes into the local repository, and the version-control badges in the Project navigator disappear.

Adding a Remote Repository

Version-control systems (particularly Git) are useful even for single-programmer projects, but they are also important tools for collaborative work. In Git, this involves hooking up to a *remote repository*, in essence a duplicate of the users' local repositories, without an attached working directory. Let's set up a remote. This will be a simple one—just a shared directory on the same computer as the two clients—but it's enough to demonstrate the principles.

Setting Up the Remote

Start by creating a "bare" (no working files) repository in /Users/Shared/, where all users can get to it. Open the Terminal, and do this:

```
$ # Work on the "Shared" user
$ cd /Users/Shared
$ # Create a directory for Git repositories...
$ mkdir git
$ # ... and work on that
$ cd git
$ # Create a "bare" repository named passer-rating.git
$ git init --bare passer-rating.git
Initialized empty Git repository in /Users/Shared/git/passer-rating.git/
$ # The directory contains just the repository infrastructure
$ ls -al passer-rating.git/
total 24
```

```
drwxr-xr-x  10 fritza  wheel  340 Jun 13 13:55 .
drwxr-xr-x   3 fritza  wheel  102 Jun 13 13:55 ..
-rw-r--r--   1 fritza  wheel   23 Jun 13 13:55 HEAD
drwxr-xr-x   2 fritza  wheel   68 Jun 13 13:55 branches
-rw-r--r--   1 fritza  wheel   85 Jun 13 13:55 config
-rw-r--r--   1 fritza  wheel   73 Jun 13 13:55 description
drwxr-xr-x  12 fritza  wheel  408 Jun 13 13:55 hooks
drwxr-xr-x   3 fritza  wheel  102 Jun 13 13:55 info
drwxr-xr-x   4 fritza  wheel  136 Jun 13 13:55 objects
drwxr-xr-x   4 fritza  wheel  136 Jun 13 13:55 refs
$ # Make sure everyone on the machine is able to modify the repo
$ sudo chmod -R a+rwX passer-rating.git/
Password:
```

With this, /Users/Shared/ includes a Git repository named passer-rating.git. It's a "bare" repository because there is no working directory containing files you can edit and check in, and never will be. Its sole purpose is to hold work from other clients.

> **NOTE**
>
> You may be feeling cheated that a "remote" Git repository isn't necessarily remote in the sense of its being on a different machine. Administering a net-served Git repository is beyond the scope of this book, but the principles are the same from the perspective of an Xcode user. There are excellent tutorials on how to do this all over the Web, including the free book *Pro Git*.

Pushing to the Remote

Now you can give the remote some content. Open the Repositories organizer (**Window→Organizer** [⇧⌘2]); then select the **Repositories** panel. Find the "passer-rating" repo in the table on the left, and select the "Remotes" folder under the repo name. The list in the main part of the window will be empty. Click the **Add Remote** button at the bottom. A sheet appears for you to enter a name and location for the remote repo (Figure 7.2).

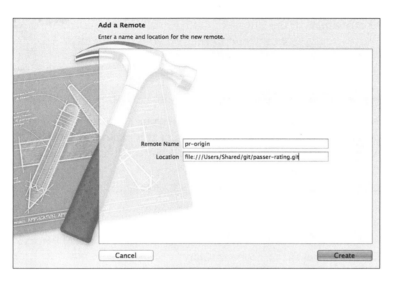

FIGURE 7.2   Clicking the **Add Remote** button in the Remotes list for a local repository yields a sheet asking for the name of the repository and its location.

For the name, enter something like **pr-origin**. The remote name is a convenience, an alias that Git can expand to the full URL for the repo when it is needed. The conventional alias for the principal remote repository for a project is "origin," but you'll have a lot of repositories, most of them will have remotes, and you'll find it easier to keep track if the name indicates the project it belongs to.

You'll be tempted to enter simply the POSIX path to the remote: /Users/Shared/git/ passer-rating.git. That's not how Git specifies repository locations; they must be URLs. So the correct location is **file:///Users/Shared/git/passer-rating.git**. Click **Create**.

> **NOTE**
>
> **Create** is succinct but a bit of a misnomer: Nothing much is created. What happens is that the settings in the .git directory in your project directory are updated to note that "pr-origin" refers to the repo in /Users/Shared/.

Xcode calls the process of updating a remote repository from local data *pushing*, after Git's term. Make sure all your changes have been checked in, and select **File→Source Control→Push**.... An alert sheet appears, asking which remote you mean to push to. There's only one known remote and therefore only one item in the popup: **pr-remote**. Click **Push**. An activity spinner appears briefly, and the sheet reports success and goes away.

That's it. You now have a repository you can share with your coworkers—or for that matter with yourself. It's not uncommon for developers to use more than one machine for work. Having a shared repository on the Internet (all that's needed is an account you can connect to with ssh) gives you your own cloud to keep all your development machines current.

Starting from a Repository

All your work so far has been done under one user account on your Mac; call that "User A." Now imagine that User A works with User B. For the sake of this example, User B will be played by a second account on the same Mac. In practice, your collaborators will be other people—or you—using different computers.

User B doesn't have a copy of the passer-rating project—that's the whole point. Xcode can get it for her. The first thing you see when Xcode launches without an open project is the Welcome to Xcode window (Figure 7.3). Issue **Window→Welcome to Xcode (⇧⌘1)** if it isn't already open. The second option in the list at the left is **Connect to a Repository**; select it to begin work with the Checkout or Clone assistant.

> **NOTE**
>
> Subversion's name for bringing in a working copy of a repository is *checking out*. Git's is *cloning*. Xcode won't know which system you'll be using until you fill in the URL and tell it.

The cloning process comes in four steps.

FIGURE 7.3   The Welcome to Xcode window (**Window→Welcome to Xcode [⇧⌘1]**) is the first thing you see when you launch Xcode with no project visible. One of the options is to check a project out from a version-control repository.

1. Fill in the **Location** field with the URL (not the path) of the shared repository: `file:///Users/Shared/git/passer-rating.git.` Click **Next**.

2. The next panel lets you name the repository; this is the name that will appear in the Repositories organizer, so make sure it's distinctive, like `passer-rating`. Xcode has guessed that the repo is managed by Git, so the **Type** pop-up shows **Git**. You could change it to **Subversion** if needed, but Xcode is right this time. Click **Clone**.

3. A save-file sheet appears for you to place and name the working directory to receive the clone. Having no imagination, I called that `passer-rating`, too, and put it on my desktop. Click **Clone** in the sheet.

4. You'll be rewarded with a panel that says, "Clone of 'passer-rating' complete." Buttons afford you the choice of seeing the working directory in the Finder, opening the project, or simply going about your business. Click **Open Project**. The Workspace window for the passer-rating project opens, exactly as it was checked in, except for some user-specific settings. User B is ready for work.

Merges and Conflicts

User A and User B now go about their work on the project. Let's give them some work to do independently to see how they fare.

User A

User A has some ideas about code style. In particular, he doesn't like the long identifiers in `rating.c` for the components of the passer rating. He does a search-and-replace (**Edit→Find→Find...**, [⌘F], and select **Replace** from the pop-up menu at the left end of the find bar) to change all instances of `Component` to `Comp`.

Also, he's noticed that Xcode has copyrighted all the files to `__MyCompanyName__` (see the sidebar). That's not right. So he replaces every instance with "Frederic F. Anderson." (The Search navigator (third tab) is introduced in Chapter 8, "Starting an iOS Application.")

He saves his changes and commits them. Eventually, he checks his accumulated commits into the shared repository with **File→Source Control→Push...**.

User B

User B is a stickler for copyright, too. She replaces all the instances of `__MyCompanyName__` in her copy with "Fritz Anderson." Also, she sets the Organization name in the Project inspector, so the problem won't come up again on her machine. She commits her changes to the local repository, and then pushes it....

And it doesn't quite work. Before User B pushed her changes, User A pushed his. The two users are contributing to a unified code base, and one or the other of them must pass on how their work will be merged into the shared repository. An alert sheet tells her, "The operation could not be performed because 'passer-rating' does not have the latest remote changes. Pull the remote changes and try again."

So User B dismisses the alert and the push dialog and does a pull: **File→Source Control→Pull...** (⌥⇧⌘X). All does not go smoothly. It isn't right to say that something has gone wrong—everything that's happening is supposed to happen; it's a normal state of affairs when two people work on the same code: They changed the same text in different ways. That's a *conflict,* and User B is on the spot for choosing how to resolve it. Xcode presents a merge sheet to show you what is to be done (Figure 7.4).

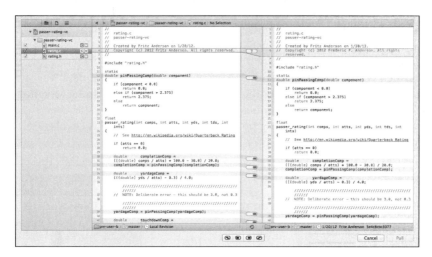

FIGURE 7.4   When you pull a revision whose changes collide with your own, Xcode presents you with a sheet that highlights the conflicts. The navigator lists all the affected files; the editor shows your local version (on the left) and the incoming version (on the right). Your version is shown with the nonconflicting changes from the pull already merged in.

> **NOTE**
>
> Even if there are no conflicts, Xcode will still show you a browser of all the changes the pull would cause. This enables you to see what changed and gives you an opportunity to reverse some of the changes if you need to.

The sheet lists all the files affected by the push in a navigator on the left. They are all badged with an "M" (the pull modifies them, and they must be committed to the local repository) and a red "C" to show that conflicts exist. Selecting a file fills the editor window with two versions of the file. The pulled version is on the right. On the left is the local version as it would look if all the changes from the pull were merged into it.

Merging

`rating.c` is a good place to start. The lines that the pull changes are marked in the scroll bar with red ticks, and in the editor with pink and blue highlights. The blue highlights do not (usually) represent a problem: These are changes User A made that User B's work did not touch. Still, she can make some choices (Figure 7.5).

She can select one of the blue highlights. The gutter between the two halves of the editor shows a toggle switch, with the mark to the right, showing that the contents of the pulled file (on the right) will be merged into the local file as shown. If she insists on her own version, she can use the control at the bottom of the merge sheet to take her local version; the toggle graphic then points to the left, and that part of the local file reverts to its pre-merged condition.

NOTE

The choice between left and right is a little confusing because the text shown on the left side of the editor always shows what the file would look like after it is merged. If the toggle is to the right, the contents of the local file before the merge are not visible; you need to switch the toggle to see them.

All the blue areas come from User A's substitution of `Comp` for `Component`. User B is okay with that, so she leaves the toggles as they are.

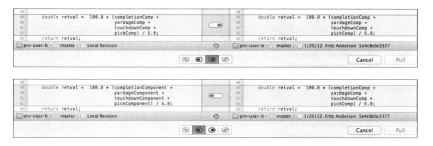

FIGURE 7.5   Selecting a blue (nonconflict) difference in the merge sheet allows you to accept the incoming change (top, the default) or stick to your own version (bottom).

Conflicts

The pink areas represent conflicts—places where both User A and User B changed the files. Git (and Subversion) do a good job of automatically interleaving the changes made in two versions, but they can't resolve a flat contradiction in a line. In this case, User A set the copyright holder to "Frederic F. Anderson," and User B, to "Fritz Anderson."

User B selects the pink area, which is badged not with a toggle, but with a ?. Xcode does not make a choice for you on conflicts. The merge control at the bottom of the sheet gives her four choices (Figure 7.6).

▶ As with the simple merges, she can choose to toggle to the right-hand version (accept the pulled text)…

▶ …or the left-hand version (her own).

▶ She can accept *both*. The choices at the sides of the control allow her to arrange the lines left-before-right…

▶ …or right-before-left.

User B is firm on her changes: The copyright holder should be "Fritz Anderson." She sets the conflicts on all three files to left-toggle.

After she makes her choices on all the conflicts, the "C" badges on the files disappear, and Xcode enables the **Pull** button. Clicking it does the merging and commits the results.

> **NOTE**
>
> In pure Git, the merged files would be carried as modified and would need to be added and committed. This isn't necessary if you use Xcode because it gives you a chance to examine all the changes right away.

FIGURE 7.6   When the merge sheet indicates a range of lines are in conflict (top), Xcode offers four options for how to resolve it.

With everything squared away, she can attempt her push again. This time it succeeds. She can send an email to User A to let him know there are changes for him to pull. (Or she could just let him discover them for himself, but that says something worrisome about how A and B get along.)

__MyCompanyName__

Xcode's templates for source files include a standard comment at the beginning showing the name of the file (which it knows because it created and named the file), the date it was created (because it knows when it created it), the name of the person who created the file, and a copyright notice (the year of which it knows from when it created the file). The names of the creator and copyright holder may surprise you. How did it get those?

Like any modern operating system, Mac OS X has user accounts, under which all user applications run. When you set up your Mac on its first run, you gave a short username and longer natural name to the first, administrative user of the computer. If you added accounts (for instance to ensure that there was a user who did not have risky access to administrative privileges), you provided natural names for those users, too. Xcode fills in the "Created by" line of the comment from that natural name.

The comment also includes a copyright notice, with a copyright holder and a year. Xcode tries to find a holder name by searching in this order:

1. In the File inspector for the project (select the project in the Project navigator, expose the Utility area, and select the first tab), there is an **Organization** field. If it's set, that's the name of the copyright holder. This works especially well if you work on different projects for different clients.

2. Failing that, if your Address Book entry (the "Me" card) has a Company name set, Xcode uses it.

3. Failing those, Xcode simply inserts __MyCompanyName__.

Setting the copyright holder for a project is easy, and it may even have been automatic in your installation of Xcode. For the purposes of some examples later in this book, however, I'll assume your headers all say __MyCompanyName__.

The Versions View

Checking files into version control, or even merging them, is not much use if you can't see what you changed. Xcode's Version editor (third segment of the **Editor** control in the toolbar) lets you do just that. Click it. The Version editor has three views (Comparison, Blame, and Log); I'll cover each, starting with the Comparison view, which you can select as the first segment in the control at the bottom-right corner of the editor.

Comparison

If you've been following along, the passer-rating project has accumulated a few revisions by a couple of authors. Select one of your source files and switch the editor to the Version view. It splits into two panels: The left side shows your file in its current state, saved or not. The right side shows what it looked like the last time you committed it. See Figure 7.7.

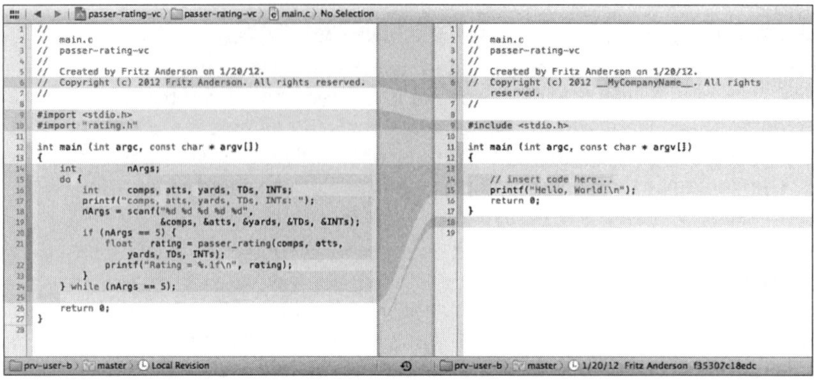

FIGURE 7.7   The Comparison view of the Version editor puts two versions of a file side by side, with a highlight connecting the changes you made between the two versions. The jump bar at the bottom lets you select among versions and branches.

Just now, they're probably identical, but try editing the current copy of the file. A blue band appears across the editor, stretching from your changes to the equivalent position in the committed version. If you made changes within a line, the differences are highlighted in a muted yellow.

The editor panes are real editors: You can make any changes you want, though any changes you make to a committed version won't stick. The idea is that you can copy code from an old version and paste it into your current version, which you can save.

NOTE

If you just want to abandon all the changes you made to a file since the last revision, there's no need to copy the old version over. Select the file in the Project navigator and expose the Utility area (**Views** control, right-hand segment). In the Source Control section, click **Discard…**, and confirm the change.

The editor isn't confined to the last two versions. There is a jump bar at the bottom of each pane, with segments representing the repository, branch, and revision the pane displays. Each segment is a pop-up menu; you can set the halves of the editor to any revision you like and see the differences between them. There's an even easier way to select revisions. Click the clock icon at the bottom of the gutter between the panes. You'll be rewarded with a timeline, a black bar with hash marks; the shorter marks represent the revisions that affect this file, the longer ones dates. See Figure 7.8. Move your mouse over the timeline; Xcode displays a popover showing the date, the revision ID, the committer, and the description for that version.

FIGURE 7.8   Clicking the clock icon at the bottom of the Comparison view's gutter changes the gutter into a timeline for you to select any two revisions in the current file's history.

There are arrowheads on either side of the timeline. Clicking the timeline to one side of a revision shows it in the editor on that side.

Blame

The Comparison view shows your revisions along one axis, the accumulated changes between two revisions. The Blame view lets you see another: Who wrote what parts of your current file, when, and why? Click the middle segment of the selector at bottom right to expose the Blame view.

> **NOTE**
>
> *Blame* is the technical name for this perspective on a version-control system, and probably reflects the mood of developers when they want to track down who came up with this or that change. Subversion tactfully offers "credit" as a synonym.

The right-hand panel in the editor goes away, to be replaced by a column of annotations. Each note matches up to lines in your code. At minimum, it shows the author, date, and revision of the last commit that changed those lines; if room permits, the annotation will include the commit message. See Figure 7.9.

FIGURE 7.9   The Blame view marks the lines in a file with the last revision and author that touched them. Clicking the gear button on the top line of the annotation gives the details of the commit.

The gear button on the top line brings up a popover showing the full details, and the popover has a tiny arrow button that exposes that revision and the revision it changed, in the Comparison view. The blue bar at the left edge gets darker the more recent the change.

> **NOTE**
>
> The log display in the Repositories organizer lets you associate an author with a card in your address book by clicking the (possibly generic) picture next to the revision. When that's done, the name (in the Repositories organizer only) yields a pop-up menu that offers to email the author.

You can display blame for any revision by selecting it from the jump bar at the bottom of the editing area.

Log

The Log view gives a third perspective on the history of a file. Click the third segment of the control at the bottom-right of the editor. Again, you see a single view of the file in the revision you select from the jump bar. The column to the right shows the full information for every revision that affected that file; you don't need to pick through revisions that didn't include changes to the file you're looking at. Clicking the arrow button on the top line of a log entry jumps you to a Comparison view between that revision and the one it changed.

> **NOTE**
>
> The Repositories organizer shows comprehensive logs when you select a repository, or file-specific logs if you select a folder under the repository and then a file within it. The disclosure line at the top of an entry lists the files that changed, as well as a **View Changes** button to bring down a sheet with a mini-Comparison view. That way, you don't need to open a project to see what happened to it.

Branching

One more thing. Programming is not a linear activity. I've gone through the revision process as though it were a unitary march of progress with every step leading surely to a bigger, better program. That's not real life. In real life, you have ideas that may or may not be useful in your product, and you shouldn't pollute the often-parallel progress of your "good" revisions while you play with them.

You do this with *branching*, which lets you accumulate revisions along separate lines (branches) of development and merge them as you need. passer-rating (so far) is too simple to provide a good example, so I'll just explain how it works; you can follow along with Figure 7.10.

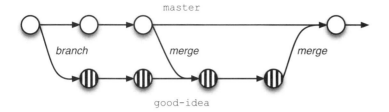

FIGURE 7.10   The main line of development of this project goes along the revisions in the
`master` branch. A developer has an idea he wants to try out, so he creates the `good-idea`
branch, occasionally merging in the improvements from `master`. When he's done, the `good-
idea` changes can be folded back into `master`.

Every project in Git or Subversion starts with one branch, which Git calls `master`. This
example begins with just the one branch. The developer comes up with a good idea, and
creates a branch he calls `good-idea`. (The quality of his ideas doesn't extend to the names
he makes up.) He does this by opening the Repositories organizer and selecting the repository for his project and the Branches folder within it. The list he sees contains only the
master branch. He clicks **Add Branch** at the bottom of the window and edits the resulting sheet to set the branch up: the name **good-idea**, that is to branch off of the latest
revision in the master branch, and in this case, that he wants to begin work on `good-idea`
immediately. See Figure 7.11.

FIGURE 7.11   The Add Branch sheet allows you to name a new branch and designate an
existing branch it is to be based on. Creating the branch designates a departure point to which
you may return to make future modifications. If you want to begin work on that branch immediately, check **Automatically switch to this branch**.

When he clicks **Create**, Xcode creates the branch and (because he checked **Automatically
switch to this branch**) puts him on the branch. How would he know this? It's a little
obscure. If he clicks the file-folder icon under the repository's name in the list on the left,
the window will show the file structure of the current branch. The name of that branch is
in a bar at the top of the listing.

He then does the normal work of revising and testing his program. In the meantime, he
also needs to maintain the program on the `master` branch, which reflects what has gone
out to users, and which other developers are using as the common meeting point for
their own revisions. So he switches back to the master branch using the **Switch Branch**
button at the bottom of the file listing in the Repositories organizer. He selects the
`master` branch from the sheet he is shown. When he's done, he switches back to `good-
idea` the same way.

Both branches progress by a couple of revisions (refer to Figure 7.10), and he decides his work on good-idea can't proceed without taking account of changes made to master. While on branch good-idea, he selects **File**→**Source Control**→**Merge**... and designates master as the source for the merge. The merge goes *from* the selected branch *into* the current one. Xcode presents a Merge sheet just like the one you saw in the "Merges and Conflicts" section.

He makes a few more revisions before he is satisfied that his idea really was good, and it's ready to go into the main branch. He switches to the master branch and merges good-idea into it.

Summary

This was a long chapter, but there's a lot to version control, and the benefits of mastering it are immense. When you created your first project, Xcode provided a Git repository automatically, just by your checking a box. In this chapter, you began to use it, committing your work step by step. Then you compared versions of your work to see what was done when, and to get a measure of forgiveness, of which there is not enough in this world.

Xcode's support for Git and Subversion is good enough for day-to-day work, but it's not comprehensive. You dipped into the command line to round out repository management. There is much more to Subversion and Git than I can cover in one chapter. The command-line interfaces to those packages are powerful, and you should at least look at them to learn what's available. The best resources are:

▶ **Git:** *Pro Git*, the best beginner-to-advanced treatment of Git. You can read it online for free at http://progit.org/book/, but consider supporting Scott Chacon, the author, by buying a physical or electronic copy.

▶ **Subversion:** *The Subversion Book*, written by (some of) the authors of Subversion and revised with each release of the tool. Find it at http://svnbook.red-bean.com/.

This takes me to the end of my generic introduction to Xcode. Now that you have a background, you can proceed to the tasks Xcode was built for: producing graphical applications for iOS and Mac OS X.

PART II

The Life Cycle of an iOS Application

IN THIS PART

CHAPTER 8

Starting an iOS Application

Now that you have the basic skills down, let's move on to a real project. You'll build an iPhone application that manages a list of quarterbacks and displays their game and career statistics.

Planning the App

Before coding, it's best (though not customary) to know what you're doing. Specifically, what are you going to present to the app's user, what data do you need to keep to make that presentation, and how do you translate between the data and the presentation?

Model-View-Controller

The Model-View-Controller (MVC) design pattern formalizes those questions into an architecture for graphical applications. The Cocoa Touch application framework is designed to implement applications that follow the MVC pattern. If you don't follow it, you will find yourself "fighting the framework": Winning through to a finished application would be difficult, and maintaining it would be miraculous. The Xcode development tools are designed to support Cocoa programming and therefore the MVC pattern.

MVC divides the functionality of an application into three parts, and each class in the application must fall into one of them:

▶ *Model objects* embody the data and logic of a particular problem domain. Models tend to be unique to each application. You can create your own subclasses of NSObject or NSManagedObject to give life to your models.

▶ *View objects* handle user interaction, presenting information and enabling the user to manipulate data or otherwise influence the behavior of the program. Views are usually drawn from a repertoire of standard elements, such as buttons, tables, scrollers, and text fields. Views ideally know nothing about any problem domain: A button can display itself and report taps without needing to know what tapping means to your application. In iOS, views are instances of UIView or its many subclasses.

▶ *Controller objects* mediate between the pure logic of the model and the pure mechanics of the views. A controller object decides how views display and how user actions translate into model events. In iOS, controllers are almost always instances of subclasses of UIViewController.

NOTE

Okay, in practice some classes won't fall exactly into model, view, or controller. If you have a view custom-built to display your particular data, making that view completely independent of your data model is foolhardy. Still, MVC is an important discipline: If you fudge on it, you should be aware that you're fudging and consider whether you can restore the MVC separation.

The Model

From the nature of a passer rating, all you need is one model class: a Passer to carry one passer's name, and the total attempts, completions, yards, touchdowns, and interceptions. Let's make this a little more interesting: Ratings can be calculated over as many attempts as you like and are usually calculated per-game as well as in a career aggregate. So Passer should "own" any number of Game objects, with details of the game (who played, what date, and so on) as well as the passing statistics for that game.

The model then looks like the diagram presented in Figure 8.1.

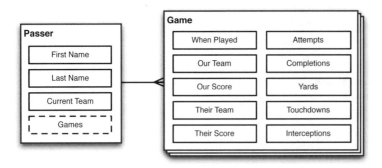

FIGURE 8.1   The summary description of what data a passer-rating app would need leads to the plan shown in this diagram: A Passer object serves only to identify a single player; his career statistics are in a set of Game objects that Passer "owns."

What about the Passer's aggregate statistics—the career yards, touchdowns, and rating? Those can be pulled out of his Games—it turns out not to be hard at all.

The Views

iPhone applications don't usually have a concept of documents, but even simple ones acquire many screens' worth of views. You'll deal in passers and their games, and you need to view and edit both.

So you need a list of passers, who can be created or edited in a separate view; and a view devoted to a selected passer, with a list of games that need a view of their own to create or edit them. A sketch of the flow appears in Figure 8.2.

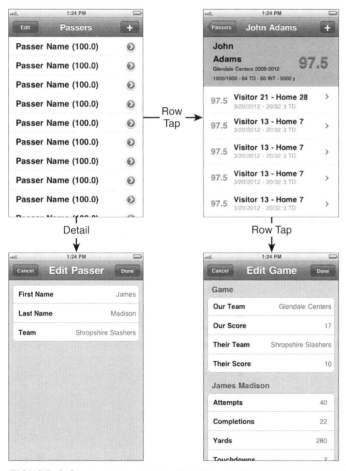

FIGURE 8.2   A rough sketch of the Passer Rating application. The initial view (top left) simply lists all the passers known to the app. Touching the + button creates a passer; touching the detail-disclosure button (>) on a passer opens it for editing. Either way, you use the view at the bottom left to edit it. Touching a passer opens his career record and a list of his games (top right). Games, too, can be added (+) or edited (touch the game), and the app needs an editor for them.

> **NOTE**
>
> That's what a full version of Passer Rating should look like, and getting it down on paper—I used the excellent Blueprint app for the iPad—is an essential step. Alas, this book will run out of Xcode examples before we complete the app.

Typically, each phase of an iPhone application displays a view object—a `UIView`—that fills the screen. That main view usually contains a hierarchy of other views. For instance, the `Passer` editor at the lower-left corner of the sketch (refer to Figure 8.2) consists of a wrapper `UIView`; it contains a navigation bar (`UINavigationItem`, at the top) which in turn contains two buttons (`UIBarButtonItem`, at either end). It also contains a table (`UITableView`) with three rows (`UITableViewCell`), each containing a label (`UILabel`) and a text-entry field (`UITextField`).

The Controllers

iPhone applications are organized around a sequence of *view controllers*, objects derived from `UIViewController`. Each view controller mediates between model objects and the views that fill the iPhone's screen. For each full-screen view you see in the sketch, you must provide a `UIViewController` subclass to link the data in the model to the views on the screen. In the life cycle of a view, the controller comes first; when it is initialized, it creates or loads the view objects and sets them up to reflect the model.

Now, even a simple application like this slides four main views onto and off of the screen, according to a precise hierarchy. Managing the relationships between them—which to slide in, which to slide back to—would seem to be an involved task—and is. But, thankfully, it is not a task you need to worry much about. UIKit, the user-facing part of iOS, provides umbrella view controllers (such as `UINavigationController`) that manage the navigation tasks for you by taking ownership of your controller objects. All you need to do is request a transition between the views, and the umbrella takes care of the rest.

> **NOTE**
>
> If you can restrict your project to iOS 5.0 or later, Xcode makes this process even easier. See Chapter 15, "Storyboard."

Starting a New iPhone Project

Start by creating a new Xcode project, selecting **File→New→Project...** (⇧⌘N). Select Application under iOS, and from the array of application types, select **Master-Detail Application**. Passer Rating follows the common pattern of presenting a progression of lists and detail views, under a navigation bar that provides a "breadcrumb" trail back up the tree. The Master-Detail Application template is a skeleton for such an app. Click **Next**. (For more on Xcode's project templates, see Appendix C, "Project and Target Templates.")

The next panel in the New Project assistant lets you name the project **Passer Rating**. That much is obvious. The next item is **Company Identifier**. Every application in the iOS universe has a string that uniquely identifies it. The app needs one. The way to ensure uniqueness is to select a name that's unique for you (ordinarily the product name) and then to prefix an inverse-dns string. I own the `wt9t.com` domain, so I'd fill in **`com.wt9t`**.

> **NOTE**
>
> You don't have a domain name of your own? Next you'll be telling me you don't have a T-shirt for the project. Get one (a domain name). They're cheap, and you don't have to do anything else with them.

Xcode generates an identifier for you and displays it just under the company ID: `com.wt9t.Passer-Rating`.

Next is **Class Prefix**. This is a string that will be prepended to the class names and associated files that the project template creates for you. If this isn't brief, you'll end up with unwieldy names, so try **PR**.

Device Family determines whether the template should include UI setups for iPhone, iPad, or both. Select **iPhone**.

There are four more options. Take two of them:

▶ **Use Core Data:** Core Data is Cocoa's object-persistence and relational framework, which is handy for keeping the database organized. The project template will add a number of convenient housekeeping methods for getting a Core Data-based application running.

▶ **Include Unit Tests:** Unit testing, the practice of automatically exercising your code to assure yourself that it works, is an important technique in modern software development. Chapter 13, "Unit Testing," covers unit testing in detail, but if Xcode's going to set it up from the start, you're going to take it up.

The other two, **Use Storyboard** and **Use Automatic Reference Counting**, take advantage of features introduced in iOS 5. Storyboard enables you to design not only the user interface for your app, but also how it transitions from view to view as the user navigates through it (see Chapter 15). Automatic Reference Counting (ARC) takes care of memory management in a transparent and reliable way. (It's available in iOS 4.3 but not fully functional.) Both are great features, but you need to target iOS 4.3.

When I get to a Mac version of Passer Rating in Part III, "Xcode for Mac OS X," I'll talk about ARC. For details on reference-counted memory management, see Appendix A, "Objective-C."

Click **Next**. You get a get-file sheet to select a directory to receive the project. Pick something convenient, such as your `Desktop` directory; that's where Xcode will put the new `Passer Rating` project directory. And because Chapter 7, "Version Control," sold you on it, check **Create local git repository for this project**. Click **Create** and look at the project Xcode has set up for you.

Target Editor

The Passer Rating project consists of two targets: "Passer Rating," which produces the app, and "Passer RatingTests," which will contain the application test suite. Xcode now shows you the Target editor. (Click the Passer Rating project item at the top of the Project navigator to bring it up yourself.) It provides an interface for the basic settings that identify your project—its identifier, target environment, orientations, and the front-end images (icons, startup screen) that are the face UIKit puts on your app.

The **Summary** tab comes in three sections:

▶ **iOS Application Target** shows the application identifier; Xcode lets you edit the prefix, but you're stuck with `Passer-Rating` until you change the product name. You can set a version number (the release version, without markers for alpha or beta status; those confuse Xcode's packaging process) and a build number (which is where you'd mark prerelease status). And you designate a target (iPhone, iPad, or both) and the "deployment target" (the lowest verson of iOS the app can run on). Xcode obligingly sets this to the latest version Apple sells, but for Passer Rating, set it to **4.3**.

Selecting the software development kit (SDK) is as important as the deployment target, even though the setting is in the **Build Settings** tab and not **Info**. This selects the libraries and headers for the highest version of the OS for which you are developing. If the SDK is set for a later version than the deployment target (it must never be set earlier), the features of the later OS are available, but linked "weakly," so your code can determine at run time whether the features are actually available before trying to use them.

▶ **iPhone/iPod Deployment Info** enables you to set the app icons and the launch images (the static PNG the OS shows the user while the app starts up). Also, you have your choice of the orientations you support, presented as a toggle button for the ones you can handle. This sets the *most* orientations the app will tolerate; your individual views may be more restrictive. You can ignore the **Main Interface** combo box; it tells the OS the NIB file (I'll get to them soon) that specifies your initial UI. For the master-detail app template, you're set up with code that creates the initial UI, and there's no need for a NIB to specify the details. Leave this (and **Main Storyboard**) blank.

If you select **iPad** with the **Devices** pop-up, you get an "iPad Deployment Info" section, laid out for iPad resources, instead. And if you select **Universal**, you get both sections.

▶ **Linked Frameworks and Libraries** is an editable list of objects that Passer Rating links to: UIKit, Foundation, and Core Data. No need to change it.

▶ **Entitlements** sets up options for compatibility with iCloud and shared access to the cryptographic keychain. You probably don't need those things, and by the time you do, you'll know what these settings mean. I won't be covering entitlements.

The **Summary** tab is just a front end for the more comprehensive settings under the **Info** tab, which in turn is a specialized editor for the `Info.plist` file. Chapter 21, "Bundles and Packages," covers the contents of `Info.plist` exhaustively, but it will be quite some time before you need to change anything.

Copyright, Again

If you browse through the source files, you can see that Xcode has once again used `__MyCompanyName__` as the copyright holder (unless you set a company name in your card in the Address Book application). This has already been covered in the "`__MyCompanyName__`" sidebar in Chapter 7. Again, you have two tasks:

▶ Make sure Xcode doesn't repeat the mistake in this project. Do this by exposing the Utility area (click the right segment of the **View** control) and its File (first tab) inspector, selecting the project (top line) in the Project navigator, and filling in the **Organization** field.

▶ Correct the existing files with a projectwide search and replace. This will be your first look at the Search navigator.

   1. Click the third tab (a magnifying glass) in the Navigator area. You see a text field labeled **Find.**

   2. Type `__MyCompanyName__` in the field; a menu pops up offering you options for the search, but the defaults (in-project, containing, match case) will do fine. See Figure 8.3, top.

   3. Press Return. The list under the search field fills with references to every file in which `__MyCompanyName__` appears, with subentries showing the found text in context. If you click one, the editor area displays the file, highlighting the match. Refer to Figure 8.3, middle.

   4. The Search navigator's **Find** label is a pop-up menu; switch it to **Replace** to expose the replacement field.

   5. The magnifying glass icon in the search field is a drop-down menu containing your search history. The first item, **Show Find Options**, lets you customize the search: literal or regular-expression; restrictions on partial-or whole-word searches; whether it's case-sensitive; and whether it extends to included frameworks.

   6. Type `Fritz Anderson` in the replacement field and click **Replace All**. You have to do the projectwide search first, or the replace buttons won't be enabled—Xcode forces you to look at what you're changing.

Figure 8.3 shows the whole process.

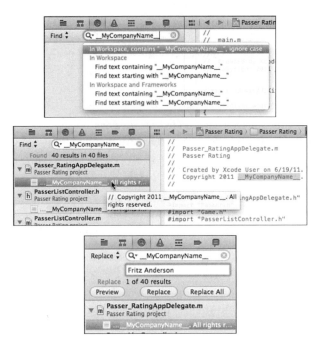

FIGURE 8.3   Expose the Search navigator to start a projectwide search and replace. (Top) Type the search string in the field; Xcode offers some common search options, but simply typing the string and pressing Return usually works. (Middle) When you press Return the navigator fills with every file that contains the string, showing each match in context. Selecting a match puts it into the Editor area. (Bottom) Use the Find/Replace pop-up to expose the replacement field. Type in your replacement string and click **Replace All** to make the change in all files.

At this point, Xcode offers to take a *snapshot* of your project. Snapshots are a supplement to version control; they copy the state of the project into a disk image before you make wholesale changes. Snapshots aren't a replacement for version control or backups—think of them as providing a mass "undo" that doesn't break your workflow as much as a commit would. Look for your snapshot history in the **Projects** panel of the Organizer (**Window→Organizer**, ⇧⌘2). From there, you can "Export" the contents of a snapshot to a new directory.

The first snapshot takes a few moments, but after that, they're cheap, so click **Enable**.

At last, you are rewarded with all instances of __MyCompanyName__ replaced with "Fritz Anderson." If you switch back to the Project navigator, you see that all the changed files' icons are dark, meaning they have unsaved changes. If you save them all (**File→Save All**, ⌥⌘S—you must hold the Option key down to see it in the menu), the "M" version-control badge will appear next to all of them. Now would be a good time to commit a revision to the repository.

The project template you chose for Passer Rating includes a lot:

▶ **Frameworks:** The Frameworks group contains UIKit, Foundation, CoreData, and SenTestingKit (which is used only by the unit-test target). They provide links into the iOS system software, and Passer Rating won't run without them. If you open the **Build Phases** tab of the Project editor, for the Passer Rating target, you'll find the frameworks in the Link Binary with Libraries phase.

▶ **Class `PRAppDelegate`:** The application is represented by an object of class `UIApplication`, which you should never need to subclass or replace. True to the delegation pattern used throughout Cocoa, all the unique behavior of the application comes through the methods of a delegate object, which the application object calls into. `PRAppDelegate` is declared as a subclass of `NSObject` and an implementor of the `UIApplicationDelegate` protocol. The template for the implementation (.m) file contains a good starter for managing the application life cycle, including setting up the Core Data database.

▶ **Class `PRMasterViewController`:** This is, as the name says, the controller for the bottom-level view of Passer Rating, which the design says is a table of passer names and ratings. Because navigation-based applications almost always start with a table, the template makes `PRMasterViewController` a subclass of `UITableViewController`, which is suited for running a table view. The implementation file includes skeletons of the methods you need to fill the table in. It also provides an instance of `NSFetchedResultsController`, which does a lot to help link tables to Core Data data stores.

▶ **Class `PRDetailViewController`:** The controller for the next layer of Passer Rating, the one that is seen when the user taps a passer's name. The template can't be sure what you'll be doing with `PRDetailViewController`, so it declares it to be an instance of the more-generic `UIViewController`.

▶ **`Passer_Rating.xcdatamodeld`:** Core Data isn't a full-service relational database (although it uses the SQLite database library internally), but if it were, the Data Model file would be the equivalent of an SQL schema. It defines the entities (think "tables") that hold the data, and the attributes (think "columns") those entities have. Xcode provides a graphical editor for data models.

▶ In the Supporting Files group, **`Passer_Rating-Info.plist`:** This is the source file that yields an `Info.plist` file to be embedded in the application. It provides basic information on what the application can do, what data it can handle, and how it is presented to the user in the Home screen. Some of that information is presented to the user as text, so its content is merged with the application's `InfoPlist.strings` for the user's language. (Chapter 20, "Localization and Autolayout," covers localization in Mac OS X, but most of the concepts apply to iOS, as well.)

▶ **Miscellaneous source files:** `main.m` is the standard container for the `main()` function where the program starts; you usually won't change it. `Passer Rating-Prefix.pch` contains common initialization for the compiler.

▶ **XIB files:** XIB files are editable files that will be compiled into NIB files and
installed in the application. They are archives, mainly of user-interface objects.
`PRMasterViewController.xib` contains the `UITableView` for the root view and links
it to the `PRMasterViewController` that runs the table. `PRDetailViewController.xib`
is a more generic layout that does the same for `PRDetailViewController`.

▶ The "Passer RatingTests" target has a class file and `Info.plist` support similar to the
app target's.

Xcode's template for the project also includes a panoply of build settings, specifying how
Passer Rating is to be compiled, linked, and organized.

The project is fully functional, as far as it goes—run it: **Product→Run**(⌘R). Xcode builds
the app, and in a few seconds, the iOS Simulator starts and launches Passer Rating. Out-
of-the-box, the app is the iOS/Core Data equivalent to "Hello World." It shows an empty
table under a navigation bar with **Edit** and + buttons. Tapping the + button adds a row
with the current date and time; tapping the new entry pushes the "detail" view into view;
the **Edit** button in the root list (or swiping across a row) lets you delete rows. You can
close and reopen the app to find that the rows you added are still there. See Figure 8.4.

FIGURE 8.4   The skeletal code that comes with the Core Data + Master-Detail Application
project template is enough to produce an app that can run in the iOS Simulator. It can add rows
to its table, and, as shown here, respond to the **Edit** button by offering to delete rows.

> **NOTE**
>
> As to whether Passer Rating is actually saving those dates and times, make sure
> there's nothing up your sleeve. Closing an iOS app usually doesn't stop it: The OS just
> puts it to sleep in the background, and its data won't be disturbed. To see a real, fresh
> restart, go to Xcode, click the **Stop** button in the project toolbar, and then click **Run**.

One More Thing

Passer Rating is supposed to calculate passer ratings, which is a problem you already
solved. Let's add your solution to the project. Select **File →Add Files to "Passer Rating"**...
(⌥⌘A). Xcode opens a modified get-file sheet (Figure 8.5). Track down `rating.h` and
`rating.c` from the old passer-rating project and command-click them to select both.
Don't click **Add** yet because there's more to do.

FIGURE 8.5   When you add files to a project, you have some options controlling whether to
use the files in-place and how to use them.

Check the box labeled **Copy items into destination group's folder (if needed)**. That
adds copies of the files to Passer Rating's project directory. It sometimes makes sense not
to do this, as when you want to share a common copy of files across projects, but for
now, this is the least complicated way to go. You'll see a better way to do the same thing
later.

Under **Folders**, you can decide how Xcode treats any directories you add. It can represent them in the Project navigator by group folders, as an organizational aid, or it can have the project refer to the directories themselves as the objects the project contains. The latter makes sense if you want to include a whole directory of data files in your product. You're not adding any directories, so this isn't an issue, but it's a good idea to make sure the setting is **Create groups for any added folders** because it's usually the safer action to take.

Now you can click **Add**.

Summary

In this chapter, you began work on an iOS application. Before doing anything in Xcode, we decided what the app would do and what it would look like.

When that was done, you knew enough to have Xcode create the project. You explored the Project editor and saw how it managed the configuration of the application. Then you explored the files Xcode's template provided and used the Search navigator to track down and simultaneously repair a bad copyright notice in seven files.

The "empty" application Xcode provided was runnable; you found that running it launched the iOS Simulator, which allowed you to use the app.

Finally, you prepared the app for your own work by adding the passer_rating function from the passer-rating project.

Now you're ready to make the empty app your own to start implementing the design you put together in this chapter. We'll start with the model.

CHAPTER 9

An iOS Application: Model

It's time to put some flesh on Passer Rating's data design. The Core Data framework for iOS and Mac OS X provides a powerful system for managing object-relational graphs and persisting them in an SQLite database.

Xcode includes essential support for Core Data. In this chapter, you'll see how to use Xcode's graphical editor to turn a data design into an executable data model.

Implementing the Model

Core Data stores the model objects for you and tracks their relationships to each other. To do that it needs a *managed-object model*, which specifies what *entities* are in the data store, and what *properties* and *relationships* they have. In the completed application, this is kept in a .mom file, which is efficient but not human-readable. For development, you edit an Xcode data-model file (.xcdatamodel) that displays all this information graphically in a format not too different from the model sketch in Figure 8.1.

NOTE

As your application evolves, so will your data model. Data files created with one managed-object model are not compatible with another. Core Data provides techniques for migrating data stores to later models if it has the full sequence of models available to it. The aggregated versions are kept in directories—.momd for use at runtime and .xcdatamodeld in Xcode.

Entities

Select `Passer_Rating.xcdatamodeld` in the Project navigator. The Data Model editor comes in two parts. The column on the left lists the top-level contents of the model, the main ones being entities. Entities describe individual records in the Core Data database. If you're familiar with SQL databases, these are roughly like tables.

The model supplied from the template is simple: There is one entity, `Event`. If you select it in the editor, you'll see its properties in three tables. (If you don't see tables, make sure the **Editor Style** control at the lower right has the first segment selected for the tabular layout.)

- ▶ **Attributes** hold simple data such as strings, dates, or numbers. `Event` has one attribute, `timeStamp`; you see in the top table that this attribute is of type `Date`.

- ▶ **Relationships** link entities one-to-one, one-to-many, or many-to-many. Core Data maintains relationships without your having to deal with keys or joins.

- ▶ **Fetched Properties** define fetch requests (queries for objects matching search criteria). These amount to relationships that are not continually updated as the database changes. To get a current object set, you need to refire the fetch. Fetched properties have their uses, but you won't have any of those uses in this project.

Click the right half of the **Editor Style** control to have a look at the other view of the model. This gives you a diagram of the whole model, in which each entity is represented by a box that contains its attributes and relationships. With only one entity, having only one attribute, there isn't much to see yet.

Now make something to see. Switch back to the Table style. Select the `Event` entity and press the Delete key. You want to add entities of your own. Referring to Figure 8.1, you need two: `Game` and `Passer`. `Game` has some interesting content, so let's start with that.

1. The bar at the bottom of the editor has two circled + buttons, and if you look carefully, you'll see the tiny triangle that tells you they are anchors for drop-down menus; they can add more than one kind of thing. The one on the left adds top-level objects to the model, and that's what you want to do.

   Hold the mouse button down on the **Add** button and select **Add Entity**. An entity named `Entity`, its name selected for editing, appears in the entities section of the editor. Name it **Passer**.

2. Click **Add Entity** again (the most recent use of the button sticks) and name the resulting entity **Game**.

Attributes

So now you have `Game` and `Passer` entities, but they don't hold any data. Entities are aggregates of simple data; these are *attributes*.

3. With Game still selected, click the + button on the right and select **Add Attribute**. This time, it's the Attributes table that acquires an entry with a generic name ready for editing.

4. Name the new attribute `whenPlayed`. You notice that the Type column for `whenPlayed` says it is of Undefined type. That's undesirable, but you'll take care of that soon.

5. Instead, create some more attributes: `ourTeam`, `ourScore`, `theirTeam`, `theirScore`, `attempts`, `completions`, `yards`, `touchdowns`, and `interceptions`.

NOTE

Remember to press Return when you finish editing a name; if you simply click the **Add Attribute** button, Xcode will abandon the edit and leave you an attribute named `attribute`.

---

6. Now take care of those undefined types. Start with `whenPlayed`: Select **Date** from the pop-up in the Type column.

7. But scalar type is not everything there is to say about an attribute. Click the right end of the **View** control on the toolbar to expose the Utility area. The Utility area is divided into an upper section, the Inspector, and a lower one, the Library. Drag the bar at the top of the Library down to make the Inspector as large as possible; click the third tab to show the Data Model inspector; and select **yards** in the Attributes list. See Figure 9.1.

The inspector has four sections, the first of which, "Attribute," is the most interesting. The name, yards, is right. The **Properties** check boxes reflect how Core Data stores the attribute. Leave **Transient** (the attribute would be in the model but not persisted) and **Indexed** (Core Data would efficiently retrieve Game objects by yards) unchecked. Uncheck Optional: The record of the game isn't complete unless it counts the yards gained.

FIGURE 9.1   The Data Model inspector, focused on Game's yards attribute. This is another way to set the type of the attribute, and it allows you to set detailed information on how Core Data is to treat it.

In the next part of the section, set the **Attribute Type** to **Integer 32**—an integer in the range of plus-or-minus 2 billion. When you do that, **Validation** fields appear for you to set a **Minimum**, **Maximum**, and **Default** for the attribute. Core Data refuses to save an object with an attribute out of range. If you make an attribute mandatory, it's wise to have Core Data initialize it to something legal. To enable a validation or default, check the respective check boxes.

NOTE

There is an argument to be made that you shouldn't make an attribute mandatory or set validation conditions until late in the development process. Core Data will raise an error if you try to save an object in which a mandatory attribute isn't set or any attribute isn't in range. If your code isn't finished, you might not have set everything yet.

The next part, **Advanced**, has to do with paralleling the Core Data store in a directory that has one file for each record in the store. This is a convenience for Mac OS X's Spotlight global-search service to find objects (such as individual emails) that can be extracted from your database. You aren't going to do anything like that, and this is an iOS application anyway.

The "User Info" section enables you to add any information you like, in key-value form, to the description of this attribute. You won't be introspecting the database's metadata, so you can ignore this section. "Versioning" gives hints to Core Data if you replace the schema for your database—it migrates your data to the new schema automatically *if it can*. Ignore it. Likewise the "Attribute Sync" section, which controls how iCloud keeps different instances of your database in sync.

So now you have yards taken care of, and six more integer attributes to go. This looks tedious. There's a better way. Click attempts; then hold the Command key down, and click completions, interceptions, ourScore, theirScore, and touchdowns. Now all six to-be-integer attributes are selected.

Turn your attention to the Data Model inspector, and change the properties as before: Not optional, integer 32, default and minimum zero. You've just set the properties of all six attributes.

ourTeam and theirTeam should be non-optional strings. There seems to be no way to set a default, so leave it blank: You'll have to remember to initialize it when you create a new Game object.

And that sets up the attributes for Game. Do the same for Passer, with three string attributes, firstName, lastName, and currentTeam.

Relationships

The data model so far is still kind of useless. You can store and enumerate Passers, and you can do the same with Games, but quarterbacks participate in games, and Game is the only thing that holds a quarterback's actual performance. Core Data calls the link between two entities a *relationship*.

8. Make sure the `Passer` entity is selected. A passer may start with no games played but eventually he will play in many. Choose **Add Relationship** from the drop-down on the right + button, click the + button under the Relationships table, or select **Editor→Add Relationship**. A new entry appears in the Relationships list.

> **NOTE**
>
> Whenever you're in doubt about what you can do in an editor, check the **Editor** menu. It shows different commands depending on the type of editor you are using, so it changes a lot. What's available now may be different from what you saw the last time you opened that menu.

9. Name it **games**. (It's a good idea to name a relationship the same as the related entity, pluralized if the relationship is to-many.)

10. Select **Game** from the pop-up in the Destination column. `Game` doesn't have any relationships yet, so there's nothing to do now with the Inverse column.

11. Turn to the Data Model inspector, which now shows options for a relationship. The items at the top reflect your choices from the table, so you can leave them alone. **Optional** is checked, which is correct because the passer may not have played.

12. Check the **To-Many Relationship** box because a passer may play in more than one game. (Core Data takes care of record IDs and foreign keys silently.)

13. There is an **Ordered** check box. Originally, Core Data acted like most relational databases: A simple reference through a to-many relationship would return an unordered set of objects; you'd have to specify an ordering to get games, for instance, by date. In Lion and iOS 5, Core Data can keep to-many relationships in an *ordered* set, which remembers the last ordering you put on it. Unfortunately, you're targeting iOS 4.3. Leave the box unchecked.

14. Don't bother with setting a minimum or maximum: The relationship is optional, so a minimum is irrelevant, and you're okay with however many `Games` may be linked to this `Passer`.

15. The **Delete Rule** is important. What happens if the `Passer` is removed from the database? You wouldn't want its `Games` to remain; there's no point in having statistics that aren't related to any passers. You have four choices:

   ▶ **No Action** does nothing when the `Passer` is deleted; the `Games` will be orphaned, *and* they will have dangling references to the now-deleted `Passer`. You don't want that.

   ▶ **Nullify** is scarcely better; the `Games` remain in the database, but at least their back-reference to the `Passer` is closed off.

   ▶ **Deny** goes too far because it would prevent `Passer` from being deleted as long as it had any `Games`. You'd need to unlink all of them before you could delete.

▶ **Cascade** is what you want; deleting a `Passer` would pursue the relationship and delete all the objects it reaches: No `Passer`, no `Games`.

16. The rest of the inspector covers the global-search, metadata, versioning, and sync attributes I showed you for attributes. Again, you don't care.

At this point, you can ask a `Passer` for all its `Games`, and it can give them to you. But you can't ask a `Game` for its `Passer`. You need to establish an *inverse relationship*. Select the `Game` entity, and create a relationship named **passer**. The destination is `Passer`; the inverse is `games`.

NOTE

It's so rare not to want an inverse for a relationship that `momc`, the compiler that translates `.xcdatamodels` into `.moms`, warns if you don't specify one.

Now that you have both ends of the one-to-many relationship, you can specify an inverse: In the **Inverse** column, specify `games`. In the Data Model inspector, the relationship is *not* optional: Again, a `Game` without a `Passer` makes no sense, and you want Core Data to enforce that. Xcode sets the minimum and maximum count to 1, which is good. And for this relationship, the **Delete Rule** should be **Nullify**—you want `Passer` to live with its relationship to this `Game` removed.

The data model is complete. Click the Graph (right-hand) side of the **Editor Style** control at the bottom to see all the entities laid out in a diagram (Figure 9.2) that looks a lot like the original design in Figure 8.1. (You need to drag the two entity blocks apart if they overlap.)

You can edit—even create—the data model in the Graph view if you want; it's just a matter of using the **Add** buttons and the Data Model inspector.

NOTE

This data model would not pass muster as a professional data design. The name `Game` is a misnomer because it implies a particular event held at a particular place and time, at which at least two quarterbacks make passes; but `Game` refers to one passer's performance at that event. A more sophisticated model would make the `Game` entity describe the event and use a join entity to link between `Passers` and `Games` and hold one quarterback's performance at that game. Further, a quarterback may play for many teams during his career, and it would be interesting to list all the games a team played; the model should normalize a `Team` entity out of `Passer` and `Game`. Noted. It's just an example.

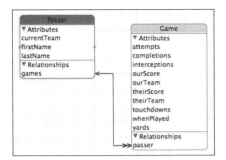

FIGURE 9.2   The Graph style of the Data Model editor shows all the entities in the model laid out in a block diagram. The one-to-many relationship between `Passer` and `Game` is shown by an arrow with one head at the `Passer` end and many on the `Game` end.

Managed-Object Classes

You could begin using the data model right away. You could ask Core Data to instantiate a `Game` as a generic object that can set, store, and return its attributes; it would be an object of class `NSManagedObject`. You could instantiate a `Passer` the same way, and it would be an `NSManagedObject` that handled those attributes. It would work. It worked for the dummy `Event` entity when you ran the project template unaltered.

But...

You might notice a lot that isn't in the data model. There is no passer-rating attribute—the point of the whole application—anywhere. `Passer` has no attributes for career attempts, completions, yards,. What are you going to do about that?

Creating the Classes

What you're going to do is to calculate them while the application runs, rather than store them. Those statistics are derived from the numbers you do store. To do those calculations, you need Objective-C methods that draw on the attributes of `Passer` and `Game`. And to have those methods, you need classes (subclasses of `NSManagedObject`, as it happens) that implement them. You need interface (`.h`) and implementation (`.m`) files for two new classes.

Make sure your data model is selected in the Project navigator. Select **File→New→File...**(⌘N). Navigate the **New File** assistant from **iOS**, to **Core Data**, to **NSManagedObject subclass.** (That last won't appear unless you have a data model in the project.) The description says that this is "An Objective-C NSManagedObject subclass, with a header," but that undersells it. Click **Next**.

> **NOTE**
>
> You can get to the same place without the template picker by selecting **Editor→Create NSManagedObject Subclass...** while the data model editor is visible.

The next page in the New File assistant sheet is new to you. It presents a list of the entities you defined in your data model. You want to create custom classes for Passer and Game, so check both and Click **Next**.

A get-file sheet appears for you to select a directory to receive the source files. Selecting a directory is your only option; Xcode names the files after the entities. Be tidy and create a directory just for the model objects: With the Passer Rating source directory selected, click **New Folder** and name it `Model`. Make sure the new directory is selected in the file browser by clicking it.

Xcode has added a few options to the sheet. The **Group** pop-up lets you select where in the organization of your project you want the files to go; they should go into the group for the Passer Rating target.

The sheet offers a list of **Targets** to which the files should belong. Definitely they should go into the application target, so leave Passer Rating checked. Xcode also offers to include the file in the Passer RatingTests target that was automatically created along with the project. Oddly enough, you don't want to include application classes in the application-test target, even if you mean to test them. Chapter 13, "Unit Testing," explains why.

If you were developing for Lion or iOS 5, you'd check **Use scalar properties for primitive data types**; internally, Core Data wraps attributes like integers in Objective-C objects, but it would be easier if you could deal in the integers directly without wrapping and unwrapping them. Checking this option makes this possible.

So only Passer Rating should be checked. Now you can click **Create**.

Now the Project navigator shows the new files. They should have "A" badges to show they have been added to the local repository; if not, select the truants and issue **File→Source Control→Add**. Because you want to keep the Project navigator tidy, select all the new files (shift-or command-clicking as necessary) and then **File→New→Group from Selection**. They'll be wrapped in a group named "New Group," which you can rename (for instance, to `Data Model`) by clicking it and pressing Return.

> **NOTE**
>
> The Project navigator represents groups with yellow folders, and your experience associates folder icons with file-system directories. That isn't so in this case. The model-class files happen to be in their own file directory, but that isn't relevant to the groups in the navigator. Groups are solely for your convenience in organizing your project. You could drag Passer Rating.xcdatamodeld into the new Data Model group, and it would remain where it was in the file system.

Now would be a good time to do a commit.

Extending the Classes

The whole point in having managed-object classes is to provide and encapsulate behavior beyond what Core Data provides. The leading example is calculating passer ratings, the purpose of the app. This section outlines how it's done; see the sample code for the full treatment.

Use the Project navigator to expose Game.h. The interesting feature is the list of @property directives that reflect the attributes you set for the Game entity, plus the reference through the passer relationship. (The .m file contains @dynamic directives to let the compiler know that Core Data will provide the accessors.) Let's add one more @property:

```
@property (nonatomic, readonly, retain) NSNumber * passerRating;
```

...which is to say, an NSNumber object, wrapping the calculated passer rating for this Game. You can read it, but you can't change it.

Import rating.h in Game.m and implement the @property between the @implementation and @end:

```
- (NSNumber *) passerRating
{
    double rating = passer_rating(self.attempts.intValue,
                                  self.completions.intValue,
                                  self.yards.intValue,
                                  self.touchdowns.intValue,
                                  self.interceptions.intValue);
    return [NSNumber numberWithDouble: rating];
}
```

You can see that except for the business of unwrapping (.intValue) and wrapping (numberWithDouble:) the numbers with NSNumber objects, the calculation is no different than it was in the passer-rating tool. Now any reference to someGame.passerRating produces an NSNumber whose doubleValue is the passer rating for that game.

Do the same thing in Passer.h and Passer.m. It's the same @property declaration, but Passer doesn't have any passer-performance statistics; all of those come through its to-many games relationship. The implementation reflects that. At the top of Passer.m, add

```
#import "rating.h"
```

to let the compiler know about the passer_rating function, and then implement Passer's passerRating @property, right after the @dynamic directives:

```
- (NSNumber *) passerRating
{
    int attempts = [[self.games valueForKeyPath: @"@sum.attempts"] intValue];
    int comps = [[self.games valueForKeyPath: @"@sum.completions"] intValue];
    int yards = [[self.games valueForKeyPath: @"@sum.yards"] intValue];
    int tds = [[self.games valueForKeyPath: @"@sum.touchdowns"] intValue];
    int ints = [[self.games valueForKeyPath: @"@sum.interceptions"] intValue];

    double rating = passer_rating(attempts, comps, yards, tds, ints);
    return [NSNumber numberWithDouble: rating];
}
```

This method works through the games relationship. It uses the key-value coding method valueForKeyPath: to pull (for instance) the attempts of each game from the games set and then to sum (@sum) the results.

You can use aggregate keypaths to derive some other interesting facts about a passer—for instance:

```
-(NSNumber *) attempts
{
    // All-career passing attempts
    return [self.games valueForKeyPath: @"@sum.attempts"];
}


-(NSDate *) lastPlayed
{
    // The date of the last game the passer played
    return [self.games valueForKeyPath: @"@max.whenPlayed"];
}


-(NSArray *) teams
{
    // The name of every team the passer played for
    return [[self.games valueForKeyPath:
            @"@distinctUnionOfObjects.ourTeam"]
            allObjects];
}
```

Some Test Data

Passer Rating won't work without data. In a finished product, that would be easy: The user provides his own data. But you don't want to wait on having a full suite of editors in the app to see how it works. So you need some test data to preload into the app.

This can take the form of a CSV file. I used a script, generate-games.rb, to produce a good-enough data set:

```
firstName,lastName,attempts,completions,interceptions, ...
Jimmy,Carter,37,11,1,0,56,2010-03-24,Boise Bearcats,2, ...
Andy,Jackson,33,8,1,1,30,2010-03-24,Modesto Misanthropes,9, ...
James,Madison,20,15,0,4,241,2010-04-14,San Bernardino Stalkers,47, ...
Quinn,Adams,9,3,1,1,17,2010-04-14,San Bernardino Stalkers,47, ...
...
```

The script runs to about 280 lines, so look for it in the sample code. The output is flawed—team A is recorded as playing at team B on the same day that team B is at team C, and Big Bill Taft turns out to be a much better quarterback than you'd expect. Those aren't relevant to exercising what the app does; for further information, check the Wikipedia entry for "YAGNI."

If the sample data doesn't exist or doesn't reflect the latest version of generate-games.rb, it should be (re)built. Can Xcode take care of this?

Yes. First, add generate-games.rb to the project by the add-files command you saw before, or simply by dragging it in from the Finder. Xcode needs to find the script wherever the project is, so have Xcode copy the file into the project directory (*not* the source directory, inside the project directory, which is what Xcode offers you at first).

Now open the Project editor (click the top line of the Project navigator), and select the Passer Rating target. Click the **Build Phases** tab to reveal the agenda for building Passer Rating. You want that agenda to include running that script.

Do this by clicking and holding the **Add Build Phase** button to drop down a menu, from which you select **Add Run Script**. A new phase, labeled "Run Script," appears. It's added as the last phase, but it's no good running generate-games.rb *after* the "Copy Bundle Resources" phase, so drag the new phase up so it comes before. Double-click the phase's title and change it to **Generate Test Data**.

The Run Script editor (click the disclosure triangle if it isn't visible) comes in three parts:

▶ At the top, you provide the script to be run. This isn't generate-games.rb: The script works by writing to standard output, which you must redirect to a file. So for the **Shell**, specify the vanilla **/bin/sh**, and for the script, the one-liner

```
/usr/bin/ruby "${SRCROOT}/generate-games.rb" \
    > "${SRCROOT}/sample-data.csv"
```

(I've broken the line with a \ for readability, but you should put it all on one line.)

The quotes are necessary. The SRCROOT shell variable expands to a path to your Passer Rating directory, and the space will confuse the sh interpreter.

▶ Next comes a table of input files. If Xcode knows what files go into and come out of a phase, its build system can skip the phase unless the inputs are newer than the outputs. Click the + button and enter

```
$(SRCROOT)/generate-games.rb
```

▶ For an output file, enter

`$(SRCROOT)/sample-data.csv`

So the run-script phase says, "run the Ruby script `generate-games.rb`, sending the output to `sample-data.csv` in the project root directory. If the output file is already there, and is newer than the script, don't bother."

Now all you have to do is make sure `sample-data.csv` is part of the Copy Bundle Resources build phase, so it will make its way inside the Passer Rating app. Click the disclosure triangle to expose the table of files to be included, click the + button to add the CSV file and...

There are a couple of problems. The first is that, not knowing what to do with an `.rb` file, Xcode dumped it into the copy-resources phase. You don't want `generate-games.rb` to be in the product. Easy enough: Select its entry in the table, and click –.

The bigger problem is a chicken-and-egg thing: `sample-data.csv` doesn't exist, so there's no way to put it into the table. The solution is to do a build (**Product→Build**, ⌘B). That runs `generate-games.rb` and puts `sample-data.csv` in the project directory. Now you can click the + button and then the **Add Other...** button to find the CSV file. Xcode offers to add the file to the project, which is just what you want.

When they're all set up, the script and resources build phases should look like Figure 9.3.

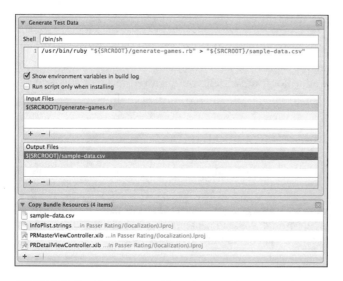

FIGURE 9.3   The Generate Test Data and Copy Bundle Resources build phases, set up to run the `generate-games.rb` script and produce `sample-data.csv`, which are then copied into the Passer Rating product.

Both the Ruby and the CSV file show up in the Project navigator with the "?" version-control badge. Select them and then **File→Source Control→Add**.

> **NOTE**
>
> There's a case to be made that `sample-data.csv` is a product file, completely repro-
> ducible from `generate-games.rb`, so it shouldn't go into a repository. If you feel that
> way, select it and issue **Ignore** from the **Source Control** menu.

In the sample code, you'll find the simple CSV parser (`SimpleCSVFile`) and the code
added to `Passer` and `Game` to make them clients of the parser. The application delegate is
set up so that when the app starts, it loads its Core Data store from the CSV.

Making the Model Easier to Debug

You've already run Passer Rating with the dummy data model from the template. This has
stored a `Passer_Rating.sqlite` file in the app's documents directory. That file must
answer to the current managed-object model (`.mom`), or an error results. But you've
changed the model. You're not sure you won't change it again.

What you can do in the early stages of development is to delete the `.sqlite` data file at
the start of every run. Eventually, of course, you'll want your persistent data to persist,
but this is a quick, easy way to save yourself some headaches.

Find the `-persistentStoreCoordinator` method in `PRAppDelegate.m`. Add some code after
the declaration of `storeURL`:

```
    NSURL *storeURL = [[self applicationDocumentsDirectory]
                        URLByAppendingPathComponent:@"Passer_Rating.sqlite"];
#if ALWAYS_DELETE_STORE
    // For ease in debugging, always start with a fresh data store.
    [[NSFileManager defaultManager] removeItemAtURL: storeURL
                                              error: NULL];
#endif
```

and `#define ALWAYS_DELETE_STORE 1` early in the file.

Summary

You've started building an iOS application in earnest. You learned how to use the Data
Model editor to construct a Core Data managed-object model that embodies your design,
making entities that describe the data types, and endowing them with attributes that
have suitable types and constraints. You also traced relationships among the entities to
express that `Passers` play `Games`.

You went one step further into the model by writing its first actual code. You had Xcode
build `NSManagedObject` subclasses from the entities and made first-class objects out of the
database records.

Finally, the need for test data drove you to your first encounter with the target Build
Phases editor. You added a script phase that generates test data and set the phase up so
that it produces it on demand.

CHAPTER 10

An iOS Controller

If I were smart, I'd start unit-testing the model as soon as the first draft was done, before adding the complexity of a human-interface layer. But I'm not smart; I'm going to put testing off until Chapter 13, "Unit Testing."

Instead, we'll go ahead with the first cut at a real app. Xcode's master-detail application template provides a working version of the first table. Let's convert that into a table of quarterbacks and their ratings.

You remember from the "The Controllers" section of Chapter 8, "Starting an iOS Application," that the view comprising a full-screen stage in an iOS application is managed by a *view controller*, a subclass of UIViewController. iOS services view controllers with a defined repertoire of method calls throughout the life cycle of the view: loading, response to events, and teardown. It is your responsibility to provide a UIViewController that supplies these methods. In this chapter, you'll fill out the initial controller, PRMasterViewController.

> **NOTE**
>
> Again, I can't supply complete listings for the files you'll be working on. The project template can provide much of what I don't show, so you'll have that in front of you already. For the rest, see the sample code you can get by following the instructions in the Introduction.

Renaming Symbols

But first: The first version of the Passer class has a convenience constructor, a class method named quarterbackWithFirstName:last:inContext:. This is wrong. By Cocoa conventions, a convenience constructor should begin with the name of the class, and it's bad style to say `last:` when the argument sets a property named `lastName:` It should be `passerWithFirstName:lastName:inContext:`.

Refactoring a Method Name

Well, you've done a global search and replace before; this is just a matter of finding every instance of `quarterbackWithFirstName:` and substituting `passerWithFirstName:`, right?

Wait. That doesn't do it. You have to take care of the second part of the selector, and that means examining every instance of `last:` to make sure it's part of the `quarterbackWithFirstName:last:inContext:` selector. To be correct, a search would need to involve a regular expression that captures all, and only, the uses of those strings that are the selector for that method. That means accounting for the arguments that come between the parts; the possibility that a call might be spread across more than one line; uses of the bare selector in `@selector` expressions; and preventing changes to a possible method named `quarterbackWithFirstName:last:team:inContext:`.

If you're a regular-expression hobbyist, you might come up with search-and-replace expressions that work. But they would take more time to formulate and verify than it would to do all the changes by hand. Refactoring does it right the first time.

`quarterbackWithFirstName:last:inContext:` is declared in `Passer.h`. Open the file, and select from `quarterback` through `inContext:` in the line containing the declaration. Select **Edit→Refactor→Rename....** A sheet appears with just the original selector shown. As you edit the selector, you find that Xcode does not accept the new name—it displays an error message—unless it has the same number of colons as in the original selector. That makes sense; if the number of arguments differs, there's no way to redistribute them.

Click **Preview** and examine the changes in the comparison sheet. Every use of the symbol—the declaration, the definition, and the calls, whether on one line or three—are changed. Xcode can do this because refactoring doesn't rely on searching: It has an index of all uses of the symbol, so it can differentiate it from near-misses and ignore issues of spacing and parameters.

Click **Save** and commit the change to version control. (Yes, really. You should commit every time you have a group of modified files that represent a single, logical change to your project. If you commit early, your commit log will reflect your intentions and not be just a list of mini-backups.)

Refactoring a Class Name

There's another naming problem, this time with the `PRMasterViewController` class. The name, provided by the project template. is descriptive in its way, but it describes the class's role and not what it does. It's a list of passers, and the name ought to reflect it: `PasserListController`. This is another case for the name-refactoring tool.

Surely this can be done with a search and replace? That doesn't quite work. For one thing, although it isn't the case here, `PRMasterViewController` might appear as a substring of some other symbol.

For another, the name of PRMasterViewController isn't just in text files. iOS apps are laid out in *NIB files*—object archives—which refer to classes by name. XIB files, from which Xcode compiles NIBs, are ultimately XML, but the XML is emphatically not human-editable. You'd have to go into a special editor, Interface Builder, and ferret out all the references.

Use the Project navigator to focus the editor on PRMasterViewController.h. Find the @interface declaration and select PRMasterViewController. Then **Edit→Refactor→Rename…**, as before. Enter PasserListController, and make sure you check the **Rename related files** box. Click **Preview** and look at the changes:

- ▶ Wherever PRMasterViewController had appeared in the source files, Xcode has substituted PasserListController. You've seen this already.

- ▶ The files whose base names had been PRMasterViewController now have the base name PasserListController.

- ▶ In the .m files for PasserListController and PRAppDelegate,

  ```
  #import "PRMasterViewController.h"
  ```
  has been changed to

  ```
  #import "PasserListController.h"
  ```
  so the renaming of the files carries over into the #import directives.

- ▶ PRMasterViewController.xib is included in the list of changed files. Look at the comparisons: You can see some complex XML, and the class-name references are changed. You also see that this isn't a simple search and replace in the XML source; the refactoring made structural edits to the files that would not have been safe for you to do by hand.

  Xcode does not offer to rename PRMasterViewController.xib. Cocoa applications often refer to NIB files through strings, and the refactoring engine can't know whether a string naming the NIB is an actual file reference or something else. It's safer to leave the strings, and the filename, alone.

- ▶ The names of the files in the header comments haven't changed. Refactoring renames only the symbols, not the contents of comments or strings. Xcode can't be sure which occurrences of a string in human-readable content are literal and not symbolic.

Save and commit the changes.

NOTE

You can also refactor @property names. However, in Xcode 4.2, if you start the rename at the *declaration* of a @property, the change won't propagate to all uses—be sure to examine the proposed changes before committing them. The workaround is to start from a use of the property or from the @synthesize directive.

Editing the View Controller

The new `PasserListController` is still set up to display the placeholder `Event` entity from the template. That's long gone, and you must substitute your own code to show `Passers`. The template code is set up to use `NSFetchedResultsController`, an auxiliary class that provides many services for listing, grouping, sorting, and editing a list of Core Data objects.

`NSFetchedResultsController` is a powerful facility, but you have to be comfortable with quite a bit of Core Data before you can use it effectively. But it's what you have now. When you read Chapter 11, "Building a New View," you'll see some of the underlying mechanism, which is simpler for simple things. For now, I'll give you a cookbook; all the changes will be in `PasserListController.m`.

Start by adding

```
#import "Passer.h"
#import "Game.h"
```

so the view controller can pull data from those classes.

The Table View

`PasserListController` is a subclass of `UITableViewController`, a standard subclass of `UIViewController` that takes care of some of the details of views that consist solely of tables. Table views fill themselves in through the *delegate* design pattern: They provide almost all the user-side behavior and call back to the controller (or other object)—the delegate—to provide the details that make a particular use of the table special. A `UITableView` doesn't keep any data itself; it pulls it from the data-source delegate.

Table-view delegates serve up the *cells* that make up the rows of the table; they create the cells and fill them in with data. Typically, this must be done only when the table asks for a row (in the method `tableView:cellForRowAtIndexPath:`), but for flexibility, the controller you get from the template fills cell data in through a custom method, `configureCell:atIndexPath:`. Find that method, and substitute this:

```
- (void)configureCell: (UITableViewCell *) cell
          atIndexPath: (NSIndexPath *) indexPath
{
    Passer * passer = (Passer *)
        [self.fetchedResultsController objectAtIndexPath:indexPath];
    NSString * content = [NSString stringWithFormat: @"%@ %@ (%.1f)",
                          passer.firstName, passer.lastName,
                          passer.passerRating.floatValue];
    cell.textLabel.text = content;
}
```

The `indexPath` indicates which section (always zero for this simple list) and row the cell is for. The method pulls the corresponding `Passer` from the fetched-results controller (which mediates between the database and this controller) and then formats a string with the Passer's information. That string goes into the text content of the cell.

Setting Up the Passer List

The fetchedResultsController method sets up a fetch request (think of it as a SELECT, if you're SQL-minded) that describes and sorts the objects for presentation to the view controller. There are two changes:

▶ The entity (table) setting becomes

```
NSEntityDescription      *entity;
entity = [NSEntityDescription entityForName: @"Passer"
                    inManagedObjectContext: self.managedObjectContext];
[fetchRequest setEntity: entity];
```

▶ Add a sort descriptor (ORDER BY) to sort by last name, then first, instead of the one descriptor that sorted Event by timeStamp:

```
NSSortDescriptor * byLast;
byLast = [[[NSSortDescriptor alloc] initWithKey: @"lastName"
                                      ascending: YES]
            autorelease];
NSSortDescriptor * byFirst;
byFirst = [[[NSSortDescriptor alloc] initWithKey: @"firstName"
                                      ascending: YES]
            autorelease];
NSArray *  sortDescriptors = [NSArray arrayWithObjects:
                                byLast, byFirst, nil];
[fetchRequest setSortDescriptors: sortDescriptors];
```

> **NOTE**
>
> Without Automatic Reference Counting, this code is wrong, but you'll fix it in Chapter 14, "Measurement and Analysis."

Creating a New Passer

The insertNewObject method gets called when the + button in the navigation bar at the top of the table is tapped; the link is made in viewDidLoad. The code in the middle inserts an Event in the database and sets its timeStamp. Apple's templates change all the time, but in the version the template gave me, insertNewObject pulled the entity (table) type from the fetchedResultsController and instantiated from there.

That's clever, but you already have a generator for Passer instances that avoids all the filibuster. Replace the body of the method with

```
- (void)insertNewObject
{
    //   Leave this in. I'll explain why.
    NSEntityDescription *entity =
        [[self.fetchedResultsController fetchRequest] entity];

    // Initialize a new Passer.
    Passer *        newPasser =
                        [Passer passerWithFirstName: @"FirstName"
                                           lastName: @"LastName"
                                          inContext: self.managedObjectContext];
    newPasser.currentTeam = @"TeamName";

    // Save the context.
    NSError *error;
    if (![self.managedObjectContext save:&error]) {
        // ...
        NSLog(@"Unresolved error %@, %@", error, [error userInfo]);
        abort();
    }
}
```

Giving every new `Passer` the same name and team isn't ideal, but you get the idea.

Live Issues and Fix-it

You've made some substantial changes, and would like to see whether the compiler will accept them. In a traditional workflow—and if you followed my advice in the "Quieting Xcode Down" section of Chapter 2, "Kicking the Tires," you're in a traditional workflow—you'd run the file through a check compilation.

But...where's the command to do that? If you've been searching for a command that lets you compile just one file, stop: There isn't one.

Try the second-best thing: **Product→Build** (⌘B), to compile the whole application. The activity view at the top of the window shows the progress of the compilation. If you and I are in sync (go to the sample code if we aren't), there won't be any errors, but there will be a warning, in `PasserListController`'s `insertNewObject` method: "Unused variable: entity."

You can see this is so. When you removed the generic Core Data methods for creating `Event` and substituted the `Passer` constructor, you cut out the need for an entity description (the constructor handles it)—but I asked you to leave it in, just for this example. So you can delete the line, and **Build** again.

There's a better way to do all this, and it explains why there is no way to compile a single file. In Chapter 2, I had you go into the Preferences window, **General** panel, and uncheck **Show live issues**. Go back and check it.

What happens now? With no errors, nothing much. Try pasting that orphaned entity line back in. The warning comes back. Now, in the expression [self.managedObjectContext save: &error], in the if statement in the middle of the method, delete the t in managedObjectContext. This time, an error badge appears, and the fragment gets a red dotted underline.

Click the red badge. A banner appears in the editor saying, "Property 'managedObjectContex' not found on object of type 'PasserListController *'; did you mean 'managedObjectContext'?"

Beg pardon? Did I *mean* managedObjectContext?

There's more: Xcode shows a popover window rooted at the misspelled symbol, with the same message, and, highlighted, the message, "Fix-it: Replace 'managedObjectContex' with 'managedObjectContext'" (Figure 10.1).

But wait—the underlying text already says managedObjectContext, with the t. That's because Xcode shows you the fix it offers. If you click away from the popover, it and the proposed fix will go away. Instead, double-click the offered fix, or just press the Return key. Xcode makes the edit, and the error disappears.

FIGURE 10.1   When you use the llvm compiler with live issues enabled, code errors are flagged almost immediately. Clicking the badge for an error may produce a Fix-it popover, offering to change the problem code to something that would cure the error. Double-clicking the fix, or pressing Return, edits the code.

Fix-it is not just a spelling checker. It uses the llvm library to gain insights into your code and to check what it finds against questionable coding practices. For instance, this sort of loop is idiomatic in C programming:

```
int     ch;
while (ch = getchar())
    putchar(ch);
```

but using an assignment (=) in a Boolean context like the condition of a while statement smells. Meaning an equality test (==) and doing an assignment is a common error. When the nested-parentheses warning is enabled, Xcode can detect that you could mean either assignment or comparison, and the Fix-it popover offers corrections that suit either interpretation. See Figure 10.2.

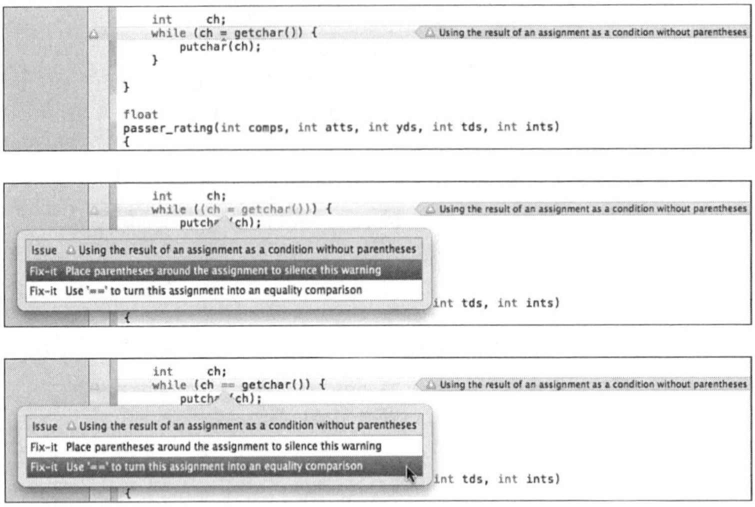

FIGURE 10.2   When more than one solution is possible (as in this assignment in the condition of a while loop), Fix-it offers alternatives and demonstrates what the corrected code would look like.

The Real Passer Rating

If all goes well, you no longer have a boilerplate application: You have an app that calculates and displays passer ratings. Now try it out. Select **Product→Run** (⌘R).

Another Bug

All has not gone well. The app crashes, the Debug navigator shows that execution was last in your code at `-[SimpleCSVFie run:]`, and the editor highlights a call to `-[NSDictionary dictionaryWithObjects:forKeys:]`. The debugger console contains a long message, including the same stack trace you see in the navigator, plus the important message:

```
Terminating app due to uncaught exception 'NSInvalidArgumentException',
    reason: '-[__NSPlaceholderDictionary initWithObjects:forKeys:]:
    number of objects (1) not equal to number of keys (12)'
```

Let's take this respite to examine the Debug navigator. The main part of the navigator is taken up by the stack trace, showing all of the pending functions from the crashed/break-pointed function at the top, to your root `main` function at the bottom. Your functions are highlighted in two ways: First, their names are shown in black instead of gray, to show that Xcode can display their source code.

Second, they are marked with a blue icon with the head-and-shoulders badge that Apple customarily uses for "user." The icon indicates the framework the function came from. Other examples are a purple mug for the Cocoa frameworks; an olive series of dotted lines (which may represent layers of bricks) for Foundation and Core Foundation; a dark-pink briefcase for the event-servicing frameworks; and a tan circle for the runtime library.

Not many of these are interesting. There is a lot that goes on inside Cocoa, and beyond knowing what called you, what you called, and what crashed, there's not much profit in watching Cocoa crawl around inside itself. Xcode understands. At the bottom of the Debug navigator is a slider (Figure 10.3) that filters the stack trace. When it's at the far right, you see everything. As you drag it to the left, Xcode edits more and more of the "irrelevant" frames out of the list.

  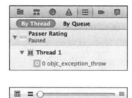

FIGURE 10.3   (left) When your application is stopped in the debugger, the Debug navigator shows the current stack trace of each of the app's threads. (middle) The slider at the bottom of the navigator controls the amount of detail in the stack trace, letting you focus on your own code. (right) Sliding the control too far to the left can elide more stack frames than is useful.

The debugger, especially the description of the exception, tells you what you need: The last of your lines to be executed was

```
NSDictionary * values =
            [NSDictionary dictionaryWithObjects: fields
                                    forKeys: self.headers];
```

and with the guidance of the message, you see in the variables display that indeed, fields contains only one object. What about self.headers? Unfortunately, I had Objective-C @synthesize an instance variable for that property, so it's not visible in the variables display. You can learn more from the debugger console:

```
(gdb) po [self headers]
<__NSArrayM 0x4d3f760>(
firstName,
lastName,
attempts,
completions,
interceptions,
touchdowns,
yards,
whenPlayed,
ourTeam,
ourScore,
theirTeam,
theirScore
)

(gdb) po fields
<__NSArrayI 0x5ee4500>(
)
```

The debugger command po means "print object." It prints the results of sending description to any object, and most system objects include details of their state. Even though there is no headers member of self visible to the debugger, [self headers] still returns an object, and po prints it out. It would be nice if you could access @propertys from the debugger command line with dot notation (self.headers), but that's not available yet.

fields is truly empty—I tried to select the line inside the array description, and there is not so much as a space character in it. So the problem then is, what would cause a line to turn up empty? Well, if the file ends with a new-line character, the "last" line, as defined by what was delimited by the last new-line, will be empty. The variable display confirms this: The method keeps a lineCount variable, and it says 1309, which is exactly the number of lines in sample-data.csv.

The solution is to add one test before the assignment to values:

```
// Skip blank lines.
if (fields.count <= 1)
    continue;
```

And because the CSV parser ought to catch some errors:

```
if (fields.count != self.headers.count) {
    // The record does not have the same number of fields as
    // specified in the header. Report the file path, line number,
    // expected, and actual field counts.
    if (error) {
```

```
    NSString *      localizedDescription =
        [NSString stringWithFormat:
            @"%@:%d: Expected %d fields, got %d.",
            self.path, lineCount, self.headers.count, fields.count];
        // The kCSV keys, errCSV codes, and WT9TErrorDomain are
        // declared in the headers.
        NSDictionary * userInfo =
            [NSDictionary dictionaryWithObjectsAndKeys:
                [NSNumber numberWithInt: lineCount],
                                            kCSVErrorLineKey,
                [NSNumber numberWithInt: self.headers.count],
                                            kCSVExpectedFieldsKey,
                [NSNumber numberWithInt: fields.count],
                                            kCSVActualFieldsKey,
                self.path,                  NSFilePathErrorKey,
                localizedDescription,       NSLocalizedDescriptionKey,
                nil];

    *error = [NSError errorWithDomain: WT9TErrorDomain
                            code: errCSVBadFormatLine
                        userInfo: userInfo];
    }
    return NO;
}
```

Running Passer Rating

Everything is fixed now, I promise. Run the app. The iOS Simulator starts up, and after a delay, you see the first cut at Passer Rating (Figure 10.4). It required a little focused effort on the controller end, but the data model seems to be holding up with some reasonable-looking results. When you swipe across a row in the table or tap the **Edit** button, the app offers to delete a passer, and when you tap **Delete**, the passer collapses out of sight. The + button creates one passer with the name "FirstName LastName," but that's all you asked for. As far as it goes, the app works.

10

FIGURE 10.4   The first real version of Passer Rating, at last. It reads the sample data, lists the passers and their ratings, and responds to commands to add and delete passers.

> **NOTE**
>
> Deleting passers in the running app is a little frightening because you can do that only so many times—at most 43, with this data set. However, you're not going to run out because I've rigged PRAppDelegate to reload the sample dataset every time the app runs.

When you're done, click the **Home** button at the bottom of the simulated iPhone, and return to Xcode. But wait: The **Stop** button in the Workspace window's toolbar is still enabled. What's going on?

Remember that from iOS 4 onward, apps don't unload when the **Home** button is pressed; they go into the background and can resume their run at any time. The **Stop** button is still active and the debugger is still running because Passer Rating hasn't quit. Tapping its icon on the home screen brings it to the foreground again, still running.

This is the right thing to do but not always what you want. If you want your app to stop, click the **Stop** button. Or simply go on with your work, and issue the **Run** command. Xcode presents a sheet offering to stop the incumbent.

> **CAUTION**
>
> The alert that offers to stop the incumbent process offers to suppress this warning in the future. *Don't check that box.* Suppose you are engaged in a long debugging session, and you are at a breakpoint. You want to resume running. You're concentrating on your work, not the tool. Which button, labeled with a triangle, would you reach for? The tiny **Continue** button tucked into the lower middle of the window? Or the large, friendly **Run** button at the top left, which would ruin your work if that alert didn't save you?

Summary

This chapter proved the data model by turning it into a real iPhone application. On the way, you got into one of the things that the Xcode refactoring engine can do: Intelligent renaming of Objective-C classes and methods in ways that a simple search-and-replace could not match.

You came across Fix-it, which offers automatic fixes of syntax errors and warnings, and Live Issues, which exposes errors and warnings as you type. The combination, made possible by the nimble llvm compiler, takes "check compiling" out of Xcode's vocabulary.

A bug in Passer Rating's CSV parser gave you a chance to get better acquainted with the Debug navigator, and see how it can do a little data mining to make debugging easier. And you used the debugger console to get a better idea of what's going on.

## CHAPTER 11

Building a New View

The passer list works well enough now. It's not fancy, but it nearly matches the wireframe in Figure 8.2. One thing it lacks is a transition from a list of passers to a passer summary and a list of games. For this, you'll create a new view controller and make a deep acquaintance with Interface Builder.

Adding a View Controller

The thing to remember is that unless you do some custom drawing or event handling, there's little reason to create a new subclass of UIView. The standard views are generic and versatile enough that making a new one is rare. What isn't rare is the need to set the content of views and respond to the events they capture. You know already that this is the business of the controller layer of the MVC design pattern, for which you need a subclass UIViewController.

The application template you started with did this for you: PRDetailViewController, with its .h, .m, and .xib files, is already in your Project navigator. Again, the default name is uninformative, so select the class name at the @interface directive in PRDetailViewController.h, issue **Edit→Refactor→Rename...**, and rename it to GameListController.

NOTE

If Xcode hadn't created the controller for you, you could get the same by selecting **File→New→File...** (⌘**N**), and pick the iOS→Cocoa Touch→Objective-C class template, subclass of UIViewController. You'd name the class, and check **With XIB for user interface**.

Version control shows the GameListController files with "A" badges because changing the name of a file is formally a delete-and-add. The PasserListController files, which referred to PRDetailViewController, are badged "M." Now would be a good time to commit a revision.

XIB Files

What is a XIB? At the first approximation, it describes the layout of your user interface. You put a top-level view into it (in this case, the app template has included one for you), and embed labels, text fields, buttons, tables, and other controls. You edit these with Interface Builder (IB), which is part of Xcode but has a name of its own because it had been a separate application for decades.

Many other platforms have such editors. Most of them emit executable code that constructs the view hierarchy described in the editor; or they work on files that the build process turns into executable code. IB is similar in that the XIB files it works on are compiled into NIB files at build time, which are installed in the target application.

That's where the similarity ends. Remember this: *There is no code.* NIBs are not executable; instead they are archives of Cocoa objects. The archives include links between objects and methods both within themselves and externally. Many newcomers who are used to other systems want code so they can "see how it's really done." NIB files *are* how it's really done. There is no code; in nontrivial cases it's hard to produce code that mimics NIB loading correctly, and in some cases (particularly on Mac OS X), it isn't possible.

> **NOTE**
>
> That is at least where you should start your thinking. On iOS, it's often useful to instantiate, arrange, and link views on your own—it's how many project templates start out—but code should not be the first technique you try. Interface Builder can be intimidating because it feels magical. As with most of Cocoa, it does things you may be used to controlling yourself. Relax. In the long run, if you learn to use Interface Builder effectively, you'll spend much less of your life fighting the operating system.

Interface Builder has peculiar needs for its editing space. Every part of the main content of the editor—your view—is significant: Ideally, you'd want to see the whole view at once. That takes space, especially if the XIB is for the iPad. Further, IB has a sidebar that you'll often want to expand, and you'll need the Utility area open to create and adjust the views you insert. What you don't need are the Navigator area, because you'll spend most of your time on one XIB, or the Debug area.

This is a job for tabs. You probably already have your workspace window set up as you prefer for editing source files. Start from there. Select **File→New→Tab** (⌘T). You're going to use this tab for all your IB work, so double-click the tab's name, and change it to **Interface Builder**.

Now configure the tab: Use the Project navigator to select GameListController.xib. With the **View** control on the toolbar, close the Navigator and Debug areas and open the Utility area. The bottom part of the Utility area is called the Library; select the **Object library** tab (the third one, with the cube) to show the repertoire of objects you can put into a XIB.

With the Project navigator gone, how can you get to other files? You've probably already noticed the bar that spans the top of the Editor area. This is the *jump bar.* It presents a number of controls for navigating your project directly. What interests you at the moment is the path control, spanning most of the bar. It takes the form of a series of arrow-shaped segments. Each segment is a link in the chain that starts with the project, goes down through the project's groups, to the file the Editor is focused on. (In the case of structured documents, it goes through the hierarchy of functions or IB objects.) If the current file has a selection, one last link identifies the selection by name. See Figure 11.1.

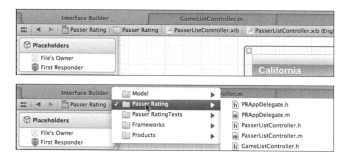

FIGURE 11.1   (top) The jump bar runs across the Editor area between the tabs and the editor. The main part of it is a path control tracing from the project through your groups to the current file and its selection. (bottom) Each level of the path control is a hierarchical pop-up menu that lets you set the path.

Clicking on a segment displays a pop-up menu offering a choice of the projects, groups, files, and selections available at that level in the hierarchy. The pop-up is hierarchical, so you can trace a new path for the editor. This suggests a strategy if you want to keep a dedicated Interface Builder tab. Open the Project navigator again. In the search field at the bottom, type **.xib** to narrow the list down to the project's XIBs. Command-click each so they are all selected. Then select **File→New→Group from Selection**. All your XIBs are now in a common group (which you can rename by double-clicking its name), which means that they are all at the same level on your jump bar. You can use the file segment of the path control to switch among the XIBs directly. Now you can close the Navigator area for good. Your workspace should look like Figure 11.2.

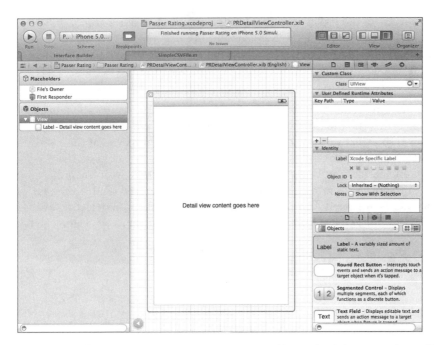

FIGURE 11.2   Interface Builder is easier to use if you give it its own tab, configured for the purpose.

Building a View

Let's get down to the business of creating the view. The `UIViewController` template starts you off with a `UIView`, sized to fit an iPhone screen, containing a `UILabel` for some sample content. If it isn't visible, click the round arrowhead button next to the bottom of the left sidebar of the editor. This switches the sidebar from icons for the top-level content of the XIB to an outline of your view hierarchy.

The design in Figure 8.2 shows a window containing (top-to-bottom) a navigation bar, a gray passer-information panel, and a table of game information. This view isn't responsible for drawing the navigation bar—it will be contained in a `UINavigationController` view that takes care of that. This means you can't use the full 320 x 480 pixel size of the view.

Interface Builder can help get the sizing right. Select the view (the View icon in the sidebar will do), and select the Attributes inspector. The Inspector area is the upper portion of the Utility view; the Attributes inspector is the fourth tab. It governs settings you can't make graphically. Different view classes have different settings, and the inspector customizes itself to match.

What you're interested in now is the "Simulated Metrics" section at the top. From the **Top Bar** pop-up, select **Navigation Bar**. The top portion of the view is now covered with a gray-gradient box that resembles a navigation bar, but it's not a live view: You can't adjust it or add subviews to it. It's just there to concede the amount of space that a navigation bar would consume. That takes care of the top part of the sketch.

You're about to add content of your own, so the sample `UILabel` in the middle isn't needed any more. Click it and press the Delete key.

The next part is the passer-detail view for the top of the view. This contains a number of uneditable text objects (labels) of various sizes and styles. First, add the container. Click in the search field at the bottom of the Object library (third tab, bottom part of the Utility area), and type `UIView`. You see an entry labeled View. Drag it out of the library and into the view in the editor. As you drag it, it transforms into a rectangle that sizes itself to the available space in the view. Let it go.

You don't want this view to take up the whole space. Click it to display resizing "handles" at the sides and corners. Drag the bottom edge up until the view takes up about the top third of the available space. This may be a bit tricky—IB clips the handles to the edge of the superview. It may be easier to grab the top handle, size it down, and then drag the resized view up until it abuts the navigation bar.

> **NOTE**
>
> If you're ambitious, you could use the Size inspector (fifth tab), which shows you the location and size of the view numerically. It should be at 0, 0, width 320 points, and height 146. (You may need to vary the size to accommodate your eventual layout.)

The detail view is supposed to be gray. In the Attributes inspector, there's a **Background** control, which has two parts: The left part is a color well, which you can click to get a color palette to edit the color. The right part is a drop-down menu containing standard colors. Select **Light Gray Color**. The inspector should look like Figure 11.3.

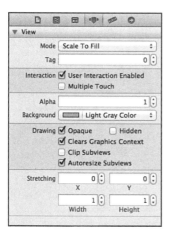

FIGURE 11.3   The Attributes inspector for the passer-detail wrapper view should look like this when you're done.

The bottom part of the view is the game list, taking the form of a `UITableView`. Typing **table** in the Library search field should show you a Table View. Drag it into the lower part of the main view. You need to expand it to fit the available space. This isn't too hard at the sides and bottom because Interface Builder "snaps" the edges to the bounds of the main view, but it won't give you any help with the top edge. Keep a sharp eye out. (Or use the Size inspector to make the y coordinate equal to the height of the top view.)

The gross layout is done. Now for the details.

Lots of Labels

The passer-detail view consists of many, many labels. Some of them are "labels" in the colloquial sense—they are permanent pieces of text that describe other things in the view. Others contain statistics and other information that can't be edited, but are dynamic in that Passer Rating can fill them with different strings for each passer it displays. All of them are "labels" in the sense that they are instances of `UILabel`.

The layout will be dominated by the passer's name and his rating, so put those in first and fit the rest around them.

> **NOTE**
>
> The cries of horror you hear will be those of professional graphic designers. Ignore them. They're used to it.

Type **label** into the Library search field to turn up the label (`UILabel`) view. Drag it into the top of the passer-detail view. The Attributes inspector has a **Text** field; fill it with **FirstName LastName**, and discover that the writing in the label has become tiny. `UILabels` adjust their text size (down to a limit you can set) to fit the content to the bounds of the label. Stretch the label across the top of the detail view so that no shrinkage is necessary.

The passer's name is important, so give it some emphasis. The **Font** element in the inspector shows the text to be Helvetica 17.0. Click the boxed-T button to open the Fonts popover (Figure 11.4). Make it bold and 18 points.

FIGURE 11.4   The **Font** popover lists all (and only) the fonts available in iOS. The **Font** pop-up menu allows you to select one of the system fonts, or **Custom.** Selecting **Custom** activates the **Family**, **Style**, and **Size** controls.

> **NOTE**
>
> As you adjust the font and content of the labels, you will find that Interface Builder tries to resize them. There's not much you can do about that, other than to drag them back into shape.

And now a label for the passer rating, on the right side, just under the name. This is really, really important, and I have no taste, so make it big, bold, and red. Fill it with **158.3** and set the font to Helvetica Bold, 52 points. For **Alignment**, choose right-aligned (the third segment), so numbers less than 100 can line up. Click the color well at the left end of the **Text Color** control in the inspector; that gets you the Colors palette. Use the fifth tab in the palette, and select the **Maraschino** crayon. The passer rating is now really, really red. Experiment with **Shadow** and **Shadow Offset**, if you like.

The statistics come next. Start with one label, `Attempts`, Helvetica 14-point regular, sized to fit, and positioned just under the left end of the name label. IB's alignment guides can help you match the left edges. You need four more captions, and you can save some effort by duplicating the one you just set up: **Edit→Duplicate** (⌘D), or hold down the Option key and drag. Line those up under the original; then edit each so that they read `Attempts`, `Completions`, `Yards`, `Touchdowns`, and `Interceptions`.

Next, create the labels that receive the numbers. Duplicate one of the captions, and make it read `30000`; size it to fit. Place it next to the Attempts caption; there are guides to align the text baselines. Duplicate it four times and align those in a column next to the remaining captions.

The numbers should line up on the right. Hold down the Shift key and select each of the statistics labels. Set the **Alignment** control in the Attributes inspector to right-justification: You can set the attributes of multiple views by selecting them all.

You want the team name to go under the rating: New label, `Tacoma Touchdown-Scorers`, Helvetica Bold, 12 point, right justified. Again the text becomes tiny, and there's no room to make the label wider. Fortunately, labels can be made to span more than one line. Use the **Lines** attribute to bump the label up to two lines, and resize the field to accommodate the necessary height.

Finally, a date label. `12/12/09 -12/12/09`, Helvetica 12, right-justified, under the team name. The layout is done. The view should now look like Figure 11.5.

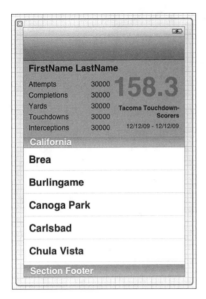

FIGURE 11.5   This is how the game-list view should look when layout is done.

First Tryout

Does it work? `PasserListController`'s `tableView:didSelectRowAtIndexPath:` is already set up to load a `GameListController` when you tap a passer and push it onto the navigation controller. So all you have to do is run the app. The simulator displays the passer list. Tap on a passer, and you can see your layout for the game-list controller, just as you laid it out. It's inert, but it's real.

Outlets

The passer-detail view has nine objects that the `GameListController` needs to fill in with names, dates, and statistics. How is the controller to connect to those `UILabel`s?

When a NIB is loaded into a running program, an object in the program is designated as the file's owner—in this case it is a `GameListController`. The NIB carries in it a list that pairs objects (your choice) to *outlets* in the owner. Originally, these were instance variables in the owner's `@interface` declaration, but now `@property`s are used because they give much better control over memory management. The `@interface` flags the outlets it wants to make available with the keyword `IBOutlet`:

```
@property (retain, nonatomic) IBOutlet UILabel *datesLabel;
```

Interface Builder can know what outlets are available because it knows what the class of the view's controller is. It knows this because when it filled in the template for this XIB, Xcode set the class of the "File's Owner." Look for yourself: The top icon in the sidebar is a placeholder for the owner. Click it, and select the Identity inspector (third tab) in the Utility area. The first element in the inspector is the class of the selected object. Xcode has set it to GameListController.

> **NOTE**
>
> "File's Owner" isn't literally present in the XIB; it's just an avatar that represents the relationship between the NIB and the object that loads it. You can set the class for File's Owner in the Identity inspector, and IB uses that as guidance for what methods and outlets the owner object has; but the actual class is that of the object that loads the NIB, not the advisory entry in the inspector.

You could type in @property declarations for all the labels you use. In fact, do that: In the **Editor** control in the toolbar, click the middle segment to establish the "assistant" editor. This splits the Editor area in two. The left half is still GameListController.xib. The right half may be blank; if it is, click the File's Owner icon in the sidebar. Now the assistant view fills with the header for GameListController. The assistant editor can be made to track the "appropriate" counterpart of any file you edit.

> **NOTE**
>
> Still not there? Click the first segment of the assistant's jump bar, and select **Automatic** from the menu that pops up.

Somewhere before the @end of the interface, type the @property for datesLabel, as I showed you. Save GameListController.h. Now go back to the sidebar, and right-click File's Owner. A small black heads-up (HUD) window appears, containing a table of outlets, among them datesLabel. There's a bubble at the right end of that row in the table. Drag from it to the label you set up with a range of dates and release; the adjoining column in the HUD fills with a reference to the label. Now, when the NIB is loaded, the owning GameListController's datesLabel property contains a pointer to that label.

However, you have to synthesize the property, unload the label when the view is unloaded, and release its memory when the view controller is deallocated. You have to do that with each of the IBOutlets you declare. This is beginning to look like work. There has to be a better way.

There is. Click the **x** next to the outlet in the HUD, and delete the @property declaration. Control-drag from the date-range label into the header file in the assistant view. As you drag within the @interface section, a horizontal insertion bar appears. Let go of the drag. Xcode displays a popover window. This window offers to declare a @property where you let go of the drag. All you have to do is type **datesLabel** into the **Name** field, click **Connect**, and the declaration appears. See Figure 11.6.

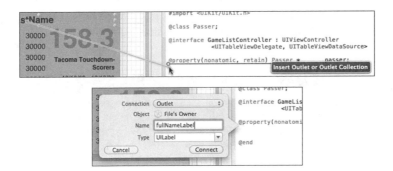

FIGURE 11.6   Right-(control-) dragging from an Interface Builder object into an associated header file offers a @property declaration linking to that object.

And not just the declaration. At the right end of the assistant editor's jump bar is a control with a "2" between two arrowheads. Click either one of them to see GameListController.m. Look through it: There's a @synthesize directive for the property, a [self setDatesLabel: nil] in -viewDidUnload, and a [datesLabel release] in -dealloc. The whole life cycle of the outlet is taken care of.

And yes, the NIB initializes the view controller's outlet with a pointer to the label. A bubble appears in the margin of the header file; the bubble signifies that the line it's next to represents an IBOutlet property. It has a dot in it to show that the outlet is connected. If you hover the mouse pointer over it, the object it connects to will highlight in the IB editor.

Before you go on a spree of making outlet connections, taking a little care can pay off: There is a + button next to the right end of the assistant's jump bar. Click it. The assistant area is now divided into two editors. Use the lower editor's jump bar to navigate to Passer.h. You want the names of the new outlets to match up with the names of the Passer properties they display, and the new editor gives you a reference for the property names.

Now control-drag from the variable labels to make new properties in GameListController. Use this convention in naming the outlets: Take the name of a Passer property, and add **Label** to it. So the name label goes into the controller interface as **fullNameLabel**, attempts as **attemptsLabel**, and so on.

> **NOTE**
>
> Interface Builder can also link controls to action methods, declared with the IBAction tag in the class @interface. When you trigger a control that you've linked to an IBAction, the action method is executed. See the "Wiring Up a Menu" section of Chapter 17, "Starting a Mac OS X Application," for an example.

GameListController needs to know about the table view, as well. Control-drag a link from the table to the @interface, and name it **tableView**.

The template put two @propertys into GameListController.h: PasserListController
sets detailItem to inform GameListController of the Passer it is to display.
detailDescriptionLabel was the outlet for the sample UILabel that you deleted early on;
delete the @property line and the references to it in GameListController.m.

Checking Connections

Check your work. This is important because the link from object to outlet is not obvious
with a graphical editor. Here's how you do it:

1. Click the File's Owner icon, and then select the Connections inspector (sixth tab).
    The inspector is a list of the selected object's connections—its outlets and its links to
    the outlets of other objects. First question: Are all the outlets connected? (You can
    ignore the searchDisplayController outlet that came with the view controller.) If
    not, drag from the bubble at the right end of the row to the object it's supposed to
    link to.

2. Move your mouse over the outlet rows in the inspector. IB highlights the corre-
    sponding objects in the editor view. Are they what you expect? The control-drag
    method of creating outlets is convenient, but it's easy to drag onto an existing
    outlet, which resets the connection. Use the x button in the outlet row to break
    erroneous connections, and then drag from the bubble to the correct object.

> **NOTE**
>
> Assuring yourself that one correct outlet connects to some object is not enough to
> guarantee that the object is connected. Outlets are just variables, and two outlets can
> have the same value. Make sure (unless you intend otherwise) that every outlet points
> to a different object.

Connecting GameListController

Interface Builder is great, but you still have to write code to get data from the model into
the view. You must make some changes to GameListController.

The template provides a setter for detailItem, setDetailItem:, which calls through to a
configureView method. That's where you move the statistics in Passer to the labels in the
view.

Here's configureView. It's a little long, but there's a point to make:

```
-(void)configureView
{
    if (self.detailItem) {
        NSString *      fieldName;
        NSString *      strValue;
        NSNumber *      numValue;

        // Set all the string labels
```

```
    for (NSString * prop in [GameListController stringProperties]) {
        NSString    *value = [self.detailItem valueForKey: prop];
        fieldName = [prop stringByAppendingString: @"Label"];
        [[self valueForKey: fieldName] setText: value];
    }

    // Set all the integer labels
    for (NSString * prop in [GameListController integerProperties]) {
        numValue = [self.detailItem valueForKey: prop];

        fieldName = [prop stringByAppendingString: @"Label"];
        [[self valueForKey: fieldName] setText:
         [NSString stringWithFormat: @"%d", numValue.intValue]];
    }

    // Set the passer-rating label
    strValue = [NSString stringWithFormat: @"%.1f",
                            [self.detailItem passerRating]];
    self.passerRatingLabel.text = strValue;

    // Set the date-range label
    strValue = [NSString stringWithFormat: @"%@ -%@",
        [sDateFormat stringFromDate: [self.detailItem firstPlayed]],
        [sDateFormat stringFromDate: [self.detailItem lastPlayed]]];
    self.datesLabel.text = strValue;
    }
}
```

I've omitted some contributors to this method—see the sample code for how they're defined:

▶ +stringProperties returns an array of the names of the string-valued properties of Passer: fullName and currentTeam.

▶ Likewise, +integerProperties returns the names of the integer-valued properties: attempts, completions, yards, touchdowns, and interceptions.

▶ sDateFormat formats dates into the current locale's "short" format—"mm/dd/yy" in the United States.

Here's where the care in naming the label outlets pays off: You can loop through the property names; use those to get the Passer values by key-value coding (see the treatment in Appendix A, "Objective-C"); add Label to get the names of the matching labels; and use KVC to set the labels' content from the Passer values. You don't have to get each property name right, and if you change your suite of labels, you only have to change the property-name arrays.

`passerRatingLabel` and `datesLabel` have one-off formats. Those can be done individually.

Code Completion and Snippets

You probably fumbled a bit as you filled in `configureView`. Cocoa Touch is a huge API, and nobody remembers every symbol and method name. `NSString` has more than 130 methods in its basic interface. If you don't have a crib, you might be pausing to look up spellings all the time. Here is where you turn on another feature I had you turn off in the "Quieting Xcode Down" section of Chapter 2, "Kicking the Tires."

Open the Preferences window (**Xcode→Preferences**, [⌘Comma]), and turn to the **Editing** tab of the **Text Editing** panel. Check **Suggest completions while typing**.

Now try the line `fieldName = [prop stringByAppendingString: @"Label"];` again, typing **stringB**. Xcode pops up a window offering to complete the symbol and shows the proposed completion in gray in the editor (see Figure 11.7). There are a lot of methods beginning with `stringB`, so you can scroll the pop-up through all of them. Pressing the up-or down-arrow key lets you choose among them. The completions all have the common prefix `stringBy`. The proposed completion puts a dotted underline under that prefix, and if you press Tab, the match advances to that point.

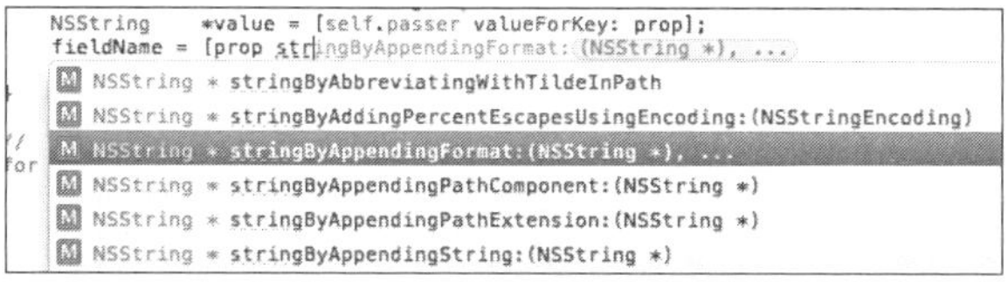

FIGURE 11.7 With code completion on, a window pops up as you type, offering to fill in any symbol you start.

Automatic completion is surprisingly good. It's context-sensitive, and I've found that when I'd recently used one symbol from an `enum` list, the next suggestions for the same prefix prefer other members of the same `enum`.

Continue typing to refine the completion list. When the selected completion shares a prefix with other suggestions, pressing the Tab key advances the cursor through the common prefix, narrowing the completion list. If you're satisfied with the current suggestion, press Return and continue editing.

Completion is sometimes perverse, offering suggestions that have nothing to do with what you want. This is particularly painful when you want to type a symbol (`completion`) that shares letters, but not case, with another (`COMPLETION`). You can type to the end of your desired spelling, but Xcode insists on the other one. If this happens (or you simply want to suppress the pop-up), press Escape, and the completion will go away.

NOTE

Don't like automatic completion? If **Escape key shows code completions** is checked, you can summon the code-completion window whenever you want it. Even with escape-completion turned off, you can still invoke completion with **^Space**.

Code completion doesn't stop at spelling. Xcode supports *code snippets* (see the second tab, marked with braces, in the Library section of the Utility area), which are blocks of code you can insert and edit for your purposes.

When I initialized the arrays and formatters for `loadProperties` to use, I used the `dispatch` once function from Grand Central Dispatch (look it up; even if you don't have a use for GCD in general, `dispatch_once` is very useful). When I typed **disp**, the main completion Xcode offered was "`dispatch_once -GCD: Dispatch Once.`" (See Figure 11.8.)

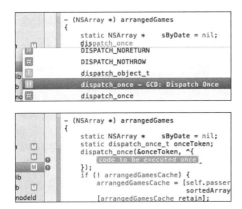

FIGURE 11.8   If you type the beginning of a snippet's completion tag, Xcode will preferentially offer to insert the snippet.

If you press Return to accept the completion, Xcode will insert the whole snippet, including placeholders for your own substitutions (such as `code to be executed once`). The Tab key jumps you through the placeholders. You can create snippets of your own; see the example in Figure 11.9.

FIGURE 11.9   Drag code of your own into the Code Snippet library to create a new snippet. Click the badge to open an editor in which to refine it (for instance, surrounding some text with <##> changes it into a placeholder), describe it, and restrict it to a particular context. In this case, typing **logerror** triggers code completion for the snippet.

Testing the Passer Detail View

Everything should be in place now. Run Passer Rating. Xcode builds the app and installs it in the iOS Simulator, which launches it. (The app takes a long time to load that CSV file—long enough that you might worry that iOS would kill it for being nonresponsive, but there are things you can do about that. See Chapter 14, "Measurement and Analysis.")

Select a passer from the initial view. Something like the view in Figure 11.10 should appear. All the labels are filled in. It works. The game table is still empty, but you've made progress in making the data available to the user.

Summary

This chapter added a view to the Passer Rating application. You had your first workout with Interface Builder, adding subviews, setting properties, and linking the views to outlets in the view controller. By now, you should be able to use Interface Builder effectively to design your user interface and hook it up to your data.

I also had you turn on code completion, which opened you up to code snippets, adding the ability to insert entire blocks of code. You learned how to add snippets of your own.

Now let's finish the game-list view.

FIGURE 11.10   Running Passer Rating and selecting a passer shows that the passer-detail view works.

## CHAPTER 12

Adding Table Cells

You've filled the game-list view with everything but...a list of games. In this chapter, you'll hook up the game table, produce a custom view for the table cells, and pick up some techniques along the way.

The Game Table

The table of `Passers` used the `NSFetchedResultsController` provided by Xcode in its template code for a `UITableViewController` subclass. `GameListController` is not a table-view controller; it's just a `UIViewController` for a view that happens to include a table. Table-view controllers are already connected to their tables; for `GameListController` you'll have to do the connecting yourself.

The first thing to do is to modify the `@interface` for `GameListController` to promise that it will implement the methods the table needs to display cells and respond to events:

```
@interface GameListController :
    UIViewController <UITableViewDelegate,
    UITableViewDataSource>
```

When the `llvm` compiler catches up to the change, the activity view in the middle of the toolbar will flag three warnings. The error/warning icon with arrowheads, at the right end of the jump bar, offers quick navigation to the sites of the issues, but to see them all at once, select the Issues navigator (fourth tab). The first entry is simply, "Incomplete implementation"—something the `@interface` promised wasn't provided.

The other two warnings give the details. They have disclosure triangles next to them that mark your source with the particulars. For each, they are "Method declared here" / "Required for direct or indirect protocol 'UITableViewDataSource'." Clicking the declared-here item opens UIKit's `UITableView.h` header and highlights a method in the `UITableViewDataSource` protocol: `tableView:numberOfRowsInSection:` in one case, `tableView:cellForRowAtIndexPath:` in the other.

Copy the declaration of `tableView:numberOfRowsInSection:`, paste it into `GameListController.m`, and fill it out:

```
#pragma mark - UITableViewDataSource


- (NSInteger) tableView: (UITableView *) tableView
  numberOfRowsInSection: (NSInteger) section
{
    Passer *        passer = self.detailItem;
    return passer.games.count;
}
```

> **NOTE**
>
> The `#pragma mark` directive puts the text in the rest of the line into the function pop-up in the last segment of the jump bar. If you prefix it with a hyphen, the label will be preceded by a dividing line.

You could do the same for `tableView:cellForRowAtIndexPath:`, but there's a snippet to help you. Expose the Utility area, and type **cell** in the Code Snippet library. You see **Reusable UITableView Cell**. Drag the snippet by its badge into the implementation file, where a method definition would be legal. The snippet expands to a template for the method you want.

There are two placeholders. One is for a string that identifies the kind of cell you'll be creating. (Cells are cached when they aren't visible, and the identifier lets you pull the right kind of cell out of the cache when one is needed.) The other says "customize cell before it is shown." Here's what should go there:

```
Game *      game = [self.arrangedGames objectAtIndex: indexPath.row];
NSString * content = [NSString stringWithFormat: @"vs. %@ %@ -%@",
                        game.theirTeam,
                        [sDateFormat stringFromDate: game.whenPlayed],
                        [sNumberFormat stringFromNumber:
                                                game.passerRating]];
    cell.textLabel.text = content;
```

This results in a number of error messages because the compiler doesn't yet know what a Game is, nor has it heard of the property `arrangedGames`. Cure the first by putting

```
#import "Game.h"
```

at the top of the file. `arrangedGames` requires more effort. There are many ways to collect the objects to be displayed in a table, but it all comes down to retrieving a specific object for a given row. The easiest way to do this is for `GameListController` to keep an array of Games in the proper order.

The template put a *class extension*—an `@interface` qualified by "`()`"—that defines private API for `GameListController`. Edit it so it adds an instance variable and a `@property`:

```
@interface GameListController () {
    NSArray * arrangedGamesCache;
}
-(void)configureView;

@property(nonatomic, readonly) NSArray *      arrangedGames;
@end
```

`arrangedGames` is read-only, so all you need is a getter method:

```
- (NSArray *) arrangedGames
{
    // Set up a sort by the whenPlayed date
    static NSArray     * sByDate = nil;
    static dispatch_once_t onceToken;
    dispatch_once(&onceToken, ^{
        NSSortDescriptor * desc =
        [NSSortDescriptor sortDescriptorWithKey: @"whenPlayed"
                                      ascending: YES];
        sByDate = [[NSArray alloc] initWithObjects: desc, nil];
    });

    // If the game array isn't known, fetch it from
    // the Passer, and apply the whenPlayed sort to it.
    if (! arrangedGamesCache) {
        arrangedGamesCache = [[self.detailItem games]
                          sortedArrayUsingDescriptors: sByDate];
    }
    return arrangedGamesCache;
}
```

When you get a new passer, in the `setDetailItem:` method, clear the cache out before reloading the views:

```
-(void) setPasser: (Passer *) newPasser
{
   if (passer != newPasser) {
       [passer release];
        passer = [newPasser retain];
```

```
        [arrangedGamesCache release];
        arrangedGamesCache = nil;
        [self loadProperties];
        [self.tableView reloadData];
    }
}
```

Be sure to include `[arrangedGamesCache release]` in the `-dealloc` method.

You have to connect the table view to the controller. That's been done at the controller's end—you set the `tableView` property when you built the view in Interface Builder (IB). But the table view has to know where it can get its data (its `dataSource` property) and what will handle its events (the `delegate` property). Return to your Interface Builder tab, make sure it's focused on `GameListController.xib`, and right-click the table. Drag connections from both the `delegate` and the `dataSource` bubbles to File's Owner. Now go back to your code-editing view because you're about to run the app.

Run it, and select a passer. It seems to work: The table is filled. It's less informative than you'd like because one large text label doesn't leave much room, but it's enough to show the right thing is going on. Scroll down…

Oh. The app crashes. The stack trace doesn't say much; the only place it touches your code is `main()`, and the crash itself occurred at `objc_msgSend`.

Actually, crashing at `objc_msgSend` is informative. If you crash there, or in any method with a similar name, you have almost certainly mismanaged memory, in particular by trying to use an object that has been deallocated. This is an extremely common error, and there are a number of tools to detect it.

NOTE

With iOS 5, Mac OS X 10.7, and Xcode 4.2 or later, these errors are a lot less common. The LLVM 3 compiler can recognize the events in your code where you need to retain, release, or autorelease objects. When you enable Automatic Reference Counting (ARC), the compiler inserts the proper calls without your having to bother with them—ARC makes it *illegal* to use the reference-counting methods yourself. This cuts out a lot of code and a lot of bugs. Alas, ARC (in its complete form) is an iOS 5 technology; Passer Rating is targeted at iOS 4.3, which doesn't fully implement ARC; and I am left to make this highly instructive error.

If you set the environment variable `NSZombieEnabled` when a Cocoa application is run, Cocoa will not return a deallocated object's memory to free storage. Instead, the object is replaced with a "zombie" object that remembers the class of the original. If you send *any* message to a zombie, it will halt your application. With luck, it does so close enough to the bug that it is obvious. You'll see an even better way to handle zombies in Chapter 14, "Measurement and Analysis."

Schemes

How do you set that environment variable? This is your introduction to *schemes*. Put roughly, every product of an Xcode project has a scheme associated with it. A scheme governs five actions: **Run** (you've been doing that all along), **Test** (Chapter 13, "Unit Testing"), **Profile** (Chapter 14), **Analyze** (also Chapter 14), and **Archive** (Chapter 16, "Provisioning"). For each action, the scheme selects the build settings to be used, the tools to be applied, and, if the product is to be executed, the circumstances under which it is run.

Environment variables are such a circumstance. Select **Product→Edit Scheme**...(⌘<, which on a U.S. keyboard amounts to ⇧⌘**Comma**). This drops the Scheme Editor sheet. At the left you see a list of actions (plus "Build," which takes care of the case in which more than one target contributes to a product). Select "Run Passer Rating" and then the **Arguments** tab. See Figure 12.1.

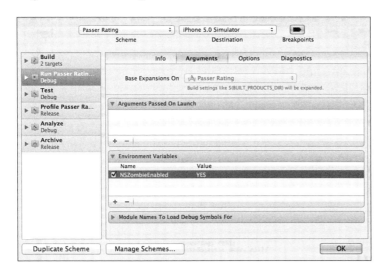

FIGURE 12.1   The Scheme editor sheet controls how your product will be built and run in response to five commands.

You see three tables; "Environment Variables" is the second. Click the disclosure triangle to open the table, if it isn't open already, and click the + button below the table. There are two columns; type **NSZombieEnabled** into the first and **YES** into the second. Make sure the box next to the name is checked—if you have an argument or variable you don't want to set, you can uncheck it.

Click **OK** to dismiss the sheet, and run Passer Rating again. Do what you did before: Tap a passer, then scroll the game list.

NOTE

A snappier way to edit a scheme is to command one of the actions—with the keyboard, the big button in the tool bar, or the **Product** menu—while holding down the Option key. The Scheme editor appears, and when you click **Run**, the action proceeds.

NOTE

The Scheme editor lets you set distinct options depending on the destination platform on which the product is to be run, but in practice it's rare to do so.

The app still crashes—now that you're prosecuting a bug, you want it to— but this time the debugger helps you: The stack crawl includes the method `tableView:cellForRowAtIndexPath:`, at the line

```
Game *     game = [self.arrangedGames objectAtIndex: indexPath.row];
```

There are three message sends here. It's not likely that the problem is with `indexPath`— that comes straight from the table, and you haven't done anything to release it. `self` should be good, or the table view's call to this method would have failed. That leaves `self.arrangedGames`, which at this point should just be the contents of `arrangedGamesCache`. So that's the culprit.

When `arrangedGames` is first called, it sets `arrangedGamesCache` to the `NSArray` returned by `[self.detailItem games]` in response to `sortedArrayUsingDescriptors:`. Methods whose names do not start with `new`, `alloc`, `init`, `copy`, or `mutableCopy` return objects the caller does not own; they are subject to deallocation. You have to retain `arrangedGamesCache`:

```
if (! arrangedGamesCache) {
    arrangedGamesCache = [[self.detailItem games]
                      sortedArrayUsingDescriptors: sByDate]
    [arrangedGamesCache retain];
}
```

Make the correction and run Passer Rating one more time. This time there's no crash. See Figure 12.2.

FIGURE 12.2   With the overrelease bug taken care of, Passer Rating can scroll the game list without crashing.

Having zombies enabled means that every object you ever allocate—between you and Cocoa, there can be hundreds of thousands—stays in memory. Even in a debug build, that takes up a lot of memory and may obscure other errors (such as a genuine memory runaway). Open the Scheme editor and uncheck `NSZombieEnabled`. Keep it around though; it's a good idea to test with it enabled to make sure you haven't introduced any new bugs.

A Custom Table Cell

The default table cell leaves practically no room for information about games. If you want to see your data, you have to make a cell of your own.

Start with a new XIB file. Select **File→New→File…**(⌘N), and in the New File assistant, navigate to **iOS→User Interface→Empty**. Click **Next**. The device family is **iPhone**, and in the save-file sheet, put `GameTableCell.xib` somewhere in the project directory; select your XIBs group as the destination within the project. As is usual, the Project navigator shows the new file with the "A" source-control badge.

Switch to your Interface Builder tab, and use the jump bar to open the new XIB. If you left IB as you had it at the end of Chapter 11, "Building a New View," the assistant editor area is split into two views. You can close one of them by clicking the **x** button at the right end of its jump bar. Leave the assistant open, though; you'll edit GameListController as you go along.

You asked for an empty XIB because otherwise you'd start off with a full-screen UIView. You don't want a UIView; you want the XIB to contain only a single UITableViewCell. Make sure the Object library (third tab) is visible in the Utility area, and type **cell** in the search field. You are left with an object named "Table View Cell." Drag it into the editor.

This is a standard-size table-view cell, 320 points wide (the width of an iPhone screen) and 44 points high (the recommended minimum size of a tappable object). You want a custom cell because the standard size can't accommodate all the information you want to show. So drag the top or bottom edge of the cell (or use the Size [number-five] inspector) to make it taller; my experiment left me with a cell 92 points high.

Now you go through much the same drudgery as for the passer-detail view in Chapter 11:

▸ A large label for the game rating. I used **158.3**, Helvetica Bold, 36 points, blue. Put it in the upper-left corner. Remember to resize the label as you make your changes because IB tries to keep it the same size and compresses the font to make the content fit.

▸ At the top right, a label for the teams, scores, and the date of the match. For size, fill it with

Tacoma Touchdown-Scorers 88
Tacoma Touchdown-Scorers 88
12/12/99

Make it Helvetica Oblique, 12 points, right-justified.

▸ Across the bottom, a label in Helvetica Regular 14 points, left-justified. Size it with **999/999 -999 yd -99 TD -99 INT**.

When you're done, you should have something like Figure 12.3.

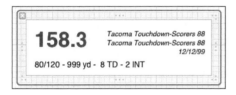

FIGURE 12.3   The finished layout of the game-list cell.

What about connecting the cell to `GameListController`? For the passer-detail view, you used `IBOutlets` for the connections, but the controller manages only one of those views at a time. For the game cell, it will be reloading this NIB over and over again. There can't be a single outlet for the cell or its labels. What the controller will have at any moment is a pointer to the cell it is working on right then. It can pull pointers to the labels from that.

This is done by setting the *tags* of the labels. Every `UIView`—cells and labels included—can have an integer associated with it, so it can be identified. If you have a superview (a container, like the cell), you can send `cellWithTag:` to it with the subview's tag. That will fetch the desired view from the hierarchy. By default, the tag is `0`. Use the **Attributes** inspector to set the rating label's tag to **1**, the scoring label to **2**, and the statistics label to **3**. You can find the **Tag** field low in the inspector, in the "View" section.

You remember that cells have identifiers so that they can be recycled as they come into and out of view. You won't create these cells programmatically any more, so you have to set the identifier in the XIB. Select the cell in the XIB and expose the Attributes inspector (fourth tab). The first item is **Identifier**, which you set to `Game Cell` to match the key used in `tableView:cellForRowAtIndexPath:`

Finally, with the cell selected. expose the Size inspector. Take note of the height (92 points in my case). `UITableView` normally doesn't measure the rows it presents; there's one height for all of them, and by default it's 44 points. Focus Interface Builder on `GameListController.xib` and select the game table. Tables put a "Table View Size" section at the top of the Size inspector. Set **Row Height** to the height of your cell.

Save all your work, and check it in.

Now modify `tableView:cellForRowAtIndexPath:` to load the compiled `GameTableCell` NIB whenever it needs a fresh cell. The method can then find the labels and format the game data into each.

```
// Tag values for the labels in the game cell
#define CELL_RATING_LABEL   1
#define CELL_SCORE_LABEL    2
#define CELL_STATS_LABEL    3

- (UITableViewCell *) tableView: (UITableView *) aTableView
        cellForRowAtIndexPath: (NSIndexPath *) indexPath
{
    static NSString *cellIdentifier = @"Game Cell";
    UITableViewCell *  cell =
        [tableView
        dequeueReusableCellWithIdentifier: cellIdentifier];

    // Could we get the cell out of recycling?
    if (cell == nil) {
        // No. Load a fresh cell from the NIB.
```

```
            NSArray * nibContents;
            nibContents = [[UINib nibWithNibName: @"GameTableCell"
                                          bundle: nil]
                           instantiateWithOwner: nil
                                         options: nil];
            cell = [nibContents objectAtIndex: 0];
    }

    // Pull data from this row's Game.
    Game *     game = [self.arrangedGames
                       objectAtIndex: indexPath.row];
    UILabel * label;
    NSString * content;

    // For each subview (label) in the cell, format the data
    // and set the label text.
    label = (UILabel *) [cell viewWithTag: CELL_RATING_LABEL];
    label.text = [sNumberFormat
                  stringFromNumber: game.passerRating];
    label = (UILabel *) [cell viewWithTag: CELL_SCORE_LABEL];
    content = [NSString stringWithFormat:
               @"%@ %d\n%@ %d\n%@",
               game.ourTeam, game.ourScore.intValue,
               game.theirTeam, game.theirScore.intValue,
               [sDateFormat stringFromDate: game.whenPlayed]];
    label.text = content;

    label = (UILabel *) [cell viewWithTag: CELL_STATS_LABEL];
    content = [NSString stringWithFormat:
               @"%d/%d - %d yd - %d TD - %d INT",
               game.completions.intValue, game.attempts.intValue,
               game.yards.intValue, game.touchdowns.intValue,
               game.interceptions.intValue];
    label.text = content;

    return cell;
}
```

Run Passer Rating one more time. When you tap a passer, his full record appears, including the complete statistics on every game. The display portions of the app behave as specified. See Figure 12.4.

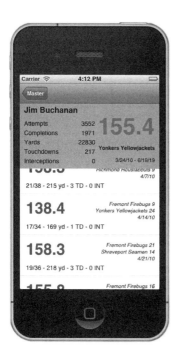

FIGURE 12.4   The finished game-list view. The table in the lower half displays the full statistics for each game.

The tagged-label approach worked well for this simple case. However, if your needs were more complex—more intricate data, or even custom drawing—tagged subviews wouldn't be enough. You'd need to create a new subclass of UITableViewCell. Xcode has a template that would start you on your way: When you create a new file, ask for an Objective-C class and specify UITableViewCell as the superclass. The resulting .m file includes skeletons of the initialization and drawing code. With a cell class specialized for displaying games, you could give the cell a game property. tableView:cellForRowAtIndexPath: could simply set cell.game, and the setGame: method you'd add to the cell class would fill in the data.

Summary

In this chapter, you filled out the game table in the game-list view. You let Xcode help you: You declared that `GameListController` would be a data source for a table, and Xcode pointed you to the methods you had to implement. One of them you copied straight out of the header Xcode showed you, but Apple supplied a code snippet that did most of your work on the other.

The first attempt crashed the app, leading you on a debugging expedition that introduced you to the important concept of schemes.

Succeeding in that, you set out to make a better game cell, creating a stand-alone XIB for the cell content and loading the independent cell.

The two display views in the plan from Figure 8.2 seem to be well in hand. There's one thing, though.

I don't trust those ratings.

CHAPTER 13

Unit Testing

All your development so far on the passer-rating projects has left out one essential consideration—one that you might have worried about at the end of the last chapter:

How do you know it works?

Yes, you know generally what to expect, and you've used the Xcode debugger to verify that what the application does makes sense, but you don't have the time, and most people don't have the discipline, to monitor for every possible error. Ideally, for every change to your application, you'd verify that everything still worked. With a prompt warning, you could isolate the problem to the last thing you did.

This discipline of verifying that each little part of your application works is called *unit testing*. The meticulous search for errors is the sort of mind-numbing, repetitive, perfectionist task that you bought a computer to do.

This is a well-enough understood problem that solutions have been devised in the form of testing frameworks. Such frameworks make it easy to take your code, more or less in the actual context in which you use it, present it with known inputs, and compare the results with what you expect. If everything is as expected, the test succeeds; otherwise it fails. The framework provides a way to run all the tests, record the results, and issue a report on them.

Xcode and its templates are set up to allow for two kinds of tests. *Logic* tests serve as test benches that support pieces of your code and challenge them to produce correct output. The tests are the hosts, and the application-supplied code is loaded under their control. Logic testing is especially good for the model portion of your application. If you want to create a logic-test suite, you must ask Xcode to add a target for it.

Application tests challenge the overall flow of your application. The application itself is the host for the tests: Executing the **Test** action executes the app, and the test code is *injected* into the running app. When Xcode creates an application project, it offers to create an *application*-test bundle along with it as a separate target.

> **NOTE**
>
> The distinction between application and logic tests is important. Apple refers to both as *unit* tests. If you're coming from Ruby on Rails, only logic tests would be called unit tests. What Apple calls application tests would be functional tests.

Logic Testing

Logic tests are the easiest to write and understand. I am anxious over the accuracy of the Passer Rating app. I don't trust the ratings. What goes into those ratings? The app has to perform a particular kind of arithmetic on a particular set of statistics. The statistics come from lines in a CSV file, which must be read and interpreted; the reader has to process all of the file; match the data to the header keys; interpret the numbers and dates as such, and correctly. passer_rating () must calculate the rating correctly. I can imagine any number of other things that must go right. Each of them should be the subject of a test.

These will be logic tests, which must be in a target of their own. Select the project in the Project navigator; then click **Add Target** at the bottom of the Project editor. Xcode presents the New Target sheet, from which you should select **iOS→Other→Cocoa Touch Unit Testing Bundle**. Click **Next**, give the bundle the name **Logic Tests**, and the company identifier you've been using, and make sure it goes into the Passer Rating project. Click **Finish**.

> **NOTE**
>
> Passer Rating isn't set up to use Automatic Reference Counting, so don't check that box.

Xcode now shows the new target in the Target editor. Xcode creates a new scheme for each new target—the target has its own life cycle, and its own way of responding to the action commands. Open the Scheme editor (**Product→Edit Scheme** ...[⌘<]), and select **Logic Tests** from the **Scheme** pop-up at the top of the sheet. See Figure 13.1.

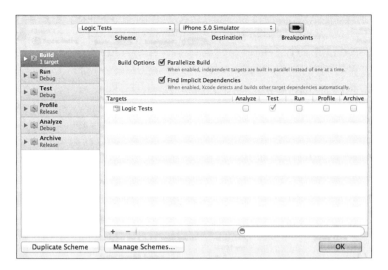

FIGURE 13.1   A unit-test target is restricted to respond only to the **Test** action. The Scheme editor shows all the options as dimmed, with Test permanently checked, and the others permanently unchecked.

The first panel of the editor, Build, shows that the target supports only one action: Test. You can't run, analyze, profile, or archive a testing bundle. This is another instance of how the type of a target determines what Xcode will do with it. After you set a type, there's no way to change it and no way to evade the restrictions.

> **NOTE**
>
> If you don't focus on Test being the only valid action, you could be in for some surprises. For instance, the **Product→Build** (⌘**B**) command is simply an alias for **Build for Run**. The Logic Tests target doesn't support Run, so Xcode complains that the target is not configured for that action.

Close the Scheme editor by clicking **OK**. If you look under the **Build Phases** tab, you'll see that the target template came with the source for a test class, Logic Tests.m, and links to SenTestingKit.framework, in addition to the usual frameworks that support Cocoa Touch development.

There's also a Run Script build phase at the end:

```
# Run the unit tests in this test bundle.
"${SYSTEM_DEVELOPER_DIR}/Tools/RunUnitTests"
```

Here's what's happening. SenTestingKit is a dynamic-library framework that, when it responds to the **Test** action, searches the current application for classes descended from the SenTestCase class. For each method in those classes with a name beginning with test, it runs that class's setUp method, then the test method, and then the class's tearDown.

A `test` method can exercise application code however it likes. For each testable result, the method calls one of the `STAssert` macros to assert that the result should have matched an expected value. If the values don't match, SenTestingKit logs an error; testing will continue, but for that particular case, the test fails.

Logic Tests is to be a logic-test suite, which means that it will run on its own and won't have direct access to classes in the Passer Rating app. If you want to test a Passer Rating component, you must link that component into Logic Tests. What should those be? My big concern is with the accuracy of the passer ratings. The app's calculation of those ratings depend, not just on the arithmetical accuracy of the `passer_rating` function, but also on its correctly reading and interpreting the CSV file that contains the raw data.

You at least need to add `SimpleCSVFile.m` and `rating.c` to the Logic Tests target. As you saw before, you could do this by dragging the files from the Project navigator into Logic Tests' Compile Sources build phase; or you could use the Command key to select both, open the File inspector in the Utility area, and check Logic Tests in the target list.

The great task is to break all the things you want to test into test methods. They could all be in one big test class, but it's easier if you create different classes to provide the unique services each kind of test needs. For instance, some of the tests you might imagine would need a fresh Core Data stack for each test. A `CoreDataTests` class could do that in `setUp` and `tearDown`, but it would be wasteful to initialize Core Data for tests that could go into a `CSVTests` class.

Creating the Logic Tests bundle created Objective-C source files for a class named `Logic_Tests`. Using your refactoring skills (from Chapter 10, "An iOS Controller"), change the class and its files to `CSVTests` because the first thing you need to be sure of is that the data file is being read.

Test Data

You need a data set that is fixed, not the one that periodically regenerates itself as a part of Passer Rating's build process, so take the current edition of `sample-data.csv`, and copy a year's worth of games—328 in the toy league I created, covering 32 passers—into a separate file.

You need an independent source for all the statistics `passer_rating()` calculates. I took my test CSV file, imported it into a spreadsheet, added columns that figure the rating and its four components, and re-exported it as a CSV that could be used to check Passer Rating's actual calculations.

> **NOTE**
>
> Unlike `sample-data.csv`, these files should be checked in—the code for the tests depends on the specific values in the files, and the tests have to be reproducible. Unfortunately, you may have changed your `.gitignore` or Subversion configuration files so that `*.csv` is excluded from listings and commits. If that's so, Xcode will refuse the **File→Source Control→Add** command. You must go to the command line and force your source-control system to accept the files.

I made more .csvs. SimpleCSVFile has to respond correctly—it should halt and return a meaningful error—if any line of a file contains more or fewer fields than there are headers. That's easy enough: Take one of the test .csvs and make one copy with an extra header field and one with one less.

When everything is prepared, add the test files to the Logic Tests target (**File→Add Files to "Passer Rating"**…, [⌥⌘A]), making sure that *only* the Logic Tests target is checked—you don't want to fold the test files into the Passer Rating app.

Testing the CSV Reader

Having given free rein to my capacity for dread and worry, I can draw up a suite of test methods for SimpleCSVFile. Create class CSVTestBase, which is a direct descendant of SenTestCase, but does no actual testing; it just provides a setup for other CSV-testing classes to use; in particular the method setCSVForFileName:. CSVOpenTests contains the real tests. Here is an abbreviated listing:

```
-(void) testNoSuchFile
{
    // Will it do the right thing if there's no such file?
    self.csvFile = [[[SimpleCSVFile alloc]
                     initWithPath: @"no-such-file.csv"]
                    autorelease];
    STAssertNotNil(self.csvFile, @"file should initialize");
    self.csvFile.delegate = self;

    NSError    *              error;
    STAssertFalse([self.csvFile run: &error],
                          @"nonexistent file should not run");
    STAssertNotNil(error, @"nonexistent file should return an NSError");
    STAssertEqualObjects(NSCocoaErrorDomain, [error domain],
                    @"Error domain was %@, not NSCocoaErrorDomain",
                    [error domain]);
}


- (void) testFileReadsCompletely
{
    // Does it read the whole file?
    [self setCSVForFileName: @"2010-data-calculated.csv"];
    self.delegateBlock = ^BOOL (SimpleCSVFile * file,
                                NSDictionary * values,
                                NSError ** error) {
        [self.records addObject: values];
        return YES;
    };
    NSError *              error;
    BOOL                   success = [self.csvFile run: &error];
```

```
    STAssertTrue(success, @"File should be valid");
    STAssertEquals(328U, self.records.count,
            @"%@ should return 328 records, returns %u",
            kGoodGameFile, self.records.count);
}

- (void) testTooManyFieldsError
{
    // Read a bad file: It has too many fields for the number
    // of headers.
    [self setCSVForFileName: @"too-many-fields.csv"];
    self.delegateBlock = ^BOOL (SimpleCSVFile * file,
                                NSDictionary * values,
                                NSError ** error) {
        STAssertTrue(NO,
                    @"File with first data line bad shouldn't call out");
        return YES;
    };
    NSError *    error;
    // run: should return NO
    STAssertFalse([self.csvFile run: &error], @"File should be invalid");

    // The NSError should be from my domain.
    STAssertEqualObjects(WT9TErrorDomain, [error domain],
            @"Field-count error should be in WT9TErrorDomain, was %@",
            [error domain]);
    STAssertNotNil(error, @"Error object after error should be non-nil.");

    // The error dictionary should report the expected
    // and actual field counts.
    NSDictionary * userInfo = [error userInfo];
    STAssertEquals(16,
            [[userInfo objectForKey: kCSVExpectedFieldsKey] intValue],
            @"expected fields should be 16, are %d",
            [[userInfo objectForKey: kCSVExpectedFieldsKey] intValue]);
    STAssertEquals(17,
            [[userInfo objectForKey: kCSVActualFieldsKey] intValue],
            @"expected fields should be 17, are %d",
            [[userInfo objectForKey: kCSVActualFieldsKey] intValue]);

    // The error should occur on line 2, the first data line.
    STAssertEquals(2,
            [[userInfo objectForKey: kCSVErrorLineKey] intValue],
            @"error line should be 2, is %d",
            [[userInfo objectForKey: kCSVErrorLineKey] intValue]);
```

```
}

- (void) testNotEnoughFieldsError
{
    // Same, but the test file has too few fields.
    // ...
}

- (void) testValidCSV
{
    // Sample a couple of records as they come in from the CSV,
    // and check all the fields against values hard-coded
    // in this method.
    // ...
}
```

13

> **NOTE**
>
> This is a severe abridgment of the test code. In particular, it doesn't show the helper methods that provide the `csvFile:readValues:error:` method and call back to the test methods' `delegateBlock`. The full example code has the details.

You can see the obsessiveness that goes into a good test; these tests are probably not obsessive enough. It's tedious, but after it's written, the test harness does the hard work, and you won't be single-stepping through every line of the parser as it plows through hundreds of records.

Now execute the test by selecting **Test** from the Action button at the left end of the workspace window's toolbar or by selecting **Product→Test** (⌘U). The first thing that happens is that Xcode reports the build succeeded (if it didn't, clean it up; I'll wait).

Soon enough, the activity view at the top-center of the Workspace window reports, "Finished Testing Logic Tests," and below it is the red badge reporting that there were two errors. If you point the editor at CSVOpenTests.m (one way to do it would be to click the arrows of the error control at the right end of the jump bar), you'll see error banners in the body of the test code, just as if the test failures had been compilation errors. See Figure 13.2.

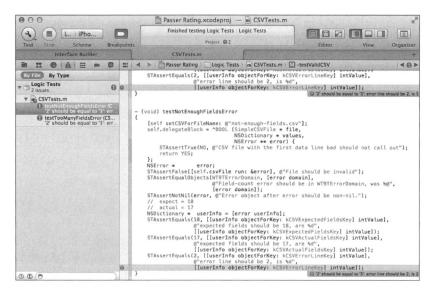

FIGURE 13.2   After a test suite has been run, Xcode flags failed assertions in the source of the test as though they were build errors. There will be one flag for each failed assertion.

The errors show up in `testNotEnoughFieldsError` and `testTooManyFieldsError`, and the code in both tests is the same:

```
STAssertEquals(2, [[userInfo objectForKey: kCSVErrorLineKey] intValue],
               @"error line should be 2, is %d",
               [[userInfo objectForKey: kCSVErrorLineKey] intValue]);
```

The CSV run was supposed to fail because the first data line (the second line in the file) had the wrong number of fields. The assertion is that the line number reported in the returned error object should be 2. The message in the red banner Xcode put next to this line in the source is:

```
'2' should be equal to '3': error line should be 2, is 3
```

`SimpleCSVFile` reported the error at line 3. What's going on? You need to see what the parser is doing on those lines. Fortunately, the debugger works in unit tests. Set a breakpoint at the start of `-[SimpleCSVFile run:]`, and run the test again.

Wait a minute, you say. Class `CSVOpenTests` already has five tests and will eventually have more. Stopping at a method that will be called repeatedly, just for one or two runs of the method, is a bad idea. Maybe you could put a breakpoint at the call site and step in?

You can do better than that. Xcode keeps track of the subclasses of `SenTestCase` in a target, and of the `test` methods in them. The Scheme editor lets you select which tests will be run when you issue the **Test** action. Open the Scheme editor, make sure the Logic Tests scheme is selected, and click the Test action in the column at the left. Xcode presents you with a table of test methods, organized by class. They have check boxes next to them; check only the tests you want. That way you can concentrate on the tests you are working on right now without getting static from the ones you aren't. See Figure 13.3.

FIGURE 13.3   The setup for the Test action for the Logic Tests target shows all the tests you define. You can use the check boxes to identify the classes and test methods you want to run.

So issue the **Test** command. The breakpoint at run: fires, and you can step through the method. It reads the CSV data into a string and then bursts it into an array of lines:

```
NSArray * lines = [contents componentsSeparatedByCharactersInSet:
                       [NSCharacterSet newlineCharacterSet]];
```

…then it steps through the array, bursting each line at the commas to get fields.

If you watch the variables display in the Debug area, you'll see something on the second pass through the loop, which you'd expect should be the first line of the data: The string for that line is empty! The first line of data doesn't come through until the *third* pass through the loop, and the method reports the error line as number three.

With a little thought, it should come to you: This is the CSV file that was exported from the spreadsheet of precalculated statistics. CSV has its origins in Microsoft Excel, and to the extent CSV has any standards at all, it can be expected to have Windows line endings—carriage-return, line-feed. The componentsSeparatedByCharactersInSet: method burst the file at each occurrence of a character in the newlineCharacterSet, not caring that in this file, the CRLF pair represents a single line separator.

Fight down the temptation to simply open the file in a text editor and convert the line endings. SimpleCSVFile is supposed to work with real CSV files (as long as they don't have any commas or quotes in the fields); it may have a life beyond this one project; and it should handle a line delimiter that will appear in most of the files it sees.

Replace the simple line-bursting code with a category on NSString that parses line endings more carefully and try again.

```
@interface NSString (LineBreakingExtensions)
-(NSArray *) componentsBrokenByLines;
@end


@implementation NSString (LineBreakingExtensions)

-(NSArray *) componentsBrokenByLines
{
    NSScanner *        scanner = [NSScanner scannerWithString: self];
    NSCharacterSet *   lineEnders =
                            [NSCharacterSet newlineCharacterSet];
    NSMutableArray *   retval = [NSMutableArray array];

    [scanner setCharactersToBeSkipped: nil];
    while (! [scanner isAtEnd]) {
        NSString * token;
        [scanner scanCharactersFromSet: lineEnders intoString: NULL];
        if ([scanner scanUpToCharactersFromSet: lineEnders
                              intoString: &token]) {
            [retval addObject: token];
        }
    }
    return retval;
}
@end
```

This time all the methods in CSVOpenTests come through clean.

Now that you're sure the data is coming in as you expect it, you can build a RatingTest class to read the CSV that contains the precalculated values for the rating and its completion, yardage, touchdown, and interception components, and compare their presumably-correct (or at least independently calculated) values against the values the passer_rating function produces. The function doesn't export those intermediate results, so I created a little support method that would do those calculations just the way that passer_rating did:

```
-(double) calculateFromRating: (ComponentKey) key
                    attempts: (int) atts
                        stat: (int) stat
{
    double      retval = 0.0;
    switch (key) {
```

```
    case kCompletion:
        retval = (((double) stat / atts) * 100.0 -30.0) / 20.0;
        retval = pinRating(retval);
        break;

    case kYardage:
        retval = (((double) stat / atts) -0.3) / 4.0;
        retval = pinRating(retval);
        break;

    case kTouchdown:
        retval = 20.0 * (double) stat / atts;
        retval = pinRating(retval);
        break;

    case kInterception:
        retval = 2.375 -(25.0 * (double) stat / atts);
        retval = pinRating(retval);
        break;

    default:
        break;
    }

    return retval;
}
```

...and then I wrote a very dense `testCalculation` method that goes through every record in the CSV, reworks every statistic, and compares it all to the precalculated results. In part, the tests look like this:

```
yards = [[game objectForKey: @"yards"] intValue];
component = [self calculateFromRating: kYardage
                            attempts: attempts
                                stat: yards];
accum += component;
expectedComponent = [[game objectForKey: @"yComp"] doubleValue];
STAssertEqualsWithAccuracy(component, expectedComponent, 0.01,
                        @"Yardage for game %d (%d / %d)",
                        index, yards, attempts);
component = (100.0 / 6.0) * accum;
expectedComponent = [[game objectForKey: @"rating"] doubleValue];
STAssertEqualsWithAccuracy(component, expectedComponent, 0.051,
                        @"Rating for game %d", index);

rating = passer_rating(completions, attempts,
```

```
                        yards, touchdowns, interceptions);
STAssertEqualsWithAccuracy(rating, expectedComponent, 0.051,
                          @"passer_rating for game %d", index);
```

...and if you looked up the passer-rating formula on Wikipedia, you won't be surprised that the three assertions you see here—that the yardage component and the rating, calculated two ways, should match the "right" answers—generated more than 800 test failures. The calculation

```
retval = (((double) stat / atts) -0.3) / 4.0;
```

in my helper method, and in `passer_rating`, was wrong. The subtrahend should be 3.0, not 0.3. My unease about the ratings I was seeing was right, and now I have a test of 328 games to make sure that if it ever goes wrong again, I'll know right away.

> **NOTE**
>
> When you program a Cocoa application, you get used to referring to embedded files through [NSBundle mainBundle]. This doesn't work for test classes because the main bundle—even for logic tests—is the application, not the test suite. The right frame of reference is [NSBundle bundleForClass: [self class]].

Application Testing

Testing the components of an application is useful, and it's a prerequisite to gaining confidence that the app is sound at its foundation. But logic testing doesn't take you all the way. You can verify that `SimpleCSVFile` and `passer_rating` work in isolation, but that doesn't tell you whether they work as Passer Rating uses them. For instance, the tests use a unique harness that has `SimpleCSVFile` call back into the test object for each record, and the test object does only simple things with results. Passer Rating's `Game` class takes the callbacks as *class methods* and does a lot of Core Data business in the mean time. There is a lot of potential for mismatches between the logic tests and the application.

It's possible to incorporate Core Data `Game` into the test suite and have it do the load, but that just shifts the mismatch. The test is the code that sets up the Core Data stack, selects the CSV file, and loads it—and not the app delegate.

Application tests exercise your application code in place. When you trigger the Test action for your application target, Xcode launches the application and lets it initialize, and then it *injects* the tests into the app to verify that the app is in the expected state. An application test for Passer Rating can query the `Game` and `Passer` classes and verify the database that was read is the one you expect.

You can also go quite a ways into the behavior of the app. Cocoa Touch provides access to singletons like your application delegate, and through that and your own globals, you can pick your way down to view controllers and their views. You can simulate user actions by sending control-and table-action messages to the controllers. You can examine the values displayed by controls after the controllers handle the actions.

However, application testing has limitations.

▶ If you test an IBAction handler that relies on the value of a control (like a UISlider), your test must set the control's value itself, or (if the IBAction uses the "sender" parameter) pass in a "mock" object that returns the values the handler expects.

▶ A test can't do much to verify the actual appearance of your views.

▶ Tests occur in a fixed order, and the application accumulates state from each. In logic tests, the setUp and tearDown methods guarantee a "clean" state for each test. Application test methods can't assume the application is in a "clean" state when they run.

▶ Tests are synchronous. As soon as your UI gets into animations or other asynchronous behavior, your tests won't be able to wait for the asynchronous business to end, and you can't test the result.

When you create an application project, one of your choices is a check box labeled **Include unit tests**. If you check it, Xcode will include an application-testing target in your project. Targets usually get schemes of their own, but an application-test target is different: The only action that makes sense for it is Test, and the only thing that makes sense when you choose the Test action for the *application* is to execute the application tests.

So Xcode doesn't create a scheme for the app tests. Instead it blends the two targets into one scheme. In the **Build** panel of the Scheme editor, the app target is enabled for all actions, as you'd expect, but for the Test action, the application-test target is also enabled. The editor won't permit any other combination. See Figure 13.4.

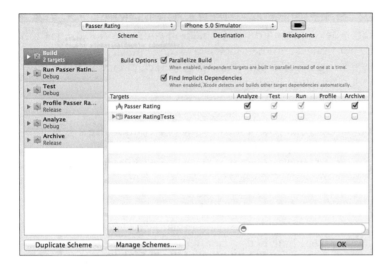

FIGURE 13.4   The first panel of the Scheme editor controls how the targets in a project coordinate for each of the five actions. The Passer Rating project has an application target, Passer Rating, and an application-test target, Passer RatingTests, created when the project was instantiated. Xcode sets the two up so that when you choose the Test action for the Passer Rating scheme, Passer Rating and Passer RatingTests are both built, and then the test suite is run.

SenTestingKit Assertions

Assertions—statements that test for expected conditions—are the core of unit testing. If the condition is not met, SenTestingKit logs it as a test failure. Assertions are made through preprocessor macros that begin (with one exception) with STAssert. The initial parameters to the macros vary as necessary, but you are always allowed a format string (as an NSString literal), followed by values to fill the format in. Hence

```
STAssertEqualsWithAccuracy(component, expectedComponent, 0.01,
                           @"Yardage for game %d (%d / %d)",
                           index, yards, attempts);
```

if it fails, would produce an error message like

```
'1.8096 should be equal to '1.135' + or -'0.01':
                           Yardage for game 97 (98 / 13)
```

Notice that your annotation has to describe only the circumstances of the test; Sen-TestingKit prints out the particulars of any mismatch.

Here are the available assertions. See SenTestCase Macros.h for the details of how to call them and what they do. The easiest way to get to the header is to use the Project navigator and open Frameworks→SenTestingKit.framework→Headers.

Simple Tests

These are the simplest assertions—true or false, nil or not:

▸ **STFail:** This is the simplest of them all. SenTestingKit logs a failure, plus your formatted message

▸ **STAssertTrue:** Fails if the Boolean expression you test is false (zero). Use this or STAssertFalse if you have complex conditions that the more-specific assertions don't handle.

▸ **STAssertFalse:** Fails if the Boolean expression you test is true (nonzero).

▸ **STAssertNil:** Fails if the object pointer you test is not nil.

▸ **STAssertNotNil:** Fails if the object pointer you test is nil.

Equality

These assertions test for whether two things are equal, in three senses of the word. SenTestingKit is picky about the values you pass for comparison because it uses the Objective-C @encode directive to check *at run time* that the expression types match. If you use STAssertEquals to test the count of an NSArray, the test value had better be unsigned (for example, 230U and not just 230), or the test will fail every time.

▸ **STAssertEquals:** Fails if the values you test are not equal. SenTestingKit applies the == operator to make the test.

▸ **STAssertEqualsWithAccuracy:** Never test floating-point values for exact equality; you must assume there are rounding errors with anything but trivial calculations on trivial values. Instead, decide on an *epsilon* value—how close the two can be for you to call them equal—and test whether the values are within *epsilon* of each other. Pass the two values and your epsilon to the macro; it fails if they fall outside the interval.

▸ **STAssertEqualObjects:** Fails unless [value1 isEqual: value2]. This is equality of the values of two objects and not just their pointers (for which you'd use STAssertEquals). Take care for the order of the objects because isEqual: doesn't have to be reflexive.

Exceptions

Cocoa throws exceptions if it is called under improper conditions, like being on the wrong thread or receiving illegal parameters. You might throw some exceptions of your own. You'll want to verify that code that should give rise to an exception does so; and if your code has triggered exceptions in the past, you'll want to keep up a test to verify that your fixes have suppressed them.

A further advantage of these macros is that they *catch* the exceptions. Ordinarily, if a test method triggers an exception, the whole method exits without attempting its remaining tests. Because they trap the exceptions within the method, these macros allow the test to continue.

These assertions can be a little tricky. With STAssertTrue, you can do a long calculation, distill it into one value, and pass that to the macro. You can then use the value for calculations later in the test.

Exception assertions deal with expressions that have two effects: Some sort of calculation as well as the presence or absence of a throw. The expression parameter to the macros may be more elaborate. Assignments and comma expressions are legal, so you can still capture values while you test for exceptions. The SenTestingKit macros evaluate the expressions only once.

- ▶ **STAssertThrows:** Fails if the expression you submit does not raise an exception.

- ▶ **STAssertNoThrow:** Fails if the expression you submit raises an exception.

- ▶ **STAssertTrueNoThrow and STAssertFalseNoThrow:** Here you deal with the two-effects (value and exception) property of an expression. You want to validate the result of an expression (true or false), but you also want to be sure the expression doesn't fail completely and throw. These assertions cover both the value and the absence of an exception.

- ▶ **STAssertThrowsSpecific and STAssertNoThrowSpecific:** Fails if the exception of a specific class is not (or is) thrown. This way you can test that your code is doing what you expect with your own subclass of NSException, while distinguishing different exceptions thrown by other libraries.

- ▶ **STAssertThrowsSpecificNamed and STAssertNoThrowSpecificNamed:** Some exceptions (usually NSExceptions) aren't distinguished by class but by a subtype indicated by the exception's name. These assertions fail upon the absence or presence of an exception of the given class and name.

Summary

Automated testing is a liberating discipline for a programmer. Any change you make *probably* won't have any effect on anything else, but most bugs live in the space between "probably" and "actually." A good testing régime relieves you of obsessive audits that never answer the question: Does it all still work? You'll know, and with that confidence, you can make bold changes to your application.

In this chapter, you learned about SenTestingKit, the Xcode framework for unit-testing applications, and the two kinds of automated tests you can put into an Xcode project: logic tests and application tests. I walked you through part of the exhaustive task of producing a logic test suite that would verify that the process of reading a CSV and pulling accurate statistics from it works correctly. In the course of it, you found a couple of bugs that would be at least tedious to discover by checking the whole application by hand. Now that you have this test, you won't need to worry that something you do in the future might bring those bugs back.

You looked briefly at application tests, which execute from within a running application. You saw the advantages—the ability to exercise some application-level logic and to verify your code's behavior as Passer Rating uses it—and the limitations.

Finally, you learned about the assertions that SenTestingKit makes available to verify that what you expect is what actually happens.

Now, move on from *whether* Passer Rating works, to *how well*.

13

Measurement and Analysis

P asser Rating has quite a way to go before it's useful for the general public, but you've run it several times and begun a testing régime, and you're fairly confident that to the naked eye, it works.

As usual, the qualifier ("to the naked eye") means more than "it works." There are issues in Passer Rating of speed and memory performance. Before you can act, you have to know what's going on—you have to profile the app. The Instruments application is the tool for profiling applications.

Speed

Passer Rating takes an appreciable amount of time to start up. If you run it on a device, it won't start: When you launch it, the screen stays black for 21 seconds, and then you're back to the home screen. It takes too long: If your app doesn't respond to user actions for more than 20 seconds, the system watchdog timer kills it. It has to be faster.

> **NOTE**
>
> In crash dumps, you'll know that the watchdog killed the app if the exception code is `0x8badf00d`.

To analyze speed, I'll be working with Passer Rating on an iPhone. The iOS Simulator provides a lot of insight into how an app works, but it is only a simulator: It has multiples of the RAM available to a device, and if it should run out, it will page memory to disk. It exposes Mac OS X API, and the shared API is optimized for a completely different processor. The simulator has a much faster processor. To install Passer Rating on a device for testing, you have to be a paid member of the iOS Developer Program, register the device, and obtain a signing certificate. All the details are in Chapter 16, "Provisioning." By default, the **Profile** action uses the Release build configuration. Go to the **Build Settings** tab of the Target editor and make sure that the Code Signing Identity for **Any iOS SDK** under the Release configuration is properly set.

My first guess was that `SimpleCSVFile` was so simple that it was inefficient. I was tempted to dive into the parser code, audit it, tinker with the works, introduce "speed optimizations" and maybe a little assembly, and try again.

Don't do this. Don't guess. Instruments can tell you *exactly* where your app spends its time. That's the "low-hanging fruit;" make those parts of your code faster, and you've done more to solve the problem than if you'd nibbled around the periphery.

To start, plug in the iOS device you registered with Apple, and use the **Scheme** pop-up in the toolbar to make it the destination for your actions.

Profiling an application is easy. Xcode provides an action for it. Trigger the **Profile** action by selecting it from the **Action** button at the left end of the Workspace window's toolbar, or by selecting **Product→Profile** (⌘I). The profiling application, Instruments, launches and offers you a choice of what kind of profiling you want to do. See Figure 14.1.

> **NOTE**
>
> Not finding what I'm calling "the Action button?" You may be thinking of it as the **Run** button, but that's not strictly accurate. If you hold down on the button, you'll get a choice of four actions to perform on the current scheme, of which running is only one. If you select **Test**, **Profile**, or **Analyze**, the icon in the button changes to match, and a short click will trigger that action.

In the new-template sheet, select **iOS→CPU→Time Profiler**, and click **Choose**. After a brief pause, Passer Rating launches on the phone, and the Instruments window begins to fill with the record of what the phone was doing from moment to moment.

FIGURE 14.1   When you start Instruments or request a new Instruments trace document, you are presented with an empty window and an assistant sheet allowing you to select a template for your profiling session.

NOTE

Xcode has a shortcut for selecting Instruments templates. Open the Scheme editor (**Product→Edit Scheme**..., [⌘<]) and select the **Profile** panel. Select **Time Profiler** from the **Instrument** pop-up, and click **OK**. Even more convenient, if you hold down the Option key while triggering the Profile action, the Scheme editor will drop down for you to select an instrument, and then you can proceed.

iOS and Instruments give you some grace when you measure performance: The watchdog timer does not fire, and Passer Rating is allowed to run as long as you need, even though it is unresponsive. It takes about a minute and a quarter to present the initial passer list—not quite four times as long as iOS would permit. Embarrassing. See Figure 14.2.

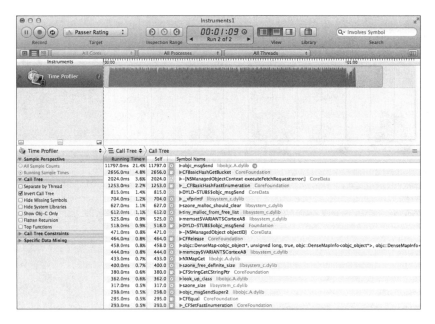

FIGURE 14.2   The trace of Passer Rating paints a discouraging portrait of the CPU being nearly saturated for more than a minute. The top part of the window is the Trace area, with a track showing CPU usage over time. Below it is the Detail area, for cumulative stack traces of the code that was executing.

Your business with Passer Rating is done for the moment, so click the **Stop** button at the left end of the Instruments toolbar. Turn your attention to the lower half of the trace window. This is the Call Tree listing of your session. Instruments' time profiler does "statistical profiling" of your code: At short intervals, it records what part of your code executes and what the call stack is at the time. The call tree in the Detail area summarizes the samples; Table 14.1 shows the first few lines.

TABLE 14.1   A Statistical Trace of Passer Rating During Its Long Startup

Running	(Self)	Symbol Name
6047.0ms	10.3%	objc_msgSend
3916.0ms	6.7%	CFBasicHashGetBucket
3617.0ms	6.1%	-[NSManagedObjectContext executeFetchRequest:error:]
2829.0ms	4.8%	CFBasicHashFindBucket Linear
2656.0ms	4.5%	access
2287.0ms	3.9%	CFRetain

NOTE

Always use Instruments' **Stop** button to end a profiling session. Just closing an app in iOS doesn't end its run—it may be preserved in the background indefinitely, and profiling will continue with it.

This doesn't seem to leave much scope for improvement. Every call tree is rooted in a function or method deep in the runtime, Foundation, or Core Data. You're not responsible for the performance of those functions. Besides, `objc_msgSend`, the hottest function, accounts for little more than one-tenth of the app's business. Where's the low-hanging fruit?

NOTE

The trees I'm showing are "inverted"—what you see are the functions in which the profiler caught the CPU. A noninverted call tree, going from the root of all call trees, would be much less informative; the only root would be the runtime `start` function, in or beneath which an unsurprising 100% of all time was spent, and you'd have to navigate down every fork of execution to individual calls. Make sure **Invert call tree** in the options bar at the left of the Detail area is checked.

You can find your own code further up the call tree; if you click the disclosure triangle next to `objc_msgSend`, you find an entry for Passer Rating:

1421.0ms   2.4%   +[Passer existingPassersWithLastName:firstName:inContext:]

Again, where's the low-hanging fruit? In the worst branch of the call tree, your code accounts for 0.024 of what Passer Rating was doing.

Not so fast. In the options area to the left of the Detail area, click **Hide system libraries**. This removes from the tree every function that isn't in your code and charges those system functions' time to the methods in your code that called them (Table 14.2).

TABLE 14.2   Time Profile of Passer Rating Without System Libraries

Running	(Self)	Symbol Name
47888.0ms	82.0%	+[Passer existingPassersWithLastName:firstName:inContext:]
3350.0ms	5.7%	+[Game csvFile:readValues:error:]
3244.0ms	5.5%	-[Passer RatingAppDelegate application:didFinish...
1388.0ms	2.3%	-[Passer passerRating]

Oh. 82% of the startup time—not quite 48 seconds—was in one method, `existingPassersWithLastName:firstName:inContext:`. That *is* your problem.

Double-click that top line of the call-tree list. Instruments fills the Detail view with the source for `existingPassersWithLastName:firstName:inContext:`. What's more, some of the lines in that method are highlighted, showing what proportion of the CPU samples occurred at what lines (Figure 14.3).

```
≡ Call Tree ≑ ⟩ Call Tree    ⟩ Ⓜ +[Passer existingPassersWithLastName:firstName:inContext:]                              ≡
                                              ▣ Passer.m                                      ▤ ▣ ▣ ▣ ▣ ✿▾
52    NSArray *      result;
53    if (passer)
54        result = [NSArray arrayWithObject: passer];
55    else
56        result = [NSArray array];
57 #else  // Use core data:
58    NSFetchRequest *   req = [[NSFetchRequest alloc] init];        ⓘ 0.1%
59    #if ! ALL_IN_MEMORY
60    NSPredicate *      byName;
61    #if TWO_LEVEL_FETCH
62    byName = [NSPredicate predicateWithFormat: @"firstName = %@", first];
63    #elif COMPOUND_FETCH
64    byName = [NSPredicate predicateWithFormat:                     ⓘ 3.8%
65             @"firstName = %@ AND lastName = %@",
66             first, last];
67    #endif  // Core Data predicate.
68    req.predicate = byName;                                        ⓘ 0.0%
69    #endif  // using Core Data
70    req.entity = [NSEntityDescription entityForName: @"Passer"     ⓘ 0.0%
71                    inManagedObjectContext: moc];
72
73    NSArray *      result = [moc executeFetchRequest: req
74                        error: NULL];                              ⓘ 95.9%
75 #endif //   ! NO_CORE_DATA
76
77 #if ALL_IN_MEMORY
78    result = [result filteredArrayUsingPredicate:
```

FIGURE 14.3   When you double-click a line in the call tree that points to your code, Instruments displays the source to that method in the Detail view. "Hotspots," where the CPU spent the most time, are highlighted.

Here's the method:

```
+ (NSArray *) existingPassersWithLastName: (NSString *) last
                              firstName: (NSString *) first
                              inContext: (NSManagedObjectContext *) context
{
    NSFetchRequest *    req = [[NSFetchRequest alloc] init];
    NSPredicate * byName;
    byName = [NSPredicate predicateWithFormat:
            @"firstName = %@ AND lastName = %@",
            first, last];
    req.predicate = byName;
    req.entity = [NSEntityDescription entityForName: @"Passer"
                        inManagedObjectContext: context];
    NSArray *           result = [context executeFetchRequest: req
                                                error: NULL];

    return result;
}
```

The listing shows the hotspot, at nearly 98% of the time spent in the method, is the call to executeFetchRequest:error:. So now you know: Speeding up the database search for a Passer with a given last and first name should relieve the problem.

Maybe it's simple: The data model doesn't call for any indexes for Passer. It would be easy to go back to Xcode and check the **Indexed** boxes on lastName and firstName. Issue the **Profile** action again. The binding between Passer Rating and Instruments' time-profiling document guarantees that it won't try to open a fresh trace document. Instruments can store more than one session in a document.

So make the profile run; it doesn't look good. Stop Passer Rating when it finally displays the passer table, and look at the time trace. If you click and drag in the time-scale ruler at the top of the Time Profiler track, you'll find you're dragging a "playback head" through the record. A tooltip near your mouse pointer shows you the time, and another down in the track shows the CPU usage at that moment. Initialization took 1:14.8. Click the disclosure triangle to the left of the Time Profiler label; this exposes the track for the previous run. Dragging the playback head across it shows that without indexing, initialization took 1:15.1.

> **NOTE**
>
> The activity view in the middle of the toolbar gives you a way to navigate among the runs without opening the stack of runs: It shows "Run 2 of 2," and you can use the arrowheads on either side to step from run to run.

Indexing isn't the answer—time for something more radical.

Maybe the compound search predicate is the problem. If you specify the first name of a Passer, you narrow the list down considerably; you could pull the results in and filter them in-memory:

```
+ (NSArray *) existingPassersWithLastName: (NSString *) last
                           firstName: (NSString *) first
                           inContext: (NSManagedObjectContext *) context
{
    NSFetchRequest *    req = [[NSFetchRequest alloc] init];
    NSPredicate *       byName;
    byName = [NSPredicate predicateWithFormat: @"firstName = %@", first];
    req.predicate = byName;
    req.entity = [NSEntityDescription entityForName: @"Passer"
                        inManagedObjectContext: context];

    NSArray *           result = [context executeFetchRequest: req
                                            error: NULL];

    result = [result filteredArrayUsingPredicate:
            [NSPredicate predicateWithFormat:  @"lastName = %@", last]];
    return result;
}
```

...and profile again. It helped; initialization is down to 1:09, only three times the amount of time the watchdog timer will tolerate.

Enough of the suspense. Here's a radical step—if executeFetchRequest:error: is a big time sink, don't call it:

```
static NSMutableDictionary *  sAllPassers;
+ (void) initialize
{
    static dispatch_once_t onceToken;
    dispatch_once(&onceToken, "{
        sAllPassers =   [[NSMutableDictionary alloc] init];
    });
}


+ (NSArray *) existingPassersWithLastName: (NSString *) last
                             firstName: (NSString *) first
                             inContext: (NSManagedObjectContext *) unused
{
    NSString *          key = [[NSString alloc] initWithFormat:
                                          @"%@|%@", last, first];
    Passer              passer = [sAllPassers objectForKey: key];
    NSArray *           result;
    if (passer)
      result = [NSArray arrayWithObject: passer];
    else
      result = [NSArray array];

    return result;
}
```

And then create the passer in passerWithFirstName:lastName:inContext after insertion and setting the first and last names:

```
NSString *      key = [[NSString alloc] initWithFormat:
                                    @"%@|%@", last, first];
[sAllPassers setObject: retval forKey: key];
```

Profile it again. It worked: Initialization takes a hair under 14 seconds. The watchdog timer won't kill Passer Rating. See Figure 14.4.

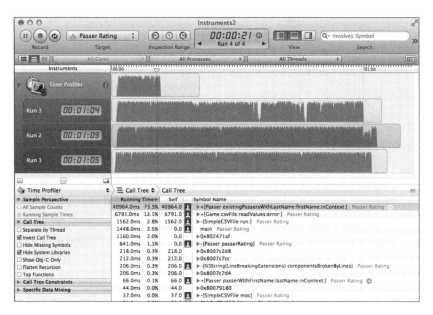

FIGURE 14.4   By avoiding Core Data fetch requests (top timeline), you cut the startup time for Passer Rating down dramatically.

CAUTION

This is an outrageous hack made possible because Passer Rating happens to use only one managed-object context. With only one table of Passers, I was able to write a version of existingPassersWithLastName: firstName:inContext: that ignores the context parameter and uses a single global lookup table instead. When I get to Chapter 17, "Starting a Mac OS X Application," where there is a separate managed-object context per document, I'll have to fall back on the original, Core Data-based version.

Okay, can you go back to the well? Table 14.3 shows the new call tree (still filtered to application code):

TABLE 14.3   Time Profile of Passer Rating Without Core Data

Running	(Self)	Symbol Name
6237.0ms	58.8%	-[Passer RatingAppDelegate application:didFinish. . .
2420.0ms	22.8%	+[Game csvFile:readValues:error:]
630.0ms	5.9%	-[SimpleCSVFile run:]
546.0ms	5.1%	main
1164.0ms	9.4%	+[Passer existingPassersWithLastName:firstName:inContext:]

The distribution is a bit flatter, which is a good sign; it means that there isn't a function that's an horrific consumer of resources. But `application:didFinish-LaunchingWithOptions:` is worth looking at. Here is the line on which `application:didFinishLaunchingWithOptions:` spends 65% of its time:

```
if (! [gMOC save: &error]) {
```

That's a problem. There's no avoiding saving the database, and `save:` is a black box with no way to affect how it does its job. If the strategy is simply to optimize the way the code reads and saves its data, you're at a dead end.

You've relieved of the problem for this particular 10-year CSV, but it's not a general solution. The file doesn't need to get much bigger to time Passer Rating out again. (I tested on an iPhone 4; who knows how soon the problem bites on a 3GS?)

The mere speed of the CSV load is not the real issue; the real issue is that the user doesn't get control soon enough. The real solution is to put the load on a background thread, and display the passer table, updating it as data comes in. This book isn't going to do that; Core Data is thread-safe, but you must painstakingly divide your code between the background and foreground tasks. It's kind of fun, but it's beyond the scope of a book about development tools.

Memory

You're not done with Instruments. iOS devices have a limited amount of memory, and although the OS does have virtual memory (it remaps the address space, shares read-only data between processes, and doesn't use actual RAM for unwritten addresses), it does not page memory out to permanent storage. iPhones and iPads have only a fraction of the RAM that a desktop machine has, and after you run it out, iOS can kill your app. Instruments provides powerful tools for monitoring your memory usage and diagnosing problems.

> **NOTE**
>
> The iOS Simulator uses the Mac OS X virtual-memory system, so a runaway app won't likely be killed for exhausting memory. But if you're just looking for bad behavior, the simulator gives you useful information on a quick turnaround. The rest of this chapter switches back to the simulator.

Allocations

Close the Instruments document you've been using for time profiling and bring the Passer Rating project in Xcode to the front. Set the **Scheme** pop-up to target the iOS Simulator; use the Scheme editor to change the Instruments template for the **Profile** action to **Allocations**. Take the **Profile** action, and let Instruments run Passer Rating. Scroll the passer list a bit, select a passer or two, scroll the game lists—give the app a workout—and then tell Instruments to **Stop** the app.

Again, you see a document window with timelines on the top and a Detail area at the bottom. This time there are two tracks in the timeline, for the Allocations instrument and the VM Tracker instrument. Ignore VM Tracker; it's useful only when you test on a device because the simulator's virtual memory system doesn't behave the same as a device's.

The Allocations track shows an area graph that traces how much memory your app has allocated. The shape of the graph isn't surprising: For a few seconds, memory plateaus at approximately 2MB, followed by a sharp spike above 9MB, and then back down below 3MB. See Figure 14.5.

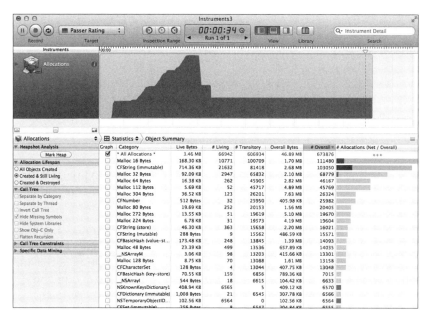

FIGURE 14.5   Running the Allocations instrument against Passer Rating produces an area graph showing the total active memory held by the application as time goes by.

NOTE

Instruments assumes your runs will last more than a few seconds, so this short run will be jammed into a narrow space at the beginning of the timeline; you may find it difficult to drag the head along the actual run to read times and sizes. There is a slider under the names of the instruments that lets you zoom in, but it's clumsy—it's meant to scale the display down to microseconds. For a gentler zoom, hold down the Shift key while you drag across the area of interest. The interval you swipe is scaled to fit the width of the window.

Click the Allocations track to make sure the Detail area contains the statistics the Allocations instrument collected. The statistics take the form of the number of objects of various types that were allocated any time during the run, the total amount of the memory they took up, and the number and size of the objects that were "still living"—had not been released—by the end of the run. Table 14.4 shows what the first few lines look like.

TABLE 14.4   Passer Rating's Memory Usage Before Optimization

Category	Live Bytes	# Living	# Transitory	Overall Bytes	# Overall
* All Allocations*	2.93MB	45373	432972	106.21MB	478345
Malloc 16 Bytes	168.62KB	10792	71471	1.26MB	82263
CFString	280.41KB	8410	55947	1.76MB	64357
Malloc 32 Bytes	83.34KB	2667	44729	1.45MB	47396
Malloc 64 Bytes	13.69KB	219	36813	2.26MB	37032
Malloc 112 Bytes	5.25KB	48	23174	2.48MB	23222
Malloc 336 Bytes	672 Bytes	2	16778	5.38MB	16780
Malloc 128 Bytes	6.50KB	52	16557	2.03MB	16609

You can see that Passer Rating allocated 478,345 objects of all types (the top line), totaling 106.21MB; 432,972 of these were "transitory"—they had been deallocated by the end of the run—and 2.93MB, in 45,373 objects, persist.

The rows that follow list each kind of object that was allocated. The most common allocation was of 16-byte blocks out of the malloc() heap: 10,792 blocks living and 71,471 born-and-died. The last column of the object-category rows show the transitory and living object counts graphically, with the number of living objects shown in a dark color and the number of transitory ones shown pale. If the proportion of living objects is small, Instruments colors the bar red/pink. If you have control over how your objects and buffers are allocated, you should consider reusing them instead of churning through allocation and deallocation.

If you click one of the category rows, you'll see a small arrow button next to the category name. Click it. The Detail area fills with a table of every allocation of that type in the time span you're examining. There will be a lot of them; Table 14.5 shows an excerpt from the Malloc 16 Bytes category.

TABLE 14.5   Instruments Will Track Every Allocation of a Given Type

#	Object Address	Creation Time	Live	Responsible Caller
46480	0xc154fc0	00:06.945.486		getObjectValue
46481	0xc153bd0	00:06.945.615		-[NSString componentsSeparatedByString:
46482	0xc154720	00:06.945.687		-[NSManagedObject initWithEntity:. . . ing:]
46483	0xc154570	00:06.945.696	•	PF_CALLOC_OBJECT_ARRAY
46484	0xc154f30	00:06.945.800		getObjectValue

Of these objects, only number 46483 was still alive at the end of the time span. All the rest were later deallocated. Now, there could be millions of a particular kind of object going through memory in the course of a profiling run. There has to be a way to filter them. The first way is to confine the list to whether the object is alive or deallocated at the end of the span you're looking at. The **Allocation Lifespan** radio buttons at the left side of the Detail area gives you the choice:

▶ **All Objects Created** lists all the objects that had been created in the span you examine, whether they survived or not.

▶ **Created & Still Living** lists only the objects (or categories) that were created during the span and were still in memory at the end. In the excerpt in Table 14.4, only object 46483 would remain in the list.

▶ **Created & Destroyed** focuses on transient objects that were created during the span but did not survive to the end. In the excerpt in Table 14.4, 46483 would be removed.

There's a further way to filter the list: by time interval. There are two ways to focus the object list on a portion of the profiling run. The easiest is to hold down the Option key and drag your mouse across the span that interests you. It's easy but imprecise. The precise way is to drag the head to the beginning of the interval and click the left segment in the **Inspection Range** control in the toolbar; then drag the head to the end of the interval and click the right segment. Clicking the middle segment clears the selection.

Either way, the segment you selected is highlighted in the timeline, and the object list is reduced to objects that were created in that interval. Figure 14.6 shows an example: Instruments is focused on the up-slope of the memory spike in the initialization of Passer Rating. Selecting **Created & Still Living** restricts the list to the objects that contributed to the spike. Each row shows where the allocation was made. If you expose the Extended Detail area on the right (use the **View** control in the toolbar), you can see the full stack trace at the moment of creation. (It appears that most of them came within your call to `save:` at the end of the process).

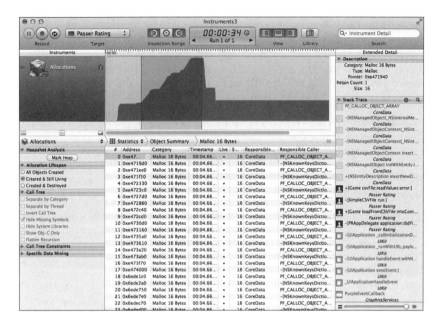

FIGURE 14.6   By selecting the time span from the beginning of the spike in allocations to its peak, and restricting the list to objects "Created & Still Living," you get a complete listing of 16-byte `malloc()` blocks created in the spike. Opening the Extended Detail area (left segment of the **View** control) shows a stack trace for each allocation in the table.

There's more. If you hover the mouse pointer over a row, you will see an arrow button next to the object's address. Click it, and the Detail table shows you the complete history of the object, when it was allocated and freed, and what the stack trace was at the time.

The bar at the top of the Detail area is a hierarchical jump bar; click a segment to back out to that level.

Allocations, too, has a Call Tree option—select it from the menu that pops up from the first segment of the jump bar. Select the **Invert Call Tree** and **Hide System Libraries** options, and if you're still focused on the memory spike, you'll see 100% of your allocations attributed to `application:didFinishLaunchingWithOptions:`; you can ask for a source listing from there and see the call to `save:` highlighted as the hotspot.

The spike is only 9MB high, but maybe there's something to be done for it. The steepest part of it is in the Core Data `save:`, and there's nothing to be done for that. But what about the slow buildup just before? Swiping across that area shows there are a *lot* of strings being created (Table 14.6):

TABLE 14.6   Examining the Early Startup of Passer Rating Shows it Allocates Many Strings

Category	Live Bytes	# Living	# Transitory	Overall Bytes	# xOverall
* All Allocations *	3.28MB	84946	165055	19.62MB	250001
CFString	803.12KB	36878	2849	892.12KB	39727

Tracing into the **CFString** category shows almost all of them come from a call to `componentsSeparatedByString:` inside SimpleCSVFile's `run:` method. This makes sense: These are the CSV fields, of which there must be—well, 12 fields in 3,293 lines in a 10-season file. The numbers match up. All those strings go unused after their record is read and assimilated. Cocoa turns their memory over to an *autorelease pool*, a kind of broker holding memory to be released later, but the default autorelease pool doesn't get drained until control is turned over to the main event loop, which you have painfully learned doesn't happen until all the initialization is done. No wonder almost all those strings are still alive.

So now put an autorelease pool of your own into the CSV-read loop:

```
- (BOOL) run: (NSError **) error
{
    NSString *  contents = /* read from file... */
    if (! contents)
        return NO;

    NSArray *   lines = [contents componentsBrokenByLines];
    NSArray *   fields;
    int         lineCount = 0;
    NSAutoreleasePool * pool;

    for (NSString * line in lines) {
        // CREATE the pool
        pool = [[NSAutoreleasePool alloc] init];

        lineCount++;
        fields = [line componentsSeparatedByString: @","];

        /*  ...Process the lines... */
        //   DRAIN the pool
        [pool drain];
    }
    return YES;
}
```

...and profile again. Now, when you survey the same stretch of the initialization, most of the strings allocated are transitory, leaving their memory free for reuse. Peak memory goes down 9MB to 6.7MB. Any day you can reduce your peak memory demand by a quarter is a good one.

Leaks

You've ministered to the gross behavior of memory management, so now let's focus on a specific topic: Leaks. In Cocoa, you are responsible for releasing the memory you allocate. This is done through a *reference-counting* scheme, in which every consumer of an object registers that it needs the object to persist by sending it the `retain` message. When it's no longer interested, it sends the object `release` (or refers it to the autorelease pool with `autorelease` for disposal later). When the retain count goes to zero, the object's memory is freed.

It is very, very easy to forget to release an object when you're done with it. If it turns out that an object is no longer in use but it still has a retain count, the object is *leaked*—it takes up memory, even though nobody wants it.

Leakage is a bad problem. If it happens enough, your application runs the device out of memory, and iOS kills it.

Instruments has a template that can track down leaks by periodically scanning memory and seeing if there are any blocks that have no references from active variables or through objects referenced from active variables. If the block is alive but unreferenced (as far as the scanner can tell), it's leaked.

Go back to the Passer Rating project in Xcode, and use the Scheme editor to select the **Leaks** instrument for the **Profile** action. Profile the app.

Instruments displays a trace document with two tracks, Allocations and Leaks. It takes time for the scanner to do its work, and leaks don't happen unless the program code does enough work to lose track of objects, so put Passer Rating through its paces: Scroll the passer list, select passers, scroll through their games, go back to the passer list—do it a few times.

As you proceed, dark-red bars appear in the Leaks timeline. This is what you're looking for. Use the **Stop** button in Instruments to end the trace, and select the Leaks instrument. Table 14.7 shows what I saw in the Detail area.

TABLE 14.7   The Leaks Instrument Summarizes Leaked Objects by Type and Allocator

Leaked Object	#	Address	Size	Responsible Frame
NSCFString	2	< multiple >	64 Bytes	-[NSCFString newSubstring...
NSCFString	1	0x7a43330	32 Bytes	-[NSString componentsSeparatedBy…
NSCFString	903	< multiple >	28.22KB	-[NSPlaceholderString init...

903 objects—that's worth pursuing. Because it tracks the history of every object allocated in the course of a profiling run, Instruments knows that the leaked objects came from `-[NSPlaceholderString initWithFormat:locale:arguments:]`, and it has a stack trace from when the allocation occurred. Click the disclosure triangle next to the row for the 903 leaks to expose the full list of the leaked objects.

Click one of them, and then expose the Extended Detail area. (Use the right segment of the **Views** control in the toolbar.) The stack trace is the same for every row, and the responsible method in Passer Rating's code is `+[Passer existingPassersWithLastName:firstName:inContext:]`. Double-click that row in the backtrace, and if you paid attention when the performance problem was "fixed," it won't surprise you to find that

```
NSString *      key = [[NSString alloc]
                    initWithFormat: @"%@|%@", last, first];
```

is the line that caused the trouble. The `alloc` method returns a retained object, `Passer` is the only object interested in its survival, and the method never releases it. Replace the line with

```
NSString *      key = [NSString stringWithFormat:
                    @"%@|%@", last, first];
```

and the leak goes away.

There were two other leaks. One of them was attributed to

```
BOOL    accepted = [self.delegate csvFile: self
                    readValues: values
                    error: error];
```

in [`SimpleCSVFile run:`]. One leak in thousands of loop iterations, and the line doesn't allocate any memory. Leaks isn't perfect; it could be a false alarm. Still, I looked further up the stack to find

```
+ (BOOL) loadFromCSVFile: (NSString *) path
        intoContext: (NSManagedObjectContext *) moc
            error: (NSError **) error
{
    SimpleCSVFile *    csv = [[SimpleCSVFile alloc] initWithPath: path];
    csv.moc = moc;
    csv.delegate = (id<SimpleCSVDelegate>) self;
    BOOL success = [csv run: error];
    return success;
}
```

Again, I `alloc`ed an object without releasing. Inserting [`csv release`] before returning cures that leak, as well as the other. Passer Rating is clean for leaks.

Zombies

The business of tracking leaks led me to an audit of all my memory practices, turning this up in -[`PasserListController fetchedResultsController`]:

```
NSSortDescriptor * byLast;
byLast = [[NSSortDescriptor alloc] initWithKey:@"lastName"
                                ascending:YES];
NSSortDescriptor * byFirst;
byFirst = [[NSSortDescriptor alloc] initWithKey:@"firstName"
                                ascending:YES];
NSArray * sortDescriptors;
```

14

```
sortDescriptors = [[NSArray alloc] initWithObjects:
                                  byLast, byFirst, nil];

[fetchRequest setSortDescriptors:sortDescriptors];
NSFetchedResultsController *    aFetchedResultsController;
aFetchedResultsController = [[NSFetchedResultsController alloc]
                            initWithFetchRequest: fetchRequest
                            managedObjectContext:
                                    self.managedObjectContext
                            sectionNameKeyPath: nil
                                    cacheName: @"Root"];
aFetchedResultsController.delegate = self;
self.fetchedResultsController = aFetchedResultsController;

[aFetchedResultsController release];
[fetchRequest release];
[sortDescriptors release];
```

Something is wrong. The sort descriptors, byLast and byFirst, are alloced but never released. Leaks never detected it because the array of sort descriptors holds them and is in turn held by the fetched-results controller, which is held by the passer controller, which never goes away. There's a valid reference to those descriptors somewhere, so they're never orphaned, and Leaks doesn't see them as such.

This should be fixed as a matter of general principles, so in my enthusiasm I did this:

```
NSSortDescriptor * byLast;
byLast = [[[NSSortDescriptor alloc] initWithKey: @"lastName"
                                    ascending: YES]
        autorelease];
NSSortDescriptor * byFirst;
byFirst = [[[NSSortDescriptor alloc] initWithKey: @"firstName"
                                    ascending: YES]
        autorelease];
// ...etc...
[sortDescriptors release];
[byLast release];
[byFirst release];
```

And so I passed that through the Leaks instrument and found...that Passer Rating crashes as soon as I tried to scroll the passer list.

If you do a Run, to trap the crash in the debugger, you find that control was last in Passer Rating's code at -[PasserListController configureCell:atIndexPath:]:

```
passer = (Passer *) [self.fetchedResultsController
                    objectAtIndexPath: indexPath];
```

The stack is 25 levels deep beyond that, passing through some SQL classes. The debug log contains an exception message headed:

```
-[NSCFString key]: unrecognized selector sent to instance 0xa332880
*** Terminating app due to uncaught exception
    'NSInvalidArgumentException',
    reason: '-[NSCFString key]: unrecognized selector sent
    to instance 0xa332880'
```

Now, it's obvious that the last modification to `-[PasserListController fetchedResultsController]` caused the problem, but I'll play dumb.

Instruments has a tool to help, but the configuration isn't among the templates offered in the Scheme editor for the **Profile** action. Instead, do a Profile run, selecting the Allocations template. Instruments runs Passer Rating and encounters the crash, but ignore that. You're interested in running again, after reconfiguring the Allocations instrument.

You can configure how an instrument behaves and how it displays its trace by clicking the small **i** button next to the instrument's name. This brings up a popover. Many of the controls for the Allocations instrument apply to future runs, but the **Track Display** group can change the display of the current trace; feel free to play with that. See Figure 14.7.

FIGURE 14.7   Clicking the **i** button next to the label of the Allocations instrument opens a configuration popover for the instrument. The popover offers controls to set up future runs of the instrument and to adjust the display of existing traces.

For the moment, you want to check two boxes: **Record reference counts**, which adds retain and release events to the history of memory blocks, and **Enable NSZombie detection**.

Zombies? The normal behavior when the reference count of a Cocoa object goes to zero is that its memory is returned to the heap, leaving an invalid object in its place until the block is reallocated to something else. But you can opt never to return object memory to the heap and instead replace the dead objects with "zombies"; if you send a message to a zombie object, it crashes your program and logs the class of the original object.

This facility has been available in Cocoa for a long time; all you had to do was set the NSZombieEnabled environment variable to YES. You did this in the "Schemes" section of Chapter 12, "Adding Table Cells." Enabling zombies from Instruments lets you take advantage of the Allocations instrument's record of object histories, so you can see not just where the over-release made trouble (which may be far from where you made your mistake), but also where the over-release occurred.

With the settings done (click the x button in the upper-left corner of the popover), click the **Record** button to make a new trace. Because released blocks never return to free storage, the allocated-memory graph doesn't come down much. (Nonobjects are released as before, so there's some retreat.) Induce the crash by scrolling the passer list.

Passer Rating crashes, but a flag appears in the ruler of the timeline, and from it a popup emerges: "Zombie Messaged—An Objective-C message was sent to a deallocated object (zombie)…". There's an arrow button next to the address it reports for the object. Click it.

Table 14.8 (abbreviated) appears in the Detail area.

TABLE 14.8   The Allocations Instrument, with Zombie Detection and Allocation History Turned on, Shows the Life History of an Over-Released Object

Category	Event Type	RefCt	Responsible Caller
NSSortDescriptor	Malloc	1	-[PasserListController fetchedRes...]
NSSortDescriptor	Autorelease		-[PasserListController fetchedRes...]
NSSortDescriptor	Retain	2	-[PasserListController fetchedRes...]
NSSortDescriptor	Release	1	-[PasserListController fetchedRes...]
NSSortDescriptor	Release	0	-[NSAutoreleasePool release]
NSSortDescriptor	Zombie	−1	-[NSSQLOrderIntermediate generateSQLStr..

Four of the entries fall in -[PasserListController fetchedResultsController]. First, the sort descriptor is alloced, giving it a reference count of 1; then a deferred release via autorelease; another retain when the array takes possession; and a release at the end of the method. Eventually, control reaches the main event loop, where the autorelease pool executes that deferred release, the reference count goes to zero, and the memory goes back to free storage. And then an SQL class tries to use it, triggering the zombie crash.

If you double-click any of the lines for PasserListController, you get a listing of fetchedResultsController with hotspots at

```
byLast = [[[NSSortDescriptor alloc] initWithKey: @"lastName"
                                  ascending: YES]
autorelease];              // twice; 50% of the hits
```

```
sortDescriptors = [[NSArray alloc] initWithObjects:
                                    byLast, byFirst, nil];
[byLast release];
```

...which tells you the whole story. Get rid of the `autorelease` or the `release` on both `byLast` and `byFirst`, and both the over-release and the leak are cured.

> **NOTE**
>
> Why did the log say that the crash was due to sending a strange message to a string? The sort descriptors were over-released. Their memory blocks were returned to the `malloc` heap for reuse. Apparently one of the descriptors' blocks was reused for a string. When you see an exception due to sending a strange message to an object, consider that you may have an over-release problem.

> **NOTE**
>
> Even if you have Cocoa memory management all squared away, you'll probably have some memory, obtained through the `malloc` family of functions, that you must manage unassisted. The Object Alloc and Leaks instruments can help, but be sure to review the environment variables in `man malloc` for useful tools for debugging low-level memory management. Most of these are available through the **Diagnostics** tabs in the Scheme editor.

Analysis

Most of these memory exercises are moot. Apple's adoption of the `llvm` parser gives Xcode intrinsic insight into your code, especially in Cocoa memory management. Taking advantage of these facilities would have saved a lot of problem solving.

The Analyzer

The first technique is *static analysis*, enabled by extra compiler flags that are set when you choose the **Analyze** action. If you leave the over-release bug in `fetchedResultsController` and select **Analyze** from the **Action** button at the left end of the Workspace window's toolbar (or **Product→Analyze**, [⇧⌘B]), Xcode compiles the project.

Because there are issues to report, the Issue navigator appears. In a normal compilation, the Issue navigator contains yellow warning and red error flags if there are any. The analyzer produces blue "notes." As with errors and warnings, clicking a note jumps the editor to the place where the problem was detected.

Select the one in `PasserListController.m`; this flags the release of `byFirst` with a banner saying "Object sent -autorelease too many times." There's a blue badge at the left end of the banner. Click it. Now the editor shows a banner at each memory-management event for `byFirst`; a series of arrows appears, linking lines with these annotations:

1. On the creation of `byFirst`: Method returns an Objective-C object with a +1 retain count.

2. On the same line—click the 2 button next to the note: Object sent -autorelease message.

3. At the release of `byFirst`: Reference count decremented.

4. At the end of the method: Object over-autoreleased: object was sent autorelease but the object has zero (locally visible) retain counts.

Again, that tells the story, and you don't need to go through a crash and an Instruments analysis to find it out. See Figure 14.8.

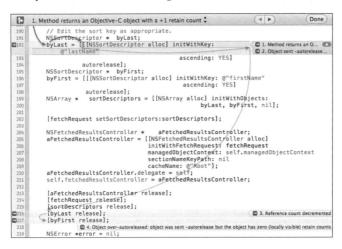

FIGURE 14.8   Clicking an analysis issue in the editor reveals the code path through a method that results in a memory issue.

The arrows, sweeping through the execution path that resulted in the over-release, are not decorative. Not all methods run straight from beginning to end. They have multiple conditional branches inside loops that may or may not exit, and may return from the method within one of those branches. You could audit the reference counts for the objects you create in these tangles, but you probably can't account for every possible combination. llvm can. It analyzes every possible code path, and the code-path arrows it draws on your code show the combination of events that result in an over-or under-retained object.

There are naming conventions for whether a method returns a retained or unretained object. llvm knows the conventions, and if you write a method that breaches them, it will object. In turn, when you get an object from such a method, it infers the retain count and critiques your memory management from that knowledge.

The analyzer is not just for memory. It can catch variables that are uninitialized or that are assigned values but never again referenced. It knows about other coding conventions.

For example, it is common for methods to pass NSError objects back to their callers through a parameter of the type NSError **; but if the caller isn't interested in the error value, it can pass NULL as the error-return pointer. The first lines of -[SimpleCSVFile run:] are

```
-(BOOL) run: (NSError **) error
{
    *error = nil;
```

llvm annotates the assignment with, "Potential null dereference. According to coding standards in 'Creating and Returning NSError Objects' the parameter 'error' may be null."

Automatic Reference Counting

It gets better. If llvm can tell you what went wrong with your memory allocations, and if it is capable of offering "Fix-It" suggestions as to how to correct your code, it should be able to set your memory practices to rights, shouldn't it?

The LLVM 3 compiler does exactly that. Automatic Reference Counting (ARC) is an advancement to the Objective-C language that builds reference-counted memory management into the language. Reference counting is still done, but the compiler does it, and it is illegal for you to try.

Internally, the process is something like this:

▶ Every assignment of an object is guarded by the equivalent of a retain.

▶ After the last reference to an object, it is sent the equivalent of a release.

▶ Every value that is returned from a method whose name does not indicate that it returns a retained object is sent the equivalent of retain and then autorelease.

▶ The preceding three actions result in many redundant actions—retains followed immediately by releases, for instance. llvm detects redundancies and eliminates them.

▶ At run time, when an object's retain count goes to zero, the runtime library releases the objects it holds in its instance variables.

There are subtleties. ARC knows only about Objective-C objects. Dynamic entities like malloc blocks, or objects managed by Core Foundation, still must still be managed in your code. Many Core Foundation objects are "toll-free bridged" to Foundation objects—you can exchange the same object between the two libraries. You must use the __bridge family of type qualifiers to flag such objects for ARC to accept them.

But basically your memory-management code goes away. dealloc methods that merely clean up an object's memory references can be eliminated entirely, clearing up a fruitful source of leaks.

Xcode's templates for projects and targets offer ARC as an option. It makes your code much more robust, but if you have to support systems older than iOS 5 or Mac OS X 10.7, you should think hard before using it. (ARC has limited support in 4.3 and 10.6.8; see the ARC release notes for details.)

Converting to ARC is tempting, but poring through a large project to revamp its memory management is a daunting task. Fortunately, the refactoring suite in the **Edit** menu includes a conversion tool. See the extended treatment in the "Automatic Reference Counting" section of Chapter 17.

Try the conversion. Does it work? *Mostly.* I can't get zombie detection to trigger, and there are no leaks. The Allocations instrument shows that the heap starts and ends with about as much memory as it did before the conversion.

But peak allocation creeps up to about 7.6MB. If you remove the autorelease pool (now @autoreleasepool) in the CSV run loop, the peak is 10.7MB, so even with ARC, doing some memory analysis with Instruments would still have paid you 3MB.

Here's the question: Is the slightly higher peak a reasonable price to pay for more concise code that gets memory management right without debugging sessions that took hours for a simple program like this? I think it's worth it.

Summary

In this chapter, I showed you two tools for testing performance and memory bugs in Cocoa applications: Instruments and the code-analysis powers of the llvm compiler.

Instruments served well in tracking down a fatal performance bug in Passer Rating. It relieved you of trial-and-error fixes to code that wasn't the problem, by pointing you to the exact parts that were the problem. It provided the tools to measure what you did and the courage to take radical steps when they were needed.

Likewise with the memory-management instruments: The Allocations instrument showed how the app was using memory from moment to moment, block by block. It showed peak memory usage and what code was causing it. By reading the subtle clues, you found a build up of temporary objects, and a simple fix dropped the peak usage by nearly 3 megabytes out of 9.

There were some leaks; the Leaks instrument found *some* of them, providing the exact location from which they were allocated. Leaks isn't perfect, but it helped.

I introduced an over-release bug, of a kind that manifested far from the code in which I made the error. That separation was no obstacle to the Allocations instrument after it was set up to detect zombies. It gave the whole history of the errant object and how it was mishandled.

Finally, you saw how the modern tools introduced with Xcode 4.2 made most memory debugging obsolete: The code analyzer, available through the **Analyze** action, finds memory bugs and demonstrates graphically how they happen. And Automatic Reference Counting all but eliminates such bugs. (Although careful analysis of your usage still pays.)

There is a *lot* more to Instruments, and I'll cover it in depth in Chapter 27, "Instruments."

CHAPTER 15

Storyboard

I've had you work on an app targeted at iOS 4.3, which means you were working the hard way. iOS 5 introduces a number of facilities that make an iOS programmer's life much, much easier. This chapter covers the crown jewel, *Storyboard*; you'll rebuild Passer Rating around a storyboard and use it to add a Passer editor.

What Storyboard Is

There was some calculation and record-keeping to Passer Rating, but it seems that much of the work went into designing views and handling the data communication among them. Some of that is unavoidable: You need to specify what the application will look like, you have to fill in the data displays, and you have to hand data off between views. But even with the abbreviated example of Passer Rating, you saw that there was a lot of work that was simply boilerplate.

A storyboard is a plan for the appearance and flow of an application. In its details, you still lay out views and connect them to view controllers. What sets a storyboard apart is that you also lay out the transitions between one view and the next. In a storyboard, the views are called *scenes*, and the transitions, *segues*.

Consider this method from `PasserListController`:

```
- (void)  tableView:  (UITableView *)  tableView
didSelectRowAtIndexPath: (NSIndexPath *)  indexPath
{
    //  Find the selected Passer
    Passer *            passer;
    passer = [self.fetchedResultsController objectAtIndexPath:
            indexPath];
    //  Create the next view controller
    GameListController * glController;
    glController =  [[GameListController alloc]
                                initWithNibName: @"GameListController"
                                        bundle: nil];
    //  Tell the next controller what it's working on
    glController.passer = passer;

    //  Push the next controller onto the navigation stack
    [self.navigationController pushViewController: glController
                                        animated: YES];

    [glController release];
}
```

Only two statements in the method relate to the actual logic of the program: They identify the selected `Passer` and tell the ensuing `GameListController` what `Passer` to focus
on. The rest is boilerplate to build the `GameListController` and install it in the navigation
controller—the template provided much of the code, with placeholders for you to fill in
the details.

Storyboard gets rid of the boilerplate. A storyboard contains a scene for every controller
and layout in your application. You draw a segue between a UI element (such as a table
cell) and a destination scene, and specify what kind of transition (such as pushing onto
the current navigation controller) is to be made. When the user triggers the segue,
Storyboard loads the successor controller and its views and pushes it onto the navigator
stack. On the way, it asks you for your application-specific logic:

```
- (void) prepareForSegue: (UIStoryboardSegue *) segue
            sender: (id) sender
{
  if ([[segue identifier] isEqualToString: @"showDetail"]) {
      NSIndexPath *           indexPath;
      Passer *                passer;
      PRSDetailViewController * pdc;
      indexPath = [self.tableView indexPathForSelectedRow];
      passer = (Passer *)[[self fetchedResultsController]
                                objectAtIndexPath: indexPath];
      pdc = (PRSDetailViewController *)
```

```
                      segue.destinationViewController;
        pdc.detailItem = passer;
    }
    // ... else clauses with code for other transitions...
}
```

The handler for the segue has only two tasks for the transition. If I wanted to ruin the method's readability by eliminating intermediate results, there would be only two statements. Storyboard takes care of identifying the event that causes the transition, instantiating the `GameListController`, and putting it on the screen.

A Storyboard Project

It is not hard to port an existing project over to Storyboard; it's even fun to see the excess code melt away. But just to show off Xcode's support, start a fresh project. Select **File→New→Project...** (⇧⌘N) to create a new project. In the assistant, select **iOS→Application→Master-Detail Application**, and click **Next**. For the **Product Name**, give **PR-Storyboard**; use whatever reverse-DNS **Company Identifier** you like; **Class Prefix**, **PRS**; **Device Family, iPhone**; check **Use Storyboard, Use Core Data**, and **Use Automatic Reference Counting**; don't check **Include Unit Tests**; click **Next**. Find a place to put the new project, and create a Git repository if you want.

The **Summary** tab of the Target editor shows a **Main Storyboard** field, containing **MainStoryboard**. That's the base name (always just the base name) of the `.storyboard` file created by the application template. This is the equivalent of the `UIMainStoryboardFile` (Main storyboard file base name) key in `Info.plist`. The summary editor permits you either a main storyboard or a Main Interface (root NIB) file, but not both.

> **NOTE**
>
> The templates for non-Storyboard applications don't specify either a storyboard or a NIB. Instead, they create the `UIWindow` and its initial view controller in the application delegate.

Now is the time to do the __MyCompanyName__ dance: Do a projectwide search-and-replace to change it to your name, and in the File inspector for the project file (top of the Project navigator), set the **Organization** field.

Make a new tab (**File→New→Tab** [⌘T]), point it at `MainStoryboard.storyboard`, and arrange the workspace as you like. You'll see something like Figure 15.1.

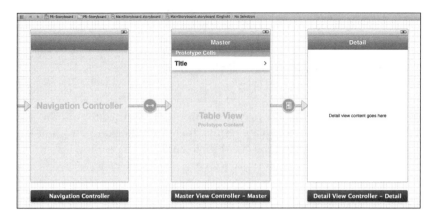

FIGURE 15.1   `MainStoryboard.storyboard` as provided by the iPhone Storyboard application template for a master-detail app. The initial scene is a navigation controller (left), which
contains a master controller (middle), which has a segue to a detail controller (right).

The storyboard is displayed as a canvas containing three scenes. The first represents a
navigation controller (`UINavigationController`); a bare arrow on its left side shows that it
is the initial controller for the storyboard. The second is the root view controller
(`PRSMasterViewController`), linked to the navigation controller by a "relationship" segue
to indicate that it is embedded in the nav controller. The third is an instance of
`PRSDetailViewController`, linked to the master controller by a "push" segue.

> **NOTE**
>
> Use the gray control panel overlaid in the lower-right corner to zoom into and out of the
> canvas. There are magnifying glasses with a + to zoom in, a – to zoom out, and an =
> button to zoom in to the maximum (100%) level.

There are six kinds of segue, distinguished by round badges on the segue arrows. Figure
15.2 illustrates them and their purposes. When you select a segue, you can use the
Attributes inspector to change its type. Depending on the type, you can also refine the
presentation of the transition between views or set the `UIStoryboardSegue` subclass that
performs the transition.

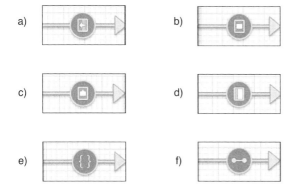

FIGURE 15.2   The Storyboard editor represents segues by six types of arrows: a) Push, for pushing the next controller onto a navigation stack; b) Modal, to present the next controller as a modal view;. c) Popover, a `UIStoryboardPopoverSegue` to present the next controller in an iPad popover; d) Replace, to change the content in the other half of an iPad split-view controller, e) Custom, representing a `UIStoryboardSegue` class you write yourself; and f) Relationship, which isn't a `UIStoryboardSegue` at all—it represents that the container view on the left contains the view on the right.

Reconstructing Passer Rating

Most of the NIB-based Passer Rating can be pulled over to the Storyboard version unchanged. It can use the same models, and many of the view layouts can be copied out of Interface Builder (IB) and pasted straight into the scenes. All you have to do is get the two projects onto the screen so that you can work with both...and that's not going to work. Xcode's project windows don't *have* to be full-screen, but they are surely unusable when you try to give two of them half a screen each.

Workspaces

If you're going to work with two projects on the same screen, now is a good time to get acquainted with workspaces. A *workspace* window looks like a project window, but it can contain more than one project.

With the PR-Storyboard project window active, select **File→Save as Workspace**.... You'll be given a save-file sheet to name and place the workspace file. (Hint: Don't place it in any project folder. A workspace contains references to projects, but there is no file-system relationship between it and any project it refers to.) Call it **PR for iOS**. The window you're looking at looks the same, except that the title bar now shows the icon and name for the workspace file you created.

The workspace contains the PR-Storyboard project. Now you want to add the old Passer Rating project. This can be tricky. The obvious gestures for adding something to the workspace are also obvious gestures for embedding it in an existing project, which you don't want.

In the Project navigator for the PR for iOS workspace, scroll down so that some empty space is visible. In the Finder, open a window on the directory containing the `Passer Rating.xcodeproj` file. Drag it into the empty space at the bottom of the Project navigator.

Watch closely! The Project navigator will show an insertion bar where the file is to go. Drag as far down and left in the navigator as you can so that the insertion bar is at the bottom and the indentation bubble on the bar is at the left margin. If instead it's indented below the last item in PR-Storyboard, it will insert the project you're dragging into the PR-Storyboard project.

Release the drag, and see that the Passer Rating project is now in the workspace. The effects are:

▶ You can work on and build both projects in a single window.

▶ In particular, you can now have PR-Storyboard's storyboard in one half of an assistant editor and one of Passer Rating's XIBs in the other, making it easier to copy and paste between them.

▶ You can create cross-project (not just cross-target) dependencies.

▶ All build products are directed to a shared build tree, so projects can refer to each others' products through the standard build settings (see Appendix B, "Some Build Variables").

▶ A snapshot of the workspace encompasses all projects.

▶ The find options in the global Search navigator add a pop-up menu to restrict searches to a single project or extend them through the whole workspace.

▶ Any new projects you create are added to the workspace.

▶ New breakpoints are kept by the workspace, although they can be moved to a project.

▶ The Scheme editor encompasses all targets in all projects. Schemes are kept in the workspace.

▶ You can still open the individual project files. The only difference is that settings stored in the workspace are not available.

Related to this is the Projects organizer, the third tab in the Organizer window. Every project and workspace known to Xcode is listed in the source list at the left side of the window. When you select one, you are shown:

- The name and location of the project/workspace file.

- When it was last opened.

- Where its "derived data" (build products) directory is; there is an arrow button to show it in the Finder, and a **Delete...** button to delete it.

- The same, for the directory that accumulates the project/workspace's snapshots.

- A list of all snapshots; buttons at the bottom of the table allow you to save a snapshot or delete it.

> **NOTE**
>
> The default location for snapshots, derived data, and archives is inside your ~/Library directory. You can change any of these in the **Locations** tab of the **Locations** panel of the Preferences window.

Each project in a workspace can be managed by a separate version-control repository or system. The commands in **File→Source Control** apply uniformly (a commit goes through one sheet for all changed files), but every action goes through the proper repos for the respective projects.

Think of workspaces as a convenience for your own work on multiple project trees or as a way to make up for the fact that separate project windows would be too big for it to be convenient to work with more than one at a time. It's a personal resource containing absolute paths to unrelated directories. Because of that, workspaces aren't actually shareable across machines or between people and are bad candidates for version control themselves.

Copying the Model

All the model files can just be transferred. Select the data model file, rating, SimpleCSVFile, Passer, Game, and sample-data.csv files in the original project, and drag them up into the list for PR-Storyboard. You'll be presented with the familiar add-to-project sheet; accept what you find there. Delete the PR_Storyboard.xcdatamodeld file from the project.

> **NOTE**
>
> When you drag between projects in a workspace, there's no option for *copying* the files into PR-Storyboard's directory tree. This poses some problems: The receiving project picks the files up as path references, which are fragile; and you don't get a complete file set in the receiving project's version-control repository. Both make it hard to share the projects with others, or to reorganize your disk storage. A more thoughtful approach would be to do the file-dragging between separate project windows, or directly from the Finder—you'd be given the option of copying the files. For now, accept the convenience of working in one window.

The transition is *almost* seamless. There are two catches.

First, this project uses Automatic Reference Counting (ARC), so Xcode objects to the memory-management calls in the imported code. If you go through the error messages, it should be clear what you need to do. Mostly you remove all the calls to retain, release, and autorelease, and eliminate dealloc methods. In one case, you replace an [[NSAutoreleasePool alloc] init] ... [pool drain] pair with @autoreleasepool { ... }. Object @propertys should be converted from retain to strong and assign to weak.

NOTE

LLVM 3 gives you a bonus: Unlike other ARC features, the @autoreleasepool directive is available to replace NSAutoreleasePool allocation and draining even for targets older than Mac OS X 10.6 and iOS 4.3.

Second, the project template for the application delegate produced code that depends on the name of PR_Storyboard.xcdatamodeld. Make it independent (and therefore tolerant of the model you dragged in) by replacing

```
NSURL *modelURL =  [[NSBundle mainBundle]
                      URLForResource:@"PR_Storyboard"
                        withExtension:@"momd"];
__managedObjectModel =  [[NSManagedObjectModel alloc]
                        initWithContentsOfURL:modelURL];
```

with

```
__managedObjectModel = [NSManagedObjectModel
                        mergedModelFromBundles: nil];
```

Edit PRSAppDelegate.m to include the database-deletion code described in the "Making the Model Easier to Debug" section of Chapter 9, "An iOS Application: Model." Also, make sure that application:didFinishLaunchingWithOptions: loads up the sample data before returning:

```
NSString *   path =  [[NSBundle mainBundle]
                      pathForResource: @"sample-data"
                            ofType: @"csv"];
BOOL         success;
NSError *    error;
success = [Game loadFromCSVFile: path
                    intoContext: self.managedObjectContext
                        error: &error];
```

Coding the Passer List

The master view the template gave PR-Storyboard is, by coincidence, nearly perfect for what you want to do: It's a table-view controller embedded in a navigation controller. There are only two differences, both having to do with the navigation bar: Double-click the title (Master) and change it to **Passers**. And find a UIBarButtonltem in the Object library (bottom of the Utility area), and drag it into the right end of the bar. With the Attributes inspector (fourth tab), set the **Style** to **Bordered** and the **Identifier** to **Add**. Connect the button to a new @property named addButton.

> **NOTE**
>
> Interface Builder sometimes fills new bar button items with placeholder titles such as "Item." You can have a written title like that, or you can use one of the standard system titles from the **Identifier** list, but you can't have both. If you use a system button (it will give you free localization and a blue color for **Done** and **Save** buttons), clear out the **Title**.

Class PRSMasterViewController, from the template, adds an **Add** button of its own; edit viewDidLoad to remove the creation of a local addButton and its insertion into self.navigationltem.

Filling the passer list is a little different from what you did in the "The Table View" section of Chapter 10, "An iOS Controller." The coding is done in PRSMasterViewController.m.

Remember to edit configureCell:atIndexPath: and fetchedResultsController as in the earlier example. Option-click on PasserListController.m in the original project to put the old code next to the new.

One thing to notice is that the tableView:cellForRowAtIndexPath: method, as supplied by the template, no longer tries to create a new cell if dequeueReusableCellWithldentifier: returns nil. With Storyboard, dequeueReusableCellWithldentifier: never fails. Look at the Main View Controller scene in the storyboard, and you can see that the table view contains one cell instead of the stack of cells you'd see in an ordinary XIB. This cell is literally in the storyboard. You can lay it out in-place. The important thing for now is that you can set the cell's identifier in the Attributes inspector; when you call dequeue... with that identifier, UIKit replicates the cell.

By this point, you should be back where you were at the end of Chapter 10: a list of passers and their ratings. Run PR-Storyboard to see.

Copying Views

It's also convenient that PRSDetailViewController is laid out as a plain UIViewController. It's a good place to start. There's a lot to the detail-view (game-list) controller in the original project, but most of the view work can be done by copy-and-paste.

To start, delete the dummy label in the middle of the view and all reference to detailDescriptionLabel in the header and implementation files for PRSDetailViewController.

Take advantage of the workspace: Select the .storyboard file in the Project navigator, and then option-click GameListController.xib from the original project to put it into the assistant editor. Select the gray header view from the XIB, and **Edit→Copy** (⌘C). Select the detail view in the storyboard (be sure to click inside the scene) and paste the header view into it (**Edit→Paste** [⌘V]). You need to drag it a bit to align it at the top of the view, but most of your work is done. See Figure 15.3.

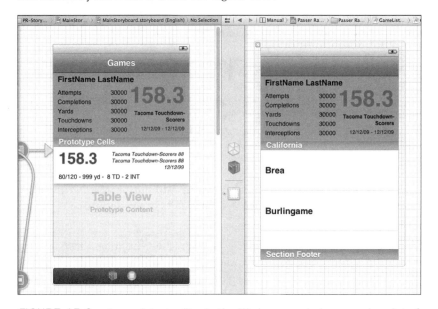

FIGURE 15.3   An assistant editor in the Workspace window can show Interface Builder files from different projects side by side. On the left is the detail-view controller from the new project, PR-Storyboard. On the right, the GameListController.xib file, from which the gray header view was copied, and pasted into the view in the storyboard.

Change the title in the navigation bar from **Detail** to **Games**.

Switch the assistant view to show PRSDetailViewController.h, and control-drag from the data labels into the @interface to create IBOutlets, just as you did in the "Outlets" section of Chapter 11, "Building a New View." While you're in the header file, add a @class Passer directive to the top, and change the declaration of detailItem from id to Passer—it will save a lot of casting.

You can copy the workings of the old GameListController to PRSDetailViewController.m practically verbatim. Just leave the table-view methods alone for the moment.

Replace the prepareForSegue:sender: method in PRSMasterViewController with the one you saw in the "What Storyboard Is" section that began this chapter.

Run PR-Storyboard one more time. Now selecting a passer in the master list shows the detail (games) view with the passer-detail view filled in.

A Custom Table View Cell

You still don't have a list of games in the "Games" view. With the Storyboard editor focused on the Detail View Controller, search the Object library for a table view, and drag it into the view. Size it to fill the whole space below the gray passer-detail view, lamenting that the editor won't snap its upper margin against the other view. Control-drag from the table into `PRSDetailViewController.h` to create a `tableView` outlet, and promise the `PRSDetailViewController` will implement the table-support methods:

```
@interface PRSDetailViewController  : UIViewController
        <UITableViewDelegate, UITableViewDataSource>
```

Supporting the table-view support protocols makes `PRSDetailViewController` eligible to fill the table view's `delegate` and `dataSource` outlets. Hook them up in the Storyboard editor.

In Chapter 12, "Adding Table Cells," I had you construct a custom cell in its own XIB; the table controller filled it in by addressing the labels through view tags. I mentioned that a more-sophisticated approach would be to create a `UITableViewCell` subclass that would handle its data directly. That's what you'll do now. And because this is a storyboard, there's no need for a separate XIB.

Select **File→New→File...** (⌘N) to bring up the New File assistant, and choose **iOS→Cocoa Touch→Objective-C class.** Name it **GameTableCell** and make it a subclass of `UITableViewCell`. Declare it in the header file:

```
@class    Game;

@interface GameTableCell  : UITableViewCell

@property(nonatomic,  weak)  Game *        representedObject;

@property(nonatomic,  weak)  IBOutlet UILabel * passerRatingLabel;
@property(nonatomic,  weak)  IBOutlet UILabel * outcomeLabel;
@property(nonatomic,  weak)  IBOutlet UILabel * statsLabel;

@end
```

In the implementation, `@synthesize` the storage and accessors for the `@property`s:

```
@synthesize representedObject;
@synthesize passerRatingLabel, outcomeLabel, statsLabel;
```

Remember that this is ARC memory management: There's no need for a `dealloc` method to release the objects.

NOTE

You can't control-drag from cell subviews to connect or create outlets in the cell's @implementation. It's a limitation of the Storyboard editor, which may have been lifted by the time you read this. You have to declare the outlets and use other means to connect them.

Provide the simple workings of the cell:

```objc
- (void) fillValues {
    // Make a formatter for the short date
    static NSDateFormatter *   sDateFormat = nil;
    static dispatch_once_t     formatOnceToken;
    dispatch_once(&formatOnceToken, "{
        sDateFormat = [[NSDateFormatter alloc] init];
        sDateFormat.dateStyle = NSDateFormatterShortStyle;

    }}

    self.passerRatingLabel.text =
            [NSString stringWithFormat: @"%.1f",
                    self.representedObject.passerRating.floatValue];
    NSString *      content;
    content = [NSString stringWithFormat:
            @"%@ %d\n%@ %d\n%@",
            self.representedObject.ourTeam,
            self.representedObject.ourScore.intValue,
            self.representedObject.theirTeam,
            self.representedObject.theirScore.intValue,
            [sDateFormat stringFromDate:
                    self.representedObject.whenPlayed]];
    self.outcomeLabel.text = content;

    content = [NSString stringWithFormat:
            @"%d/%d - %d yd - %d TD - %d INT",
            self.representedObject.completions.intValue,
            self.representedObject.attempts.intValue,
            self.representedObject.yards.intValue,
            self.representedObject.touchdowns.intValue,
            self.representedObject.interceptions.intValue];
    self.statsLabel.text = content;
}

- (void) awakeFromNib
{
    [self fillValues];
```

```
}

(void) setRepresentedObject: (Game *) newRepresentedObject
{
    representedObject = newRepresentedObject;
    [self fillValues];
}
```

With the workings of the cell in place, it's time to lay it out. The table view in the storyboard has one cell in it—the prototype cell. Select the prototype cell, and drag its lower resizing handle (or use the Size inspector) to make its height 92 points.

Put `GameTableCell.xib` from the original project into the assistant editor—the XIB contains a bare `UITableViewCell`. Select all the *contents* of the cell (you don't want to copy the cell itself), copy them, and paste them into the prototype cell in the storyboard. Close the assistant editor.

Select the prototype cell, and in the Identity inspector (third tab) change its class to `GameTableCell`. (Xcode should help you with an autocompletion.) In the Attributes inspector (fourth tab), fill in the **Identifier** with **GameTableCellID**. The `dequeueReusableCellWithIdentifier:` method won't find the cell unless you set an identifier for it.

Now you can connect the detail labels in the cell to their outlets. These have to be connected to the *cell* as it is represented in the storyboard; connections to the outlets in the `@interface` don't work for cell prototypes. Control-click the cell (it might be easier to do this with the cell as it appears in the outline sidebar), and drag to the large, blue passer-rating label. Release, and select the `passerRatingLabel` outlet in the heads-up window that appears. Connect the other two labels similarly.

That's all you have to do for the custom cell.

Of course, you won't see any cells unless `PRSDetailViewController` provides the `UITableViewDataSource` methods to fill them in. Be sure you've copied the `arrangedGames` @property and method (and the `arrangedGamesCache` instance variable) from the original `GameListController`, and add these methods to `PRSDetailViewController.m`:

```
#pragma mark - UITableViewDataSource

- (NSInteger) tableView: (UITableView *) tableView
  numberOfRowsInSection: (NSInteger) section
{
    return self.detailItem.games.count;
}

(UITableViewCell *) tableView: (UITableView *) aTableView
        cellForRowAtIndexPath:  (NSIndexPath *) indexPath
```

```
{
    GameTableCell *    cell =
                [aTableView dequeueReusableCellWithIdentifier:
                        @"GameTableCellID"];
    cell.representedObject = [self.arrangedGames
                        objectAtIndex: indexPath.row];
    return cell;
}
```

Again, notice that unlike the original GameListController, there's no need to load a separate XIB file to instantiate the cell: Give dequeueReusableCellWithIdentifier: a cell ID, and it will do the rest. Also, there's no need to crawl the views inside the cell; now that there's a custom cell class to manage the labels, all you have to do is supply the Game the cell it is to display.

Run PR-Storyboard again. The Games list now shows the games for the passer you select. You're now (almost) back to the full functionality of the original app, with much less code and a much clearer design.

Adding a Passer Editor

I said you're *almost* back to the original app. There's one difference: You took down the original Add (+) button and dropped in a button of your own. You didn't connect it to anything. In this section, you do something with the button, but rather than simply adding a dummy Passer to the list, you'll edit the new Passer's details.

An editor view on an iPhone should be self-contained, filling the screen, with **Cancel** and **Save** buttons in a bar at the top. It should be presented modally—sliding up from the bottom when activated, and out through the bottom when dismissed by one of the bar buttons. The content should be a stack of labeled text-editing fields—and in iOS, any stack of views is a table until proven otherwise. See Figure 15.4.

Creating the Editor View

Start by finding a table controller in the Object library, and drag it into the Storyboard canvas. It expands to a full scene, which you can drag below the master and detail scenes; the canvas grows to accommodate it. See Figure 15.5. You need a bar for the top of the view. The way to do this is to select **Editor→Embed In→Navigation Controller**. This creates a navigation view controller scene to the left of the new controller, linked by a Relationship segue to show the table view is embedded in the navigation view.

> **NOTE**
>
> You could also have dragged a UINavigationController into the canvas, but that would also create a plain UIViewController as its root view. You want a table-view controller instead. You'd need to delete the controller and drag a UITableViewController in anyway, and then drag a Relationship segue to embed it.

FIGURE 15.4   How the finished passer editor should look.

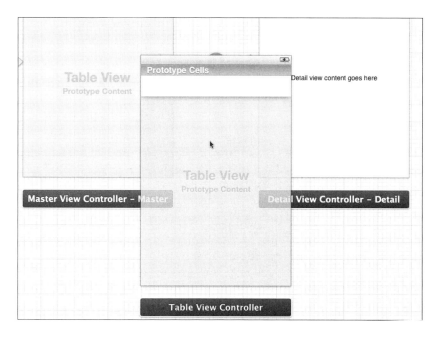

FIGURE 15.5   Dragging a table-view controller into the storyboard canvas from the Object library expands the icon to a full-size scene that you can drop into the canvas.

Before Storyboard, if you wanted to present a static table—one that has an unchanging list of cells, not data-driven—you had to provide the count-generate-fill methods just as though you had to compute the number and placement of the contents. If you had editable content in the cells, you had to be ingenious to find each `UITextField` control and hook it up to the correct model object.

Storyboard changes this by letting you construct static tables directly. Select the table view in the new scene (click the empty area, not the prototype cell), and in the Attributes inspector, change the **Content** from **Dynamic Prototypes** (which you used for the data-driven passer and game tables) to **Static Cells**. The table is now shown with three cells. Change the **Style** to **Grouped** to wrap the cells in the gray background of a grouped table.

You can create another wrapped group by incrementing the **Sections** stepper, but you need only one section. Similarly, if you click in the lower or upper margin of a section, the Attributes inspector will let you set the number of cells in the section. (Selecting a group in the graphical editor can be tricky; you'll have better luck in the outline sidebar.) You want three cells, but decrement the count to 1 anyway; it makes it easier to replicate your layout.

The editing cell needs a label and a text field. Drag a label from the Object library into the left end of the cell. Size it so it takes up one-third of the width of the cell. Set the **Text** to **First Name**; **Alignment** to right-justified; **Font** to **System Bold**, **14** points; and **Text Color** to a medium bluish-gray.

Drag in a text field to take up the remaining two-thirds of the cell's width (with a little bit of margin from the label). Give it a **Placeholder** of **First**; **Border Style** none (first segment); **Clear Button** should be **Appears While Editing**; **Font**, **System**, **16** points; **Min Font Size**, **10** points, with **Adjust to Fit** checked; **Capitalization** should be **Words**.

Select the table-view section again. Increment the **Rows** stepper to produce three rows. Xcode duplicates your existing cell, so all you need to do is correct the label and placeholder text.

Coding the Editor Controller

As with any scene, you must provide your own controller; when you dragged the table-view controller into the canvas, Xcode bound it to a generic `UITableViewController`, but that doesn't help you. Create a new Objective-C class, `PRSPasserEditController`, a subclass of `UITableView`. Before you forget, go to the storyboard, select the new table-view controller, and in the Identity (third) inspector, set **Class** to match.

Put the new `PRSPasserEditController.h` into the assistant editor. (Selecting **Automatic** as the first element in the assistant's jump bar should do it.) You'll connect the field editors in the static cells straight to the controller. Because you're going to the controller, and not a cell subclass, you can control-drag to create the `IBOutlets`.

Add the **Cancel** and **Save** buttons for the navigation bar: Find "Bar Button" in the Object library, and drag one button into each end of the bar. Use the Attribute inspector to set the standard **Cancel** and **Save** identifiers. (The latter turns the **Save** button blue.) You need the buttons to tell the controller to do something when they are tapped;

Control-drag to create IBAction methods for them. (See the "Wiring Up a Menu" section of Chapter 17, "Starting a Mac OS X Application," for an example.)

The easiest way to run an editor under Storyboard is for the editor to communicate with the owner of the object being edited through a delegate @protocol.

When you've added the protocol declaration, PRSPasserEditController.h should look like this:

```
@class PRSPasserEditController;

@protocol PasserEditDelegate <NSObject>
- (void) passerEditorSaved:  (PRSPasserEditController *) editor;
- (void) passerEditorCanceled: (PRSPasserEditController *) editor;
@end

@interface PRSPasserEditController  : UITableViewController

@property(weak, nonatomic) IBOutlet UITextField *firstNameField;
@property(weak, nonatomic) IBOutlet UITextField *lastNameField;
@property(weak, nonatomic) IBOutlet UITextField *currentTeamField;

@property(nonatomic, weak) id <PasserEditDelegate> delegate;
@property(nonatomic, weak) id representedObject;
@property(nonatomic, copy) NSDictionary * values;

//  Action for the Cancel button:
- (IBAction) cancelTapped: (id) sender;
//  Action for the Save button:
- (IBAction) saveTapped: (id) sender;

@end
```

The implementation isn't complicated:

```
@interface PRSPasserEditController ()
- (void) fillValueFields;
@end

@implementation PRSPasserEditController
@synthesize firstNameField, lastNameField, currentTeamField;
@synthesize delegate, representedObject, values;

#pragma mark - View lifecycle

- (void)viewDidLoad
{
```

```objc
  [super viewDidLoad];
  [self fillValueFields];
}


- (void)viewDidUnload
{
  [self setFirstNameField:nil];
  [self setLastNameField:nil];
  [self setCurrentTeamField:nil];
  [super viewDidUnload];
}


- (BOOL)shouldAutorotateToInterfaceOrientation:
        (UIInterfaceOrientation) interfaceOrientation
{
    return   (interfaceOrientation == UIInterfaceOrientationPortrait);
}


- (void) fillValueFields
{
    self.firstNameField.text = [self.values objectForKey: @"firstName"];
    self.lastNameField.text = [self.values objectForKey: @"lastName"];
    self.currentTeamField.text = [self.values objectForKey: @"currentTeam"];
}


- (void) setValues: (NSDictionary *) newValues
{
    values = newValues;
    [self fillValueFields];
}


- (IBAction) cancelTapped: (id) sender
{
    [self.delegate passerEditorCanceled: self];
}


- (IBAction) saveTapped: (id) sender
{
    NSMutableDictionary *   results = [NSMutableDictionary dictionary];
    [results setObject: self.firstNameField.text forKey: @"firstName"];
    [results setObject: self.lastNameField.text forKey: @"lastName"];
    [results setObject: self.currentTeamField.text forKey: @"currentTeam"];
    self.values = results;

    [self.delegate passerEditorSaved: self];
}
@end
```

Take note of a couple of points:

▸ Even though `PRSPasserEditController` is a subclass of `UITableViewController`, there are no data-source or delegate methods to support the table. They aren't needed; UIKit supplies that functionality for static tables.

▸ When **Save** or **Cancel** are tapped, the editor communicates with its delegate (the client that asked for the editor) through the `PasserEditDelegate` protocol.

▸ The client and the editor pass the values for the editor through a `values` dictionary property; the client sets the values when it creates the editor, and if the user taps **Save**, the editor returns them through the `values` property. By working through a dictionary, instead of directly with a `Passer`, you avoid the problems of rolling back changes to (or the creation of) a `Passer` if the user taps **Cancel**, and of validating the values before committing them to the database.

Adding a Segue

The editor has everything it needs to operate, except that there is no way to display it, and it has no client. At last, we get to segues.

Arrange the storyboard so you can see both the master scene and the scene for the *editor's* navigation controller. Hold down the Control key, and drag from the + button in the master's navigation bar to the editor's navigation controller. A heads-up window, labeled **Storyboard Segues**, appears, giving you a choice of the type of segue you want. Select **Modal**.

A controller can originate many segues, and there needs to be a way to distinguish them. Select the new segue, and in its Attributes inspector give it the name **EditPasser**. (This is also where you can change the **Style** of the segue to **Modal** if you missed it before.)

If you ran PR-Storyboard now, you'd find that the editor does appear when you tap the + button, but it won't contain any data, and tapping the **Cancel** or **Save** buttons won't dismiss it. The master controller must prepare the editor and establish communications with it.

Open `PRSMasterViewController.m`, and look for the method `prepareForSegue:sender:`. You already edited this method to provide the passer/game transition (the `showDetail` segue). Now add code that responds to the EditPasser segue you just added:

```
- (void) prepareForSegue: (UIStoryboardSegue *) segue
                  sender: (id) sender
{
    if ([[segue identifier] isEqualToString:  @"showDetail"]) {
        //  ... existing code for a tap on a Passer cell ...
    }
    else if ([segue.identifier isEqualToString: @"EditPasser"]) {
        // Collect the destination (navigation) controller
        UINavigationController * dest;
```

```
            dest = segue.destinationViewController;

            // Find the actual editor controller in the nav controller
            PRSPasserEditController * pec;
            pec =   (PRSPasserEditController *) dest.topViewController;

            // Tell the editor that I'm the client
            pec.delegate = self;

            if (sender == self.addButton) {
                // The Add button was tapped.
                // Have the editor remember that there's no
                //      existing Passer being edited.
                pec.representedObject = nil;

                // Supply dummy data for the editor to display.
                pec.values = [NSDictionary dictionaryWithObjectsAndKeys:
                            @"First", @"firstName",
                            @"Last", @"lastName",
                            @"Team", @"currentTeam",
                            nil];
            }
            else {
                // ... we'll get to this later ...
            }
        }
    }
}
```

prepareForSegue:sender: tells the originating (master) controller that a particular segue has been triggered by a particular UI element. The segue has created the controller for the destination scene, so the master controller can initialize it. In this method, dig past the UINavigationController at the root of the editor to get to the editor itself. Set its delegate to make the master the editor's client, and supply default values for editing.

Add to PRSMasterViewController.h the promise that the master controller can be a client of the editor:

```
#import "PRSPasserEditController.h"

@interface PRSMasterViewController : UITableViewController
        <NSFetchedResultsControllerDelegate, PasserEditDelegate>
```

and provide the delegate methods you just promised to implement:

```
#pragma mark - PasserEditDelegate

- (void) passerEditorSaved:(PRSPasserEditController *)editor
```

```
{
    Passer *    passer = editor.representedObject;
    if (! passer) {
        // There's no existing Passer being edited. Create one.
        passer = [NSEntityDescription
                    insertNewObjectForEntityForName: @"Passer"
                          inManagedObjectContext:
                                  self.managedObjectContext];
    }
    // Harvest the new attribute values
    [passer setValuesFromDictionary: editor.values];
    // Remove the editor from the screen
    [self dismissModalViewControllerAnimated: YES];
}


(void)  passerEditorCanceled:(PRSPasserEditController *)editor
{
    // The user canceled;  don't do anything with the data
    // Remove the editor from the screen
    [self dismissModalViewControllerAnimated: YES];
}
```

That's everything you need to do in `PRSMasterViewController` to support the editor. Run PR-Storyboard again, and tap the + button. The editor appears with the default strings prefilled. Tap the **Cancel** button, and the editor goes away. Tap the + button again, edit the strings, and tap **Save**. This time, when the editor slides out, a new passer is added to the Passers list, with the name you entered.

> **NOTE**
>
> A real product would validate names, prevent duplications, and maybe offer a picker, rather than free-form input, for the team name. That's beyond the scope of an example.

Editing an Existing Passer

`PRSPasserEditController` is general enough to edit an existing `Passer`. Carry that feature through to the master controller.

It's common in iOS to present a master table in which the elements can be expanded—tap a cell to bring up a detail view—*and* edited. Applications signal that they offer editing by marking the table cells with a *detail disclosure* accessory, a blue circle with a right-pointing caret. Go to the storyboard, select the master view's prototype cell, and in the Attributes inspector, set **Accessory** to **Detail Disclosure**.

It would be nice to link up the disclosure button's action straight to the editing scene, but the Storyboard editor won't let you do it; you can't select the accessory. Instead, you must use a table-view delegate method to capture the tap on an accessory view:

```
- (void) tableView: (UITableView *) tableView
    accessoryButtonTappedForRowWithIndexPath:
                             (NSIndexPath *) indexPath
{
    // Capture the cell that was tapped
    self.accButtonlndexPath = indexPath;
    // Perform the segue
    [self performSegueWithldentifier: @"EditPasser"  sender: nil];
}
```

▶ The big thing this method does is to trigger the `EditPasser` segue programmatically. The Storyboard editor didn't let you set up a segue to pick up a UI action automatically, but you can fetch one by name and trigger it yourself.

▶ When an accessory view is tapped, the enclosing cell is not selected. The `prepareForSegue:sender:` method can't use the table's `indexPathForSelectedRow` method to find the associated Passer. So create a strong @property named `accButtonlndexPath`, of type NSIndexPath*, and @synthesize it.

Now you can fill in the last bit of `prepareForSegue:sender:`:

```
if (sender == self.addButton) {
    // ... the Add button was tapped ...
}
else {
    // Not the add button;  assume it's an accessory button
    // Collect the Passer at the saved index path
    Passer *   passer =
        (Passer *) [self.fetchedResultsController
                        objectAtlndexPath: self.accButtonlndexPath];

    // Tell the editor it's editing an existing passer
    pec.representedObject = passer;

    // Load the editor with the existing values
    pec.values = [NSDictionary dictionaryWithObjectsAndKeys:
                    passer.firstName, @"firstName",
                    passer.lastName, @"lastName",
                    passer.currentTeam, @"currentTeam",
                    nil];
}
```

`passerEditorSaved:` is already written so that if the editor were holding a reference to an existing `Passer`, that's what would receive the edited values. If you run PR-Storyboard again and tap the detail-disclosure accessory on a passer cell, you get the passer's information to edit. When you tap **Save**, the magic of `NSFetchedResultsController` updates the passer list to reflect the changes (including re-sorting the item by its new name).

The thing to take away from this exercise is that segues are first-class objects that you can retrieve by their identifiers and use, even if they aren't anchored in the storyboard to a UI element. You can draw a purely programmatic segue from a view controller without linking it to a cell or button. It won't be triggered automatically, but you can trigger it by the identifier you give it.

Summary

This chapter showed you how Xcode supports Storyboard, which can radically simplify the design and operation of your application. I showed you how to create a Storyboard project and use its familiar Interface Builder features to create scenes and lay them out. You then added segues to manage transitions between scenes.

There is still a lot to be done before Passer Rating fulfills the vision laid out in Chapter 8, "Starting an iOS Application." But when you look at the storyboard (Figure 15.6), it's beginning to look a lot like the plan in Figure 8.2.

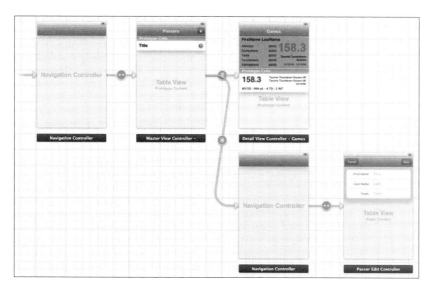

FIGURE 15.6   The PR-Storyboard storyboard after the work done in this chapter. The application is far from finished, but it reflects more of the vision drawn out in Figure 8.2.

I also covered the expanded support for creating static and dynamic table views, which were so simple, you could add a `Passer` editor to Passer Rating with little trouble.

On the way, you saw how Xcode projects can aggregate into workspaces, making it much easier to build new products from existing ones.

You also learned something that you may have to explain to your managers: Storyboard saves a lot of effort and cuts the opportunities for errors down dramatically, but it's not magical. You can't build an application "just by drawing." Every scene must be backed by a controller object you provide, at least as a skeleton, in advance. The demos that look magical (and seduce nontechnical managers) hand-wave the significant coding effort you still have to put in.

## CHAPTER 16

Provisioning

Here's the short of it: Apple does not want any app running on any iOS device that isn't written by someone it trusts. It doesn't want any apps in general circulation that it doesn't curate through its App Store. At each stage of the life cycle of your app—from testing on your desktop, to circulating it among beta testers, to final distribution—you have to jump through some hoops.

This chapter shows you the triangle of identities—signing, application, and device—that go into provisioning an iOS app for installation on a device and what Apple's procedures are for turning those identities into provisioning profiles.

Developer Programs

To get your app onto a device, Apple has to trust you. (Or if it can't, it at least has to be able to identify you and track you down.) It needs your name and address, your assent to the licensing terms, and a payment that both defrays its costs and verifies you are who you say you are. So, early on, you have to pony up for a paid iOS developer program ($99 in the United States as I write this).

There are two kinds of registration for the general iOS developer program.

Organizations

Organizations (companies) are corporate entities with credentials such as a DUNS number from the Dun & Bradstreet credit-rating organization. Apple allows them to have more than one developer working on the company account; these are organized into a hierarchy of actors, with different levels of privilege.

▶ **Members** are authorized to install apps for development purposes, subject to the approval of senior members of the team. Members can't authorize anything; they can only post requests to Admins or the Agent.

▶ **Team Admins** can invite others to the Organization account, authorize devices for use in development, issue non-generic development profiles, approve requests from Team Members, examine sales reports, and do all the things Team Members can do.

▶ There can be only one **Team Agent** because the Agent represents the legal authority and identity of the Organization. The Agent can make financial arrangements, authorize new applications, and clear apps for beta and App Store distribution. The Agent has custody of the signing certificate that validates an app for distribution beyond a handful of development devices and can also do anything an Admin can do.

Individuals

The story is much simpler for developers registered in the Individual program: Access is available to only one person, who acts as the equivalent of a Team Agent. No permissions, no restrictions.

The Enterprise Program

Apple has a separate Enterprise developer program for organizations developing apps for in-house use. Member organizations can distribute their apps, strictly within themselves, without having to publish apps like company directories through the App Store. The apps can be installed on an unlimited number of devices, subject to a provisioning profile that must be renewed every 6 months. Enterprises have Members, Admins, and Agents, as with the Organization account.

The Provisioning Story

The saga of getting your app into a device comes in three parts: development, ad-hoc distribution, and App Store distribution. The first round comes early in the development process.

You can get a lot done toward developing an app using just the simulator, but there is no substitute for putting it on a device. The simulator relies on Mac hardware and Mac system software, and iOS devices are severely limited by comparison. If your app does anything but the most trivial tasks, it will probably crash, or at least be unacceptably slow, the first time you try it on a device. So early on, you must satisfy the device that it's okay to install and run your app.

Authorization to install an app *always* consists of three identities:

▸ **Signature:** The app must be cryptographically signed by a developer (or in the case of general distribution, the Team Agent) to identify it with the developer-program membership. The certificate represents a *signing identity*. Apple issues the signing certificate.

▸ **Application ID:** This identifies the particular app. It's a simple string, made unique through the reverse-domain convention, that you register to your program membership through Apple. For Passer Rating, this is `com.wt9t.Passer-Rating`.

▸ **Authorized device:** App Store and Enterprise applications can be installed on any iOS device in the world. For development and beta, the device has to be registered with Apple for your program membership. Your program has 100 registrations, and each lasts a year; you can unregister a device, but its slot won't be available to you until the anniversary of your membership.

On the basis of these, Apple issues a *provisioning profile*. It binds your app ID, one or more authorized signers, and one or more devices together into a cryptographic bundle that assures your iOS device that it's permitted to accept the app.

For the purposes of development, installation is done directly from Xcode to a device, as an automatic consequence of a **Product→Run** with the device you designate in the **Scheme** control in the toolbar.

In the early days of iPhone development, all these registrations and certifications had to be done one step at a time, by hand, through the iOS Provisioning Portal site (see "The Provisioning Portal" later in this chapter). The Portal is still there for management tasks, obtaining profiles for distribution, and other special cases. For most purposes, though, Xcode can take care of everything for you.

Automatic Device Provisioning

The mechanism is called Automatic Device Provisioning (ADP). Turn it on by selecting the Devices organizer (**Window→Organizer** [⇧⌘2]**→Devices** panel, Figure 16.1) and clicking **Provisioning Profiles**. This panel lists all the profiles allowing your apps to run on devices for development and distribution. Click the **Automatic Device Provisioning** check box to turn ADP on.

Now click **Refresh**. Xcode asks you for your Apple Developer Programs credentials, and if you belong to more than one development team, you'll be asked to pick one. The overall function of ADP is to make sure all the certificates and profiles associated with your membership in that team are made current and loaded into your machine.

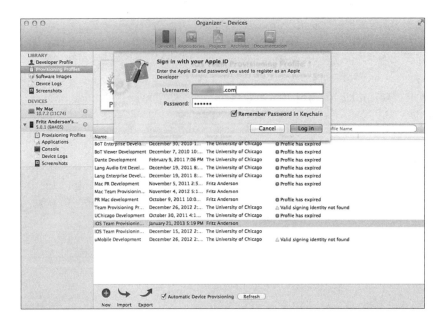

FIGURE 16.1 When you click the **Refresh** button in the **Provisioning Profiles** panel, you will be asked for your Apple developer credentials and to select the team membership you want to use if you belong to more than one.

▶ If you don't have a *development* certificate (one is issued to each member of a team for the purpose of debugging an app on a tethered device), Xcode will offer to apply for one.

▶ If your development certificate is about to expire, Xcode will apply for a renewal.

For either new or renewal applications, Xcode will download and install the certificate automatically if you have authority to approve certificate requests. If you don't have the authority, Apple will notify your Team Admins and Agent, and when one of them approves the request, you'll get an email instructing you how to install the new certificate.

▶ If you are an individual developer, or the Team Agent for a company, Xcode will offer to apply for and install a generic *distribution* certificate, for signing release builds for beta (ad-hoc) or App Store distributions.

▶ If a device is connected at the time you clicked **Refresh**; if you clicked the **Use for Development** button in the device's information panel in the Organizer; and if you have enough privilege (individual developer, Admin, or Agent), Xcode will register it to your team.

▶ Xcode will download and install a Team Provisioning Profile, authorizing a development install of any "generic" app under development, on registered devices. If the refresh registered a new device, the profile will be reissued to cover it.

► If any certificate or provisioning profile to which you are entitled is missing from your system, Xcode will download and install them.

The Provisioning Portal

Originally, the iOS Provisioning Portal (go to `http://developer.apple.com/ios`, log in, and click the link in the sidebar) was the only way to get certificates, application IDs, and development or distribution provisioning profiles. Apple has been steadily developing Xcode to take care of most provisioning tasks. However, you still need to work through the Portal if you need to customize a profile or issue a distribution profile.

Development Certificates

Individuals, Team Admins, and Team Agents can issue development signing certificates for themselves through ADP. Team Members don't have approval authority; they can use ADP to generate a signing request for their development certificates, but these must be approved by an Admin or an Agent.

When a Team Member submits a signing request, the Admins and Agent receive an email notifying them that a request is pending. The email contains a link to the approval page in the Provisioning Portal. The approval page displays a table of pending requests; check the ones you want to approve, and click **Submit**. The approved Members receive emails instructing them how to download the certificates from the Portal, or they can use ADP to download and install them automatically.

Development Certificates expire after 6 months.

Distribution Certificates

Only the Team Agent (or the Individual) may request a distribution certificate—one only for a membership. This can be done only through the **Distribution** tab of the Certificates page of the Provisioning Portal. When you first use the page, the table of certificates is empty. Click **Request Certificate**, and you see the first of a series of pages that instruct you how to generate a Certificate Signing Request (CSR) for upload to the portal. The short of it is:

► Find the Keychain Access application (`/Applications/Utilities/Keychain Access`, or in the Utilities group in Launchpad), and open it.

► Select **Keychain Access→Request a Certificate from a Certificate Authority…**. The Certificate Assistant appears.

► Enter your email address. For the **Common Name:**, enter a distinctive name, identifying your organization uniquely. (If your organization has both an Enterprise and an App Store account, make the two common names different.) Select **Saved to disk**.

► Click **Continue**, and save the CSR file.

▶ Use the Portal page to upload the CSR. You return to the certificate list, which shows that the request is pending.

▶ Refresh the page every few seconds until the certificate is approved. Click **Download**.

▶ Double-click the downloaded .cer file to marry the public key in that file to the private key the Certificate Assistant put in your keychain.

CAUTION

This will be the only instance of the complete public/private signing pair in the world. The .cer file is not enough to sign applications. Save the certificate by selecting it in the certificates list of the Local keychain, issue **Keychain Access→Export Items...** (⇧⌘E), and export a .p12 file to create an archive. Or use the **Export** button in the **Provisioning Profiles** panel of the Devices organizer to export all your identity certificates into a single, shareable, archive.

NOTE

As far as your Mac is concerned, Apple's signature on signing certificates isn't valid; it was not in turn signed by a well-known and trusted certificate authority such as Thawte or Verisign. Apple doesn't want trust of its signing-certificate authority to be universal, so it offers, just to its developers, a root-authority certificate to validate the signing certificates. There is a link on the Certificates page; download it, open it so that Keychain Access can install it, and now Apple, too, is "well known and trusted."

Distribution certificates expire after 1 year.

Device IDs

If you're an Agent or Admin for your developer account (or the individual enrollee), registering a device is simple: Use Automatic Device Provisioning.

If you're not a privileged team member, you'll have to pass your device's UDID, a 40-digit hexadecimal number that uniquely identifies it, to a privileged member who can enroll it manually through the Provisioning Portal.

You can collect a UDID in two ways. First, connect the device to your Mac:

▶ In iTunes, select the device and the **Summary** tab in the main view. Among the information it displays is the device's serial number. *This is not what you want.* Click the serial number, and it changes to the UDID. You can't select the string, but **Edit→Copy** puts it on the clipboard. This works on Windows as well as on the Mac.

Or:

▶ In Xcode, open the Devices organizer and right-click the device in the Devices list. Select **Copy Device Identifier**. Or select and copy the **Identifier** string in the device summary.

As an Admin or Agent, when you get a UDID, go to the Provisioning Portal and select the **Devices** page. You have two options:

▶ You can do it en masse with the **Upload Devices** button, which you can read about under the **How To** tab.

▶ To do it one at a time, click the **Add Devices** button. The page will show spaces where you can enter a name and UDID for your device; if you want to submit more than one, there's a + button to add rows to the form. Click **Submit**.

Registering a device adds it automatically to development profiles; developers can download the revised profile with ADP. If you have an Ad Hoc (beta) profile, you must add the device to the profile manually, reissue the profile, and redistribute it.

Application IDs

The wildcard ID "*" suffices for profiles for generic applications. If an app needs any service that requires it to be uniquely identified:

▶ Game Center

▶ iCloud storage

▶ In-app purchasing

▶ Push notification

...it isn't generic. If you need any of those services, even for development, a wildcard ID won't do. You'll need to go to the Provisioning Portal to register the app ID and the special services it requires.

When you set up the template that created your app's project (Chapter 8, "Starting an iOS Application"), you gave a reverse-DNS identifier for your "company," to which Xcode appended the name of your app, thus creating a unique bundle identifier for the app.

Select **App IDs** in the Portal, and click **New App ID**. Enter a description of the app. (Make sure it's succinct and distinguishable from any of your other apps—it's surprising how hard it is to tell them apart just by the bundle identifiers.) Then type in the bundle identifier (the one that Xcode produced for you from your company prefix and app name).

The app ID isn't exactly the same as the bundle ID you entered. Apple prepends a unique hexadecimal "seed" number to the bundle ID, and the result is the app ID. If you have two apps that you want to share Keychain information, there's a pop-up to force Apple to use the same seed for their IDs.

There's no approval necessary, and you can register as many IDs as you like, as long as they aren't already taken by someone else. After your app is registered, you can click the **Configure** link next to its entry to turn on push notification and iCloud. In-app purchase and Game Center are enabled automatically as long as the ID doesn't contain a wildcard (*).

Remember: You can register *only* 100 devices in a given year. It isn't a rotating 100: If you sell your iPhone, and remove it from your list, Apple will withdraw it from the devices you're allowed to install on, but you won't get the slot back until the anniversary of your membership. At the anniversary date, your deletions take effect, and you'll be allowed to delete additional devices with immediate effect; the free-deletion period ends as soon as you add another device.

Development Profiles

A development provisioning profile authorizes a developer with an individually issued development signing certificate to use Xcode to install an app on a registered device for the purpose of testing and debugging. The *Team Provisioning Profile* is issued against the wildcard application ID. If your application is not generic, you have to present a full, registered ID to Apple's servers. That requires an Admin, Agent, or Individual to use the Provisioning Portal to issue a custom development profile.

In the Portal, select **Provisioning** and the **Development** tab. You see an (empty) table of provisioning profiles. Click **New Profile**. The resulting form asks you a lot of questions that you know the answers to. You're given the raw materials, and all you have to do is pick the ones that go into the profile.

1. Enter the profile name. The thing to remember is that when you get the provisioning file, the name of the file will be derived from what you enter here. Make it pithy, but also make it distinctive. Be sure to include something like "dev" in the name because you're going to issue three profiles over the life of an app—development, ad-hoc, and for the App Store. If you just enter the name of your app, you will not know which is which.

2. Select the development signing certificates that can install under this profile. If you've been following along, you've already issued development certificates. If you're an Individual developer, there's only one choice.

3. Select an App ID from the pop-up. You already created one of these; it's not the wildcard ID because the Team Provisioning Profile would cover that already.

4. Check all the devices you want to install your development builds on.

Then click **Submit**. You'll be taken back to the profile list, with your profile marked "Pending." Wait a minute, and then start refreshing the page. Soon, the status becomes "Active," and you can click **Download**.

Because you chose a pithy, distinctive name for the profile, you found the file easily. It has the suffix .mobileprovision. Drag it onto the Xcode icon in the Dock. Xcode assimilates it into its list of profiles in the Devices organizer, where you can examine it by clicking its pithy and distinctive name in the Provisioning Profiles list. It can authorize installations on devices registered to the profile, and the build system uses it to automatically determine which of your signing certificates to use.

The provisioning profile is valid for 6 months, after which you must return to the Portal to renew it.

Distribution Profiles

Apple calls any installation that doesn't require Xcode "distribution." This represents a major break in the lifetime of an application, and only a Team Agent (or an Individual) can create profiles that authorize it, and only that person has the signing certificate that seals an application for distribution. There are three kinds of distribution:

▶ Ad Hoc distribution is used for beta testing. Ad Hoc distribution is restricted to devices drawn from the same list of devices as you registered for development. The only difference is that users can drop the `.mobileprovision` file and the `.ipa` application archive into iTunes and sync their devices to install it; there's no need to tether the device to Xcode.

Apple promises that developers who use Ad Hoc distribution for purposes other than testing will be terminated.

▶ Enterprise distribution is a hybrid between Ad Hoc and App Store distribution. As with Ad Hoc, you issue the `.ipa` and the `.mobileprovision` files to your users, but distribution is not limited to registered devices.

Your Enterprise development agreement forbids you to distribute applications to people outside your organization. The best assurance of this is to put the files behind a password wall on your company's server.

You can distribute Enterprise apps over-the-air by providing a URL that leads to a manifest file linking to the app and its profile. See "Distributing Enterprise Apps for iOS 4 Devices" (available through `developer.apple.com`—I presume the title will be updated soon) for details. When you **Product→Archive** your app, and elect to **Share**... the app as an `.ipa`, there will be a check box for Enterprise distribution, which will help you compose the manifest.

▶ App Store distribution uses an App Store distribution profile to seal the app and prepare it for submission to the App Store approval process, which I discuss in the "Preparing an App Store Release," section in this chapter.

> **NOTE**
>
> Ad Hoc distribution may pose a political problem if you develop for an organization. The 100-device registry is a finite resource of the organization and must be managed. You can't develop if you can't register new devices, but there will be pressure to authorize copies for the CEO, your boss's boss, your boss's boss's committees.... Before the question arises, make sure your organization establishes a policy that conserves the device registry for testing and development.

For each kind of distribution, go to the Provisioning Portal, and select the **Distribution** tab of the **Provisioning** section. Click **New Profile**. You have a choice between an App Store (or Enterprise) or an Ad Hoc certificate. Give the profile a pithy, distinctive name. There's only one certificate you can use. Set the App ID, which might be **Xcode: Wildcard AppID**;, although ADP should take care of that one for Agents and individuals.

If the distribution is to be Ad Hoc, you can check boxes to select which of the registered devices the profile is good for; App Store and Enterprise distributions will be unrestricted, so the check boxes will be disabled. Click **Submit**, and wait for the profile to be approved.

You can distribute the resulting .mobileprovision as you like, but it will be usable only with a distribution signature on the app.

Ad Hoc provisioning profiles are good for 6 months; the others are good for a year.

Using a Signing Identity

How do you use a signing certificate? It's a complicated process, but Xcode's iOS build-settings automation set it up so that you usually don't need to do anything.

Xcode knows about your provisioning profiles—Automatic Device Provisioning fetched everything you're entitled to, and you've dragged in any .mobileprovisions that fall through the cracks. Each profile matches an application ID to the signing certificates that are valid for that ID. So for any target, Xcode can find the profile that matches its ID and can identify which of your signing certificates go with it.

> **NOTE**
>
> Developer certificates are tagged in Xcode and Keychain Access as "iPhone Developer"—Xcode can inspect the certificate and determine that that's the purpose. When you get to distribution, the distribution certificate is labeled "iPhone Distribution."

See for yourself: In the Project navigator, select your project, and in the Project editor, select the target that builds your app. Choose the **Build Settings** tab, and display **All**, **Combined**. Type `sign` in the search field.

You'll see a number of settings, including a group labeled "Code Signing Identity." At the top level of the group, it says "Don't Code Sign," which looks bad. At the next level, there are two configurations, Debug and Release, and they say "Don't Code Sign," too. But under *those* are conditional settings, in this case for the condition "Any iOS SDK," which in this case means always.

If you open the pop-up for those settings, you'll see that the selection is **Automatic Profile Selector (Recommended)—iPhone Developer**. In gray, on the same line, you should see the common name and profile that match the target. Below that, you can see an explicit list of development and distribution certificates, so you can force the use of one, but almost always, Xcode selects the right one automatically.

So don't do anything.

> **NOTE**
>
> If you are on multiple teams—one for yourself, one each for your organization's App Store and Enterprise accounts, for instance—make sure that all your certificate requests have different common names. This might entail using the Provisioning Portal instead of ADP for your development certificates—ADP autogenerates the CSR in your Developer Programs name. Worst of all is if you end up with two distribution certificates issued with the same common name. Xcode keys on certificate type and common name in selecting signing identities, and you have only a sporting chance that it will pick the right one. If you are in this bind, remember that Xcode looks for signing identities in the default keychain. Create a new keychain for one of the certificates, and switch default keychains as you need.

Distribution Builds

You prepare an app for **distribution** by using the one build action that doesn't have a key equivalent or item in the Action button at the left end of the project window's toolbar: **Product→Archive**. The menu item is normally disabled. You must meet the following prerequisites:

- ▶ The destination (right) part of the Scheme control must name a connected device or **iOS Device**.

- ▶ The target must have a matching distribution profile.

- ▶ The build settings must name the distribution signing identity that matches the profile.

- ▶ The signing identity must be in your keychain.

When all these are done, issue the **Archive** command. If all goes well, the Archive organizer appears, showing all the applications you've archived and focused on the app you just built. See Figure 16.2.

16

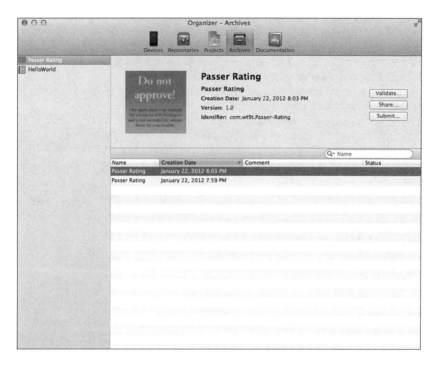

FIGURE 16.2   When an Archive build succeeds, the result is added under your app's name to the **Archives** panel of the Organizer. From there, you can share the archived app, verify that it meets some of the criteria for App Store acceptance, or submit it directly to the App Store.

Select the latest archive of your app, and click the **Share…** button. A sheet appears, giving you your options. See Figure 16.3. If you mean to share the executable app (the .ipa, a ZIP archive of the .app bundle), select **iOS App Store Package (.ipa)**.

FIGURE 16.3   Selecting **Share**… from the Archives organizer displays a sheet allowing you to choose the shareable form of your iPhone application.

The **Identity:** pop-up lets you choose the signing identity to use to seal the `.ipa`—as with the build settings, Xcode automatically matches the identity to the app's distribution profile, and if you use a nonmatching identity, the archiving will fail, so leave the pop-up alone unless you know what you're doing.

Click **Next**. A save-file sheet allows you to place and name the `.ipa` file. There is a check box, **Save for Enterprise Distribution**, that can help you prepare a manifest for over-the-air installations. Click **Save**, and you're done.

Sharing Identities and Profiles

You may have more than one development machine. That isn't a problem: You can use ADP to download and install all the certificates and provisioning profiles that your program and team memberships entitle you to.

What if you need to share with others? If you need to share provisioning profiles, select the **Provisioning Profiles** panel in the Devices organizer, select the profiles you want to export, and click the **Export** button. Use the save-file sheet that appears to name and place the archive file. There's no need to add a password because provisioning profiles aren't secret; you'd need the matching signing certificates to create apps that use them.

You can take two approaches if you want to share or archive signing identities:

▶ Open Keychain Access and find the certificate pair you're interested in. Select **Keychain Access→Export Items**… (⇧⌘E), and save the pair as a password-protected `.p12` file. Double-clicking the `.p12` opens Keychain Access, and on presentation of the password, installs the certificate.

▶ In the Devices organizer, select **Developer Profile**, and click the **Export** button. You get a save-file sheet with added fields to enter and confirm a password. Click **Save**, and you get a `.developerprofile` archive containing all your profiles and signing identities. Use the **Import** button to load them into another user's development environment.

Preparing an App Store Release

It all comes down to getting your work out into the world. Repeat the provisioning dance, prepare your app for the App Store, and submit it.

Final Provisioning

You already have the tools to build an App Store release: The only differences are that when you get to the **Distribution** tab of the **Provisioning** panel in the Portal site, you select **App Store** instead of **Ad Hoc**, and you don't need to select any devices. Click **Submit**, wait for Apple to approve the profile, download it, and install in Xcode.

iTunes Connect

App Store distribution entails legal obligations and money. You must sign up with iTunes Connect to sign the necessary contracts and provide bank-account and tax information. Sign in to iTunes Connect at `http://itunesconnect.apple.com/`. If this is your first time, you'll have to complete some registration chores. The main page gives you access to reports, contracts, finances, and app management.

People

iTunes Connect keeps contacts for your organization so that information and authority are given only to the specific people who need them. Contacts are assigned one or more roles from the categories Admin, Legal, Finance, and Technical. At this writing, an iTunes Connect contact can take 10 actions—things such as managing your apps' presence and pricing in the App Store, reviewing sales figures, signing contracts, and providing tax and banking information. Different roles permit different subsets of those actions.

> **NOTE**
>
> You can distribute free apps without having to sign a paper contract or share financial information with Apple.

Entering an App

When you have identity, contract, and financial matters squared away, click the **Manage Your Applications** link on the main iTunes Connect page. You will be rewarded with an empty table of apps; click **Add New App**. If this is your first time, you will be asked, *once and for all*, for a primary language and a company name. You can never change these, so spell the name out to yourself before you click **Continue**.

You now embark on a series of forms to identify and characterize your application. You are asked for:

- The name, version number, SKU number, and bundle ID for the app.

- A public description, store categories (such as Sports), and keywords (such as quarterback, passer, statistics, rating, football).

- When you intend to make it available.

- Price.

- A contact email for this app and URLs for the product and support.

- Copyright notice.

- Whether, and to what extent, your app contains material of concern to parental controls, such as violence, drugs, or sexual content.

- Whether you use encryption other than that supplied by Apple. (You may need to secure government licenses if you do.)

- Any end-user license agreement you want to attach.

- A 512x512 icon.

- At least one screenshot. The web application checks images immediately for format and size.

- Notes to assist Apple's reviewers, such as test accounts for servers the app may contact.

When everything is in, you're brought back to the Manage Your Applications page. Your app is marked as being in the "Prepare for Upload" stage. You have a limited time (120 days) to upload it; if you don't meet the deadline, Apple will ban you from using the application name you chose. When you think your app is in releasable shape, come back to this page, and click its entry. Click the **Ready to Upload Binary** button. This takes the status of your app to "Waiting for Upload."

Validating and Submitting

If you're "Waiting for Upload," you are ready to validate and submit your app.

Select **Product→Archive** to put a finished version into the Archives organizer. Select that version and click **Validate**.... Xcode asks for your login credentials for iTunes Connect; enter them and click **Next**. It presents pop-up menus for you to verify that the application is to be submitted against a specific version registered with iTunes Connect and to select the signing identity to be used. Click **Submit**....

An activity spinner appears while Xcode checks your app against the initial, automated criteria that Apple uses in the App Store acceptance process: Are the icons present and the correct size? Is the app signed properly? Is there an App Store distribution profile? Was it built with approved tools, and does it avoid unpublished API? And so on.

When the evaluation is done, either you'll be told you're ready, or you'll be given a list of reasons why you're not. Keep fixing and revalidating until you're clear.

At last, you're ready to turn your work over to the App Store. Select your final archive in the Archives organizer, and click **Submit**…. Repeat the authentication and signing process, but this time Xcode uploads your application. You are now in the hands of the approval process.

The App Store approval process is beyond the scope of a book about Xcode. The criteria are simple, if not always fair: Apple curates the App Store and won't associate itself with anything it suspects would damage its reputation, the reliability and performance of its products, its relations with its partners, or its standing with the law. The iOS Dev Center links to a summary of its criteria, but Apple emphasizes that it's not exhaustive, and it has discretion to stop developers' gaming the letter of the standards.

There are horror stories about unexplained rejections. There are tales of long waiting times—expect 2 weeks, but it varies widely. Apple says that more than 90% of apps are approved. Good luck!

Summary

In this chapter, I gave an overview of the three identities that go into iOS provisioning: signing identity, application identity, and device identity. You saw how to marry those identities into a provisioning profile for development and in-house distribution—and how Xcode's automatic management of devices and team provisioning profiles makes it easier to test apps under development.

You saw how the provisioning story ties into the various developer-program and iTunes Connect memberships. And you had a glimpse of the process of bringing your app to the brink of distribution through the App Store.

PART III

Xcode for Mac OS X

IN THIS PART

CHAPTER 17

Starting a Mac OS X Application

Now you can advance to Xcode skills that apply to Mac OS X development. If you're a Mac developer, I hope you haven't skipped Part II, "The Life Cycle of an iOS Application." Most of what I showed you in the iOS part of this book applies to Mac projects as well and isn't repeated in these chapters.

By the same token, if your interest is in iOS, *don't stop reading.* You aren't done yet! Bundles and property lists aren't the priority for you that they are in Mac OS X, but you must know about them and their place in Cocoa development. In particular, have a look at the section on Info.plist in Chapter 21, "Bundles and Packages."

What you're going to do now is port the Passer Rating iPhone app to Mac OS X. Because you kept a good separation in the model-view-controller design, the model layer of the application could come through unchanged (although you're going to expand it a bit). The view and controller layers are new; the human-interface layers for the two platforms, UIKit on iOS and AppKit on the Mac, share some concepts but are fundamentally different.

The Goal

A desktop application is a different sort of thing from a mobile app. Desktop apps present their information in windows, and users expect data-handling windows to be *documents*, each of which stores its data in its own file. Mac Passer Rating *could* present only one window for only one data set, but as you'll see, it's not much more trouble to work with documents. That way, the user can organize passer statistics into leagues, which he can exchange with others.

The top level of the iOS Passer Rating app was a list of passers. Does that make sense if you have more than one document? If you have discrete leagues, it may be better if you take *teams* as the root of the dataset. This entails a slight rework of the data model, which I'll get to presently.

So a league (the document) has a list of teams. Each team has a list of passers who have (at least for a time) played for it. Each passer has a list of game performances. When you were working on the iPhone screen, you were restricted to showing only one level of the hierarchy at a time. On the desktop, you can make it all visible. Something like Figure 17.1 is what you'll be shooting for.

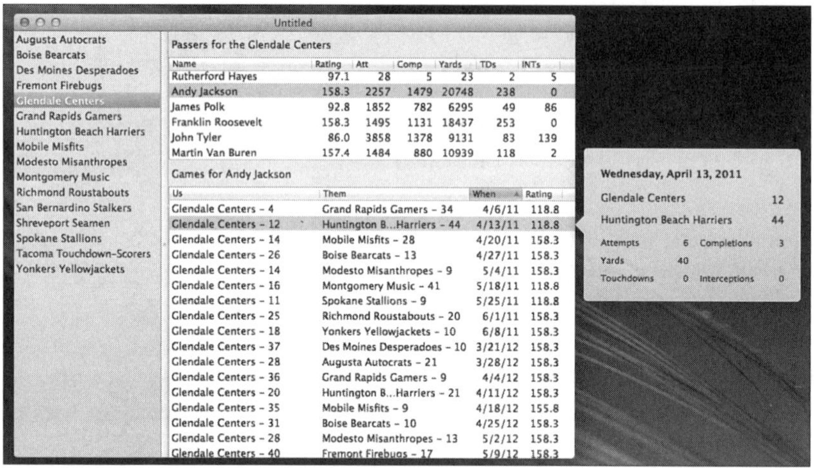

FIGURE 17.1   Mac Passer Rating as we want it to look, at least for the purpose of this example. A document represents a "league" composed of teams (left table). Selecting a team fills the upper table with the passers who have played on it. Selecting a passer lists his game performances in the lower table. Clicking a game brings up a popover window with the details.

Getting Started

Starting a Cocoa application project is scarcely different from what you saw in Chapter 2, "Kicking the Tires": Select **File→New→Project...** (⇧⌘N), which gives you an empty workspace window and a New Project assistant sheet. Select **Mac OS X→Application** from the master list at the left and the Cocoa Application icon from the array at the right. Click **Next**.

Now you come to the panel of project options, and there are quite a few of them.

▶ **Product Name** will be **Mac Passer Rating**. It's a dumb name for an application— the user knows she's using a Mac and probably doesn't care that there are other versions—but it helps you keep track of things if the project has a distinctive name. You can rename the product later by seeking out "Product Name" in the **Build Settings** tab of the Target editor.

- **Company Identifier** forms the prefix for the application ID. For my purposes, this is `com.wt9t`. Enter your own.

- The **Bundle Identifier** concatenates the company identifier and the product name. This is how the application will be identified to the system and (if you intend to sell through the Mac App Store) to Apple. The field isn't editable; it's just for your information.

- **Class Prefix**. Depending on whether you check **Create Document-Based Application**, Xcode creates either an `NSDocument` subclass (for your document), or an application-delegate class (to control the application as a whole). The template generates the name for that class by prepending what you type in this field to `Document`, or `AppDelegate`, as the case may be. Enter **League**.

- You're given an opportunity to choose an **App Store Category** from a pop-up list. Apple allows more than one category, so if you want more, or you change your mind, you can edit `Mac Passer Rating-Info.plist` later. **Sports** fits this app.

- Check **Create Document-Based Application** because the app produces documents. The document options in this panel have big effects on the boilerplate code Xcode's template produces for you.

- Mac OS X relies on filename extensions to regulate which files go with what applications. Mac Passer Rating won't be sharing any common document types, so fill **Document Extension** with something distinctive such as `prleague`—you shouldn't include a dot. Don't feel you have to restrict yourself to three or four characters: The people who use Mac Passer Rating won't ever have to type the extension.

- You used Core Data for iOS Passer Rating, and you'll use it here. Check **Use Core Data**.

- Check **Use Automatic Reference Counting**.

- For this example, skip **Include Unit Tests**.

- If you check **Include Spotlight Importer**, the template will add a target that produces a plug-in for the Spotlight systemwide search utility. You could imagine making league documents searchable by team and player names, but this is just an example. Leave it unchecked.

Now click **Next**, which drops a select-directory sheet for you to place the project directory (which will be named `Mac Passer Rating`, like it or not). Make your choice, check **Create local git repository for this project**, and click **Create**. The Workspace window now fills with the skeleton of the application.

- `LeagueDocument.h` and `LeagueDocument.m` define the class that loads and stores the league data, and presents it for display and editing. `LeagueDocument` is the controller class in the Model-View-Controller pattern. AppKit, the Cocoa framework for Mac applications, encompasses a sophisticated scheme for managing documents centered on the NSDocument class. NSDocument responds to requests to read, save, present, and edit its data; your document subclass merely customizes the standard behavior.

Because you asked for a document that uses Core Data, LeagueDocument is a subclass of NSPersistentDocument, which does even more for you. It takes care of loading and saving data and handles undo and redo events.

> **NOTE**
>
> It would be better to leave LeagueDocument to the tasks of reading and writing the document data (as a *model controller*) and provide an NSWindowController subclass for running the details of the document window (as a *view controller*), but I'll do everything in the document class for simplicity.

▶ LeagueDocument.xcdatamodeld is an empty data model (actually, a directory containing .xcdatamodel files representing versions of a data model) for LeagueDocument. Throw it away by selecting it in the Project navigator and pressing Delete; when Xcode asks what you want to do with it, click **Move to Trash**. You'll replace it with a copy of the model from the iOS Passer Rating app. The name of the model file doesn't matter; by default NSPersistentDocument loads all the compiled .mom files and merges them into a single model.

▶ Mac Passer Rating-Info.plist is a precursor to the Info.plist file that describes the properties and behavior of the application to the Finder and Launch Services. The **Summary** and **Info** tabs of the Target editor provide a (relatively) simple way to customize this file. Again, Chapters 21 and 23 will tell you more about Info.plist. InfoPlist.strings provides a dictionary that matches Info.plist entries to translated versions.

▶ Mac Passer Rating-Prefix.pch is a *prefix* file and the source for the project's precompiled header. Review the "Precompiled Headers" section of Chapter 5, "Compilation," for a review.

▶ MainMenu.xib and LeagueDocument.xib will be compiled into NIB files. They specify the human interface for the application and LeagueDocument, respectively.

▶ Unless you build one of your own, AppKit composes an About box from information in Info.plist. If a Credits.rtf file is part of the application bundle, its contents appear in a scrolling subview.

▶ main.m is the main entry point into the application. All it does is call the AppKit NSApplicationMain function. You never edit main.m.

As with the iOS template, Mac Passer Rating is runnable as-is. Select **Product→Run** (⌘R). In a moment, you'll be running the application, which won't look like much—just a menu bar with **Mac Passer Rating** in it. Select **File→New** (⌘N), and see a document window that you can close, resize, and even save a file that will reopen if you double-click it in the Finder. See Figure 17.2.

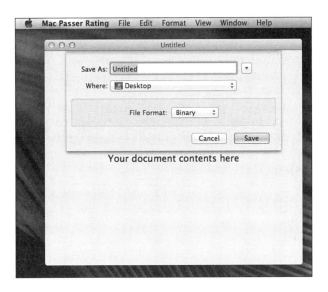

FIGURE 17.2   The document-application template is runnable as-is. You can create a new document and save it to a file that you can reopen in the Finder.

When the novelty has worn off, you can turn this application into something about football.

Model

As I said, adding a third level to the hierarchy—the team—requires a rework of the model. The data model and supporting classes from the iOS Passer Rating app are a good place to start from.

Porting from iOS

Select **File→Add Files to "Mac Passer Rating"**… (⌥⌘A) to drop a get-file sheet. (The command is available only if the Project navigator is visible.) Navigate to the directory containing the source for the iOS Passer Rating app, and select these files (hold down the Command key to select more than one file):

▶ SimpleCSVFile.h and SimpleCSVFile.m

▶ rating.h and rating.c

▶ Game.h and Game.m

▶ Passer.h and Passer.m

▶ Passer Rating.xcdatamodeld

NOTE

If you didn't follow along in the iOS part of this book, you can recover these files from the sample code. If you arranged your iOS source directory so that some files are in different subdirectories, you must make a different add-files pass for each directory.

Check **Copy items into destination group's folder (if needed)**, make sure **Mac Passer Rating** is checked in the **Add to Targets** table, and click **Add**. The files appear in the Project navigator; select them all, issue **File→New→Group from Selection**, and rename the resulting group something like `Model`.

The next step is to factor (database-savvy developers would say *normalize*) `ownTeam` out of `Game` and into a new entity, `Team`. Click `Passer Rating.xcdatamodeld`, and (using the skills you picked up in Chapter 9, "An iOS Application: Model") create the `Team` entity, with one attribute, `teamName`. `teamName` should be a string, indexed, not optional, and with an obviously bogus default name such as **UNASSIGNED_NAME**. Add a relationship, `games`, tracing to many of the `Game` entity; deletion should cascade.

`Game` can lose the `ourTeam` attribute, and gain `team`, a to-one relationship to `Team`, nullifying on delete. Be sure to set this relationship up as the inverse of `Team`'s `games`. When you're done, the diagram view of the data model should look like Figure 17.3.

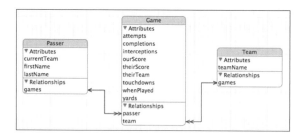

FIGURE 17.3   For the Mac, the Passer Rating model adds a `Team` entity. Each `Team` relates to many Games. Game's `ownTeam` string attribute goes away, as its purpose is served by `team.teamName`.

As with `Passer` and `Game`, you'll want to add a convenience method that generates a `Team`; that requires an Objective-C class to wrap the `Team` entity.

The first step, as it was for the others, is to make sure the data model is visible, and select **File→New→File...** (⌘N). Navigate to **Mac OS X→Core Data→NSManagedObject subclass**. Click **Next**. Back in Chapter 9, Xcode asked what entities should be backed with new classes. Not this time: There's only one entity—Team—that doesn't have a class associated with it. Xcode goes straight to the get-file sheet for you to place the implementation and header files.

The sheet offers to declare scalar values as scalar `@property`s, a feature available in Mac OS X 10.7 and iOS 5. It's a good idea, but preserve uniformity with the existing classes by leaving the box unchecked. Finally, the sheet offers a pop-up to select the project group to receive the new files and a check box list of targets to add the class to.

If you don't have a data model in the editor, Xcode will insert a panel in the New File assistant asking which model you want to use as the basis for the new NSManagedObject subclass. It then gives you a choice among that model's entities, including those you've already made classes for. Tread carefully because the version of Xcode you are using might lose track of files and crash when it gets into unusual situations with Core Data.

Create a factory method and a couple of derived properties:

```
+ (Team *) teamWithName: (NSString *) aName
              inContext: (NSManagedObjectContext *) moc
                 create: (BOOL) doCreate
{
    NSFetchRequest *   fetch = [[NSFetchRequest alloc] init];
    fetch.entity = [NSEntityDescription entityForName: @"Team"
                            inManagedObjectContext: moc];
    fetch.predicate = [NSPredicate predicateWithFormat:
                            @"teamName = %@", aName];
    NSError *          error;
    NSArray *          result;
    result = [moc executeFetchRequest: fetch error: &error];
    if (! result) {
        NSLog(@"%s: Bad query for Team %@, %@",
            __PRETTY_FUNCTION__, error, [error userInfo]);
        return nil;
    }

    if (result.count > 0)
        return  [result lastObject];

    if (! doCreate)
        return nil;
    Team *              retval =
        [NSEntityDescription insertNewObjectForEntityForName: @"Team"
                                inManagedObjectContext: moc];
    assert(retval);
    retval.teamName = aName;
    return retval;
}

- (NSUInteger) ownTotalScore
{
    NSNumber *    total =
              [self.games valueForKeyPath: @"@sum.ourScore"];
```

```
    return total.unsignedIntegerValue;
}


- (NSUInteger) oppTotalScore
{
    NSNumber *    total =
            [self.games valueForKeyPath: @"@sum.theirScore"];
    return total.unsignedIntegerValue;
}
```

and declare them in the header file. That's it.

You need to pull the model changes through to the classes that implement Passer and Game. Remove the ourTeam property from Game.h and Game.m. Where you create a new Game, in csvFile:readValues:error:, use teamWithName:inContext:create: to link up to a Team rather than recording the ourTeam string directly:

```
NSString *       teamName = [values objectForKey: @"ourTeam"];
retval.team =  [Team teamWithName: teamName
                       inContext: file.moc
                          create: YES];
```

Elsewhere, wherever a team name was referenced through ourTeam in Game, refer to team.teamName. For instance, in Passer.m

```
- (NSArray *) teams
{
    return   [[self.games valueForKeyPath:
            @"@distinctUnionOfObjects.ourTeam"] allObjects];
}
```

becomes

```
- (NSArray *) teams
{
    return [[self.games valueForKeyPath:
            @"@distinctUnionOfObjects.team.teamName"] allObjects];
}
```

Remember to revert existingPassersWithLastName:firstName:inContext: to the version that looked up Passers in a particular NSManagedObjectContext, instead of keeping one in-memory table for the whole app.

Automatic Reference Counting

With everything cleaned up, it's time to make sure it compiles. Select **Product→Build** (⌘**B**).

All does not go well. Some of it comes from straightforward blunders, and those are easy enough to fix. But there's an additional class of errors. In `SimpleCSVFile.m`, llvm objects to lines such as

```
NSAutoreleasePool *     pool = [[NSAutoreleasePool alloc] init];
...
[pool drain];
```

and

```
- (void) dealloc
{
    [path release];
    [headers release];
    [super dealloc];
}
```

What's happening here? I had you turn on Automatic Reference Counting (ARC) when you created the project. Under ARC, reference-counting methods are illegal. The iOS 4.3-friendly memory management in these files won't do for Mac Passer Rating.

You could plod through all the ARC-related errors and patch them, but that's not a complete process: llvm tells you what was there that shouldn't be, but it can't tell you what should be there but isn't.

There's a better way. Xcode can examine your code and convert it to ARC for you. Unfortunately, the first thing Xcode does is to check whether ARC is enabled in the current target, and if it is, it happily tells you there's nothing to be done. Not helpful.

So again, go to the **Build Settings** tab of the Target editor, type **reference** in the search field, and set "Objective-C Automatic Reference Counting" to **No**.

Now select **Edit→Refactor→Convert to Objective-C ARC...** and Xcode first does a check compile; if it finds non-ARC issues in your code, it will tell you that it can't proceed until you fix them. So fix them.

Start the refactor again. If everything is clean, Xcode will drop an assistant sheet, the first panel of which summarizes what it's about to do. Be aware that you must ask Xcode to change your code in-place; it offers to capture a snapshot as a first step.

Next comes the ubiquitous comparison sheet. Among other things

▶ Properties with the `retain` attribute become `strong`.

▶ Object properties that were `assign` become `unsafe_unretained`. If you won't be running on iOS 4.3 or Mac OS X 10.6, you can convert them to the safer `weak`.

▶ The `NSAutoreleasePool` that was allocated and drained in the `run:` method of `SimpleCSVFile` is replaced by an `@autoreleasepool` block.

17

▶ Messages such as retain, release, and autorelease disappear.

▶ Entire dealloc methods disappear.

Examine the changes, and if they make sense, click **Accept Changes**. You're done.

Making the Application Twitch

Now get this thing doing *something* before you go much further. Can LeagueDocument load up some sample data (yes, the same .csv sample you labored with on iOS) and display at least some team names?

Wiring Up a Menu

The first thing to do is to add a menu item to Mac Passer Rating's **Edit** menu to load up a document. Select MainMenu.xib in the Project navigator; Interface Builder (IB) appears with a menu bar at the top of the editor area. (If the bar isn't there, click the menu icon in IB's sidebar.)

If you click a title in the menu bar, the corresponding menu appears. Add an item to the **Edit** menu that can trigger the load. Click **Edit**; you can find a lot of items having to do with searching and speech that don't fit Mac Passer Rating. Click each, and press Delete.

While you're at it, delete the **Format** and **View** menus, too; but take care to close the menus before pressing Delete: In the peculiar hierarchy of AppKit menus, the menu bar is a menu; it contains menu *items*, whose contents may themselves be menus. If you try to delete an open **Format** menu (for instance), Xcode deletes the *menu*, but not the menu *item* that contained it. You can tell because a gap remains in the menu bar where the menu was. Select that and delete it; or close the menu so the Delete key kills both the item and the menu it contains.

You add a menu item by dragging it from the Object library (in the lower part of the Utility area, third tab) into the menu. Type **menu** into the library's search field. Find "Menu Item," and drag it to the bottom of the open **Edit** menu. See Figure 17.4.

FIGURE 17.4   Dragging a new menu item into a menu.

Double-click in the **Item** label, and replace the name with **Fill with Test Data**; and in the blank area at the right end of the menu item, double-click, hold down the **Command** key, and press **t** to make the key equivalent ⌘T.

When I did this, I held down the Shift key to get what I thought would be an uppercase T. This resulted in a key equivalent of ⇧⌘T—not what I wanted. I reselected the field and pressed Delete; this made the key equivalent Delete. This is a good time to make friends with the Attributes inspector, the fourth tab in the upper part of the Utility area. When you have a menu item selected, the top two fields are **Title** and **Key Equivalent**, and the latter has an **x** button to clear it.

Now you want the menu item to do something. As in the iOS app, user-interface elements direct a message (an *action*) at an object (the *target*) when they are triggered. You haven't written the action method yet, but you can make up a name for it: `fillWithData:`.

What about the target? You'll search `MainMenu.xib` in vain for a reference to `LeagueDocument`—that's a class that's associated with individual documents, not the application as a whole. To what Cocoa object will you assign the task of responding to `fillWithData:`? *I don't know*, says a stubborn part of our subconscious, *anything that wants to respond to it, I guess.*

This turns out not to be a stupid answer in Cocoa. AppKit keeps a continually updated *responder chain*, a series of potential responders to user actions. The chain begins at the "first responder," which may be the selected view in the front window, and then proceeds to the front window, the window's document, and finally to the application itself. You have probably noticed that the second icon, a red cube, in the Interface Builder sidebar represents the First Responder. A user interface control can designate the First Responder, whatever it may be at the time, as the target of its action, and AppKit shops the action up the responder chain until it finds an object that can handle it.

The responder chain is a little more complicated than that. For more information, consult Apple's documentation for `NSApplication`, `NSResponder`, and the related Programming Topics articles.

Like the other icons above the dividing line in the Interface Builder sidebar, First Responder does not literally exist in the XIB. It is a *proxy*, a way for objects within the XIB to make reference to outside objects. These are File's Owner, which is the object that caused the NIB compiled from the XIB to load; First Responder, the current starting point for the responder chain; and Application, the `NSApplication` object that embodies the application as a whole. When the sidebar is expanded to the outline view, IB helpfully labels these as Placeholders.

If you try control-dragging an action link from the new menu item to the First Responder icon, you're balked. Interface Builder presents a HUD for the link, asking you to choose the method selector for the desired action. The list it presents does not include `fillWithData:` because you just made that up. Before you can make the link, you have to tell Interface Builder that `fillWithData:` is a possible action.

Interface Builder allows you to do this by editing the properties of the First Responder object in the Attributes inspector (fourth tab). Select the First Responder icon. The inspector shows an empty table for user-defined actions that a responder might answer to. Click the + button, and type **`fillWithData:`** in the Action column. The Type column presents a pop-up menu of possible control types that might send that action; you can leave it blank unless you want IB to offer the action only to senders of that type. It's fine to leave it blank (for `id`). IB now knows that in this NIB, `fillWithData:` is one of the actions a first responder might perform.

> **NOTE**
>
> In AppKit, action methods must take one argument: `fillWithData:`, with a colon, not `fillWithData`, without—the names are distinct. If you leave the colon off, IB will supply it.

Now you can control-drag from the new menu item to First Responder, and the HUD contains `fillWithData:`. The display will even be scrolled to it, as a rough match for the item's label. Make the connection.

> **NOTE**
>
> The Connection inspector (sixth tab in the inspector portion of the Utility area) affords another way to make the connection—and to break it. Select First Responder and the Connection inspector. The Received Actions section fills with the same long list of actions you saw in the connection HUD when you control-dragged to the FR icon, but it's larger and easier to scroll. Next to each selector is a bubble; dragging from it to the menu item would make the connection, and a label would appear showing where the connection went to. An **x** button next to the connection label lets you break the connection.

Loading Data into `LeagueDocument`

Importing the `.csv` file is simple—most of the work was done on the iOS side. Add `sample-data.csv` to the project, and declare

```
- (IBAction) fillWithData: (id) sender;
```

in `LeagueDocument.h` and put

```
#import "Game.h"

    .

    .

    .

- (IBAction) fillWithData: (id) sender
{
```

```
    NSString *   dataPath =
          [[NSBundle mainBundle] pathForResource: @"sample-data"
                                         ofType: @"csv"];
    [Game loadFromCSVFile: dataPath
            intoContext: self.managedObjectContext
                error: NULL];
}
```

into `LeagueDocument.m`.

> **NOTE**
>
> Action methods, which respond to triggers from user-interface elements, are by convention given the return type `IBAction`, rather than `void` (for which `IBAction` is a synonym). This signals to IB that the method should be listed among the actions the class handles. Xcode puts a connection bubble next to any declaration or definition of an `IBAction`, so you can link it to a control action in IB.

This is enough for you to see whether the menu command works. Set a breakpoint at the beginning of `fillWithData:`. Run Mac Passer Rating. With Lion's state-restoration feature in place (you can turn it off in the **Options** tab of the Scheme editor's **Run** panel), you'll probably see the document window from your first run; if not, make a new one with ⌘N. Save the document (anywhere, any name). Then select **Edit→Fill with Test Data** (⌘T).

A couple of things happen. First, the breakpoint you set at the beginning of `fillWithData:` triggers, so you know the menu item worked. Second, if you continue, the title bar adds the gray **Edited** flag to show that the command resulted in a change of the document's contents—even if you can't see it.

In the next chapter, you'll see it.

Summary

This chapter started you on some new Xcode skills, against the background of a Mac OS X version of the passer-rating project. To do this, you had to go through some conversions: You created a document-based Core Data application, and imported existing code. On the way, you discovered that Automated Reference counting requires changes from a non-ARC code base; I showed how to get Xcode to make those changes and how you can direct and refine the process.

You saw that document-based Mac applications are different from iOS applications in that they are based on at least two separate NIBs, one (`MainMenu.xib`) for the application as a whole and another to be instantiated for each document window. This posed a conundrum when an app-wide facility—a menu command—had to communicate with a document-specific facility—editing the content of one document among potentially many. You learned how the First Responder proxy in Interface Builder and the responder chain bridge the gap.

CHAPTER **18**

Wiring a Mac Application with Bindings

If you have another look at Figure 17.1, you'll see that even in the abbreviated form Mac Passer Rating can take, there can be more than 20 pieces of information, distributed across four displays, to be filled in, edited (in some cases), and coordinated across updates. This is going to involve some tedious, repetitive code and a lot of communications infrastructure through the network of objects, isn't it?

No. AppKit (the Mac-specific part of Cocoa) offers a facility called *bindings*, supplemented by `NSController` classes, which are a bit subtle when you first encounter them but after you master them can cut your coding burden by an order of magnitude.

> **NOTE**
>
> Experienced Mac programmers—and Apple—warn you: Bindings are an advanced topic. If this were a book about AppKit, you'd go through an initial round of doing it the "easy," although verbose, way. My purpose in this book is to show you how to take advantage of Interface Builder's (IB) support of bindings, which is a major feature.

Filling the Document Window

You lay out the document window and its contents with Interface Builder, an editor for XIB files. You'll start with adding a view to the window that came with the document XIB in the same way you saw when you built the views for the iOS Passer Rating app. But in this chapter, you'll go beyond that to add and configure objects that run the links between your data and the screen automatically.

A Table View

First, you should have something that can display some data—a simple table to display the names of teams and the total points they and their opponents have scored.

Select `LeagueDocument.xib` in the Project navigator; you'll need the editor area for the window and the Utility area for the Object library. Select the **Your document contents here** label in the middle of the document window, and press Delete to be rid of it. Type **table** in the Object library's search field, and drag a Table View into the document window you're editing. Make sure you put the table *inside* the window: You want to contain it, not make it a top-level object.

Drag the table to the upper-left corner of the window; it "snaps" to the corner when it's aligned. Next, drag its lower-right corner so it snaps to the lower-right corner of the window. This is more than you need, but it's just to get something working.

This table is going to list team names with their total scores for themselves and their opponents. This requires three columns, and the canned table from the library has only two. With the table still selected, turn to the Attributes inspector (fourth tab), and find… attributes for a scroll view.

Many of the views in the IB library are not simple objects. They represent a hierarchy of views; in this case, a scroll view, which contains two scrollers, a table header view, and a table view, which contains two columns, to each of which is attached a text-field cell. See Figure 18.1.

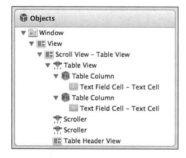

FIGURE 18.1   The "table view" you dragged into the document window is not as simple as it looked.

There are three ways to navigate this hierarchy. The first is to move your mouse pointer to the object you want to select, and press the mouse button repeatedly until your intended object is highlighted. Each click goes one level deeper. The second is to expand the sidebar to an outline view by clicking the round arrowhead button next to its lower end. You can then expand the hierarchy and select what you want. Third, you can navigate the whole XIB hierarchy with the jump bar. Pick your method and go one level down from the scroll view to select the table.

The Attributes inspector gives you three levels of settings, for each level in NSTableView's place in the class hierarchy: First as a table view, then as a control view, and finally just as a view. Make these changes to the Table View section:

▶ For **Columns**, set 3.

▶ For **Column Sizing**, set **Sequential**. That way, when resizing the table makes it wider, the first column grows wider until it reaches a maximum width you set, and then the second up to its maximum, and then the third.

Everything else can remain as it is.

So you've set three columns—where's the third? When you resized the table to fill the window, the second (and then-last) column resized to fill the available space. The third column was added to the right, out of sight. Click the second column—below the header—until it highlights, grab the graphical handle that appears on its right edge, and set it to the size you want. (Remember it has to accommodate only a four- or five-digit total score). That should bring the third column into sight, which you can resize the same way. You should also adjust the first column so that it can accommodate team names.

While you're selecting columns, you can see that the Attributes inspector offers a **Title** field. Name the columns `Team Name`, `Own`, and `Opp`, respectively. The **Size** inspector (tab 5) is also of interest: You can set the starting, minimum, and maximum widths there.

Let's get an idea of how this window works. It's not necessary to run Mac Passer Rating to do this—not much of a consideration now, when the app is so small that it builds and shows a window quickly; but in a big project, you'd like to test the window just on its own.

Select **Editor→Simulate Document**. You get the window you've been building, with the minimal behaviors the contents can show without being connected to an application. The header titles appear; you can drag at the edges of the column headers to resize them; if you add to the total width of the columns, you can scroll the table from side to side; you can drag columns to reorder them; and you can resize the window...

Autoresizing

Wait. This isn't right (Figure 18.2). The window resizes, but the table doesn't. It just sits in the upper-left corner of the window at the same size it had when you created it.

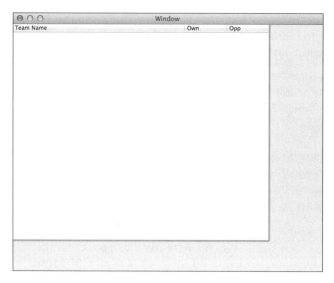

FIGURE 18.2   When you resize the document window in the Cocoa Simulator, the table doesn't resize with it.

Cocoa has two ways to manage sizing problems like this: Autoresizing, which has been available on the Mac and iOS from the beginning; and autolayout, which is new in Lion. Autolayout is powerful but can't be demonstrated with a single-view window; see the "Making the Text Fit—Autolayout" section of Chapter 20, "Localization and Autolayout," for much more.

> **NOTE**
>
> If you quit the Cocoa Simulator and then reopen it, Lion's state restoration gives you the same window with the same dimensions—and misalignments—you left it with. Close the window before quitting the simulator to have a fresh view of your work.

Autoresizing adjusts the size of a view in relation to its superview (the view that contains it). When the superview changes size, the view is moved and resized automatically. How this is done, on the horizontal axis, is determined by answering three questions:

1. Should the view change its width?

2. Does the left edge of the view stick to its position relative to the left edge of the superview?

3. Does the right edge of the view stick to its position relative to the right edge of the superview?

Three similar questions must be answered on the vertical axis.

You want the table to grow or shrink along with the window (so the answer to question 1 is "yes, both horizontally and vertically"); you want it to remain flush with each edge of the window. (So the answers to questions 2 and 3 are also "yes," for both ends of both axes.)

Select the scroll view enclosing the table view (not the table view itself), and bring up the Size (fifth) inspector. The upper part of the inspector contains what you might expect—fields to set the location and dimensions of the view inside its container.

The lower part is more graphical: It has an **Autoresizing** control with red lines and a square, with which you answer the three questions, and an **Example** view that does a trippy animation showing the effects. See Figure 18.3.

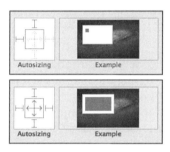

FIGURE 18.3   The **Autoresizing** control determines whether a view can be resized on the horizontal and vertical axes (the inner arrows) and whether each edge keeps a constant distance from its superview's edges (the outer struts). (top) By default, views don't resize and keep their distances relative to the top-left corner. (bottom) The scroll view containing the Team table should resize and stick to the window's edges, so the table can always fill the window.

The **Autoresizing** control consists of an inner box representing the view and an outer box representing the superview. The view's box (the inner one) contains two double-headed arrows (called *springs*, for historical reasons); these answer question 1 in each direction. Click an arrow, and it turns from dotted pink to solid red, indicating that the view should resize on that axis. Click both arrows to see that the **Example** view shows the view (represented by a red rectangle) resizes in both directions as its animated superview varies.

Surrounding the inner box in the **Autoresizing** control are four I-bar lines, extending from each edge to the edge of the superview box. (These are called *struts*.) By default only the top and left struts are solid red—you can see by the **Example** animation that the view stays a constant distance from the superview's top-left corner, while the other distances vary. Click the other two struts to require that all four edges should stick to the superview, and see that the view in the **Example** animation resizes in unison with its container.

Now run the XIB in the Cocoa Simulator: The table (strictly speaking, its scroll view) resizes along with the window, and (if you set minimum and maximum sizes for the columns) the column widths adjust to fit.

18

NOTE

UIKit, on iOS, uses the same autoresizing mechanism as Mac OS X's AppKit. It's the usual way to ensure that views and table cells are laid out properly when the user rotates the device.

Your First Object Controller

You're still in LeagueDocument.xib. Type **array** in the Object library's search field, which should narrow the list down to "Array Controller," an instance of NSArrayController, which is a kind of NSController that provides automated access to groups of objects. Drag the icon into the editor view. The controller won't show up in the view, but it appears as a top-level item in the sidebar.

Make sure the array controller is selected, and use the Attributes inspector to set **Mode** to **Entity Name**, and the **Entity Name** field to **Team**. Check **Prepares Content**, which tells the array controller that it is responsible for loading instances of the entity. (If you weren't using Core Data, it would authorize the array controller to start off with a new array containing one newly created object.)

In the **Editor** control in the toolbar, select the Assistant (middle) view. (The window is probably getting crowded; try hiding the navigator area and switching the Workspace window to full-screen.) The assistant half of the editor should be showing you LeagueDocument.h; if it isn't, click the first segment of the assistant editor's jump bar, and select **Automatic**. The project template set LeagueDocument as the class of File's Owner for this XIB, so LeagueDocument.h is the natural counterpart to the XIB file.

Create an outlet in LeagueDocument for the array controller just as you learned in the "Outlets" section of Chapter 11, "Building a New View:" Hold down the control key and drag from the array controller icon into the header file, just above the @end directive. When an insertion bar appears where you want it, release the drag, and fill out the resulting popover with the name of the outlet, **teamArrayController**. Click **Create**. See Figure 18.4.

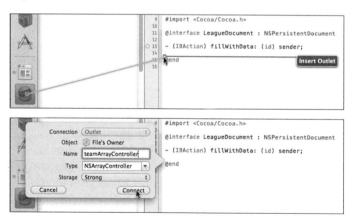

FIGURE 18.4   (top) Control-dragging from the array-controller icon into the header file in the assistant view shows an insertion bar in the class's interface. (bottom) Releasing the drag produces a popover window to create an outlet @property holding a reference to the controller.

This will not be the only NSArrayController in this XIB; eventually you'll have tables for passers and games, each with its own array controller, and if you don't do something, they will all be listed in the sidebar as "Array controller." With the array controller selected, turn to the Identity (third) inspector, and type **Team Array Controller** in the **Label** field in the Identity section. Be sure to press Return or Tab to commit the change. The outline shows the new label.

Now we start getting into bindings. Bindings rely on Cocoa's *Key-Value Observing (KVO)* protocol. Any object can ask to be notified when any specified property of another object changes. There are many details, conditions, and caveats to that—look up KVO in the Documentation organizer for the authoritative information—but the short of it is that @propertys of objects, and attributes of Core Data objects, can be observed for changes.

NSController and its specializations, like NSArrayController, use KVO to link the values of the objects they manage to user-interface elements. The links go both ways—a model object's values get propagated to the screen as they change, and editing a value on the screen updates the model automatically. These links are called *bindings*. (Again, this is a gross oversimplification, but it's enough to get you through IB's support for bindings.)

You've set up what is now Team Array Controller so that it observes objects of the Team entity. Where are those objects to be found? In the managed-object context (NSManagedObjectContext) of the current document. The array controller must be told what the context is, and this will be your first binding.

With Team Array Controller selected, go to the Bindings (seventh) inspector. You see a list of properties of the array controller that it can take from bindings. You're interested in the last one, Managed Object Context. Click the disclosure triangle to open it. What you see (Figure 18.5) is a relatively simple binding editor; all other binding editors build on these elements.

FIGURE 18.5   The Managed Object Context binding for Team Array Controller shows the common elements of all binding subeditors.

▶ The **Bind to:** check box determines whether a binding is active. Check it.

▶ The pop-up next to it gives you a choice of sources for bindings. This includes **File's Owner**, the **Shared User Defaults Controller** (so you can control preferences directly), and any NSController objects in the XIB. Team Array Controller should pull its managed-object context from the LeagueDocument, so pick **File's Owner**.

▶ If you had chosen an object controller, **Controller Key** would be where you'd specify which part of the selected controller would provide data to the binding. In this case, ignore it.

- **Model Key Path** is the interesting one. You want to draw on LeagueDocument's managedObjectContext property. Type that in—Xcode should offer to complete the name before you finish.

- **Value Transformer** is used for user-interface bindings. A value transformer is like an adapter between one form of data (for example, whether a property is nil) to another (whether a button should be enabled). It saves having to create additional properties in model objects just to accommodate particular views. You want managedObjectContext to come through unchanged, so leave this blank.

- Check **Raises For Not Applicable Keys**. If it is checked, and the property (model key path) you bind to can't be accessed through key-value coding, AppKit will raise an exception at runtime. It's imaginable that you wouldn't want that condition flagged, but usually it's an error, and you want to halt when it happens.

Binding the Team Table

Team Array Controller is now set up and ready for use as a broker between Team objects and the user interface. Select the first (Team Name) column of the Team table. You see any number of attributes that could be bound for this column, but for the moment, the only thing you care about is how to fill in the names.

> **NOTE**
>
> Xcode treats these bindings as though they were to the columns themselves, but that isn't true. Few of these properties are properties of table columns. The real links are between individual Team objects in the array controller's array of Teams and each row in that column. Because the bindings are uniform, it's more convenient to treat them as being to the whole columns.

Disclose the Value binding, and bind it to Team Array Controller. By default, the **Controller Key** is set to **arrangedObjects**, which is what you want: It's the *controller* outlet that contains all the Teams, net of sorting and filtering. The **Model Key Path** should be **teamName**—that's the Team property the column is to display. If Team Array Controller is hooked up properly, Xcode knows the property keys for Team, and it offers teamName as a completion. The rest of the binding editor controls the details of how the column acts as a display and editor for teamName. The details are beyond the scope of this book.

Now do the same thing for the second (Own) column, binding its value to ownTotalScore; likewise the third column, to oppTotalScore.

Running Bindings

Make sure all the bindings are set up, the **Fill with Test Data** menu item points at fillWithData:, and sample-data.csv is part of the project and select **Product→Run** (⌘R). You should see something like Figure 18.6: A blank window fills with team names and scores at your command. The table sorts when you click a column header. Save the document; then double-click on a team name, and edit it. The gray **Edited** badge appears in the title bar, and if you click it and select **Browse All Versions...**, you're shown the current version alongside the one you saved.

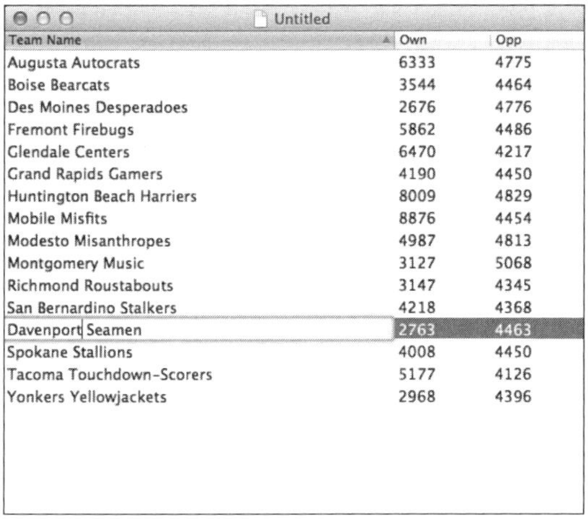

FIGURE 18.6   The first iteration of Mac Passer Rating reads the sample data and displays the `Teams`. Clicking column headers sorts the table, and you can edit team names.

Mac Passer Rating still has a way to go, even for this early milestone, as you'll find if you try to edit one of the scores. The console side of the Debug area fills with a lusty exception trace, the gist of which follows:

```
Mac Passer Rating[27928:707]   Error setting value for key path
    ownTotalScore of object <Team:   0x10018fe70>   (entity: Team;
    .
    .
    .
    teamName = "Spokane Stallions";
}) (from bound object <NSTableColumn: 0x1001774b0>
    [<Team 0x10018fe70> setValue:forUndefinedKey:]:
    the entity Team is not key value coding-compliant for
    the key "ownTotalScore".
```

meaning that `ownTotalScore` is backed only by a getter (it's a computed property, after all) and not a setter (which is what would have been needed to save the edited value).

It's likely you'll be left hanging with the score cell still open for editing—handling the exception jumped the portion of the code that would have closed the cell. The application isn't hung; you can, for instance, **Edit→Undo** your typing. But the document is unusable.

The immediate thing to do is go to LeagueDocument.xib, select the score columns, and uncheck **Editable** in the Attributes inspector. But the larger question is: How can you get a better handle on this kind of error? There are two things you can do.

The first is specific to bindings. **Product→Edit Scheme** (⌘<) gets you the Scheme editor sheet. Select the **Run** panel and the **Arguments** tab. Click + under the Arguments table, and enter

```
-NSBindingDebugLogLevel 1
```

which logs to your debugger console whenever AppKit detects something amiss in your use of bindings. This may produce many long logs. You can use the **Clear** button in the Debug area to remove old output so that you can concentrate on what comes later. The console content won't be lost; you can find the whole log in the Log (seventh) navigator.

NOTE

An easy way to get a "not key value coding-compliant" exception is to rename a property out from under a binding. If you do the renaming without using refactoring, your XIB still contains a binding that refers to the old name. When you load the NIB, the controller looks for the value in the model object; it isn't there, and you get the exception. Refactoring automatically edits your XIBs to match the new name. If you must rename by hand, be sure to audit your bindings. The same problem can occur with IBOutlets.

The second is generally applicable. Select the Breakpoint navigator (sixth tab), and click the + button at the bottom. Select **Add Exception Breakpoint...** from the pop-up menu, and click **Done** in the settings popover that appears. This drops you into the debugger, and stops, whenever an Objective-C or C++ exception is thrown. With this, Xcode will interrupt execution at the point at which it happened.

NOTE

The other option from the **+** button is **Add Symbolic Breakpoint....**. This allows you to name a method or function at which to break, rather than having to supply a line number in source code. If you want to catch all calls to the standard printf function, just create a symbolic breakpoint, and enter **printf** as the symbol. The facility is intelligent: Give it the name of an Objective-C method or a C++ template function, and it can intercept any function with the given name.

If you retry this bug, Xcode will jump to the foreground. The stack trace doesn't go through any of your code—bindings are handled completely within AppKit—but the stack trace will be full of references to the binding system. (Move the detail slider at the bottom of the Debug navigator to the right to show more frames from the call stack.)

Use this moment to glean the context of the bug; then click the **Continue** button in the debugger bar until the exception dump appears in the debugger console. Unfortunately, the dump can't be had at the point at which the exception was thrown, which is where you need it.

Laying Out Views

This is progress, but it's only about a quarter of the way to the app you saw in Figure 17.1. Mac Passer Rating has a cascade of tables, from Team to Passer to Game.

The Team table has shown you're on the right track, and now you can repurpose it into a "source list" at the left side of the window. Select the table in LeagueDocument.xib and expose the Attributes inspector. Drop the column count to **1**, uncheck **Headers**, and set the **Highlight** style to **Source List** (a blue-gradient background). Click the color well at the left end of the **Background** control, and in the Color picker use the gray-scale slider (second tab, pick **Gray Scale Slider** from the pop-up) to set the table's color to about 80% white.

Sizing requires a little work. Select the enclosing scroll view and resize it to a width of about 180 points. Unset the flexible-width spring, and clear the right-edge strut; this parks the view on the left side of the window, resizing vertically with the window, but always keeping its width.

Now drag in two labels (type **label** in the Object library's search field) and two tables into the window to the right of the Team list, as shown in Figure 18.7. (You can use **Editor→Canvas→Show Layout Rectangles** to highlight the bounds of each element. **Show Bounds Rectangles** would have done the same thing but would have shown the actual view boundaries instead of the visual extents, which is what the Aqua layout standards use.)

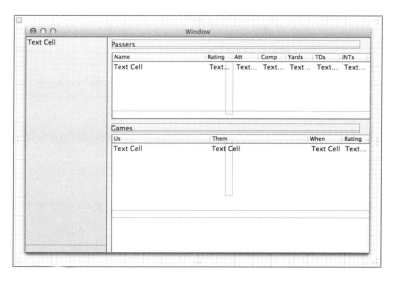

FIGURE 18.7 The next step in developing Mac Passer Rating is to resize the Team table (on the left) and add labels and tables for Passers and Games. Set **Editor→Canvas→Show Layout Rectangles** to have IB draw rectangles around the visible extent of the views.

18

Here are a few points to keep in mind:

▸ As you drag and resize the elements, Xcode pops blue alignment guides, showing where they align with each other and suggesting offsets and insets to suit the Aqua layout standards. By default, your drags snap to these guides; use **Editor→Canvas→ Snap to Guides** to control it.

If you use Lion autolayout, those guides become more than advisory; they are how you create constraints for AppKit to enforce at runtime. Read more in the section "Making the Text Fit—Autolayout," in Chapter 20.

▸ When your layout is mature, you can turn on **Editor→Canvas→Live Autoresizing** so your general layout is preserved if you have to resize a superview.

▸ You'll now have three scroll views (one for each table) in the main view, all bearing the same name in the outline sidebar. Select each, and use the Identity inspector to set the **Label** to something that will identify each.

▸ The Passer table (the upper one) has one column for the passer name and then six numeric columns. Use the outline sidebar: Fully expand the items under the Passer table, hold down the Command key, and select those six columns. Now you can use the Size inspector to set the initial, minimum, and maximum widths. (I used 50, 40, and 80.)

▸ For all columns, uncheck **Editable** in the Attributes inspector.

▸ Similarly, select the text-cell objects inside each numeric column, and in the Attributes inspector use the Alignment control to set them right-justified (fourth segment).

▸ The principle is the same for the four columns of the Game table, at the bottom.

▸ Set up autoresizing for the Passer table's enclosing scroll view: Fixed to left, top, and right, *but not bottom*; flexible in both directions. For the Game table's scroll view, it's fixed left, bottom, and right, *but not top*—flexible in both directions. When a view is flexible on an axis, but not fixed, the unfixed edge floats so that it maintains the same proportion from the corresponding edge of the superview.

▸ The Passer label should be flexible in width, and fixed left, top, and right. The Game label should be the same but floating both top and bottom.

The Passer and Game Array Controllers

You have two tables that display objects based on Core Data entities. You need array controllers. Find Array Controller in the Object library and drag two of them into the editor. Use the Identity inspector to give them distinctive names such as `Passer Array Controller` and `Game Array Controller`.

The Team Array Controller picked up every Team in the LeagueDocument's managed-object context. The point of these tables is to display only the passers for the selected team and only the games for the selected passer. The Passer and Game controllers focus on specific collections. How do they know what collections to use?

You can start thinking about this by remembering that bindings are two-way streets. The Team array controller supplies information to the Team table, but the Team table also sends information back to the Team controller. Specifically, when you select a Team in the table, the Team controller records the selection in its selection property.

What would the Passer array controller want to know? First, it wants to know that it's handling instances of the Passer entity. Second, it wants to know how to get the collection it is supposed to display. You need to tell it that it is to watch the selection object of the Team controller and pull the passers set from that object. This is another binding.

First, you need to take care of the fact that in the simple data model I've set up, there is no passers relationship in the Team entity—it relates to a set of Games and nothing else. So synthesize a passers relationship:

```
- (NSSet *) passers
{
    return   [self.games valueForKeyPath:
                   @"@distinctUnionOfObjects.passer"];
}
```

which goes through all the games, find all the passers, and reports each Passer only once. Be sure Team publishes the new relationship:

```
@property(nonatomic, readonly) NSSet *     passers;
```

The setup for Passer Array Controller is like this:

1. In the Attributes inspector, set the Object Controller properties to **Entity Name Passer**; check **Prepares Content**.

2. In the Bindings inspector, bind **Content Set** to **Team Array Controller**, through the selection controller key, to obtain the set through the passers model key path.

3. Also, bind Managed Object Context to **File's Owner**, key path managed-ObjectContext. (File's Owner isn't a controller, so it doesn't take a controller key.)

Do the same for the Game Array Controller. It controls Game entities, binds to the selection of the Passer Array Controller, and pulls the selection's games as its content set. Conceptually, the controller stack should look like Figure 18.8.

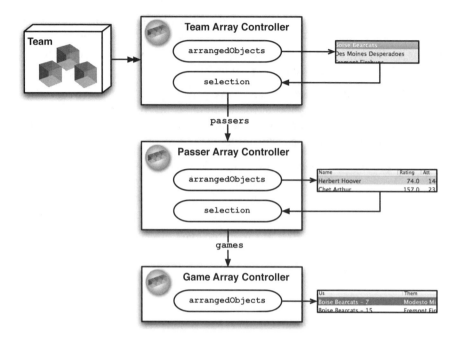

FIGURE 18.8   The completed network of array controllers. Team Array Controller at the top feeds directly from the Team objects in the document's managed-object context. It sorts and filters the list into arrangedObjects, which populates the Team table. Selecting a row in the Team table sets the Team controller's selection; the selected Team's passers are what Passer Array Controller pulls in and assorts into its own arrangedObjects, and so on.

Binding the Passer Table

It's time to wire the Passer table to the Passer Array Controller. Start by binding the numeric columns. This isn't much different from what you did for the first draft of the Team table—bind the Value of each column to Passer Array's controller, through its arrangedObjects, at the key path corresponding to the column. Table 18.1 shows the matchups, which shouldn't surprise you.

I've held out on the first column, the passer's name—one column for a full name, not separate columns for firstName and lastName, which are the attributes defined for the Passer entity. How are you going to fill this column?

The solution the iOS Passer Rating used was to have a computed read-only property, fullName, which concatenated firstName, a space, and lastName. That's simple, and probably the right answer; it generates a full name in one place, in code. But I'm going to do it another way to demonstrate another feature of bindings.

TABLE 18.1   Property Names for the Numeric Columns in the Passer Table

Column Head	Property
Rating	passerRating
Att	attempts
Comp	completions
Yards	yards
TDs	touchdowns
Ints	interceptions

Select the Name column, and bring up the Bindings inspector. *Do not* bother with the Value binding. Instead open Display Pattern Value1. Bind to **Passer Array Controller**→arrangedObjects→firstName.

When you completed the Value1 binding, a new binding became available: Display Pattern Value2. Bind to **Passer Array Controller**→arrangedObjects→lastName.

In both binding editors, you saw a unique field, **Display Pattern**. It is a formatting string; the value that comes from the Value1 binding is substituted into %{value1}@ , Value2 into %{value2}@, and so on. Fill the field with

%{value1}@ %{value2}@

which gets you firstName-space-lastName. Don't worry about which editor you should put the format string into; setting one sets them both.

Do the same trick with the label above the Passer table: Bind it to **Team Array Controller**→selection→teamName, with the format string **Passers for the %{value1}@**.

NOTE

Bindings even automate special cases for you. Suppose no Team were selected, or the selected Team had no teamName set. You might enter **Passers** in the **No Selection Placeholder** and **Null Placeholder** fields, respectively, and the bindings mechanism would fill the label with that string.

Check your work by running the app. Everything is as expected, but there's a problem. Passer ratings should come with one digit (always) after the decimal point, and the Rating column shows values like 158.3333.... At least the formatter is courteous enough to put in an ellipsis to mark the truncation. See Figure 18.9.

Passers for the Glendale Centers		
Name	Rating	Att
Rutherford Hayes	85.8333...	28
Andy Jackson	158.333...	2257
James Polk	81.5110...	1852

FIGURE 18.9   The bindings for the Passer table work, but there's a formatting problem with the passer rating.

If a bound value is numeric, and you don't specify a format, the bindings mechanism will render it in a generic format. This is fine for the integer stats, but you'd be more particular about the floating-point rating. You want 158.3, not 158.3333.... The solution is to attach a *formatter* object to the Ratings column's text cell.

> **NOTE**
>
> Before Lion, you'd have gotten into formatters a lot sooner than this. The bindings mechanism did not have a default formatter for numbers; if the bound cell did not have a formatter, and the binding delivered a number (or NSNumber), AppKit would give up and throw an exception.

Type **number** into the Object library's search field to find Number Formatter. Drag it onto the "Text Cell" label under the header of the Rating column—the cell is represented only there, so just dragging into the column won't do. When the cell highlights, drop the formatter on it. The cell label changes from "Text Cell" to "123."

You must now edit the formatter so it renders numbers as you want. It is not obvious how to do this; the formatter is not represented in the graphical editor. You have to use the outline sidebar, where you can find the formatter indented under the cell, or the jump bar.

Select the formatter and the Attributes inspector. For **Behavior**, you want **Mac OS X 10.4+ Custom** because you want to specify the format precisely. You don't have to bother with format strings; just scroll down to **Fraction Digits** and set both **Minimum** and **Maximum** to **1**. At the bottom of the editor is a **Sample** view. Type some trial numbers in the **Unformatted** field (you have to press Return to commit it), and satisfy yourself that everything that shows up in the **Formatted** field is what you want.

The Game Table—Truncation and Dates

If you got through the Passer table, the Game table is going to be a breeze.

▶ The first two columns (Us and Them) should be a display pattern for the team name and the game score: **%{value1}@ - %{value2}@**. Value2 should be ourScore and theirScore, respectively, and Value1 for the Them column should be theirTeam.

What about the team name for the Us column? Game doesn't have a direct reference to it. Attend to the label on the key: **Model Key Path**. You can trace through relationships and @ sign aggregators, so the key path should be team.teamName.

▶ For the When column, use whenPlayed.

▶ For Rating, use passerRating. Add a number formatter to restrict the display to one fractional digit.

▶ The label above the table should be the display pattern **Games for %{value1}@ %{value2}@**, from Passer Array Controller→selection, firstName, and lastName.

Run Mac Passer Rating to check your progress. There are a couple of problems yet remaining. See the Us and When columns in Figure 18.10: If the team name is long, the team-and-score value can overflow the column; the column truncates the value with ellipses, obscuring the score. Also, the default format for the When column spells the date out fully, which overflows that column.

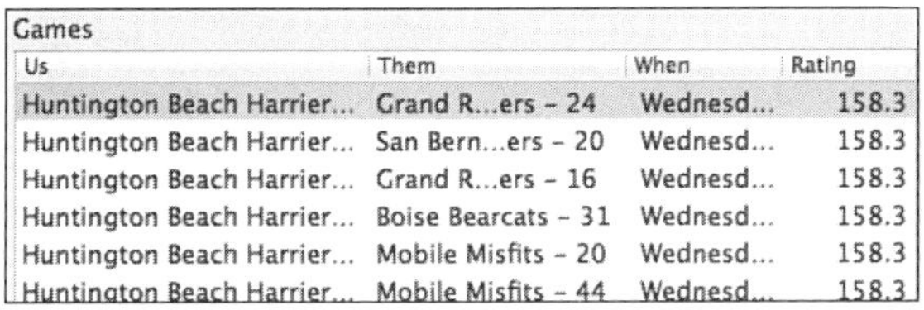

Games

Us	Them	When	Rating
Huntington Beach Harrier...	Grand R...ers - 24	Wednesd...	158.3
Huntington Beach Harrier...	San Bern...ers - 20	Wednesd...	158.3
Huntington Beach Harrier...	Grand R...ers - 16	Wednesd...	158.3
Huntington Beach Harrier...	Boise Bearcats - 31	Wednesd...	158.3
Huntington Beach Harrier...	Mobile Misfits - 20	Wednesd...	158.3
Huntington Beach Harrier...	Mobile Misfits - 44	Wednesd...	158.3

FIGURE 18.10 The table cell for the Us column was left at its default **Line Break** setting of **Truncate Tail**. When the column gets too narrow, the end of the team name, and the score, are replaced with ellipses. The Them column sets line breaks to **Truncate Middle**, which preserves the score and puts the ellipses where the omission is less significant. Also, the default format for dates is full-text, which is too wide for the When column.

For the team columns, the significant parts are the team name (even a part of one) at the beginning, and the score at the end. Text cells can take care of that automatically: Drill down to the text cells for the two team columns (again, the ability to command-click them in the outline sidebar helps), and look for the **Line Break** pop-up; select **Truncate Middle**. That makes the columns look like the Them column in Figure 18.10.

Next select the text cell for the When column. You used a number formatter for the Rating cells, so you've probably guessed there is a date-formatter object as well. Find it in the Object library by typing `date` in the search field, and drag it onto the cell for that column. The **Mac OS X 10.4+ Default** behavior will do because you can select **Short Style** from the **Date Style** popup.

The Game Popover

The plan from Figure 17.1 shows a popover window attached to a row in the Game table. I'm going to run through this quickly—mostly it involves binding work that you know how to do by now—but there are a couple of points to take note of: Setting an `IBAction` to detect a click on the table and using `NSObjectController` to mediate single objects.

An `NSTableView` is a complex apparatus, but it descends from `NSControl`, which is simple. Like a menu item, a control has a target (where to send commands) and an action (the name of the method that handles the command). Different controls trigger their actions on different events—text fields send their action messages when you finish editing them—but tables, like most controls, trigger when you click them.

`LeagueDocument.xib` should still be open. You'll need `LeagueDocument.h` open in the assistant editor, which you can open with the middle segment of the **Editor** control in the toolbar. If the first segment of the assistant's jump bar is set to **Automatic**, you should see `LeagueDocument.h`; if you don't, click File's Owner to get its attention. (For this step, you can hide the Utility area.)

You created an IBOutlet by control-dragging from a UI element to an @implementation in the "Outlets" section of Chapter 11. You're going to do the same thing with an IBAction for a table click. Select the Game table (it may be easier to do this from the outline sidebar), hold the control key down, and drag into the header file so an insertion bar shows just above the @end directive. Release, and fill in the popover to describe an IBAction named gameTableClicked:. See Figure 18.11.

FIGURE 18.11   Control-dragging from the Game table into the @interface in LeagueDocument.h pops up a window to create an IBAction that responds to a click in the table.

NOTE

By default, Xcode's linking popover offers an **Outlet**, not an **Action**. Remember to set the **Connection** popup.

A connection bubble, filled, should appear next to the new IBAction declaration. Xcode adds a stub for gameTableClicked: to LeagueDocument.m; fill it out like this:

```
@interface LeagueDocument ()
@property(strong) NSPopover *    gamePopover

// Use IB to link these outlets:
@property(nonatomic, weak) IBOutlet NSArrayController *
                                gameArrayController;
@property(nonatomic, weak) IBOutlet NSTableView *
                                gameTable;
@end
    .
    .
    .


@synthesize gamePopover, gameArrayController, gameTable;
 .
 .
 .
- (IBAction) gameTableClicked: (id) sender
{
    NSInteger        row = self.gameTable.clickedRow;
```

```
// row is -1 if the click was outside any row

if (row >= 0) {
    // Close the popover if one was already visible
    [self.gamePopover performClose: nil];

    // Create a view controller for the popover's content
    NSViewController *  gvc =
        [[NSViewController alloc] initWithNibName: @"GameViewController"
                                          bundle: nil];
    // Ask the array controller for the row'th game
    id     aGame = [self.gameArrayController.arrangedObjects
                        objectAtIndex: row];

    // Tell the view controller what game it's to show
    gvc.representedObject = aGame;

    // Create a popover and fill it with the view controller
    self.gamePopover = [[NSPopover alloc] init];
    self.gamePopover.contentViewController = gvc;
    self.gamePopover.behavior = NSPopoverBehaviorTransient;

    // Place the popover next to the row, and show it
    NSRect rowRect = [self.gameTable rectOfRow: row];
    [self.gamePopover showRelativeToRect: rowRect
                                 ofView: self.gameTable
                          preferredEdge: NSMaxXEdge];
}
}
```

CAUTION

I have you connecting to outlets and actions declared in a *class extension*, an additional @interface declared with the class's name and empty parentheses, usually in the class's .m file. Xcode 4.2 could make such connections into an extension interface but was unstable afterward. Later versions should fix this. If not, move the declarations in to the main @interface in the header file.

The method picks up three properties. You can figure out how to use Interface Builder to create the gameArrayController and gameTable IBOutlets; and gamePopover is a simple, synthesized @property.

NOTE

While you're at it, link up passerArrayController and passerTable IBOutlets as well. They'll come in handy later.

What about that `NSViewController`? View controllers are analogous to their counterparts in iOS, but they run single views within a window's hierarchy, rather than a single window-filling view as is typical in iOS. `NSPopover` is built to support an `NSViewController`.

For this purpose, everything you need to do can be handled by bindings. There is no need to subclass `NSViewController`. Use **File→New→File...** (⌘N), the **User Interface** panel, to create a View XIB, named `GameViewController.xib`. Select File's Owner and set the class, in the Identity inspector, to `NSViewController`.

Add an `NSObjectController`; you've dealt with `NSArrayController` before, and this is its superclass, which manages single objects. In the Attributes inspector, the mode is **Class**; the class is **Game**; it **Prepares Content** but is not **Editable**.

The object controller has to obtain an object to manage. In the Bindings inspector, bind Content Object to File's Owner, with the model key path `representedObject`. View controllers come with a generic object pointer, `representedObject`, that holds the object the view is to display.

The base view is already in the XIB; if you don't see it, click it in the editor's sidebar. This is an instance of `NSView`, the root class for things that know how to draw and lay themselves out. You're going to use it simply as a container for a group of labels. Drag in labels to match the layout shown in Figure 18.12.

FIGURE 18.12   The completed layout for `GameViewController.xib`. It's all labels with no need for autoresizing.

The small detail labels are done by selecting the Size (fifth) inspector and selecting **Small** for **Size**. There's no need to set autoresizing for any of the views; the game popover won't be resizable.

Don't bother creating any outlets. The whole thing can be done with bindings. The labels and contents in the layout in Figure 18.12 should tell you what labels need to be bound to what properties. All of them need to be bound to the appropriate key path for the `selection` key of the object controller. Remember that the first team must be bound to the path `team.teamName`!

Run Passer Rating one more time. You should see the application we plotted out at the start of Chapter 17, "Starting a Mac OS X Application." As a bonus, if you left the name column of the Team table editable, you can edit the team name and see it propagate through the labels and Game stats.

It's annoying that the tables are in random order. As with many database systems, to-many relationships have no inherent ordering (although the latest versions of Core Data offer it). Array controllers have a `sortDescriptors` property that lets you specify an initial ordering of their contents. This method, added to `LeagueDocument.m`, assigns sort descriptors to the controller objects:

```
- (void)windowControllerDidLoadNib:(NSWindowController *)aController
{
    [super windowControllerDidLoadNib:aController];
    // Sort teams by name
    self.teamArrayController.sortDescriptors =
        [NSArray arrayWithObject:
            [NSSortDescriptor sortDescriptorWithKey: @"teamName"
                                          ascending: YES]];
    // Sort passers by last name, first name
    // If you don't have a passerArrayController property,
    // go to LeagueDocument.xib and control-drag from Passer
    // Array Controller and establish the link.
    self.passerArrayController.sortDescriptors =
        [NSArray arrayWithObjects:
            [NSSortDescriptor sortDescriptorWithKey: @"lastName"
                                          ascending: YES],
            [NSSortDescriptor sortDescriptorWithKey: @"firstName"
                                          ascending: YES],
        nil];
    // Sort games by date
    self.gameArrayController.sortDescriptors =
        [NSArray arrayWithObject:
            [NSSortDescriptor sortDescriptorWithKey: @"whenPlayed"
                                          ascending: YES]];
}
```

The user can reorder the tables by clicking column headers.

Summary

Bindings are a tremendous convenience in Mac OS X programming, and even this long chapter can't cover everything. In this chapter I gave you an introduction to what bindings can do for you, but more to the point, you saw what Xcode can do to support them. It is *possible* to set up bindings in code, but Interface Builder is indispensable to getting them right, easily (comparatively) and quickly.

I showed you how bindings and formatters can render your data in forms that your model classes don't directly support, saving you from having to alter your model to accommodate per-view variations in presentation.

You also saw how to set up autoresizing to ensure that when you resize a window, your contents adjust to keep themselves visible and take advantage of any added space.

You used number and date formatters, and truncation controls, to control how information is presented in table cells and labels.

Finally, you created a XIB for a complex data view that, thanks to bindings, didn't need any code at all.

## CHAPTER 19

A Custom View for Mac OS X

Let's extend Mac Passer Rating by one more step, and in the process see how to handle custom classes in Interface Builder (IB). In this chapter we'll add another popover, to be shown when you double-click a row in the Passer table. The popover will show a simple scrolling bar graph comparing pass attempts and completions, by game.

You already know how to create and populate an NSPopover. The popover needs an NSViewController. It turns out that the view controller must do a little bit of work, so you need to use **File→New→File…** (⌘N) to create an Objective-C subclass of NSViewController named PasserGraphController. (Be sure to use the Mac OS X section of the New File assistant, so you can get the benefit of the view-controller template.)

This gets you header and implementation files and a XIB. Select PasserGraphController.xib to find that you already have an empty custom view. The class of File's Owner (select it and choose the Identity inspector) is the generic NSViewController; change it to PasserGraphController.

Drag another custom view (search the Object library for **custom**) inside the root view, and snug its edges against the root's sides. (This will make sense soon.) Use the Identity inspector to set its class to PassCompletionView. Xcode won't offer to complete the name for you because you haven't defined it yet.

With the PassCompletionView still selected, issue **Editor→Embed In→Scroll View**. The PassCompletionView is now wrapped in a scroll view. Expand the sidebar to the outline view (or navigate in the jump bar) to see it, because it's hard to make out visually with all three views being the same size. Select the scroll view and in the Attributes inspector, uncheck **Show Vertical Scroller.**

> **NOTE**
>
> The **Embed In** commands are useful. In the `LeagueDocument` layout, you could have embedded the tables and labels in the right side of the window in a custom view, selected that new view and the Team scroll view, and then embedded them in a split view. After you made the views on both sides of the split flexible-width, and stuck to that edge, you could reapportion the amount of horizontal space between the two sides.

Choose the assistant editor, and click **File's Owner** to focus it on `PasserGraphController.h`. Control-drag from the `PassCompletionView` into the `@interface` to create:

```
@property (strong) IBOutlet PassCompletionView *completionView;
```

That's the end of the first cycle with `PasserGraphController`.

A Graphing View

I've begged the question of what `PassCompletionView` is. Create a new Objective-C subclass of `NSView` with that name. You get header and implementation files. `PassCompletionView` will use the delegate pattern to pull its data from the model. That requires a `@protocol` to define the method through which the delegate provides the data. Put this in `PassCompletionView.h`:

```objectivec
#import <Cocoa/Cocoa.h>

@class PassCompletionView;

@protocol PassCompletionDelegate <NSObject>

- (NSManagedObject *) passCompletion: (PassCompletionView *) view
                        gameAtIndex: (NSUInteger) index;

@end

@interface PassCompletionView  : NSView

@property(nonatomic, assign) IBOutlet id<PassCompletionDelegate>  delegate;

@property(nonatomic, assign) CGFloat       cellWidth;

@property(nonatomic, assign) NSUInteger    attRed;
@property(nonatomic, assign) NSUInteger    attGreen;
@property(nonatomic, assign) NSUInteger    attBlue;
@property(strong) NSColor * attColor;
@property(nonatomic, assign) NSUInteger    compGreen;
```

```
@property(nonatomic, assign) NSUInteger      compRed;
@property(nonatomic, assign) NSUInteger      compBlue;
@property(strong) NSColor * compColor;
@property(nonatomic, assign) NSUInteger      gameCount;

@end
```

`PassCompletionView.m` involves a lot of detailed drawing and preparation. I'll summarize it here; the complete file is in the sample code:

```
-  (id) initWithFrame: (NSRect) frame
{
    self = [super initWithFrame: frame];
    if (self) {
        // Default colors:
        self.compColor = [NSColor blueColor];
        self.attColor = [NSColor redColor];
        self.cellWidth = 15;
    }

    return self;
}

- (void) awakeFromNib
{
    if (self.compRed || self.compGreen || self.compBlue) {
        self.compColor =
            [NSColor colorWithDeviceRed: (self.compRed / 255.0)
                                  green: (self.compGreen / 255.0)
                                   blue: (self.compBlue / 255.0)
                                  alpha: 1.0];
    }
    // Set self.attColor similarly,
    // from .attRed, .attGreen, .attBlue
}
- (void) recalculateFrame
{
    // Set the width of the view to accommodate all the games
    // and tell AppKit to redraw the view.
}
- (void) setCellWidth: (CGFloat) newCellWidth
```

```objc
{
    if (cellWidth != newCellWidth) {
        cellWidth = newCellWidth;
        [self recalculateFrame];
    }
}

- (void) setGameCount: (NSUInteger) newGameCount
{
    if (gameCount != newGameCount) {
        gameCount = newGameCount;
        [self recalculateFrame];
    }
}

- (void) drawRect: (NSRect) dirtyRect
{
    // First fill the view with light gray
    // Then an inset rectangle with white, making
    // a blank area framed in gray.
    // ...

    for (NSUInteger index = 0; index < self.gameCount; index++) {
        // For each of the passer's games...
        // get this column's game from the delegate
        NSManagedObject *    game = [self.delegate passCompletion: self
                                                    gameAtIndex: index];
        NSRect barRect;
        NSUInteger stat;
        // Calculate the bounds of the attempts bar
        barRect.origin.x = GRAPH_PADDING +
                        index * (CELL_PADDING + self.cellWidth);
        barRect.origin.y = GRAPH_PADDING;
        barRect.size.width = self.cellWidth;

        // Use Core Data to pull in the number of attempts
        stat = [[game valueForKey:  @"attempts"] unsignedIntegerValue];
        stat = MIN(stat, MAX_ATTEMPTS);

        barRect.size.height = stat * pixPerAttempt;
        // Fill the bar with the "attempt" color
        [self.attColor setFill];
        [NSBezierPath fillRect: barRect];

         // ...
         // Calculate a bar rectangle for game.completions
```

```
        // ...
        [self.compColor setFill];
        [NSBezierPath fillRect: barRect];
    }
}
```

The result can be seen in Figure 19.1. Not fancy, but good enough for a demo.

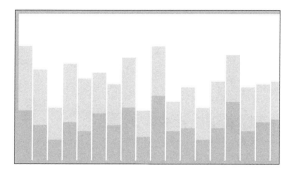

FIGURE 19.1   The `PassCompletionView` graph is not elaborate but does the job of comparing one quantity as a fraction of another.

Back to the View Controller

With `PassCompletionView` defined, you can fill the gaps in `PasserGraphController`. As an `NSViewController`, it has a `representedObject` property to refer to a model object that supplies its content. As a controller, it acts as an intermediary between the represented model object and its views. It should keep a reference to a `PassCompletionView`, and be that view's delegate, supplying it with `Games`.

All of which is to say that `PasserGraphController.h` should look like this:

```
#import <Cocoa/Cocoa.h>
#import "PassCompletionView.h"


@interface PasserGraphController : NSViewController
                            <PassCompletionDelegate>


@property(nonatomic, strong) IBOutlet
            PassCompletionView * completionView;


@end
```

PasserGraphController.m is nearly as simple:

```
#import "PasserGraphController.h"

@interface PasserGraphController ()
@property(nonatomic, strong) NSArray * gameArray;
@end

@implementation PasserGraphController

@synthesize gameArray, completionView;

- (void) awakeFromNib
{
    // Get the passer's games
    NSSet *   games = [self.representedObject valueForKey: @"games"];
    // Sort them by date
    self.gameArray =
        [games sortedArrayUsingDescriptors:
            [NSArray arrayWithObject:
                [NSSortDescriptor sortDescriptorWithKey: @"whenPlayed"
                                              ascending: YES]]];
    // Let the graph view know how many games there are
    self.completionView.gameCount = self.gameArray.count;
}


#pragma mark - PassCompletionDelegate

- (NSManagedObject *) passCompletion: (PassCompletionView *) view
                         gameAtIndex: (NSUInteger) index
{
    return [self.gameArray objectAtIndex: index];
}

@end
```

...just enough to set up a list of games and parcel them out to the graphing view.

Complete the completion-graphing package by returning to PasserGraphController.xib.
You've defined PassCompletionView's delegate and PasserGraphController's
completionView to be IBOutlets, so you can hook them up in IB.

▶ Control-drag from the graph view to File's Owner, and select **delegate** from the
  HUD.

▶ Make sure File's Owner's completionView outlet is connected to the graph view.

Using `PasserGraphController`

The pass-completion graph package is finished. Here's how you use it:

1. In `LeagueDocument.m`, add a `passerPopover` `@property` to the class extension (the abbreviated `@interface` at the top of the file):

```
@interface LeagueDocument ()
@property(strong) NSPopover *   gamePopover;
@property(strong) NSPopover *   passerPopover;
@end
```

   and make sure you `@synthesize` it in the `@implementation`.

2. Still in `LeagueDocument.m`, add this to the top:

```
#import "PasserGraphController.h"
```

3. Add these lines anywhere after the call to super in the `-windowControllerDidLoadNib:` method:

```
// You can't wire the double-click action in Interface Builder,
// so you have to do it in code:
self.passerTable.doubleAction = @selector(passerTableClicked:);
self.passerTable.target = self;
```

4. ... which obliges you to supply a `passerTableClicked:` method:

```
- (IBAction) passerTableClicked: (id) sender
{
    NSInteger     row = self.passerTable.clickedRow;
    if (row >= 0) {
        [self.gamePopover performClose: nil];
        [self.passerPopover performClose: nil];

        // Create a graph controller
        PasserGraphController *    pgc =
                [[PasserGraphController alloc]
                    initWithNibName: @"PasserGraphController"
                        bundle: [NSBundle bundleForClass:
                                    [PasserGraphController class]]];

        // Get the Passer corresponding to the double-clicked row
        id     passer =
                [self.passerArrayController.arrangedObjects
                        objectAtIndex: row];
        // and point the graph controller at it
        pgc.representedObject = passer;

        // Set up the popover
```

19

```
        self.passerPopover =   [[NSPopover alloc] init];
        self.passerPopover.contentViewController = pgc;
        self.passerPopover.behavior = NSPopoverBehaviorTransient;

        // Show the popover next to the double-clicked row
        NSRect     rowRect = [self.passerTable rectOfRow: row];
    [self.passerPopover showRelativeToRect: rowRect
                                    ofView: self.passerTable
                             preferredEdge: NSMaxXEdge];
    }
}
```

Run Mac Passer Rating, and find that if you double-click a passer in the Passer table, a lovely scrolling game-by-game graph of completions appears in a popover window. See Figure 19.2.

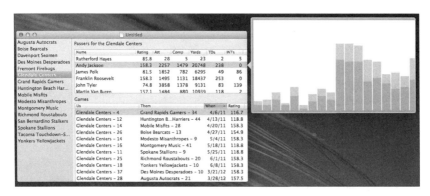

FIGURE 19.2   Double-clicking a row in the Passer table reveals a popover window with a scrolling bar graph comparing passing attempts to completions for that passer.

Custom View Properties

We're not quite done with PassCompletionView. You saw that its awakeFromNib method initialized attColor and compColor, the colors for the attempt and completion bars, from the corresponding red, green, and blue numbers. I had you set aside properties for those values, but not respond to changes in them—they'd normally have setters that took new values and forced a redraw of the view to reflect them. What's the point in having properties that aren't fully supported?

Let me step back in history a bit. Before Xcode 4, when Interface Builder was a stand-alone tool, it supported plug-in bundles (.ibplugin). These were challenging to write but a boon to developers of custom views. An IB plug-in would incorporate the code to draw a view and an Attributes inspector panel to configure its particular features. Users could adjust the attributes and see them reflected in the editor.

Xcode 4 does not support any plug-ins, including .ibplugins. Custom views are shown as featureless blue-gray rectangles. The history of Xcode 4 has been that lost features from Xcode 3 have been gradually restored, but there are good reasons not to include plug-ins: Apple has become sensitive about admitting arbitrary code to its software. It's a security hole, it commits them to an application architecture they want the freedom to change, and it adds to their support burden. Don't expect Xcode plug-ins to return.

Xcode gives back a little through key-value coding: You can set an object's properties by adding key-value pairs to it. In PasserGraphController.xib, select the PassCompletionView and the Identity inspector to find a section labeled "User Defined Runtime Attributes." See Figure 19.3.

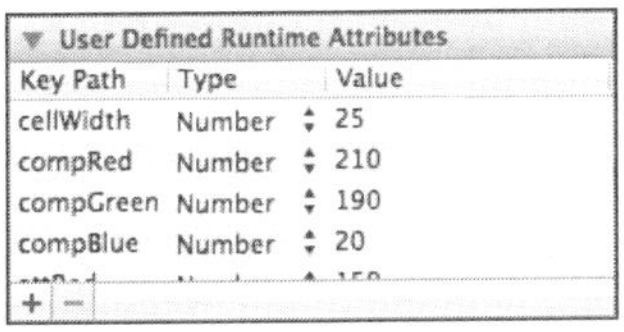

▼ User Defined Runtime Attributes			
Key Path	Type		Value
cellWidth	Number	⬍	25
compRed	Number	⬍	210
compGreen	Number	⬍	190
compBlue	Number	⬍	20
+ −			

FIGURE 19.3   The Interface Builder Identity inspector includes a section for setting key-value pairs for a view's properties.

Here's where you can set those colors. Click the + button, and type the name of a property of PassCompletionView. Be careful! If you enter a key that doesn't correspond to a property, you'll get a KVC exception when the NIB loads, and loading will fail. Select the type of the property; you can have a Boolean, number (restricted to integer), string, key into a string-localization dictionary, or you can explicitly set the property to nil. Then type in the value. The default colors for the bars, set in the view's initializer, are red and blue, which didn't show up well in the monochrome images for this book's figures. Using this feature, I could set up something with more contrast.

> **NOTE**
>
> I'm using the term *property* loosely here. Key-value coding requires only that an object implement getter and setter (if any setting is done) methods for an attribute. The @property and @synthesize directives are just the easiest way to generate those methods.

19

Summary

This was a short chapter, but it covered some important features of Interface Builder.

You saw how to create an NSViewController subclass, with a XIB for its contents and code to mediate between a model object and its views.

You created a custom view that draws its contents and renewed your acquaintance with the near-universal Cocoa design pattern of delegation.

You used Interface Builder to automatically wrap an existing view in a scroll view and considered how to use the other wrapping commands in your development.

And you took advantage of a feature that, although it doesn't make up for the lack of true interactive editing, does let you set the parameters of a XIB object that IB doesn't provide an Attributes editor for.

CHAPTER 20

Localization and Autolayout

Mac Passer Rating is a good example, but what would make it perfect would be if I could see it in French (they play football in Québec)—using an application named Quart-Efficacité. Users of Mac OS X specify what languages they understand by setting a list of available languages in order of preference in the **Language** tab of the **Language & Text** panel of the System Preferences application. When a user's list sets French at a higher priority than English, MPR should present menus, alerts, and labels in the French language.

> **NOTE**
>
> The localization techniques I'll show you are identical to the ones you'd use for an iOS app.

Cocoa applications load resources through the NSBundle class. When asked for a resource, NSBundle first searches the subdirectories of the application bundle's Resources directory, in the order of the user's preferences for language. Language subdirectories are given such names as English.lproj, fr.lproj, or en-GB.lproj. (Plain-text language names are now deprecated; you should use ISO-standard language abbreviations, optionally suffixed with a code to identify a regional variant.)

If a directory that matches the user's language and region (fr-CA.lproj) can't be found, Mac OS X falls back to the language-only variant (fr.lproj); then to the localization for the "development region" (usually en.lproj); and finally to strings and layouts in unlocalized resources, not in any .lproj directory.

If you look at the Mac Passer Rating project directory in the Finder, you'll see an en.lproj directory is associated with MPR and contains Credits.rtf, Info-Plist.strings, MainMenu.xib, and LeagueDocument.xib.

Click those files (as well as the other XIBs) in Xcode's Project navigator, and look at the jump bar above the Editor area. As you expect, it progresses from the project, through the enclosing groups, to the file. But there's one more level: It has the name of the file, to which is appended (English). As far as Xcode is concerned, what you see is only one of many possible variants on that file—the one that appears in en.lproj.

Adding a Localization

All right then. You want a French (specifically a French-Canadian) variant on those files. How do you get it?

Start with the simplest. Credits.rtf appears in a scrolling view in the automatically generated About box. The file you got from the application template contains a brief, humorous list of credits (such as **With special thanks to:** Mom). Brevity and humor are virtues, so I'll just translate it.

Select Credits.rtf in the Project navigator and expose the Utility area (third segment in the toolbar's **View** control). Choose the File (first) inspector, and find the Localization table. Click the + button, and select **Other→French—Canada (fr-CA)**. Three things happen: "French—Canada" appears in the Localizations list; Credits.rtf picks up a disclosure triangle in the Project navigator, which shows the two versions when you expand it; and the jump bar offers the variant along with English. In the Finder, the project has picked up a fr-CA.lproj folder containing a Credits.rtf file.

> **NOTE**
>
> If you regret adding a localization for a file, you'll find that you can't just select it in the Project navigator and press Delete. You have to select the file and click the – button in the Localization table.

Replace the contents of the French-Canada file (be sure you have the right one!) with the following:

- **Les ingénieurs:** Certains gens
- **Conception d'interface humaine:** D'autres gens
- **Test:** On espère que ce n'est pas personne
- **Documentation:** N'importe qui
- **Nous remercions particulièrement:** Maman

> **NOTE**
>
> Putting the two variants side-by-side in the assistant editor can be helpful. Be sure to bless Xcode for providing an RTF editor and for changing the spelling dictionary to match the locale.

Trying It Out

The obvious way to test this localization is to shuffle your language preferences in the System Preferences application, launch Mac Passer Rating, and see whether the About box contains the new text. This would, however, also make any other application you launch use its French localization until you switch the preference back. This is inconvenient unless you prefer to work in French.

> **NOTE**
>
> Changing the systemwide language preference is necessary when you edit `InfoPlist.strings` to localize things such as the display name of the application. You have to build the app, change the preference, and relaunch the Finder using ⌥⌘**Esc**.

A command-line option is available to change your language preference only for the application being launched. Select **Product**→**Edit Scheme** (⌘<), and the **Arguments** tab of the **Run** panel for the Mac Passer Rating scheme. Click the + button at the bottom of the Arguments Passed on Launch table, and enter

```
-AppleLanguages (fr-CA)
```

in the new row that appears. Run the app and examine the menus. AppKit generates some menu titles that appear in French automatically. Select **Mac Passer Rating**→**About Mac Passer Rating**; the About box shows the content of the localized `Credits.rtf`. It's a start. See Figure 20.1.

> **NOTE**
>
> Some developers wonder if it's possible to pass command-line arguments to Mac OS X applications when users launch them from the Finder. No; command-line arguments are useful for development, but there's no way for users to specify them unless they execute an app's binary from the Terminal. If you're looking for file parameters, write handlers for open-file events in the application delegate or a custom `NSDocumentController`, or handle Apple Events.

20

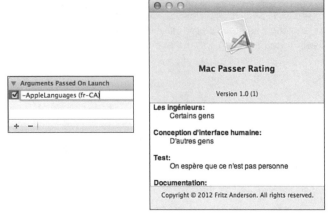

FIGURE 20.1   Use the **Arguments** tab of the **Run** panel of the Scheme editor (left) to add an -AppleLanguages command-line parameter to Mac Passer Rating, so its locale will be fr-CA. When a localized Credits.rtf file is in place, it is used in the automatically generated About box.

Localizing `MainMenu.xib`

Credits.rtf was easy enough; styled text is fluid, and you have continuous access to the contents. Not so with a menu bar. If you took the same approach, added a localization to MainMenu.xib, and attacked it with Interface Builder (IB), you'd click and double-click continually to get at all the menu and item titles.

Don't create a localization that way. There is a shortcut in the form of the ibtool command-line tool. ibtool is a general-purpose utility for manipulating XIBs and NIBs, with many commands, but I'm going to show you only two, for extracting and importing strings. For more, enter man ibtool at the command line.

Open the Terminal application (/Applications/Utilities/Terminal) and make sure your working directory is the Mac Passer Rating *inside* the directory that contains the project file. An easy way to do this is to type **cd** and a space; then drag the directory into the terminal window. Check your setup:

```
$ pwd
/Users/xcodeuser/Mac Passer Rating/Mac Passer Rating
$ ls
...
en.lproj
fr-CA.lproj
$
```

You want ibtool to read MainMenu.xib from the en.lproj directory and extract a .strings file to go into the fr-CA.lproj directory. The command line is

```
ibtool --export-strings-file fr-CA.lproj/MainMenu.strings \
       en.lproj/MainMenu.xib
```

NOTE

Be sure to type both hyphens in `ibtool` options; if you type only one, the best you can hope for is that it will fail silently.

`.strings` files are specialized versions of the text property list format (see Chapter 23, "Property Lists"), encoded in UTF-16. They contain key-value pairs, with the key being an identifying token for a user-visible element, and the value being the text the element is to display for a particular localization. Usually, `.strings` files are copied into the `.lproj` directories in the application bundle, but in this case, `MainMenu.strings` is just a container to extract and inject translated strings.

NOTE

The issue of how Xcode handles .strings files is in flux. Mac OS X `.strings` files must be encoded as UTF-16, and that's the encoding emitted by `genstrings` and `ibtool`. Many command-line utilities assume that any text file is encoded as UTF-8 (if not ASCII), making it inconvenient to apply some useful tools to them. A solution is dawning, whereby Xcode can accept UTF-8-encoded `.strings` files and transcode them to UTF-16 before copying them into the application bundle. Given that few `.strings` files are created in Xcode, that's not as useful a solution as it sounds.

Open `MainMenu.strings` in your favorite text editor, and find a list that looks like this:

```
/* Class = "NSMenuItem"; title = "Bring All to Front"; ObjectID = "5"; */
"5.title" = "Bring All to Front";

/* Class = "NSMenuItem"; title = "Window";  ObjectID = "19"; */
"19.title" = "Window";

/* Class = "NSMenuItem"; title = "Minimize";  ObjectID = "23"; */
"23.title" = "Minimize";

/* Class = "NSMenuItem"; title = "Mac Passer Rating";  ObjectID = "56"; */
"56.title" = "Mac Passer Rating";
...
```

The title for object 19 in the XIB (tagged as `19.title`) is "Window." The comments (between `/* */`) are there to guide you as to what is being translated, and when the translation is done, what the original context was. If you were preparing a translation of `MainMenu.xib` *into* English, this is what it would look like.

Apple can give you a little help here. It has a localization-support page at `http://developer.apple.com/internationalization/`, where you can download tools (developer registration required). The tools, such as AppleGlot, haven't been updated in some years, and in any event are meant for much bigger jobs than Mac Passer Rating. The real trove is in the glossary files that Apple used to translate its applications and system software. They're in many languages, among them French.

Dig through the example localizations, edit the file, and this is what `MainMenu.strings` comes to look like:

```
/* Class = "NSMenuItem"; title = "Bring All to Front"; ObjectID = "5"; */
 "5.title" = "Tout ramener au premier plan";

/* Class = "NSMenuItem"; title = "Window"; ObjectID = "19"; */
"19.title" = "Fenêtre";

/* Class = "NSMenuItem"; title = "Minimize"; ObjectID = "23"; */
"23.title" = "Placer dans le Dock";

/* Class = "NSMenuItem"; title = "Mac Passer Rating"; ObjectID = "56"; */
"56.title" = "Quart-Efficacité";
...
```

> **NOTE**
>
> The **Fill with Test Data** item becomes **Remplisser avec les données de test**.

Now use `ibtool` to read the English `MainMenu.xib`, merge in the translated `MainMenu.strings` from `fr-CA.lproj`, and output a new `MainMenu.xib` file into `fr-CA.lproj`:

```
ibtool --import-strings-file fr-CA.lproj/MainMenu.strings \
       --write fr-CA.lproj/MainMenu.xib \
       en.lproj/MainMenu.xib
```

Now you need to get Xcode to recognize the Canadian-French localization so it can copy it into the application. Xcode is touchy about localizations it did not create, so follow along carefully:

1. In the Project navigator, select the unlocalized `MainMenu.xib`. If you do not do this, Xcode will add the new file as a separate file and not as a localization.

2. Issue **File→Add Files to "Mac Passer Rating"**... (⌥⌘A).

3. Locate the `MainMenu.xib` file that `ibtool` put in the `fr-CA.lproj` folder, and click **Add**.

4. Click the newly found localization and browse it to see whether it's as you expect.

5. Remember to add the new file to source control (**File→Source Control→Add**).

Build and run, maintaining the -AppleLanguages (fr-CA) argument in the Scheme editor. All the translations should be there. You may wonder about the key equivalents—they don't change between English and French.

There is, however, one other thing: The application menu is still labeled Mac Passer Rating. What's going on?

The application menu is not named out of the menu XIB. AppKit derives it from the "Bundle name" (CFBundleName) key in Info.plist. I'll get to localizing Info.plist soon.

Localizing the Window XIBs

Menus are only part of the story—obviously. Strings appear elsewhere in Mac Passer Rating's human interface. As before, you must inject your translations into the window XIBs, but because text usually becomes longer when you translate it from English, you must pay attention to layout as well. There are two ways to deal with the layout problem.

Translating View Strings

Rough localization of Mac Passer Rating's windows goes about the same:

```
$ ibtool --generate-strings-file fr-CA.lproj/xib-base-name.strings \
 en.lproj/xib-base-name.xib


.
.   edit the  .strings file
.


$ ibtool --import-strings-file fr-CA.lproj/xib-base-name.strings \
   --write fr-CA.lproj/xib-base-name.xib \
   en.lproj/xib-base-name.xib
```

> **CAUTION**
>
> In the version I am using, Xcode would not recognize files as localizable if they were not in an .lproj directory. If you try to import a localization for a XIB from any other directory, Xcode will treat the localization as an independent file. This is a frequent problem because a new-file template that creates a XIB in addition to source files places all of them in the same directory, which is inappropriate for one or the other. To keep the tool chain happy, delete the XIB from the Project navigator (making sure to delete only the reference); go to the command line and use the mv subcommand of your source-control tool to put the XIB in the appropriate .lproj; and put the XIB back in the project. Select the XIB and add your localization as usual.

20

Making the Text Fit—by Hand

But this is an example of how your localization work isn't done when you translate the labels. Open both versions of `GameViewController.xib` in Interface Builder (Figure 20.2, top). The layout that worked well for English doesn't leave enough room for the French labels. You need to stretch the labels to accommodate the longer strings and adjust the enclosing view to match.

> **NOTE**
>
> The use of *passe* in the labels is probably unnecessary for French readers, but the principle is the same: English is generally the tersest of the languages that use the Latin alphabet. View boundaries that look good for English won't look good for other languages, and vice versa.

You'd then save the edited French files, build again, and verify that the content fits nicely in its windows.

Making the Text Fit—Autolayout

In Chapter 18, "Wiring a Mac Application with Bindings," I mentioned Lion's autolayout feature as an alternative to autoresizing for managing view layouts. Autolayout has many applications, but the simplest example is in making a master XIB that can accommodate itself to different text content. In this section, I'll demonstrate autolayout as an alternative way to produce the Canadian-French game popover.

What is autolayout? When you dragged views into your XIBs, IB provided some guides to help you: The edges of the views snapped to line up with other views, or with the suggested spacing for the Aqua human interface. When you'd sized and placed the views, that was it; the guides were just a convenience in lining things up. After that, everything was left to autoresizing. Autoresizing has a limited vocabulary: Can the view resize horizontally or vertically? Does it keep its distance from any of the edges of its container?

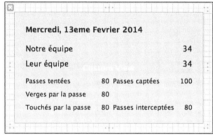

FIGURE 20.2   (top) Merely applying a translated .strings file to GameViewController.xib doesn't do everything. Because other Latin-alphabet languages are usually more verbose than English, the layout of localized XIBs often have to be redone (bottom).

Autolayout is different. Basically those Aqua guides become Cocoa objects that constrain your views to maintain the relationships you set in IB. A view could have many constraints: A label might be constrained

▸ To be a fixed distance from the left edge of the containing view

▸ To be as tall as the text it contains

▸ To be of a minimum, maximum, or fixed size

▸ But to balance that size against the goal of being wide enough to display its full contents

▸ To line up its baseline with an adjacent label

▸ To observe a minimum, maximum, or fixed distance from its neighbors

▸ To line up its sides with the sides of labels above and below, subject to their own priorities for width

▸ Or to line up with the horizontal or vertical center if its container balanced in priority against whether it should shift to let other views maintain their minimum widths and separations

Most views start out with only two or three constraints attached to them, but you can see that across a container with many subviews, the constraints can multiply, and resizing a window can cascade effects through the whole tree. Further, the constraints propagate *up*:

20

Adding more text to a label can push out against the constraints of its neighbors and force the window to a new size.

That's what you'll do here: You'll edit the English version of `GameViewController.xib` as a kind of template and create the Canadian-French version with `ibtool`. The constraints you put in your template XIB can, if you do them right, produce a XIB that accommodates the longer strings.

The process starts by bringing up the English version of `GameViewController.xib` in your Interface Builder tab. Converting to autolayout involves nothing more than checking a box in the File inspector, but don't do that yet—you'll want to make some adjustments before turning the process over to Xcode.

> **NOTE**
>
> When you convert to autolayout, Xcode changes the "deployment version" of the XIB to Mac OS X 10.7 if it isn't there already. The deployment version can be set through a pop-up menu in the File inspector. Usually, you'll be happy to set it to **Project SDK Version**, the default. However, if you need backward compatibility, set it to the earliest OS you want to run on. If you use objects or attributes that are available only in later OSs, Xcode will raise a warning pointing to the incompatibility.

When I dragged the labels that make up this XIB into the view, I didn't pay any attention to the autoresizing settings. The view wasn't going to resize during its lifetime, and there was no point in bothering. Everything is fixed-width and anchored to the top-left corner of the enclosing view. If you were to convert now, Xcode would produce a nest of constraints that you'd have to undo.

So adjust the autoresizing properties of the subviews as though the main view could resize: Make the non-numeric labels flexible-width. Stretch the date label so its right edge hits the Aqua guideline, and make it flexible-width and anchored to the top and both sides. Make the labels in the right-hand column anchor to the right edge of the superview. Don't put any anchors on the numeric labels.

> **NOTE**
>
> You wouldn't have to do this if the XIB were a fresh one, and you set autolayout from the start. You could watch the constraints (what had been guides) pop up as you dragged the subviews in, and adjust your placement so you have the right set of constraints from the start.

Now expose the File inspector (first tab in the Utility area) and check **Use Auto Layout**. Xcode warns you that it will start generating constraints automatically, but you want this, so click **Continue**.

Nothing much seems to have happened until you click one of the labels in the view, such as "Yards" in Figure 20.3. Then you see a spiderweb of constraint lines surrounding the view.

For **Yards**, these are

> ▶ An Aqua-standard inset from the left edge of the superview

> ▶ A fixed vertical separation from the view above

> ▶ The same, for the view below

> ▶ Alignment of the right (actually, the trailing) edge of the label with the one above

> ▶ The same, with the view below

> ▶ Alignment of the baseline with that of the "80" label to the right

What *isn't* set is a width constraint—I'll show you why shortly. Most of what you see in autolayout is nebulous this way: You express desires about relationships among views, but there are fewer absolutes than you're probably used to.

If you select one of the constraint lines, (as in the lower trailing-edge constraint in Figure 20.3), IB highlights both labels to which the constraint applies. This points up an important fact: Constraints (except for width) are not a property of any one view; they are independent objects that relate to two views equally. A constraint affects the views at both ends of the relationship, and which ends up influencing the other depends on how the network of constraint priorities works out.

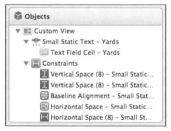

FIGURE 20.3   Selecting the Yards label in the game view displays six constraints that apply to it. Clicking a constraint highlights it and the two views to which it applies; the constraints on both views are shown. If you type the name or content of a view into the search field at the bottom of the document outline, you can see the full set of constraints that apply to that view.

Like anything else in a XIB, constraints have attributes you can edit in the Attributes inspector. For alignment constraints, there is only a slider, setting the priority of the constraint. Priorities start out at 1000, the maximum. As you drag the slider up and down the scale, a popover appears, explaining how the selected priority measures up against intrinsic constraints like views' desire to be large enough to show all their contents, or the user's desired size for a window.

> **NOTE**
>
> Adding priorities to your constraint model makes it infinitely more complex. Apple advises that you not change your priorities from 1000 unless you *really* need to.

Constraints that have values, like widths or spacing between views, can be set as minima, maxima, or exact values. If the constraint isn't exact, it is shown in the canvas with a badge. See Figure 20.4. But give some thought to whether you need to constrain a size. The case you're probably thinking of is to ensure that a view is never too narrow for its content. That constraint is *already there*—an important part of autolayout is that views "know" what size they have to be to display their content. If they are pushed to be smaller, they will push back, possibly preventing the enclosing window from being resized too small. Remember: Whereas autoresizing propagates *down* so that a superview stretches and compresses its subviews, autolayout propagates *up*.

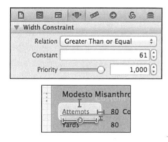

FIGURE 20.4   A constraint like a width or offset, which has a numeric value, can set the value as a minimum, maximum, or exact quantity. Setting a **Relation** of **Greater Than or Equal** labels the constraint graphic with a ≥ badge.

As you browse through the labels, you see that the grooming before converting to auto-layout paid off. The constraints mirror the autoresizing struts: What is on the left is bound to the left edge, and on the right, the right. It's good that this worked out because once Xcode establishes an automatic constraint, you can't just select it and press Delete. You can break it by moving or resizing the view; then the constraint becomes a *user* constraint (shown with a thicker line on the canvas and with a darker icon in the outline sidebar), which you can edit or delete as you desire. But if you delete a constraint that just happens to coincide with what would be an automatic one, the automatic constraint comes back.

You'll have to fish around to get the resizing behavior you need; the dependencies are a net, not a tree. Here is the simplest arrangement that worked for me.

Vertical Spacing

Arranging the view vertically is simple: There is no need to respond to resizing vertically; it's okay if it's impossible. You create new constraints with the **Align** and **Pin** submenus of the **Editor** menu.

▶ For the date, pin the top spacing to the superview.

▶ For each pair of labels along the left edge, pin the vertical spacing between them.

▶ For each label/number pair, Xcode automatically aligns the baselines.

▶ Align the baselines of the Attempts number and the Yards label.

▶ Align the baselines of the Touchdowns and Interceptions labels.

▶ Pin the bottom spacing of Touchdowns to the superview.

In other words, the labels on the left form a rigid stack, and they pull everything to their right along with them. Try resizing the view in IB: You can't make it taller or shorter. This isn't a matter of the view having a fixed vertical size of its own; its rigidity is a consequence of the constraints on the views inside.

> **NOTE**
>
> When you select labels for pinning and alignment, be careful to select the views and not the *cells* they contain. A selected view has resizing handles on the edges; if you click once more, IB grays out the canvas and highlights the label to show that the cell is selected. The **Align** and **Pin** menus are inactive.

Horizontal Spacing

Distributing the labels horizontally is trickier. In the Attempts—80—Completions—80 row in the lower part of the view, you have four labels, which have to observe buffers between each other, and must align with the labels above and below them. This makes for a lot of constraints, and you need to build them carefully to keep them to an understandable number.

> **NOTE**
>
> If you're not working with Interface Builder as you read this, try to follow along with the layouts shown in Figures 20.2 or 20.5.

20

▶ The date label is the only one that spans the whole view, and it sets the keynote for everything below. Adjust its width and placement so that it triggers the standard Aqua spacing from the left and right edges. If IB doesn't cooperate, use the **Pin** menu to pin the leading and trailing space to the superview, and use the Attributes inspector to select **Standard** spacing.

▸ The left (leading) edges of the labels on the left side are pinned automatically to the superview. (Move them left or right if that isn't so.) That's fine.

▸ Go down the labels on the right edge of the view (date and numbers), selecting each pair and aligning the right (trailing) edges. They will be positioned to match the trailing-space pin you put on the date label. In other words, the horizontal position propagates from that of the data label.

▸ For the upper team name (Huntington Beach Harriers), align its right edge (position) with the other team name (Modesto Misanthropes), and pin the horizontal space (width) with the team's score.

▸ The second team name picks up its width from its alignment with the first.

▸ IB automatically pins the widths of the scores and of some of the other numeric labels.

▸ Attempts, Yards, Touchdowns, Completions, and Interceptions labels should have fixed horizontal spacing (position) with their respective numeric labels.

▸ The numbers for Attempts, Yards, and Touchdowns in the left stack should be left-aligned (positions) by selecting the adjacent pairs and issuing **Editor→Align→Left Edges** (⌘[).

▸ The numbers for Attempts and Touchdowns (on the left edge) should be pinned to a standard horizontal spacing (relative position) with the labels to their right (Completions and Interceptions). This should come automatically; move or resize those labels to trigger the automatic spacing if you need to.

▸ Make sure the Yards number is properly positioned (it doesn't have a label to the right to hang onto), by aligning right edges with the Touchdowns number below it.

> **NOTE**
>
> The **Align** submenu shows **Left Edges** and **Right Edges**, but if the views involved are labels or text fields, the document outline will call them Leading or Trailing alignments. This is because autolayout is sensitive to whether the current language runs left-to-right or right-to-left.

That's a lot. The search field at the bottom of the outline sidebar makes it a bit easier: Entering the name or content of a view filters the outline to that view and its associated constraints. Entering the type of the constraint (such as `leading`) filters down to constraints of that type.

> **NOTE**
>
> You can also see all the constraints associated with a view by selecting the view with the jump bar; the constraints appear in a submenu.

But here's where your work starts to pay off: Try resizing the overall view so that it is narrower. Autolayout lets you get down to a size that won't truncate or overlap the text in any of the labels, but it stops you there. The effect is less dramatic if you widen the view: Everything stays in alignment, but the space between the labels and numbers in the left column grows, and the right column doesn't grow to match. This can be debugged, but it's good enough.

Make the view as small as you can esthetically tolerate, and save the English GameViewController.xib. Now return to the Terminal; you can generate a new Canadian-French XIB from the English one. Make sure the working directory is the source directory for Mac Passer Rating (ls and verify that the .lproj directories are visible), and type

```
ibtool --import-strings-file fr-CA.lproj/GameViewController.strings \
    --write fr-CA.lproj/GameViewController.xib \
    en.lproj/GameViewController.xib
```

Return to Xcode, and switch to the Canadian-French version of GameViewController.xib. (The jump bar is handy for switching localizations.) You find that the view has been redistributed to accommodate the new strings, thanks to autolayout's priority on sizing views to accommodate their natural content. See Figure 20.5.

FIGURE 20.5   With constraints correctly set in the English version of GameViewController.xib, all that is needed to produce a properly laid-out Canadian-French version is to import the translated .strings file and let autolayout do the rest.

It might seem like less work just to redo the layout by hand, but your first draft of a view will probably not be your last. If you stick to manual layout, changing the content of a XIB requires a messy merging operation into the localized ones, as well as a manual layout session with each localization. Autolayout lets you edit one XIB, and create the localized XIBs from scratch, confident that the layout will be done for you.

Autolayout is not merely a feature of IB; its principal use is in AppKit at runtime. Run the English localization of Mac Passer Rating, select a game, and take note of the compact presentation of the popover. Now select a team name in the source list, and change the name to something lengthy. Click a game for that team. Autolayout redoes the popover view to accommodate the longer name. See Figure 20.6.

20

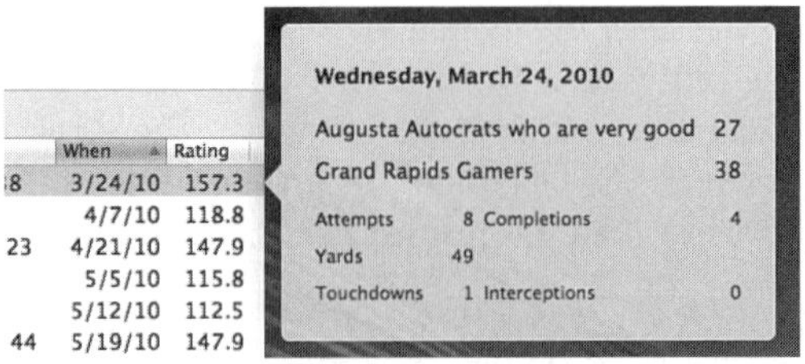

FIGURE 20.6   Autolayout resizes and realigns the popover view to accommodate a long team name at runtime. The layout of the table at the bottom may not be ideal but can be tuned by judicious use of constraint priorities.

> **NOTE**
>
> The layout scheme isn't ideal—Figure 20.6 shows that making a team name long results in a lopsided table in the lower part of the view. With a bit more work, and Apple's programmatic debugging tools (including the Cocoa Layout instrument), you can produce a layout that looks a lot better. You can find detailed techniques in the Documentation organizer in the *Cocoa Autolayout Release Notes*, which may be folded into a programming guide by the time you read this.

Localizing `Info.plist`

You saw earlier that localizing `MainMenu.xib` didn't take care of the application menu (**Mac Passer Rating**). There are other gaps, as well: The automatically generated About box contains the English application name and copyright notice; if you viewed MPR's icon on a French localization of the Finder, it would have the English name, and its documents would be labeled League Document.

All these strings come from `Info.plist`, which I cover in Chapter 21 and Chapter 23. There must be only one `Info.plist` in a bundle directory (such as an `.app` bundle), but you can change how its contents are presented through a `.strings` file in the `.lproj` directory corresponding to the user's locale. Unlike the `.strings` files you saw earlier in this chapter, these are not merely intermediate files; they are meant to be incorporated into the application.

The Cocoa Application project template starts you with the English version of the localization file, `InfoPlist.strings`. The file starts out empty, which is fine for applications running in the development region (usually `en` but settable by the `Info.plist` key `CFBundleDevelopmentRegion`). For localization, you select `InfoPlist.strings`, add the localized version you want, and edit the file.

The file has the same format as the intermediate `.strings` files you saw earlier in this chapter. There are two kinds of keys to identify the strings to be localized: If you want to set a value corresponding one to one with an `Info.plist` key, use that key as the key for the translation. Otherwise, use the string that appears in the base `Info.plist`.

To do what Mac Passer Rating needs, this is all `fr-CA/InfoPlist.strings` need contain (some lengthy strings are elided):

```
/* One-to-one values for Info.plist keys */
"NSHumanReadableCopyright" = "Copyright   ...   Toutes droits reservées.";
"CFBundleDisplayName" = "Quart-Efficacité";
"CFBundleName" = "Quart-Efficacité";
/* The file-type string is inside an array, and a single plist key
   doesn't correspond to it. Use the untranslated value as the key: */
"League File" = "Fichier de Ligue";
```

> **NOTE**
>
> CFBundleDisplayName isn't in the `Info.plist` precursor for new projects. If a key does not appear in `Info.plist`, the system won't bother trying to localize it. For the translated app name to be displayed, you have to add the key to `Mac Passer Rating-Info.plist`, with the value **Mac Passer Rating**.

Testing the `Info.plist` localization comes in two parts. The first is easy: Run Mac Passer Rating, and verify that the application menu and About box are as you expect.

Finder behavior is trickier because you have to set your preferred language in the **Language & Text** panel of System Preferences, and then relaunch the Finder so it pulls the localized strings. System Preferences tells you to log out and log back in to see the results of the change. There's another way: Press ⌥⌘**Escape**, select **Finder**, and click **Relaunch**. Finder reappears in your selected language.

> **NOTE**
>
> While you're in **Language & Text**, visit the **Formats** tab to be sure that the **Region:** matches the language you chose. The switch should be done automatically, but if you created a custom format set, it will stick. If it does, you won't see localized date and time formats in your applications.

If all went well with the `InfoPlist.strings` modification, Finder should present Mac Passer Rating as Quart-Efficacité. See Figure 20.7.

FIGURE 20.7   When displayed in a Canadian-French Finder, Mac Passer Rating should display as Quart-Efficacité.

Strings in Code

What you've done so far completes the localization of Mac Passer Rating (Figure 20.8). You've been fortunate because the application keeps all its user-visible content in localizable resources. Not every app is so fortunate; some user-visible strings may be embedded in code. This is especially the case with alerts and other constructs that need strings formatted on-the-fly. Let's make a ridiculous change that illustrates the problem and its solution.

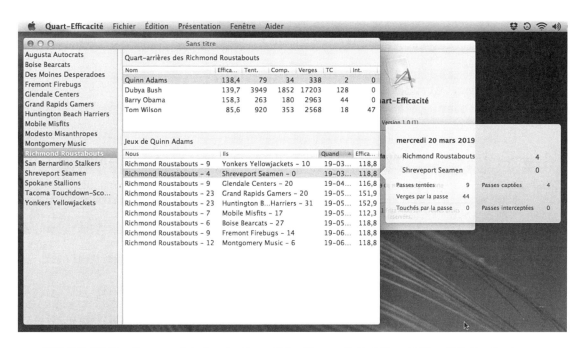

FIGURE 20.8   The complete localization of Mac Passer Rating (Quart-Efficacité). It reflects the XIB translations, the changed layout of `GameViewController.xib`, and the `InfoPlist.strings` file. Because the app always used the standard formatters, numeric and date formats were translated automatically.

Most of the team names in the `sample-data.csv` file are alliterative—the team's name begins with the same letter as the city it represents. You conceive the prejudice that *all* team names should be like this, and any attempt to edit a name that violates the rule should be refused.

The restriction goes into the setter for `teamName` in `Team.m`:

```objc
- (void) setTeamName: (NSString *) newTeamName
{
    NSArray *   words =   [newTeamName componentsSeparatedByString: @" "];
    NSString *  firstOfTeam = [[words lastObject] substringToIndex: 1];
    NSString *  firstOfCity = [newTeamName substringToIndex: 1];
    if (! [firstOfCity isEqualToString: firstOfTeam]) {
        NSAlert *  alert =
            [NSAlert alertWithMessageText: @"Illegal team name"
                           defaultButton: nil // Autolocalized
                         alternateButton: nil otherButton: nil
                 informativeTextWithFormat:
            @"\"%@\" must be the first letter of the team name, not \"%@\""
            firstOfCity, firstOfTeam];
        alert.alertStyle = NSCriticalAlertStyle;
```

20

```
    [alert runModal];
    return;
  }
  [self willChangeValueForKey: @"teamName"];
  [self setPrimitiveTeamName: newTeamName];
  [self didChangeValueForKey: @"teamName"];
}
```

CAUTION

Remove this method if you intend to keep using Mac Passer Rating. The sample data contains team names that violate the constraint, and attempting to add it to a document gets you nothing but hundreds of alerts.

Sure enough, if the Modesto Misanthropes move to Carmel and want to keep their team name, Mac Passer Rating objects. In English. Every time. See Figure 20.9.

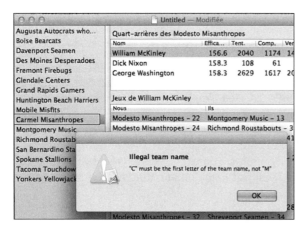

FIGURE 20.9   Setting alert text in code means you get the same text no matter what the locale is.

A bundle, including an application bundle, can have .strings files of its own. In Cocoa, the NSBundle method localizedStringForKey:value:table: returns the string, from the named .strings table, for the best current locale for a given key. The value: parameter is a default in case no value is found in a .strings file.

Most commonly, the localizedStringForKey:value:table: method is wrapped in one of a family of macros. These macros have two advantages. First, they provide convenient defaults for the bundle—the application main bundle—and the table file (Localizable.strings). Second, the genstrings command-line utility can scan source code for these macros and generate .strings files automatically.

The simplest macro is NSLocalizedString, which takes a key string to identify the string and a comment string to clarify, in a comment in the .strings file, the purpose of the string. The NSAlert setup then becomes

```
NSAlert *     alert =
    [NSAlert alertWithMessageText:
     NSLocalizedString(@"Illegal team name",
                   @"alert title for non-aliterative team name")
              defaultButton: nil    // Autolocalized
            alternateButton: nil otherButton: nil

      informativeTextWithFormat:
     NSLocalizedString(@"\"%@\" must be the first letter of the "
                   team name,   not \"%@\"",
                @"alert format for non-aliterative team name"),
      firstOfCity, firstOfTeam];
```

Without a localization, this code behaves the same as before. There must be a .strings file to back it up. genstrings gets you started. In the Terminal, set the current working directory to the directory containing the Mac Passer Rating Source, and issue:

```
$ genstrings *.m
$ # Put it in en.lproj before you add it to the project:
$ mv Localizable.strings en.lproj/
```

This produces a file, Localizable.strings, in the same directory. It summarizes the strings you marked for localization. Make sure it's in en.lproj, and add it to your project; then add the French-Canada localization. Here's the entry for the alert title; the informative text is too long to fit this page:

```
/* alert title for non-aliterative team name */
"Illegal team name" = "Illegal team name";
```

The key and value are for the default string you specified; the comment appears before them. The same pair, in French, would be

```
/* alert title for non-aliterative team name */
"Illegal team name" = "Nom de l'equipe interdit";
```

genstrings has done something strange to the format string for the alert's informative string. The %@ format specifiers have been replaced by %1$@ and %2$@. Why is this? Different languages don't have the same word ordering. What works in English may be infelicitous or ungrammatical in another language. The number n in a specifier says that the nth value in the arguments is to be used at that position, regardless of where the specifier appears in the format string. As an example that is probably infelicitous itself, the format string could be parenthesize:

```
/* alert format for non-aliterative team name */
"\"%@\" must be the first letter of the team name,  not \"%@\""
    = "... ne doit pas être \"%2$@\",  il faut être \"%1$@\".";
```

Running Mac Passer Rating again, and attempting an illegal rename, now shows a localized alert. See Figure 20.10.

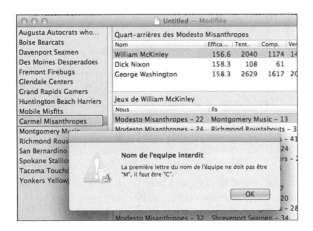

FIGURE 20.10   Adding a `Localizable.strings` file to `fr-CA.lproj` and translating the strings marked as localizable in source code produces a localized alert panel.

Summary

In this chapter, I gave you an overview of the tasks that go into localizing a Mac application; the same techniques, except for autolayout, apply to iOS. The developer tools assist in the task, but Xcode's support is incomplete and a bit touchy. You saw how to add a localization to a file that the application template put into the default `en.lproj` directory, as well as the importance of making sure your localizable files start out in an `.lproj` file before you add a localization.

You went through converting a XIB to Lion autolayout, which is hard work to get right, but when it's done, AppKit eliminates most of the work of keeping your localizations up to date even if you make radical changes to your master UI.

I went on to techniques for translating menus (easy) and UI layouts (a little harder). Then came techniques that require embedding `.strings` files in the application—`InfoPlist.strings` for Finder strings, and `Localizable.strings` for strings that would otherwise be hard-coded in your source.

And I covered how to test your localization at runtime and in the Finder.

CHAPTER 21

Bundles and Packages

Many of Xcode's products take the form of *packages*, directory trees that the Finder presents as single files. Let's pause now to consider the problem of resources. Resources are the sorts of data that are integral to an application, but for one reason or another aren't suitable to incorporate into source code: strings, lookup tables, images, human-interface layouts, sounds, and the like.

In the original Mac OS, applications kept resources in *resource forks*, mini-databases kept in parallel with the data stream you normally think of as a file. The problem with the Resource Manager was that it did not scale well to sets of many, large, or changeable resources. The catalog written into each resource file was fragile, and any corruption resulted in the loss of every resource in the file. With the multiplicity of large resources—images, sounds, human-interface layouts, and lookup tables—needed to support modern applications, the tasks involved in managing them became indistinguishable from the tasks of a file system. File systems are a solved problem; they do their work as efficiently and robustly as decades of experience can make them. Why not use the file system for storing and retrieving resources?

One reason to avoid shipping application resources as separate files is that an application that relies on them becomes a swarm of files and directories, all critical to the correct working of the application, and all exposed to relocation, deletion, and general abuse by the application's user. Meanwhile, the user, who simply wants one thing that does the application's work, is presented with a swarm of files and directories.

Mac OS X provides a way to have the flexibility of separating resources into their own files while steering clear of the swarming problem. The Finder can treat directories, called *packages*, as though they were single documents.

A Simple Package: RTFD

A package can be as simple as a directory with a handful of files in it. The application that creates and reads the package determines how it is structured: what files are required, the names of the content files, what sort of subdirectory structure is used.

A common example of an application-defined package is the RTFD, or rich text file directory. The Apple-supplied application TextEdit, in its Info.plist file, specifies what kinds of documents TextEdit can handle; among these is NSRTFDPboardType, which is listed as having extension .rtfd and is designated as a package file type. When it catalogs TextEdit, the Finder notes that directories with the rtfd extension are supposed to be packages and treats them as if they were single files, not ordinarily displaying the files within.

It is sometimes useful to look inside a package, however, and the Finder provides a way to do that. Right-clicking a package file produces a pop-up menu containing the command **Show Package Contents** (see Figure 21.1). Selecting that command opens a new window showing the contents of the package directory, which can be further navigated as in a normal Finder window.

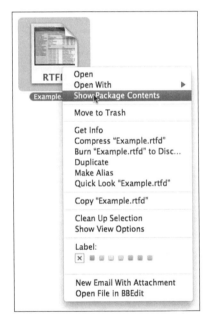 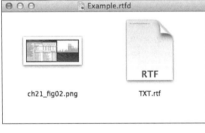

FIGURE 21.1   (left) Right-clicking a package document in the Finder presents a menu that includes the command **Show Package Contents**, which (right) shows the files within the package.

In the case of RTFD, the package directory contains one plain RTF file, TXT.rtf. The RTF file incorporates custom markup, such as:

```
This is the icon for an Xcode project:
    {{\NeXTGraphic Project.tiff \width400 \height400
}
```

Here, the markup refers to a graphics file—in this case, `Project.tiff`—that is also in the RTFD directory.

NOTE

Cocoa's AppKit application framework provides support for package-directory documents. NSDocument subclasses handle package reading and writing by overriding `readFromFileWrapper:ofType:error:` and `fileWrapperOfType:error:`. The NSFileWrapper class provides methods that assist in creating and managing complex file packages.

Bundles

A *bundle* is a particular kind of *structured* directory tree. Often, bundles ship as packages—the most familiar type of bundle, the application, is an example—but the concepts are separate. A directory can be a bundle without being a package, a package without being a bundle, or it can be both. Table 21.1 shows examples.

TABLE 21.1   Examples of Directories That are Bundles or Packages or Both

	Not Bundle	**Bundle**
Not Package	Other directories	Frameworks
Package	Complex documents	Applications

Mac OS X has two kinds of bundles: *versioned bundles*, which are used for frameworks—structured packages of dynamic libraries, headers, and the resource files that support them (see Chapter 22, "Frameworks")—and *modern bundles*, which are used for applications and most other executable products.

At the minimum, a modern Mac bundle encloses one directory, named `Contents`, which in turn contains all the directories and files comprising the bundle. The `Contents` directory contains an `Info.plist` file, which specifies how the bundle appears in the Finder and, depending on the type of the bundle, may provide configuration data for loading and running the bundle's contents. Beyond that, what the `Contents` folder contains depends on the type of the bundle.

Application Bundles

Mac OS X applications are the most common type of bundle (see Figure 21.2). An application directory has a name with the suffix `.app`. The `.app` directory is a file package; even though it is a directory, the Finder treats it as a single entity. This allows the author of the application to place auxiliary files for the application in a known place—inside the application bundle—with little fear that such files will be misplaced or deleted.

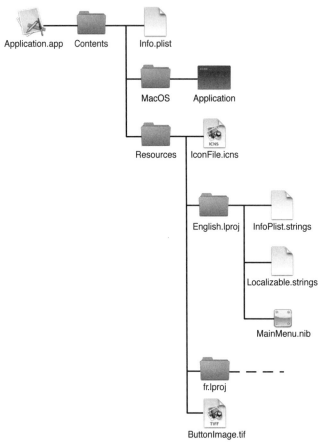

FIGURE 21.2   The structure of a typical application bundle. The executable file is at Contents/MacOS/Application. The application's human interface for English-speaking users is specified in Contents/Resources/English.lproj/MainMenu.nib; presumably, a French version of MainMenu.nib is inside Contents/Resources/fr.lproj. The custom image for a button, ButtonImage.tif, is common to all languages and therefore appears in the Resources directory.

The Contents directory of a Mac OS X application bundle most commonly contains

▶ Info.plist, an XML property list file that describes such application details as the principal class, the document types handled, and the application version. More on this file in the next section.

▶ Resources, a directory containing the application icon file, images, sounds, human interface layouts, and other parameterized content for the application. This directory may be further organized into subdirectories, according to your convenience.

In addition, there may be localization subdirectories, which have the `.lproj` suffix. When an application seeks a resource, the Cocoa or Core Foundation bundle managers looks first in the `.lproj` directory that corresponds to the current language and locale.

▶ `MacOS`, a directory containing the executable binary for the application, along with any other executables.

▶ `Frameworks`, a directory of frameworks that are versioned bundles, containing a dynamic library, resources needed by the library, and header files needed by users of the library. An application typically includes a framework because it links to the framework's library.

> **NOTE**
>
> What about iOS apps? They're packages—the Finder treats them as unitary files—but not bundles. All the files—binary and resources—are contained directly in the .app directory.

The `Info.plist` File

The `Info.plist` file, found in the `Contents` directory of any modern bundle and in the `Resources` directory of frameworks, is the locus of much of the information Mac OS X and iOS need to make sense of a bundle. This file provides icon and naming information to the Finder/Home screen, flags and environment variables to Launch Services, names of "default" screen images in various sizes and orientations for iOS apps, and specifications for the basic structure of applications and plug-ins. It's a property list (`.plist`) dictionary file, a format covered in Chapter 23, "Property Lists."

The Target editor's **Summary** and **Info** tabs form a specialized editor for the target's `Info.plist`. They give you at least a first cut at the settings you need without much trouble.

You can also edit the `Info.plist` file directly, using the Property List editor (see Chapter 23). Sort of. Actually, the file you edit is not named `Info.plist`. If you work on a target named `PasserRating`, the name will be `PasserRating-Info.plist`. There are two reasons. First, you may have two or more targets producing bundles that need their own `Info.plist`s; the different files need different sources with names that identify their use.

Second, the real `Info.plist` for a product won't exist until it is installed at build time. What you see is a source file that Xcode processes to generate the final property list. It's this processing phase that enables you to use build-variable references instead of literal values for some of the keys. The handling of the target-specific `Info.plist`s is special: They are *not* to be included in any build phase of your target—that just copies the unprocessed source file into the application's `Resources` directory. Instead, the name of the file is specified in the `INFOPLIST_FILE` build variable. The build system picks it up from there.

> **NOTE**
>
> A number of build settings control processing of `Info.plist`. Check the Packaging section of the **Build Settings** tab of the Target editor. Among them are the option to use C-style preprocessor directives in the source file. Unfortunately, when you use them, you are committed to editing the file as XML text because the Property List editor destroys all content that isn't property-list XML.

Localizing `Info.plist`

Some `Info.plist` properties are localizable. A file named `InfoPlist.strings` should be in the `.lproj` directory for each localization of your application. Localizable keys can then be assigned per-locale values. For instance, `InfoPlist.strings` in the `English.lproj` directory might include the pair

```
CFBundleName = "PasserRating";
CFBundleDisplayName = "Passer Rating";
```

The same file in the `fr.lproj` directory might include

```
CFBundleName = "Q-Effic";
CFBundleDisplayName = "Quart-Efficacité";
```

For users whose language preferences place French above English, the Mac Passer Rating icon will be labeled `Quart-Efficacité`. The name of the bundle directory, however, will still be `PasserRating.app`, even if the casual user doesn't see it.

The Xcode Property List editor customizes itself for `Info.plist`s. When the name of a file ends in `Info.plist`, it fills the dictionary key column with pop-up menus offering the keys peculiar to that kind of property list. This means that you should avoid using Xcode to edit property lists whose names end that way (like the `DirectoryInfo.plist` file you might set up for some names and addresses) but aren't actual `Info.plist`s.

`Info.plist` Keys

Here are the most frequently used keys for `Info.plist`. The dictionary keys are itemized, followed by the plain-English labels used by the Property List editor. Many of these are specific to Mac OS X, some to iOS, and some are shared.

Keys for All Bundles

The keys in this section apply to almost any kind of bundle, including applications.

▶ **Structure**

  ▶ `CFBundleExecutable` (Executable file) **also iOS**, the name of the executable file, which may be an application binary, a library, or plug-in code. It corresponds to the `EXECUTABLE_NAME` build setting; use `$(EXECUTABLE_NAME)` in the target's **Properties** tab to ensure this key is always properly set. A bundle that mismatches this entry with the actual name of the executable file will not run. Applications must specify this key.

▶ CFBundleIdentifier (Bundle identifier) **also iOS**, a unique identifier string for the bundle, in the form of a Java-style reverse domain package name, such as `com.wt9t.Passer-Rating`. Xcode initializes this to the company ID you supplied when you chose the project template, followed by `$(PRODUCT_NAME:rfc1034identifier)`, and you can expect to leave it alone. All bundles must specify this key.

▶ CFBundleInfoDictionaryVersion (InfoDictionary version) **also iOS**, a compatibility-check version number for the `Info.plist` format. Xcode injects this version number automatically when it builds bundles. I've never seen a version number other than 6.0. All `Info.plist` files should include this key.

▶ CFBundlePackageType (Bundle OS Type code) **optional on iOS**, the four-character type code for the bundle. Applications are type APPL, frameworks are FMWK, plug-ins are BNDL or a code of your choosing. See also CFBundleSignature. Mac OS X applications must specify this key.

▶ CFBundleSignature (Bundle creator OS Type code) **optional on iOS**, the four-character creator code associated with the bundle. Mac OS X applications must specify this key, but it's rare for it to be anything other than ????.

▶ **User Information**

  ▶ CFBundleGetInfoString (Get Info string) **also iOS**, a string that supplements the version information supplied by CFBundleShortVersionString and CFBundleVersion. Formerly, this key was used for copyright strings, but that is now handled by NSHumanReadableCopyright.

  ▶ CFBundleIconFile (Icon file) **also iOS**, the name of the file in the Resources directory that contains the bundle's custom icon, a file in `.icns` format for Mac, `.png` for iOS. You can omit the extension. An icns file contains images and masks at various scales to assure a good appearance at all sizes. Build one with the Icon Composer application from the **Xcode→Open Developer Tool** menu.

  ▶ CFBundleShortVersionString (Bundle versions string, short) **also iOS**, a short string with the product version, such as **4.3.4**, of the bundle, suitable for display in an About box or by the App Store. See also CFBundleGetInfoString. This key may be localized in `InfoPlist.strings`. Applications must specify this key.

  ▶ CFBundleVersion (Bundle version) **also iOS**, the build version of the bundle's executable, which may identify versions within a release cycle, such as betas: **2.1b3**, for instance. This may also be a single number, corresponding to a build number within the life of the bundle. The build version displays in parentheses in the About box. See also CFBundleShortVersionString.

▶ **Localization**

    ▶ CFBundleDevelopmentRegion (Localization native development region) **also iOS**, the native human language, and variant thereof, of the bundle, like fr-CA for Canadian-French. If the user's preferred language is not available as a localization, this is the language that will be used.

Keys for iOS and Mac OS X Applications

▶ **Structure**

    ▶ NSPrincipalClass (Principal class), the name of the bundle's main class. In a Mac OS X application, this would normally be NSApplication; in iOS, UIApplication.

    ▶ NSMainNibFile (Main nib file base name), the base (no extension) name of the application's main NIB file, almost always MainMenu on Mac OS X and MainWindow on iOS (when a main NIB is used). Use NSMainNibFile-ipad (Main nib file base name [iPad]) to specify a separate NIB for your app when it's launched on an iPad.

    ▶ UIMainStoryboardFile, the base name of the storyboard package that is the root of the application. Use this or NSMainNibFile, but never both.

▶ **User Information**

    ▶ CFBundleDisplayName (Bundle display name) the name for the Finder or Home screen to display for this bundle. The value in Info.plist should be identical to the name of the application bundle; localized names can then be put in InfoPlist.strings files for various languages. The OS displays the localized name *only* if the name of the application package in the file system matches the value of this key. That way, if a Mac user renames your application, the name he intended, and not the localized name, displays. Project templates initialize this key to ${PRODUCT_NAME}. See also CFBundleName. Applications must specify this key.

    ▶ CFBundleName (Bundle name), the short—16-character maximum—name for the application, to be shown in the About box and the Application menu. See also CFBundleDisplayName. This key may be localized in InfoPlist.strings; Xcode initializes it to ${PRODUCT_NAME}. Applications must specify this key.

▶ **Documents and URLs**

    ▶ CFBundleDocumentTypes (Document types), an array of dictionaries specifying every document type associated with the application. Use the Info tab of the Target editor for the application target to edit these; you'll save yourself some headaches.

▶ CFBundleURLTypes (URL types), an array of dictionaries defining URL schemes, such as http, ftp, or x-com-wt9t-custom-scheme, for which the application is a handler. Use common schemes *sparingly*; if your product is a web browser, you support http, but if you just happen to pull some resources from an HTTP server, don't advertise yourself to the whole system as being able to service HTTP URLs. It's much more useful in iOS, where your application's custom scheme can provide a handy interapplication communications method for other applications, email, and the Web. See Apple's documentation, and the **Info** tab of the Target editor for details.

▶ UTExportedTypeDeclarations (Exported Type UTIs), an array of dictionaries that describe the types of documents your application can write, and which you want Launch Services to know about. The entries center on declaring a UTI and the chain of UTIs the principal UTI conforms to. This key is used by Spotlight to build its list of document types. UTIs take precedence over the declarations in CFBundleDocumentTypes as of Mac OS X 10.5. Again, it's easier to manage this list through the **Info** tab of the Target editor. See Apple's documentation for the format of the dictionaries.

▶ UTImportedTypeDeclarations (Imported Type UTIs), an array of dictionaries that describe the types of documents your application can *read*, and which you want Launch Services to know about. The entries are in the same format as those used in UTExportedTypeDeclarations. The **Info** tab of the Target editor provides an easy editor for this.

▶ **Localization**

  ▶ LSHasLocalizedDisplayName (Application has localized display name), the hint, if <true/> or nonzero, to the Finder that this application has localized versions of its display name (CFBundleDisplayName). Applications must specify this key.

  ▶ CFBundleLocalizations, an array populated with codes (like en or fr-CA) for languages in an application that handles localization programmatically instead of through localized resources.

Keys for Mac OS X Applications

These keys apply only to Mac OS X applications and cover launch configurations, help facilities, and information on the documents and URLs the application handles. The Info.plist structure antedates Mac OS X, so many keys have fallen into obsolescence, but the OS has to support them for backward compatibility. The template you instantiate for a new application target gives you everything you need to start, and the **Info** tab can help you with *almost* everything you'd ever need to fit what you want to do, but there's no substitute for following the OS release notes.

▶ **Structure**

 ▶ CSResourcesFileMapped (Resources should be file-mapped), if YES or <true/>, Core Foundation will memory-map the bundle resources rather than read the files into memory.

 ▶ ATSApplicationFontsPath (Application fonts resource path), a string. If your application contains fonts for its own use, it contains the path, relative to the application's Resources directory, to the directory containing the fonts.

▶ **User Information**

 ▶ NSHumanReadableCopyright (Copyright [human-readable]), a copyright string suitable for display in an About box. This key may be localized in InfoPlist.strings. Applications must specify this key.

 ▶ LSApplicationCategoryType (Application Category). This is a string containing an Apple-defined UTI that describes for the Mac App Store what kind of application this is—Business, Lifestyle, Video, and so on. Ordinarily, you'd set this in the Summary tab of the application's Target editor, so you don't have to bother with the UTIs. When you submit your app through iTunes Connect, you will be allowed two categories for your listing; make sure the primary one is the same as your LSApplicationCategoryType.

▶ **Help**

 ▶ CFAppleHelpAnchor (Help file), the base name, without extension, of the initial help file for the application.

 ▶ CFBundleHelpBookFolder (Help Book directory name), the folder—in either the Resources subdirectory or a localization subdirectory—containing the application's help book.

 ▶ CFBundleHelpBookName (Help Book identifier), the name of the application's help book. This name should match the name set in a <meta> tag in the help book's root file.

▶ **Launch Behavior:** These keys control how Launch Services launches and configures a Mac application. iOS has a "Launch Services" framework, but there is no public interface for it.

 ▶ LSArchitecturePriority (Architecture priority), an array of strings (for example, i386, ppc64, and x86_64) indicating what architectures the application can run under. The order is significant: Launch services will use the first architecture on the list—native or emulated—that the machine supports. The user can override this in the Get Info window in the Finder.

▶ LSBackgroundOnly (Application is background only), if it's the string 1, the application will be run in the background only and will not be visible to the user.

▶ LSEnvironment (Environment variables), a dictionary, the keys of which are environment-variable names, defining environment variables to be passed to the application upon launch.

▶ LSExecutableArchitectures, an array of strings (for example, i386, ppc, ppc64, and x86_64) indicating what architectures the application can run under.

▶ LSGetAppDiedEvents (Application should get App Died events), indicates, if YES or <true/>, the application gets the kAEApplicationDied Apple event when any of its child processes terminate.

▶ NSSupportsSuddenTermination (Application can be killed immediately after launch). When you log out, restart, or shut down, Mac OS X takes care that all running applications will be given the chance to clean up, ask the user to save files, and so on. If this key is <true/>, the system can shut your application down with a BSD kill signal instead. You can still use NSProcessInfo methods to restore the ask-first policy (such as when you are in the middle of writing a file), but the kill policy makes shutdowns much quicker.

▶ LSMinimumSystemVersion (Minimum system version), a string in the form 10.x.x, specifying the earliest version of Mac OS X or iOS this application runs under. If the current OS is earlier (back through 10.4), Mac OS X will post an alert explaining that the app could not be run.

▶ LSMinimumSystemVersionByArchitecture (Minimum system versions, per-architecture), a dictionary. The possible keys are i386, ppc, ppc64, and x86_64. For each key, the value is a string containing the three-revision version number (for example, 10.6.3) representing the minimum version of Mac OS X the application supports for that architecture. You can use this, for instance, to accept 10.5 for PowerPC execution, while requiring 10.6 for 64-bit Intel.

NOTE

Bear in mind that Xcode 4 can't generate PowerPC applications at all.

▶ LSMultipleInstancesProhibited (Application prohibits multiple instances), indicates, if <true/>, that only one copy of this application can be run at a time. Different users, for instance, could not use the application simultaneously.

▶ LSRequiresNativeExecution (Application requires native environment,) if YES, the application will always run on the native processor architecture of the computer. Overrides the order of LSArchitecturePriority. Use this to prevent your universal application from running under Rosetta (on systems older than Lion).

- ► LSUIElement (Application is agent [UIElement]), if set to the string 1, identifies this application as an *agent application*, a background application that has no presence in the dock but that can present user interface elements, if necessary.

- ► LSUIPresentationMode (Application UI Presentation Mode), an integer between 0 and 4, representing progressively greater amounts of the Mac OS X UI—dock and menu bar—to be hidden when the application runs. See Apple's documentation for details.

- ► **Other Services**

  - ► LSFileQuarantineEnabled (File quarantine enabled): If <true/>, Launch Services will regard the files your application creates as though they had been downloaded from the Internet and warn the user of the possible risk in opening them. You can exempt files from quarantine with LSFileQuarantineExcludedPathPatterns.

  - ► LSFileQuarantineExcludedPathPatterns (no editor equivalent): An array of glob wildcard patterns for files (locations, extensions, and so on) that will be exempt from quarantining even if LSFileQuarantineEnabled is set.

  - ► NSAppleScriptEnabled (Scriptable), indicating that, if YES or <true/>, this application is scriptable. Applications must specify this key.

  - ► OSAScriptingDefinition (Scripting definition filename), the name of the .sdef file, to be found in the application's Resources directory, containing its AppleScript scripting dictionary.

  - ► NSServices (Services), an array of dictionaries declaring the Mac OS X services this application performs, which appear in the **Services** submenu of every application's application menu, subject to the **Keyboard Shortcuts** tab in the **Keyboard** panel of System Preferences. The dictionaries specify the pasteboard input and output formats, the name of the service, and the name of the method that implements the service. See Apple's documentation for details.

  - ► QLThumbnailMinimumSize (Quick Look thumbnail minimum size), the smallest size (in either dimension) you allow for Quick Look thumbnails of your documents. By default, this is 17 pixels.

  - ► QLPreviewHeight (Quick Look preview height), the pixel height Quick Look uses for document previews if your QL plug-in takes too long to render.

  - ► QLPreviewWidth (Quick Look preview width), the pixel width Quick Look uses for document previews if your QL plug-in takes too long to render.

  - ► QLSupportsConcurrentRequests (Quick Look supports concurrent requests), if YES, indicates that your QL plug-in can handle simultaneous requests for thumbnails or previews.

▶ QLNeedsToBeRunInMainThread (Quick Look needs to be run in main thread): Quick Look prefers to get previews and thumbnails generated on a background thread. Set to YES if your plug-in must be run on the main thread.

▶ SMAuthorizedClients (Clients allowed to add and remove tool): An array of strings describing the signing requirements for client applications that may install or remove a privileged tool under the launchd daemon.

▶ SMPrivilegedExecutables (Tools owned after installation): A list of dictionaries describing privileged helper tools for an application, to be installed by the launchd daemon. See Apple's documentation for the uses of launchd.

▶ **Obsolete:** Xcode still offers these keys in the Info.plist and Target **Info** editors, but you'll never use them.

   ▶ LSPrefersCarbon (Application prefers Carbon environment), LSPrefersClassic (Application prefers Classic environment), LSRequiresCarbon (Application requires Carbon environment), LSRequiresClassic (Application requires Classic environment): Carbon is the application framework that Apple provided in Mac OS X 10.0 to enable Mac developers to port their applications from Mac OS 9 relatively conveniently. It has been deprecated as an application framework since Mac OS X 10.5, though the nonapplication API lives on. These flags controlled whether Carbon applications should be launched natively or into the "Classic" environment that emulated Mac OS 9. Classic is long-gone, and Carbon is not for use in new development.

   ▶ LSVisibleInClassic (Application is visible in Classic): If 1, the application would be visible as a background process to applications running in the Classic environment.

   ▶ APFiles (Installation files), APInstallerURL (Installation directory base file URL): These settings seem to have been used up through Jaguar, Mac OS X 10.2. They are so far out of use that Google won't tell me what they do. They appear to relate to a self-installation technology, possibly from before Mac OS X.

   ▶ UIUpgradeOtherBundleIdentifier (Upgrade other bundle identifier): This appeared with iOS 3.2, and nobody outside of Apple seems to know what it does.

   ▶ NSPersistentStoreTypeKey (Core Data persistent store type): This is a key for use in document-type specifications that seems to have escaped into the top-level Info.plist documentation and editors by accident.

▶ NSJavaNeeded (Cocoa Java application), indicating that, if YES or <true/>, the Java VM will be started before loading the bundle. This is needed for Cocoa-Java applications but *not* for 100% Pure Java. Apple dropped support for Cocoa-Java in 2005.

▶ NSJavaPath (Java classpaths), an array of paths to Java class files, either absolute or relative to NSJavaRoot. Xcode maintains this array automatically.

▶ NSJavaRoot (Java root directory), a string containing the path to the root of the Java class tree.

iOS Keys

These tags are unique to iOS applications. *In general*, if you want to customize any Info.plist key for a particular device, create a custom key composed of the base name, followed by a hyphen, then iphoneos, a tilde, and a device specifier (one of iphone, ipod, or ipad). For example: UIStatusBarStyle-iphoneos~ipad. In practice, you can omit the -iphoneos part: UIStatusBarStyle~ipad.

▶ **Structure**

▶ LSRequiresIPhoneOS (Application requires iOS environment), whether Launch Services refuses to launch the application except on an iOS device.

▶ CFBundleIconFiles (Icon files): An array of filenames for the application icons. These are expected to be the same icon in the various sizes needed by different iOS platforms; the system looks through the files to pick the proper one. If you omit the file extensions, the system will find @2x Retina Display variants automatically. Overrides CFBundleIconFile (optional).

▶ UIDeviceFamily, 1 (the default) if the application is for the iPhone and iPad Touch; 2 if it s for the iPad. Or it could be an array containing both. *Don't* set this key yourself; the Xcode build system for iOS inserts it automatically based on your device family setting in the Target editor.

▶ UIAppFonts (Fonts provided by application), an array of paths within the application bundle for application-supplied font files.

▶ UIRequiredDeviceCapabilities (Required device capabilities), an array of strings, such as telephony, wifi, or video-camera, that describe what device features your application absolutely needs to run. This is used by iTunes and the App Store to save users who don't have those features from buying and installing your app.

Pay particular attention to the armv7 requirement: If present, your app will not be offered to devices older than the iPhone 3GS, even if you compile with the ARMv6 architecture. This array contains only armv7 by default.

▶ UIRequiresPersistentWiFi (Application uses WiFi): The Property List editor's summary is a little misleading. Ordinarily (if this key is absent or has the value

NO), iOS will shut down the WiFi connection if you haven't used it for half an hour. If YES, the WiFi transceiver will turn on as soon as your application launches and will stay on as long as it runs.

▸ UISupportedExternalAccessoryProtocols (Supported external accessory protocols), for an array of strings naming all the external-device protocols your application supports. The protocol names are specified by the manufacturers of the accessories.

▸ **User Presentation**

  ▸ UIStatusBarStyle (Status bar style), the style (gray, translucent, or opaque black) of the initial status bar. The names of the styles used in the iOS API are used, the default being UIStatusBarStyleDefault.

  ▸ UIStatusBarHidden (Status bar is initially hidden), if YES, the status bar is hidden when your application is launched. Before coveting those 20 extra pixels, consider whether you want your customers to shut your app down whenever they need to check the time or see if they're running out of power.

  ▸ UIInterfaceOrientation (Initial interface orientation), indicating the screen orientation the application starts up in. Look up enum UIInterfaceOrientation in the UIKit headers for the available values; the Info.plist entries are supposed to be the *names* of those orientations. The default is UIInterfaceOrientationPortrait.

  ▸ UIPrerenderedIcon (Icon already includes gloss and bevel effects), if YES, iOS will not clip your icon to a rounded rect or add a shine effect to it.

  ▸ UISupportedInterfaceOrientations (Supported interface orientations, Supported interface orientations [iPad], and Supported interface orientations [iPhone]), an array naming the orientations your app supports on iOS or iPad. Unless you constrain the choice with UIInterfaceOrientation, iOS will use the orientation that matches this list and the actual orientation of the device.

  ▸ UIViewEdgeAntialiasing (Renders with edge antialiasing): If you draw a Core Animation layer aligned to fractional-pixel coordinates, it normally isn't anti-aliased. You can set this key to YES if you draw that way customarily and want to take the performance hit of making it look nice.

  ▸ UIViewGroupOpacity (Renders with group opacity), if YES, allows Core Animation sublayers to inherit the opacity of their superlayers. Cooler appearance, slower performance.

  ▸ UILaunchImageFile (Launch image) and UILaunchImageFile~ipad (Launch image [iPad]), the name of the file that is shown between the time the user selects your app in the home screen and the time when it can render its content. Prior to iOS 3.2, there was no option but Default.png for the ~ipad variant; this can be a base name for an image file (such as MyLaunchImage.png); based on that, iOS seeks orientation-specific variants by inserting variant strings (such as `MyLaunchImage-Portrait.png` and `MyLaunchImage-Landscape.png`) and looking for those files. See the *iPad Programming Guide* in the Documentation organizer for details on orientation-specific keys.

▶ **Behavior**

- ▶ `UIApplicationExitsOnSuspend` (Application does not run in background): If true, tapping the Home button on the iOS device will shut your app down, rather than put it into the background.

- ▶ `UIBackgroundModes` (Required background modes): iOS typically does not allow backgrounded apps any execution time, beyond a grace period of no more than 10 minutes if they request one. There are exceptions for specific cases such as audio, VoIP, and navigational apps. Provide an array of `audio`, `voip`, or `location` to be treated as such an application. Be prepared to defend your claim in the App Store review process.

- ▶ `UIFileSharingEnabled` (Application supports iTunes file sharing): If `YES`, the contents of the app's `Documents/` directory will be visible while the device is plugged into iTunes. This allows your users to move files between their devices and their computers.

Keys for Plug-ins

These tags provide information on how a Mac OS X plug-in bundle is to be accessed and configured.

- ▶ `CFPlugInDynamicRegistration` (Plug-in should be registered dynamically), indicating that, if `YES` (`<true/>`), the plug-in in this bundle is to be registered dynamically.

- ▶ `CFPlugInDynamicRegisterFunction` (Plug-in dynamic registration function name), the name of the dynamic registration function for this plug-in, if it is not `CFPlugInDynamicRegister`.

- ▶ `CFPlugInFactories` (Plug-in factory interfaces), a dictionary used for static plug-in registration. See Apple's documentation on plug-in registration for more details.

- ▶ `CFPlugInTypes` (Plug-in types), a dictionary identifying groups of entry points for plug-in registration. See Apple's documentation on plug-in registration for more details.

- ▶ `CFPlugInUnloadFunction` (Plug-in unload function name), the name of a function to call when the plug-in in this bundle is to be unloaded from memory.

Keys for Preference Panes

Panes for the Mac OS X System Preferences application specify the icons and labels used in the application's display window with these tags.

▶ NSPrefPaneIconFile (Preference Pane icon file), the name of the image file you provide in Resources as an icon for this preference pane in System Preferences. The picture should be 32 pixels by 32 pixels in size. Lacking this image, the bundle icon will be used.

▶ NSPrefPaneIconLabel (Preference Pane icon label), the name of this preference pane, as shown beneath its icon in System Preferences. You can break the string into lines with the newline (\n) character. Lacking this string, the CFBundleName will be used.

Keys for Dashboard Widgets

Mac OS X Dashboard widgets have their own set of keys, specifying their component files, security model, and basic layout. A widget Info.plist must also contain the keys CFBundleIdentifier, CFBundleName, and CFBundleDisplayName and should include other general-purpose keys, such as CFBundleShortVersionString or CFBundleVersion, as you see fit.

You'll rarely deal with these keys in Xcode; if you develop Dashboard widgets, you will use Dashcode, available to registered (free) developers through connect.apple.com.

▶ **Layout**

  ▶ CloseBoxInsetX, specifies how far right from the leftmost possible position to place the close box.

  ▶ CloseBoxInsetY, specifies how far down from the uppermost possible position to place the close box.

  ▶ Height, the height, in pixels, of the widget.

  ▶ Width, the width, in pixels, of the widget.

▶ **Security**

  ▶ AllowFileAccessOutsideOfWidget, indicating that the widget is permitted to read and write files in the file system outside of the widget bundle itself.

  ▶ AllowFullAccess, indicating that, if <true/>, the widget is given full access to the file system, network assets, command-line utilities, Java applets, and WebKit facilities.

  ▶ AllowInternetPlugins, indicating that, if <true/>, the widget is allowed to use WebKit to access browser plug-ins.

  ▶ AllowJava, indicating that, if <true/>, the widget is allowed to use Java applets.

- ▶ AllowNetworkAccess, indicating that, if <true/>, the widget is allowed to use network or other nonfile-based resources.

- ▶ AllowSystem, indicating that, if <true/>, the widget is allowed to use command-line utilities.

▶ **Structure**

- ▶ Font, an array of strings naming fonts included in the widget bundle. Widget fonts are placed in the root of the bundle, not in a Resources directory.

- ▶ MainHTML, a required key: a path, relative to the bundle's root, to the main HTML (Hypertext Markup Language) file for the widget.

- ▶ Plug-in, the name of a plug-in used by the widget.

Summary

This chapter explored bundles and package directories, important concepts in both Mac OS X and iOS development. Most of Xcode's product types are bundles. We reviewed the structure of simple packages and application bundles and examined the Info.plist file, which communicates a bundle's metadata to the operating system.

CHAPTER 22

Frameworks

In Chapter 19, "A Custom View for Mac OS X," you constructed a bar-graph view that is isolated from the code inside Mac Passer Rating. Yes, its method selectors refer to games, and the drawing code pulls in properties with names such as attempts and completions, but the code doesn't link to any code in the rest of the application.

Once again I'm going to pretend that PasserGraphController and PassCompletionView form a package that I'd want to reuse. We did the same thing with passer_rating in Chapter 6, "Adding a Library Target."

But there's a difference this time: The graph view requires a noncode resource, PasserGraphController.xib, to link the view to its controller and to set drawing parameters. If we were building a classical Objective-C library, we'd be stuck; there's no practical way to put anything but code in a linkable library.

Mac OS X solves this problem with *frameworks*, specialized bundles (see Chapter 21, "Bundles and Packages") that incorporate dynamic libraries, headers, and supporting resource files. You're already a client of a complex set of frameworks, constituting the code and headers for AppKit, Foundation, and Core Data. In this chapter, you'll build a framework of your own.

> **NOTE**
>
> This is a Mac OS X-only chapter. iOS applications are not allowed to include loadable code, so they can't package dynamic libraries, including frameworks. They can include, but not download, script files as long as the interpreter is embedded in the application binary. JavaScript in web pages is downloadable code, but it is sequestered in the UIWebView that downloaded it.

Adding a Framework Target

The first step toward building a framework should be familiar to you: Go to the Project editor for Mac Passer Rating, and click the **Add Target** button at the bottom of the editor. A New Target assistant appears. You want **Mac OS X→Framework & Library→Cocoa Framework**. Click **Next**.

Name the framework **PasserGraph**, accept the existing **Company Identifier**, and check **Use Automatic Reference Counting** but not **Include Unit Tests**. Verify that you'll be adding the target to the Mac Passer Rating project, and click **Finish**.

Xcode adds a new PasserGraph group to the Project navigator. It includes

▶ `PasserGraph.h` and `PasserGraph.m`: Xcode assumes you're starting your framework from scratch, and provides a template for a class for the framework to vend. Select these, press **Delete**, and have Xcode delete the files.

▶ `PasserGraph-Info.plist`: As a bundle, a framework must have an `Info.plist` file. The template fills in everything you need. The Principal Class entry might tempt you, but that's for plug-ins, which get loaded once and instantiate an object to represent the plug-in. PasserGraph is a library and has no gatekeeper object. Leave it blank.

▶ `InfoPlist.strings`: It's empty. Leave it that way.

▶ `PasserGraph-Prefix.pch`: You'll use Core Data in addition to Cocoa. Add

```
#import <CoreData/CoreData.h>
```

to the file.

While you're thinking about Core Data, select `PasserGraph` in the Target editor and the **Build Phases** tab. Open the "Link Binary With Libraries" section, click the + button, and add `CoreData.framework`.

Populating the Framework

As you did in Chapter 6, reallocate some files between the application and framework targets.

1. Select `PasserGraphController.m`, `PassCompletionView.m`, and `PasserGraphController.xib`, and use the File inspector (Utility view) to take them out of the Mac Passer Rating target and put them into PasserGraph.

2. Select `PasserGraphController.h`, and add it to PasserGraph. (As a header, it couldn't be a member of an application target, but it can be part of a framework.) In the pop-up menu next to the target name, select **Public**. This embeds the file in the `Headers` subdirectory of the framework so that any project that uses PasserGraph can have access to `PasserGraphController.h`.

3. Do the same for `PassCompletionView.h`, but give it **Project** scope, so it won't be built into the framework. (**Private** scope would bundle it into a `PrivateHeaders` directory.)

The framework is more than just a library: It also includes a `.h` file and a `NIB` (compiled from the XIB file you transferred) in the single framework unit.

Using the Framework

Let Mac Passer Rating know about the new framework. In the **Build Phases** tab of the Target editor for Mac Passer Rating, open the "Link Binary With Libraries" phase and click the + button. The browser sheet that drops down includes a section for products in the project. Select `PasserGraph.framework` and click **Add**. Use the pop-up to mark the framework **Required**—you *can* make a library **Optional** if you're willing to check for the existence of its services and carry on without them if they aren't present, but PasserGraph's classes must be there.

Because **Find Implicit Dependencies** is checked in the **Build** panel of the Scheme editor for Mac Passer Rating, there's nothing you need to do to incorporate PasserGraph in the build process for the application. Xcode sees that you' re using the product of another target and makes sure it's up to date.

Try it: Run the application (**Product→Run** [⌘R] or select the **Run** action from the **Action** button at the left end of the toolbar). It works! You can summon up the graph view, and you can set breakpoints in the graphing code.

So why am I not ending this chapter?

Installing a Framework

Try Mac Passer Rating as a real application. Select **Product→Archive**. The framework and the application build from scratch. (Archive always does; it ensures that your distribution products don't carry over any products of earlier builds.) Xcode then presents you with the Archives organizer. See Figure 22.1.

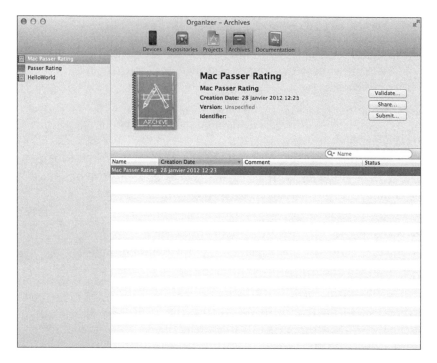

FIGURE 22.1   Executing **Product→Archive** opens the Archives organizer, focused on the archive you just created.

An archive embodies all the build products—and debug symbols—of a project, for sharing, installation, or submission to an App Store. Your freshly made archive is already selected, so click the **Share...** button in the header above the archive list. In the first sheet that appears, select **Build Products**, and click **Next**. You'll be given a save-file sheet for you to name and place a directory containing what you've built. Provide a name and location that is easy to find.

Running the Application Alone

Bring the Finder forward, and open that directory. It turns out to be surprisingly complex (Figure 22.2). Ignore your misgivings, find the Mac Passer Rating application, and double-click it.

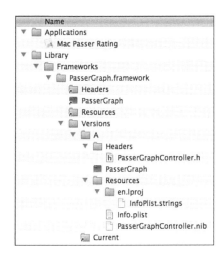

FIGURE 22.2   The built-products directory for the Mac Passer Rating archive is surprisingly complex.

The icon appears in the Dock for an instant and goes away. Instead, you see a Mac OS X crash-report window. Use the disclosure triangle to expose the details (if they aren't already visible), and inspect the wreckage. The relevant message is (truncated for space):

```
Dyld Error Message:
  Library not loaded:
        /Library/Frameworks/PasserGraph.framework/...
  Referenced from: .../Mac Passer Rating
  Reason: image not found
```

"Image not found" means that the dynamic linker couldn't find the dynamic library in PasserGraph.framework, which it looked for in /Library/Frameworks. Well, of course not: You never installed the framework in the global library directory.

But this explains the complexity of the built-products directory: It's a model of the final installation locations of the application (in the global /Applications directory) and the framework (in /Library). So do you need to install the framework as a systemwide resource? And why did it work when you ran the app from within Xcode?

The second question has a simple answer: When you develop a framework, Xcode doesn't force you to go through an installation phase. It sets up the runtime environment so that the dynamic linker looks first in the project's derived data directory where the framework was built. That way, you always run the current development version of the framework with no fuss.

The first question requires a little theory.

Where Frameworks Are Found

The core of a framework is a dynamic library—something you encountered in Chapter 5, "Compilation." The Mac OS X dynamic linker has a search path of directories it tries when looking for a dynamic library (essentially Library/Frameworks in the user, local, network, and system domains). It is not wise to rely on that search, though. First, it is bad citizenship because every library that forces a repeated search whenever it is loaded adds to the time it takes to launch applications. Second, it is bad security because you don't know whether some other framework of the same name has come ahead of you in the search path.

NOTE

The days when frameworks could be installed in Library directories for sharing among applications are all but gone. It was a great idea, but the usual problem with shared dynamic libraries caught up with it: What happens when an application that relies on version *n-1* of a framework is installed on a system where another application has already installed version *n*? The framework mechanism, with its internal versioning structure, partially solved this problem, but not fully. Nowadays, it's practical only for publishers of application suites that can update all their components simultaneously, which basically means Apple and Microsoft.

For speed and security, each time an application is built against a dynamic library, the application records the one location where it should find the correct library. That implies the framework's installed location should be known at build time. And that, in turn, implies that dynamic libraries must build their expected installation paths into themselves.

So where should the dynamic linker find PasserGraph? Hopefully, it's at the place you baked into the framework when you first built it. And the only practical place is within the .app bundle.

Which gives rise to the next question: A Mac OS X application can be run from anywhere in the file system. How do you bake the installation location into the framework?

Open the **Build Settings** tab of the Target editor for PasserGraph. The immediate setting for the baked-in name is Dynamic Library Install Name (LD_DYLIB_INSTALL_NAME)—but don't change it. If you double-click the value for that setting, you'll see it's a derived value from DYLIB_INSTALL_NAME_BASE and EXECUTABLE PATH. You want to go upstream from that derived name.

Instead, use Installation Directory (INSTALL_PATH). It, too, has a derived value, amounting to /Library/Frameworks. Change this to

@executable_path/../Frameworks

which means "user of this library, look for it in the Frameworks subdirectory of your parent directory." The @executable_path element relieves you of having to specify an absolute directory path, which would of course change as the user moved or renamed the application. It frees the framework to be available to the developer of any application without having to customize its installation path.

Putting the Framework in the Application

Now you've committed to putting `PasserGraph.framework` into the application bundle. How do you make sure it gets there?

Go to the **Build Phases** tab of the Target editor for Mac Passer Rating, and select **Add Copy Files** from the **Add Build Phase** button at the lower right. The new phase appears at the bottom of the list, which is acceptable. Click the disclosure triangle to open the phase. See Figure 22.3.

FIGURE 22.3   The "Copy Files" build phase, filled out so `PasserGraph.framework` is copied into the `Frameworks/` directory of Mac Passer Rating's `.app` bundle.

The first thing to do is to identify the file that is to be copied. Click the + button at the bottom of the phase's table, and use the browser to designate `PasserGraph.framework`.

Next, determine where in the application bundle the framework is to go. The **Destination** pop-up offers quick settings for a number of common locations in the bundle, as well as options for an absolute path or the project's products directory. The destination you want is **Frameworks**. The **Subpath** field would allow you to designate a subdirectory of the destination directory to receive the file; this would be most useful if you were building up a directory tree in the application `Resources` directory. Leave it blank.

Copy only when installing controls whether the `PasserGraph.framework` will be put into the application bundle for nonarchiving builds. Check this box; you want to rely on the framework that is built into the project's derived-data tree.

One last step. In the **Build Settings** for PasserGraph, find the **Skip Install** setting, and set it to **Yes**. Now that the install path for the library is no longer fixed in the file system— you just added a build phase that installs it manually— there is no point in setting up the mock installation that you got when you exported the archive directory. Setting **Skip Install** eliminates the creation of the separate installation tree.

> **NOTE**
>
> If you forget to set **Skip Install**, Xcode's build system will warn that you've set an installation location of your own, without suppressing the automatic installation. It will tell you to set **Skip Install**.

Building Mac Passer Rating

Select **Product→Archive** again. The Archives organizer shows you something new: Instead of the rectangular gray icon of an Xcode archive package, you see a new entry with an application icon. Click **Share**…. The export sheet is different, too. You have three options:

▸ **Mac OS X App Store Package** (.pkg) produces an installer package to be distributed through the Mac App Store. This must be signed, so if you choose this option, you must supply a distribution signing identity.

▸ **Application** saves a plain .app package that can be double-clicked to launch. There will be no directory with installation trees. Select this option.

▸ **Archive** saves an .xcarchive package that contains the application and .dSYM debugging-symbol files for the application and the framework. This package is a record of Mac Passer Rating as of the moment it was archived; you have the complete executable and enough information to debug it. With that, you can respond to a crash report by recovering the stack trace at the time of the crash.

Select **Application**, click **Archive**, and save the application. Double-click **Mac Passer Rating**, and test the graphing feature.

One More Thing

The graph doesn't appear. There's a bug that points up a trick in producing self-contained frameworks that maintain their own NIBs and other resources. You could launch the Console application (look in /Applications/Utilities) to see if there is any guidance— as it happens, AppKit prints a helpful diagnostic message. But here's a different approach.

Launch Mac Passer Rating from the Finder, and immediately turn to Xcode. Select the submenu **Product→Attach to Process**. The submenu is large—it lists every running process on your machine—but Xcode helpfully places Mac Passer Rating at the top, calling it a "likely target." Select it.

Xcode switches to debugging mode. Double-click a passer's name, which is supposed to summon the graph. Because you set a breakpoint on exceptions (Didn't you? See the "Running Bindings" section of Chapter 18, "Wiring a Mac Application with Bindings"), the debugger cuts in at the last line of the passerTableClicked: method of PasserGraphController:

```
[self.passerPopover showRelativeToRect: rowRect
                           ofView: self.passerTable
                    preferredEdge: NSMaxXEdge];
```

Unfortunately, the debugger isn't much more help. If you type **po self**, the debugger tells you it can't print a nil object. Almost all the values in the variables display are blank. The problem is that you're dealing with an optimized release build. As you saw in Chapter 5, variables come into and out of existence from moment to moment, and lines are executed out of order.

So let's take advantage of that `.xcarchive` package. Export one if you haven't yet; call it **MPRArch**. Open the terminal, and set the current working directory to the archive root. When you're there, apply the gdb debugger to the app:

```
$ # Get into the archive package
$ cd ~/Desktop/MPRArch.xcarchive/
$ ls
Info.plist  Products    dSYMs


$ # Launch a debugging session with Mac Passer Rating
$ # Typing the first few characters of a name and pressing
$ # tab makes this easier.
$ gdb Products/Applications/Mac\ Passer\ Rating.app/
GNU gdb 6.3.50-20050815 (Apple version gdb-1708)...
Copyright 2004 Free Software Foundation, Inc.
GDB is free software...
...Reading symbols for shared libraries ........ done


(gdb) # gdb found the debug symbols in the archive.
(gdb) # break on an Objective-C exception:
(gdb) br objc_exception_throw
Breakpoint 1 at 0x51eb851eab3d45


(gdb) # Run Mac Passer Rating:
(gdb) run
Starting program: /Users/xcodeuser/Desktop/MPRArch.xcarchive/
    Products/Applications/Mac Passer Rating.app/Contents/
    MacOS/Mac Passer Rating
Reading symbols for shared libraries
    ++++++++.........................done
Reading symbols for shared libraries . done
Reading symbols for shared libraries . done
.
.
.
```

By now, Mac Passer Rating is running. Reproduce the bug by double-clicking a row in the passer table. This triggers the breakpoint on objc_exception_throw (truncated and elided for space):

```
2011-11-04 19:55:20.046 Mac Passer Rating[73558:90f]
    unable to find nib named: PasserGraphController
    in bundle path: (null)


Breakpoint 1, 0x00007fff90feed45 in objc_exception_throw ()
(gdb) # Examine the stack trace with the bt (backtrace)
(gdb) # command:
(gdb) bt
#0    0x00007fff90feed45 in objc_exception_throw ()
...
#5    0x00007fff92931232 in -[NSPopover
      showRelativeToRect:ofView:preferredEdge:] ()
#6    0x0000000100002566 in -[LeagueDocument passerTableClicked:]
      (self=<value temporarily unavailable, due to optimizations>,_
      _cmd=<value temporarily unavailable,  due to optimizations>,
      sender=<value temporarily unavailable, due to optimizations>)
      at /Users/xcodeuser/Desktop/Mac Passer Rating
          /Mac Passer Rating/LeagueDocument.m:120
#7    0x00007fff8d5dfa1d in -[NSObject performSelector:withObject:] ()
...
#14   0x00007fff920e7682 in -[NSApplication run] ()
#15   0x00007fff9236680c in NSApplicationMain ()
#16   0x0000000100001be4 in ?? ()
(gdb)
```

The last contact with Mac Passer Rating code is, as the Xcode debugger said, in passerTableClicked:, and gdb can't find any variable values either. gdb, however, has the grace to print the exception message: "unable to find nib named: PasserGraphController in bundle path: (null)."

```
(gdb) # We're done. Kill Mac Passer Rating and exit.
(gdb) kill
Kill the program being debugged? (y or n) y
(gdb) quit
$
```

> **NOTE**
>
> All this time, you've probably had the Mac Passer Rating project open and were working with the last-built version of the app. Surely the gdb session would not have gone so well if the app had moved on to another version? Actually, it would. When an executable file is built, the linker embeds a unique identifier (UUID) in it and marks the debugger-symbols (.dSYM) file with the same UUID. When the Apple version of gdb loads the executable for debugging, It searches for the UUID in Spotlight and matches the application to the correct version of the debugging information.

There is a reference in code to a NIB named `PasserGraphController`, and it's in `passerTableClicked:` (**Note:** You actually made the change in Chapter 19.)

```
PasserGraphController *    pgc =
    [[PasserGraphController alloc]
        initWithNibName: @"PasserGraphController"
                bundle: nil];
```

The problem is the `nil` that is passed in for the bundle. When a `nil` bundle is passed to `initWithNibName:bundle:`, `NSViewController` searches for the named NIB in the `Resources/` directory of the main—the application's—bundle. But `PasserGraphController.xib` is in the *framework's* resource directory.

There's something else wrong: As a client of PasserGraph, Mac Passer Rating shouldn't have to worry about the name of a NIB in the PasserGraph resources. So the first thing is to take the implementation detail out of `passerTableClicked::`

```
PasserGraphController *    pgc = [[PasserGraphController alloc] init];
```

and then to give `PasserGraphController` a proper init method:

```
- (id) init
{
    self = [super initWithNibName: @"PasserGraphController"
                        bundle: [NSBundle bundleForClass:
                                        [self class]]];
    // No further initialization, so no if (self)...
    return self;
}
```

The `init` method shows the trick: `NSBundle` can identify the bundle that supplied a class—`PasserGraphController` comes from the PasserGraph framework bundle: [`NSBundle bundleForClass: [self class]`], where `self` is an instance of `PasserGraphController`.

Make these changes, archive, and save the application. Double-click, summon a graph popover, and find that the framework, at last, works.

Summary

In this chapter, I showed you techniques for breaking your Mac OS X programs into reusable modules by putting them into frameworks. The technique of putting source code into a library was already familiar to you, but you saw how frameworks can encapsulate headers and runtime resources.

You learned about the prerequisites for making a framework available to an application: Setting the dynamic library's installation path to a relative path within the owning application and adding a "Copy Files" build phase to put it there.

I finished by showing you the uses of the various archives that Xcode can export: installation trees; bare applications; and time-capsule archives that bundle one version of an application with its debugging data, so you can apply a debugger to an old release.

CHAPTER 23

Property Lists

IN THIS CHAPTER

▶ Understanding what property lists contain

▶ Creating a simple property list

▶ Editing property lists

▶ Using property list formats

Cocoa uses *property lists* (also called *plists*, after the common extension for property-list files) everywhere. They are the all-purpose storage medium for structured data, both for application resources and sometimes even application documents. Although I've put this chapter in the Mac OS X section of this book, property lists are important to iOS developers, as well.

▶ Many of Apple's standard formats for configuration files are simply specifications of keys and trees for property lists. If you want a configuration file of your own, you could do much worse than a specialized plist file.

▶ In particular, applications on iOS and Mac OS X alike include an Info.plist file that tells the system how the app is to be presented and what kinds of data it handles. See Chapter 21, "Bundles and Packages," for details.

▶ The property-list format is mature—older than Mac OS X. Cocoa can parse plist files in one line of code, directly into Foundation data types.

Property List Types

A property list is an archive for the fundamental data types provided by Cocoa's Foundation framework. It consists of one item of data, expressed in one of seven data types. Five property list types are scalar—number, Boolean, string, date, and data—and two are compound—ordered list and dictionary. An ordered list can contain zero or more objects of any property list type. A dictionary contains zero or more pairs, consisting of a string and an object of a property list type.

A property list can express most collections of data quite easily. A passer's performance in a single game could be represented as a dictionary of numbers with the keys `attempts`, `completions`, `interceptions`, `touchdowns`, and `yards`. A game could be a dictionary containing the date, team names, scores, and the performance dictionary.

Both Core Foundation and Cocoa provide reference-counted object types that correspond to the property list types (see Table 23.1). You can pass a Cocoa property list pointer to a Core Foundation routine for the corresponding type; you can also use a `CFTypeRef` for a property list type as though it were a pointer to the corresponding Cocoa object. (However, Automatic Reference Counting [ARC] has made bridging Cocoa and Core Foundation objects a little more complicated; search for "Transitioning to ARC Release Notes" in the Documentation organizer for details.)

TABLE 23.1   Property-List Types in Cocoa and Core Foundation

Data Type	Cocoa	Core Foundation	Markup
Number	NSNumber	CFNumber	`<integer>` `<float>`
Boolean	NSNumber	CFBoolean	`<true/>` `<false/>`
Text	NSString NSMutableString	CFString CFMutableString	`<string>`
Date	NSDate	CFDate	`<date>`
Binary Data	NSData NSMutableData	CFData CFMutableData	`<data>`
List	NSArray NSMutableArray	CFArray CFMutableArray	`<array>`
Associative Array	NSDictionary NSMutableDictionary	CFDictionary CFMutableDictionary	`<dict>` `<key>...` *plist type* ... `</dict>`

NOTE

The dictionary data type in Cocoa requires only that the keys in a dictionary be objects of an immutable, copyable type; Core Foundation dictionaries can be even more permissive. However, if you want to use a Cocoa or Core Foundation dictionary in a property list, all keys have to be strings.

Editing Property Lists

When you started the Passer Rating iPhone app, the first thing Xcode showed was the Target editor for the application. See Figure 23.1. The second tab, **Info**, is a specialization of the Property List editor for `Info.plist`, which contains a dictionary describing to iOS how the application is to be presented. Each line of the top section represents one key-value pair at the top level of the dictionary; the **Info** editor refines the experience by wrapping some of the top-level keys (for such as document and data types) into distinct lists of convenient graphical editors.

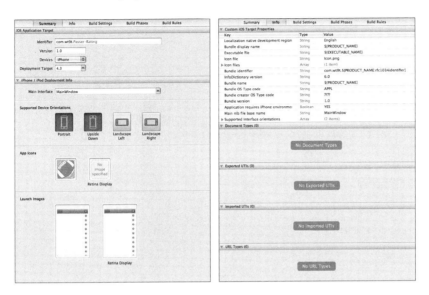

FIGURE 23.1   As soon as an application project is created, Xcode presents a Target editor to edit its `Info.plist` file. The first two tabs, **Summary** and **Info**, are specialized editors to set the application's presentation and behavior.

Still, it's just an editor for a particular kind of property list. Let's have a look at the real thing. Use the search field at the bottom of the Project navigator to search for **plist**. The only file surviving in the navigator should be `Passer_Rating-Info.plist`. Click it.

Not much to see. It's Xcode's generic Property List editor, which is just a little simpler than the Target editor's **Info** tab. What's the big deal? Do this: Right-click the file's name in the Project navigator, and select **Open As→Source Code**. Now the Editor area fills with something like this:

```
<?xml version="1.0" encoding="UTF-8"?>
<!DOCTYPE plist PUBLIC "-//Apple//DTD PLIST 1.0//EN"
            "http://www.apple.com/DTDs/PropertyList-L0.dtd">
<plist version="1.0">
<dict>
    <key>CFBundleDevelopmentRegion</key>
    <string>English</string>
    <key>CFBundleDisplayName</key>
    <string>${PRODUCT_NAME}</string>
    <key>CFBundleDocumentTypes</key>
    <array>
```

```
        <dict/>
    </array>
    <key>CFBundleExecutable</key>
    <string>${EXECUTABLE_NAME}</string>
    <key>CFBundleIconFile</key>
    <string>Icon.png</string>
    <key>CFBundleIconFiles</key>
    <array>
        <string>Icon.png</string>
    </array>
    <key>CFBundleIdentifier</key>
    <string>com.wt9t.${PRODUCT_NAME:rfc1034identifier}</string>
    <key>CFBundleInfoDictionaryVersion</key>
    <string>6.0</string>
    <key>CFBundleName</key>
    <string>${PRODUCT_NAME}</string>
    <key>CFBundlePackageType</key>
    <string>APPL</string>
    <key>CFBundleSignature</key>
    <string>????</string>
    <key>CFBundleURLTypes</key>
    <array/>
    <key>CFBundleVersion</key>
    <string>1.0</string>
    <key>LSRequiresIPhoneOS</key> <true/>
    <key>NSMainNibFile</key> <string>MainWindow</string>
    <key>UISupportedInterfaceOrientations</key>
    <array>
        <string>UIInterfaceOrientationPortrait</string>
        <string>UIInterfaceOrientationPortraitUpsideDown</string>
    </array>
    <key>UTExportedTypeDeclarations</key> <array/>
    <key>UTImportedTypeDeclarations</key>
    <array/>
</dict>
</plist>
```

You likely are relieved to see that the property list format is XML and that Cocoa's built-in writer for .plist files indents them nicely. The top-level element is <plist>, which must contain one property list element—in this case, <dict>, for the Info.plist dictionary. A <dict> element's contents alternate between <key> string elements and property list value elements. One of the keys, UISupportedInterfaceOrientations, has an <array> value. An <array> may contain zero or more property list elements, of any type, in this case, the orientations supported by the Passer Rating app. I covered Info.plist keys at length in Chapter 21.

NOTE

I'm indulging in two cheats here. First, what you're seeing is not the `Info.plist` that will be inserted into the application bundle. It's a source file for a compiler that the build system uses to fill in variables and insert some invariant keys—you see variable names such as `${PRODUCT_NAME}`. Second, the `Info.plist` in the app bundle won't be an XML file; it will be a *binary plist*, as explained later in this chapter.

What's good about XML is that it is standard: Correct XML will be accepted by any consumer of a document type definition, regardless of the source. A `.plist` file generated by any Cocoa application will be treated the same as one generated by a text editor.

What's bad about XML is that it is standard: It must be correct. If you forget to close an element or miss the strict alternation of `<key>` and property list elements in `<dict>` lists, you'll get nothing out of Apple's parser.

Usually, you don't need to worry about this sort of thing because you use the Property List editor in its graphical form. You don't see the opening and closing tags, so you can't omit them. The editor forces you to put a key on every element in a dictionary and restricts you to the legal data types. Simple.

However, sometimes it's not practical to use the Property List editor to create or maintain property lists. Let's have a look at how the editor works, and then I'll develop why it's not for every task.

A Brand New Property List

We're going to create a property list that describes how to make an omelet. (I'll leave it to you what the file would be good for.) Bring Xcode forward. Select **File→New→File…** (⌘N), and navigate the New File assistant thus: **Mac OS X→Resource→Property List**. (You can get the same thing from the iOS part of the assistant.) If you have a project window open, you see the usual put-file sheet. Call it **Omelet**. (No extension is necessary; Xcode adds `.plist` for you.) The other controls for disposing the new file in the project are now long-familiar to you.

You're presented with the same kind of Property List editor that you saw for the `Info.plist` file, only it's empty. There's no control for adding any content. What to do?

Look at the **Editor** menu. It's dynamic, adjusting its content to the type of the active editor. Now that it's a Property List editor, you find the command **Add Item**. Select it, and a new row appears in the editor. See Figure 23.2 (top).

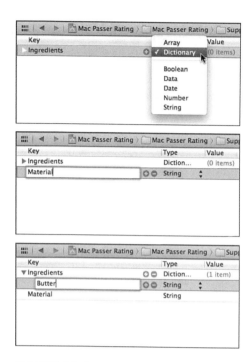

FIGURE 23.2   (top) Selecting **Editor→Add Item** inserts the first element in a new property list. Select from a pop-up menu in the Type column to indicate the data type the element represents. (middle) Pressing the Return key or clicking the **+** button when a container element is closed inserts a new element that is a sibling of the selected container. (bottom) If the container is open, pressing Return or clicking **+** inserts the new element as a child of the container.

NOTE

Because a property list can consist of a single scalar (noncontainer) object, it makes sense that if you make the new row a string, you'll get a plist that contains only a string, right? No. The Property List editor edits only container lists—dictionaries or arrays. The top-level container is there, just hidden. It starts you out with a dictionary, and as the outer container isn't selectable, you can't use the editor to change it to an array. If you want an array, there is a workaround: Right after creating the file, right-click it in the Project navigator, and select **Open As→Source Code**. Look for the `<dict/>` element and replace it with `<array/>`. The Property List editor adds new elements in the file as items in the top-level array.

The new row is a key-value pair for the dictionary, with a *key*, represented as a text field that is open for editing; a *type*, represented as a pop-up listing the possible plist types; and a *value*, which is editable if the type is a scalar.

The omelet recipe should have three sections, named Ingredients, Material, and Method. Ingredients should be a dictionary, with the keys naming the ingredients; the values should be dictionaries themselves, keyed quantity and unit. So name the first new row **Ingredients**, and set its type to **Dictionary** (refer to Figure 23.2 [top]).

You want more items in the recipe. You want the Material and Method elements to be siblings of Ingredients, and you want to add ingredient dictionaries as children of Ingredients. That's two styles of adding rows to the editor.

Select the Ingredients row, and press the Return key (or click the + button at the right of the Key cell or select **Editor→Add Item**). This produces a new sibling row, which you can name **Material** and make a dictionary. (Refer to Figure 23.2 [middle].)

Select the Ingredients row again. At the left margin of the row, there is a disclosure triangle, which is turned so that the point is to the right, indicating that the container is closed. Click on the triangle so that it points down. This opens the container, which doesn't make much difference because a new dictionary doesn't have any contents to show.

Now press Return. A new row appears, but this time, it is indented to show that the new element is *inside* the Ingredients dictionary. (Refer to Figure 23.2 [bottom].) The difference is whether the disclosure triangle points closed or open. If closed, you'll get a sibling at the same level. If open, you'll get a child, enclosed in the container.

Now you have an element inside Ingredients. Name it **Eggs**, and make it a dictionary. Open Eggs, press Return (or click the + button) twice, to create new elements, named **quantity** (type **Number**, value **3**—it's a generous omelet), and **unit** (type **String**, value **count**). You've completed your first ingredient.

NOTE

Make a mistake? **Undo** works as normal. If you want to get rid of an item, select it and press Delete, or click the − button in its Key column. Deleting a container deletes all its contents as well.

Add more siblings to Eggs—or children to Ingredients—as shown in Table 23.2.

TABLE 23.2   Remaining Ingredients in an Omelet

Mushrooms	count	2
Salt	pinch	1
Butter	ounce	2

Doing this the obvious way, clicking new-sibling and new-child buttons at each step, and setting the same unit and quantity keys for each new dictionary, is tedious. Here are some shortcuts:

▶ After you have one dictionary (Eggs) set up the way you want it, select that dictionary by clicking the container row (Eggs), and **Edit→Copy**. When you paste the row you've copied, it will be inserted as though you had clicked the + button on the selected row. So select the Ingredients dictionary while it's open, or the Eggs dictionary while it's *closed*, and **Edit→Paste**. You have to change the pasted element's key and change the values of the "unit" and "quantity" keys, but that's the minimal work you need to do anyway.

▶ When you've finished editing a key or value, the Tab key takes you to the next visible editable string.

▶ The Return key closes a text-field cell if one is open. Pressing it again creates a new element (sibling or child) as though you'd clicked the + button on the selected row. The new row has the key string (if it's in a dictionary) or the value string (if it's not) ready for editing. The initial type will be **String**, which probably is the type you'd want if you motor through several new rows at a time.

The Material dictionary should be simple key/string pairs, as shown in Table 23.3. The Method array should contain strings, as shown in Table 23.4.

TABLE 23.3   Materials for Making an Omelet

Bowl	Small
Fork	Table fork or small whisk
Crepe Pan	10" nonstick
Spatula	Silicone, high-heat
Egg Slicer	Optional, for slicing mushrooms

Method's strings must appear in order, so it has to be an array. If it's not in the order you want, you can drag items into order. See Figure 23.3.

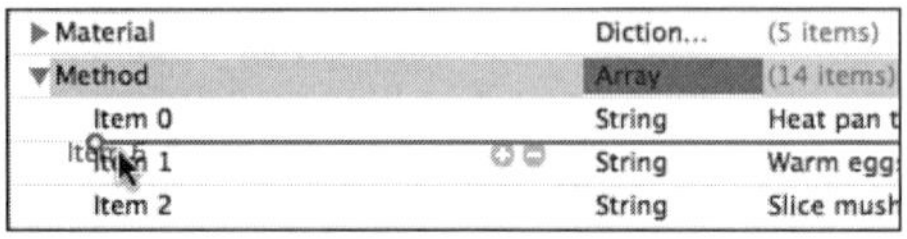

FIGURE 23.3   You can reorder array elements simply by dragging them where you want them.

TABLE 23.4   Instructions for Making an Omelet

Heat pan to medium. (Butter foams but doesn't burn.)
Warm eggs in water to room temperature. Slice mushrooms.
Sauté in 1/4 of the butter until limp; set aside.
Break eggs into bowl; add salt.
Whisk eggs until color begins to change.
Coat pan with 1/2 the butter.
Pour eggs into pan, and tilt to spread uniformly.
When edges set, use spatula to separate from pan; then tilt liquid into gaps. Leave undisturbed for 30 seconds.
Loosen from pan, and flip (using spatula to help) 1/3 over Top with mushrooms.
Slide onto plate, flipping remaining 1/3 over. Spread remaining butter on top.

When you've done it all, your Property List editor should look like the one in Figure 23.4.

Key	Type	Value
▼ Ingredients	Diction...	(5 items)
▼ Eggs	Diction...	(2 items)
unit	String	count
quantity	Number	3
▼ Mushrooms	Diction...	(2 items)
unit	String	count
quantity	Number	2
▼ Salt	Diction...	(2 items)
unit	String	pinch
quantity	Number	1
▼ Butter	Diction...	(2 items)
unit	String	ounce
quantity	Number	2
▼ Parsley	Diction...	(2 items)
unit	String	sprig
quantity	Number	1
▼ Material	Diction...	(5 items)
Bowl	String	Small
Fork	String	Table fork or small whisk
Crêpe Pan	String	10" nonstick
Spatula	String	Silicone, high-heat
Egg Slicer	String	Optional, for slicing mushrooms
▼ Method	Array	(14 items)
Item 0	String	Heat pan to medium (butter foams but doesn't burn)
Item 1	String	Warm eggs in water to room temperature
Item 2	String	Slice mushrooms
Item 3	String	Sauté in 1/4 of the butter until limp, set aside
Item 4	String	Break eggs into bowl, add salt
Item 5	String	Whisk eggs until color begins to change
Item 6	String	Coat pan with 1/2 the butter
Item 7	String	Pour eggs into pan, and tilt to spread uniformly
Item 8	String	When edges set, use spatula to separate from pan, then tilt liquid into gaps
Item 9	String	Leave undisturbed for 30 seconds
Item 10	String	Loosen from pan, and flip (using spatula to help) 1/3 over
Item 11	String	Top with mushrooms
Item 12	String	Slide onto plate, flipping remaining 1/3 over
Item 13	String	Spread remaining butter on top

FIGURE 23.4   The Property List editor showing the finished Omelet.plist. You can open or close all the subelements in a dictionary or array by holding the Option key when you click the disclosure triangle.

Search and replace works in property lists as it does in regular text files. If you Edit→Find→Find... (⌘F), the Find bar appears. If you type **butter**, the containers open to show and highlight all instances of the string. Clicking the left- and right-arrow buttons in the find bar (or pressing ⇧⌘G or ⌘G) navigates among the found rows but doesn't enable them for editing.

Edit→Find→Find in Workspace/Project... (⇧⌘F) works, too. The Search navigator appears, you enter **butter**, and the plist appears in the list of matches.

In both cases, search and replace work as they do for regular text files.

Why Not the Property List Editor?

The Property List editor generated a correct property list with all the data in what seems to be the most direct way possible. What more is there to say?

It isn't perfect. Control-click the file in the Project navigator, and select **Open As→Source Code** from the contextual menu. Again, you see the plist in the XML format in which it is stored.

You have doubts about your recipe. Maybe a little garnish would be nice, but you can't decide. So you add an XML comment to the Methods array:

```
<key>Method</key>
<array>
    .
    .
    .
    <string>Slide onto plate, flipping remaining 1/3 over</string>
    <string>Spread remaining butter on top</string>
    <!— Should I add parsley? —>
</array>
```

Now save the file. (You may already have found that Xcode won't let you switch between editors unless you save the file first.) Using the contextual menu, choose **Open As→Property List**. Make a tentative advance in presentation by adding Parsley (sprig, 1) to the Ingredients dictionary. (You need to open the dictionary; Xcode saves the open/collapsed state but reverts to all-collapsed if you change editors.) Save again, and once again **Open As→Source Code**.

The comment you added is gone. If you use the Property List editor to change a property list, it will destroy any content that isn't property list data. Similarly, if you take advantage of the build option to use a preprocessor for #includes and conditional compilation, those directives will be lost if they pass through the Property List editor.

CAUTION

If you intend to treat property lists as normal source files, using comments for notes or to comment content out, you must *never* edit them with the graphical editor. Viewing them is okay—actually, it's unavoidable because Xcode puts you back in the graphical editor every time you return to the file—but don't edit them.

That aside, a text editor can just be the best tool for the job. Large and repetitive structures are a bit easier to handle in the XML text, it's easier to handle programmatically generated files, and maybe you just like to work with source.

There's a way you can do this without forcing the Source Code editor every time. Select your property list file in the Project navigator, and open the Utilities area (using the right-hand button in the **View** control in the toolbar). Make sure the File inspector tab (the first one) is selected. You see various information about the file and its status in your project (Figure 23.5, left); the one you're interested in is the setting in the **File Type** pop-up menu.

FIGURE 23.5   The pop-up under the filename in the file inspector chooses the editor and syntax that Xcode applies to that file. You can force Xcode always to use the XML editor for a particular .plist file by selecting **XML** in the **Property List /XML** group, instead of **Property List XML**.

It starts with **Default–Property List XML**. Scroll through the menu (it will be quite a way down) until you find the **Property List / XML** group, and select **XML**.

Nothing happens to the editor. Close Omelet.plist from under the Project window by selecting **File→Close "Omelet.plist"** (^⌘W). Select the plist again in the Project navigator. Now it appears as an XML file, and always will, without your having to tell Xcode to switch.

> **NOTE**
>
> That Xcode labels **Property List XML** as a default suggests that you might change the default and get the plain-XML editor all the time without setting it for each file. In Xcode 3, you could do that. In Xcode 4, as I write this, you can't. If the feature returns, it will appear in the Preferences window.

If you commit to creating and editing property lists in XML, you lose the safety of the Property List editor in keeping the syntax correct. There are a couple of ways to reduce the risk.

First, you can start your own .plist files by editing a known-good .plist file. It's difficult to omit the processing instruction or the <plist> skeleton if they are already in the file.

Second, you can use the macro or glossary facilities of your text editor to create a document skeleton and wrap your entries in proper tags. Bare Bones Software's BBEdit comes with a .plist glossary for just this purpose.

When you have your property list file, you'll need to know if it is syntactically correct—if it isn't, you can't use it. The best way is to use the plutil tool. In the Terminal, type **plutil *pathToPropertyList***. You see either *pathToPropertyList*: OK or a diagnostic message if all is not well. See man plutil for details.

> **NOTE**
>
> One of the most common errors is forgetting that the text portions of the property list XML are parsed character data, which means that < and & must be represented by < and &.

Other Formats

If you stick to editing property lists as text, you'll find that text editors can display and edit only *most* property list files. There are two other formats a plist file may use. One is also text; the other is binary.

Text Property Lists

Property lists came to Cocoa's architecture from its ancestor framework, NeXTStep. In NeXTStep, property lists were encoded in a text format that Apple characterizes as a legacy technique but is used often enough that you should be familiar with it. defaults, the command-line interface to the preferences system, the bundle specifications for the editor TextMate, and many of the internal Xcode configuration files use the text format.

Text property lists have only two primitive types: string and data (Table 23.5). Strings are surrounded by double-quote characters, which may be omitted if there are no spaces in the string. Number, date, and Boolean values must be stored as string representations, and the application that reads them is on its own for converting them to their respective types. The convention for Boolean values is to use the strings YES and NO.

TABLE 23.5   Encoding for Text-Style Property Lists

Type	Coding
String	"Two or more words" *or* oneWord
Data	< 466f6f 626172 >
List	(Shirley, "Goodness and Mercy", 1066)
Associative Array	{ key = value; "key 2" = < 332e3134313539 >; }

Data elements are delimited by angle brackets and contain pairs of hexadecimal digits, representing the bytes in the data. Any spaces in the digit stream will be ignored.

Arrays are surrounded by parentheses, and the elements are separated by commas. Dictionaries are surrounded by braces, and the *key = value* pairs are *followed* by semicolons, which means that the last element must be closed off with a semicolon.

Binary Property Lists

With Mac OS X version 10.2, Apple introduced a binary property list format. Binary plists are smaller and load faster. Programmatically generated plists are binary by default; Xcode, for instance, writes Info.plists in binary. Property lists can be converted between XML and binary format in-place using the plutil command-line utility in the form

```
plutil -convert format pathToFile
```

where *format* is either binary1, for conversion to the binary format, or xml1 for the XML format; and *pathToFile* is the path to the file to convert.

The build settings INFOPLIST_OUTPUT_FORMAT and PLIST_FILE_OUTPUT_FORMAT influence how Xcode writes Info.plist and other-plist files, respectively, into your product. By default, these are binary, but you can set them to XML.

Specialized Property Lists

Many of Cocoa's standard "file formats" are simply property lists with stereotyped keys and enumerated values. Xcode knows about these stereotypes; you can assign a type to a plist by opening it in the editor and right-clicking. The contextual menu includes a **Property List Type** submenu. If Xcode encounters a stereotyped plist, such as Info.plist or an iOS Settings bundle, it chooses the key/value repertoire automatically.

Once a property list type is established, the Key column in the Property List editor assumes a much more active role. Xcode now knows what keys this particular plist supports and what types are appropriate to those keys.

For example: An iOS application Info.plist includes the key UTExportedTypeDeclarations. If you add a row to the plist, the key field is no longer a simple text field but a combo field (a text field with a scrollable list of choices), in which "Exported Type UTIs" is an option. If you select it, Xcode automatically changes the type of the row to array because the UTExportedTypeDeclarations element must have an array value.

If you open that array, and add a row to it, Xcode creates a dictionary— UTExportedTypeDeclarations must contain dictionaries—prepopulated with the three keys (and types) required of those dictionaries.

For a key that has a restricted set of scalar values, Xcode sets the element to the proper type, and instead of an editable value field, the value column contains a pop-up of English-language names for the legal values.

Remember that Mac OS X combo fields are text fields, not menus. Xcode offers them wherever it's legal to enter a custom value. Treat that key or value as editable text, and ignore the attached list. The list isn't comprehensive or restrictive; if something you need isn't there, type it in yourself.

The combo fields' lists scroll automatically to offer presets that match what you've typed. This is handy, but the matching is case-sensitive. If you aren't finding what you expect, try typing with an initial cap.

Having English-language equivalents for all your keys and values cuts you off from the actual content of those elements; even if XML editing isn't to your taste, you may want to audit what's going into your file. There are two strategies for this:

▶ Open the Utility (right) area, select Quick Help (the second tab), and click in a row. Quick Help shows the English name and the "declaration," the actual encoded key. You're out of luck for English-language values.

▶ Select **Editor→Show Raw Values & Keys** (or the same command from the contextual menu). The Property List editor switches over to its "normal" behavior, displaying the raw keys and values.

Summary

This chapter introduced property lists, a ubiquitous data-storage format in Cocoa. You've seen how to use the Property List editor and text tools to manage them. I showed you the other ways property lists can appear on Mac OS X and iOS and how Xcode adapts itself to the stereotyped formats of well-known specializations of the plist format. By now, you should be comfortable with the concept.

PART IV

Xcode Tasks

IN THIS PART

Xcode 4 for Xcode 3 Veterans

Depending on your experience and your cognitive style, Xcode 4 comes to you as a liberation, a disappointment, or even an outrage. My own reaction was severely negative, but I've come to respect Xcode 4, and even to like it. Mostly. This chapter, acknowledging your losses, will show you how to live with Xcode 4, and even to like it. Mostly.

The Desktop and the Browser

A key impetus in rewriting Xcode was that Xcode 3 had become a swarm of windows, some with duplicative content (such as the editors in the Debugger, Project Search, and Build Results windows) and some without a clear relationship to the entities they edited (such as file, target, project, executable, and SCM Info inspectors). The menus were dominated by commands just to activate the various editors and palettes.

Xcode 3 was a classical Mac application: You edit multiple documents, and each document can have an independent editor window. There are good reasons for this. People are meant to think and act in a real, physical world, and the "desktop metaphor," in which different entities are embodied in different, apparently physical windows, fits that natural cognitive style.

Since then, another, computer-specific metaphor has arisen, and experienced computer users have come to find it intuitive: the browser, in which one active window presents a view into a large set of data and provides many ways to navigate across it. The window isn't a simulation of a physical object but a machine that controls your work on your behalf. Xcode 4 is a browser.

A browser, because it is one machine that does everything, can become large. Your work can no longer overlap. This doesn't sound like a great loss if you work only with the browser, but nobody does. Your client emails specifications to you. You create images. You browse the Web and view PDFs for reference. The irony of a browser is that although it is intended to present "all your work" in one window, you can't readily get to all your work if part of it takes a form Xcode can't display.

This is a loss. Let's get to work.

Start Slow

Xcode 4 has a lot of features and displays, but the basics aren't that different from Xcode 3. The initial configuration of the Workspace window is simple: There's a list of files (the Project navigator) on the left. There's an editor on the right. This is *almost* what you had in version 3: The major differences are that the Project navigator contains only file references, and not targets, smart groups, and the like; the Details view that used to be above the editor is gone (and do you actually miss it?); and it's easy to lead yourself away from this simple view.

Here's how to preserve the simplicity (see Figure 24.1). At the right of the toolbar, you can see two segment controls that control what the window contains.

- ▶ On the left (**Editor**), you select the style of the main editor area. You want the first option, a simple text editor.

- ▶ On the right (**View**), you can toggle the presence of three "areas" in addition to the editor; the buttons depict where those areas go. To start with you want only the left one, the Navigator.

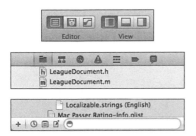

FIGURE 24.1   Four controls can keep the Xcode Workspace window simple for starting out with Xcode. (top) Set the **Editor** control to the "plain" text editor, and the **View** control to display only the left Navigator area. (middle) For a list of files (the main purpose of the old Groups & Files list), select the first, file-folder tab in the Navigator area. (bottom) At the bottom of the Project navigator, make sure none of the filter buttons are selected (blue), and the search field is empty.

The Navigator area serves many purposes, selectable with the tiny tab icons at its top. You want the Project navigator, the first (file-folder) tab. If you're unsure, hover the mouse pointer over an icon to get a tooltip.

The Project navigator can filter its contents using the small controls at the bottom. There are three buttons for common filters; the only indication that they are active is that their graphics are blue instead of black. They are tiny and out-of-the-way, and it is easy to miss that a filter is in effect. You might wonder where your files have gone. Check the filters, and turn them off if you need to. Similarly, there is a search field for filtering the list by filename (which takes care of the major use of the old Detail view and the simpler features of the old smart groups); make sure you clear it if you want to see everything.

The Sorcerer's Apprentice

Xcode 4 is *very* active in assisting you. Code completions pop over and out of your code as you type; red error flags flash at you in the moments between your using a variable and declaring it; popovers offer to rewrite your code; bubbles flash around sections of your code as you mouse over the left gutter of the editor. Some of these features were in Xcode 3, but Xcode 4 steps them up.

You may come to love this, but initially, you may find it distracting, even anxiety-provoking. You can turn it off until you're ready to deal with it. See "Quieting Xcode Down" in Chapter 2, "Kicking the Tires."

The Editor

The Xcode 4 Standard editor (select the left-hand segment of the **Editor** control in the toolbar) is straightforward and similar to Xcode 3. Type your text and save it. The completions and indentations are the same. If you click in a symbol, it highlights with a gray underline and offers a pop-up menu to edit all instances of the symbol in the current lexical scope.

In Xcode 3, you could command-double-click to be taken to the definition of a symbol and option-double-click to get a Quick Help window documenting it. Xcode 4 does the same, except that it takes a single-click. Xcode signals the feature by giving the symbol a "link" appearance; if it doesn't show up, move the mouse cursor out of the symbol and back in.

The **Editor** control can select two other editors for the Editor area. The third, the Version editor, is covered in the "Source Control" section of this chapter and in more depth in Chapter 7, "Version Control." The middle button displays the assistant editor.

The Assistant Editor

At first glance, the assistant editor (click the middle segment of the **Editor** control) is simply a split view, putting two files side by side. You can use it just that way: Xcode is full of gestures that select a file—click in any navigator, select from a jump bar, command-click a symbol—and they all put the file in the Editor area (in the main pane, on the left, if the assistant editor is visible). The same gestures fill the assistant pane if you hold down the Option key.

NOTE

You can use the **General** panel of the Preferences window to choose how gestures map to creating or switching editors. I'll just refer to the default behaviors.

What earns the editor the name "assistant" is that it can select the file it displays automatically. Clicking the first segment of the assistant editor's jump bar offers you a choice of what kind of file it is to show. Then, whatever file you choose for the main editor, the assistant displays the file that is related in the way you chose. The most common choice is **Counterparts**, which matches implementation files to headers. See Figure 24.2.

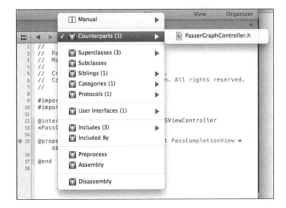

FIGURE 24.2   The root segment of the jump bar for the assistant pane offers a variety of schemes by which the pane can automatically choose its content.

This isn't confined to textual source. If the assistant view is committed to counterparts, and the main view is showing Interface Builder (IB), the assistant will show the header for the class of File's Owner.

NOTE

The **View→Assistant Editor** menu includes choices for how assistant editors are laid out relative to the main view. You can customize the layout case-by-case by adding the Shift key to any gesture that would open an assistant pane. You can have more than one assistant view; there's a **+** button at the top-right corner of the view to add another.

More Than One Editor

Xcode 4 adheres firmly to the doctrine that there should be only one editor at a time. If you're used to a desktop-model application such as Xcode 3, this is frustrating. It's not the way you're used to working. You'll want to know: Can I have more than one editor? Yes, you can. You can accomplish this in a few ways, depending on what you need.

The simplest is to use the assistant editor. If your use for separate windows was to refer to two files at a time, this should be good enough, and it's a big win if the assistant's automatic tracking of counterparts does what you need. If you need more flexibility, you can set the assistant to **Manual** and use its jump bar or Option-key navigation to fill it with whatever you want.

If your problem with the single-editor model is that Xcode disrupts the way you configured the Workspace window, you can use tabs (**File→New→Tab** [⌘T]). Other applications may have taught you that this is simply a way to switch among files, but remember that Xcode 4 works as a browsing environment, not a document editor. A tab in Xcode doesn't just carry the content of the Editor area, it also carries how you configure areas and navigators.

Editing a XIB, for instance, requires quite a large editor for laying out your views, plus the Utility area, which you rarely use in other contexts. On the other hand, you don't have much use for the Navigator area because you change files infrequently, and don't want search or error results. If you devote a tab to Interface Builder (you can even double-click the tab's title and name it **Interface Builder**), you can protect that unique layout. Tabs can be torn off into independent workspace windows.

And you can have separate windows; double-click a file in a navigator—or drag its tab out of the workspace window—and you get a window with no content other than an editor for the file you selected. You still have the problem that the main Workspace window wants to take up most of your screen, but you can have windows in the desktop style. But they aren't the same thing as Xcode 3 editor windows; they're just stripped-down Workspace windows. If you select **View→Show Toolbar** and then start selecting non-editor areas, you're back to a full-blown workspace.

Because spawned windows are just Workspace windows, closing what you think of as the "main" window does not close the project as it did in Xcode 3; the other Workspace windows remain open, and so does the project. Reopening a project restores the windows that were open when the workspace was last closed, so you could end up with just a single bare editor when you start. To get the behavior you expect, select **File→Close Workspace/Project** (⌥⌘W), or simply quit Xcode. Table 24.1 summarizes the various Close commands.

TABLE 24.1   Close Commands in Xcode

⌘W	Close the tab.
⇧⌘W	Close the window.
^⌘W	Remove the file from the tab.
⌥⌘W	Close the project.

This all comes with a caveat. Tab and window setups don't protect you from the fragility that comes with Xcode's default behavior of intruding the Debug area and the Debug navigator when you run your target. You must remember to switch to a tab in which you'd tolerate that behavior before running; you could even have a **Debug** tab for the purpose and modify the "Run starts" behavior to switch to it automatically. See the "Behaviors" section of Chapter 4, "Active Debugging," for the beginnings of a strategy.

Building

Xcode 3 started with a build process centered on *configurations*, sets of build settings you could use depending on your purpose in building a product. As it evolved, building developed on a separate axis, *actions*: building to analyze, building to sublaunch into Instruments, building to launch, and building to archive.

Xcode 4 completes that evolution. The **Product** menu offers five actions: **Run**, **Test**, **Profile**, **Analyze**, and **Archive**—as the primary things you do with your product. The details of those actions are bundled into the product's *scheme*: things such as which configuration should be used for the action, what executable should run to host the product, what parameters should be passed in, and what tools should be applied.

Actions still build targets, and schemes usually match one-for-one with targets, but because the focus is on what is to be *done*, and not what is to be *built*, a scheme may include more than one target (such as a product and its test suite). And a scheme may have variations depending on its destination (platform and operating system version). That's why the **Target** pop-up that used to be in the toolbar of the Xcode 3 Project window is now two chained pop-ups labeled **Scheme**.

This sounds complicated, and it certainly can be subtle, but you can ignore schemes most of the time. The defaults Xcode provides in its project and target templates are good enough to start with; if your needs are not complex, you may never need to change your schemes.

Schemes are a recurring theme in this book. The "Schemes" section of Chapter 12, "Adding Table Cells," provides a practical introduction, and Chapter 26, "The Xcode Build System," covers technical details.

Where Did Everything Go?

As an Xcode 3 user, you developed an instinct for where you can find your tools for the development process. It may not have made much sense, but you got used to it. Xcode 4 rearranges those tools; let's see where they've gone.

Groups & Files

You're used to the old Groups & Files list, but that's not the same as its having been simple. It did contain files, and almost everything you did with it was to select a file. But "Groups" covered a multitude of concepts, some of them quite abstract: There were groups to organize files; groups to represent targets; groups to represent executables; groups to represent file statuses; and on and on. The Groups & Files list was the one part of Xcode 3 that overloaded a single tool for many disjoint tasks.

Xcode 4 overloads screen spaces for many different purposes, but it tries to confine itself to one purpose at a time. The Project navigator—the nearest equivalent to Groups & Files—does one thing: It organizes, displays, and filters a list of files.

Where did all the other groups go?

▶ The **Products** group is still there, but it always points to actual files. The group contains icons representing the last-built version of each product; right-click one and select **Show in Finder** to go to the file. If the name is red, the file doesn't exist, at least where Xcode can find it.

▶ **Targets** are now in the Target editor you get when you click the Project icon in the Project navigator and select a target. Add a target with the large + button at the bottom of the Project/Target editor, or select **File→New→Target**…. To delete it, select a target and press Delete.

Targets in the old Targets group contained build phases, which in turn contained the files involved in each phase. The **Build Phases** tab of the Target editor gives you a list of full-size tables to add and remove files, and adding and removing phases is done directly with buttons in the editor.

Xcode 3 did not guarantee the order in which build phases would execute: You could add a "Run Script" phase, and drag it into a particular position inside the target group, but it might or might not be executed in that order. Xcode 4's Build Phases editor guarantees the execution order of the phases.

▶ **Executables** were either the directly executable products of your targets, or external applications that would host your products (such as a third-party application for which you were building a plug-in). In Xcode 4's model, executables don't exist, and aren't selectable, independent of a *scheme* (the set of contexts in which a target would be built, tested, or executed). What had been embodied in Executable objects is now subsumed into scheme options. This eliminates Xcode 3's presentation of a "current executable," which easily got to cross-purposes with the selected target and configuration.

▶ **Find Results** was a historical list of the results (it did not redo the searches) of your most recent projectwide searches. Selecting an item in the group would put the results in the Detail area, and you could use the search field there to narrow the results further.

The magnifying-glass badge in the field at the top of the Search navigator (third tab) preserves the most recent searches, and a search field at the *bottom* of the Search navigator lets you narrow them down.

▶ **Bookmarks** listed all the places you'd marked in your source for later reference. Xcode 4 doesn't offer bookmarks.

▶ **SCM** listed all the files in the project that were not marked as current with the version-control system in use by the project. The Project navigator can do the same thing with the second of the three filter buttons at the bottom.

24

▶ **Errors and Warnings** gave a cumulative list of all the files having outstanding issues from previous builds. This had already been overtaken by features in the Build Results window. The Issues navigator (fourth tab) serves the same purpose.

▶ **Project Symbols** listed all the program symbols in your project. It served best as a way to fill the Detail view above the editor in the Project window with a searchable list from which you could jump to definitions. The Symbol navigator (second tab) provides the same service.

▶ **Smart Groups**, which put all files matching a name pattern you supplied, are gone. If you want to match a substring, use the search field at the bottom of the Project navigator. If you match a particular substring all the time, consider having a separate tab to edit files of that kind (especially handy for matching .xib files to an IB setup), and leaving the pattern permanently in the Project navigator for that tab.

Detail View

The Detail view was a list at the top of the Project window that gave expanded information on what you selected in the Groups & Files list. It indicated whether files were part of the current target, how big their compiled object files were, and whether they had been compiled since they were last modified. It also served as a browser for the Symbols smart group. It included a search field to filter its contents.

This will be a short section: There is no Detail view. The specific information it provided about files isn't available any more, at least at a glance. You can filter files (in the Project navigator) and symbols (in the Symbol navigator) using the search fields at the bottom of the respective navigators.

Info Windows

In Xcode 3, selecting a file, project, executable, or target in the Groups & Files list, and issuing **File→Get Info** (⌘I) would reliably get you an Info window, showing you all the characteristics of what you selected: File properties, build settings, executable parameters, and so on. Xcode 4 abolishes Info windows, moving their function into editors, the Utility area (third segment in the **View** control in the toolbar), and the Scheme editor (**Product→Edit Scheme…** [⌘<]).

The rule-of-thumb is that settings are expressed in editors if possible, and that editors are presented by your taking direct action with the mouse, rather than through a menu command or a double-click on a placeholder.

Here's what you might remember from Xcode 3, and how you can do the same thing in Xcode 4:

▶ Double-clicking a target got you a **Target Info** window. It had five tabs:

    ▶ **General** governed target dependencies. They're now covered in the **Build** panel of the Scheme editor if you want dependencies detected automatically; or in a "Target Dependencies" list in the **Build Phases** tab of the Target editor, if you want to manage them by hand.

▶ **Build** listed all the build variables that controlled the build of the product. This has gone to the **Build Settings** tab of the Target editor. The **Build Settings** tab for projects and targets is better—simply better. The Xcode build system, you remember, keeps a hierarchy of settings, and under Xcode 3, you had to trace from defaults through the project and up to a target. You had to do most of the tracing yourself across Info windows, and it was easy to get into a place where you could try to make a projectwide change and never be sure it would propagate to all targets. Xcode 4's Target **Build Settings** editor shows the whole inheritance hierarchy at one glance, and you can edit it at any level in one view.

▶ **Rules** matched file types to the tools that were to process them. It has gone, substantially unchanged, to the **Rules** tab of the Target editor. See Chapter 26 for more about how the **Build Settings** and **Rules** tabs work.

▶ **Properties** was a high-level editor for `Info.plist`. Its has been divided into the Target editor as the **Summary** tab (for presentational settings like icons and App Store categories) and **Info**, a property-list editor that knows the specific requirements of `Info.plist`.

▶ **Comments** is dead in all the Info windows.

▶ The **Project Info** window, obtainable by double-clicking the project icon at the top of the Groups & Files list, has gone to the Project editor in the same way as the Target settings. You can find a few settings—version compatibility and organization name, most notably—in the File inspector in the Utility area. The **SCM** control for the project is now handled more-or-less automatically by Xcode; see Chapter 7 for details.

▶ **File Info** was for setting file types, line endings, text encodings, target membership, and SCM status for the files you selected in the Groups & Files list. This has all moved to the Utility area in the File inspector (first tab).

A variant on the File Info window, available when you double-clicked a file within a "Compile Sources" build phase, let you set per-file-per-target compiler flags. You can do this in Xcode 4 by editing the second column of the file's entry in the Compile Sources table in the Target editor's **Build Phases** tab.

▶ **Executable Info** let you set the arguments, environment variables, debugger, and other options for an executable, which might be your own application, or a third-party application that would host your plug-in. "Executables," as independently existing objects, don't exist in Xcode 4. The settings that were packaged in executables are now set in the Run and Profile panels of your target's Scheme editor, which you can open with **Product→Edit Scheme…**).

▶ If you double-clicked a Copy Files phase of a Target, you got a Copy Phase Info window. It's now handled by the "Copy Files" section you get when you add the phase to the **Build Phases** tab of the Target editor.

▶ Likewise, the **Script Phase Info** window has turned into a section of the **Build Phases** tab.

Special-Purpose Editors

Xcode 3 had a window for every role. Each had a list at the top, indexing into a file that would fill the attached editor when you made a selection. Each window had a menu command that summoned it.

These are all gone. Xcode maintains only one area for indexing into files: the Navigator. Different methods for indexing files—name, search results, errors, symbols—are embodied in their own navigators. Part of the rationale was that on modern screens, vertical space, where the results were, is precious, whereas horizontal space, where navigators go, is cheap. Ironically, the Navigator area must be stretched wide to show even a large fraction of the information that those specialty windows showed. It's a matter of opinion whether they show enough.

The **Project Search** window accepted a search string, some find options, and a scope, and filled its list with matches from all the files in the project. You could then supply a new string to make a global replacement. The Search navigator (third tab) does the same thing in the same way.

The search options are still there, but you have to know the trick: The magnifying glass in the search field is a drop-down menu, and one of the items in it is **Show Find Options**; this exposes the options. The options hide themselves in due course, which is a pity: Without them, there's no way to know whether your next search will be whole-word or substring; textual or regular-expression. Add the replacement field by changing the pop-up next to the search field from **Find** to **Replace**.

BEHAVIORS

You can clear up some Xcode 4 annoyances with *behaviors*. The **Behaviors** panel of the Preferences window lists events to which you can attach actions, like showing or hiding areas and navigators. See Figure 24.3.

A simple example appears in Chapter 4. Here is a deeper example, which recovers some of the feel of the Xcode 3 Project Search window:

1. Open the **Behaviors** panel of the Preferences window (**Xcode→Preferences** [⌘**Comma**]).

2. Select **Find initiates**, check **Show tab**, and enter `Search Results`. It doesn't matter that you don't have a tab by that name; Xcode creates it when you start a project search with ⇧⌘**F**.

3. Select **Find Completes with Results**, and again set **Show tab** and enter `Search Results`.

Now, when you start a project search, a new tab appears to receive the results. Type in your search and press Return. If the search succeeds, the Search navigator fills with the matches, and a fresh editor is there to display your results—without disturbing your main work area.

You can also create behavior events of your own—just click the **+** button under the behavior list, give the new entry a name, and set its actions. The "trigger" event for your behavior is the selection of its name in the menu at **Xcode→Behaviors**. You can assign it a key combination by double-clicking the Command button that appears next to its name in the list.

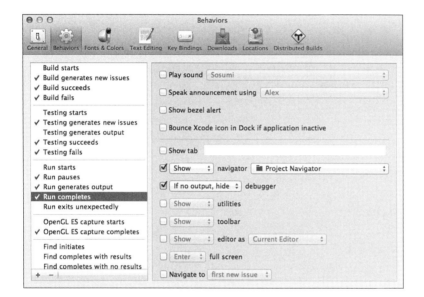

FIGURE 24.3   The **Behaviors** panel of the Preferences window lists events (on the left) that can trigger a fixed repertoire of actions. In this case, **Run completes** does some cleanup by showing the Project navigator and hiding the Debug area.

The **Build Results** window served two purposes: It navigated among compiler errors, and it was a high-level browser for the textual log of the build process. The former is now done by the Issues navigator (fourth tab) and the latter, by the Log navigator (seventh tab). They're straightforward to use, and Chapter 26 gives the details.

You may never have used the **Breakpoints** editor, which provided a global list of the breakpoints you set in your code. It was there that you could set conditions and special actions on each breakpoint and create symbolic breakpoints. (`objc_exception_throw` was always a favorite, but the Breakpoints navigator gives you a shortcut, through the + button, which breaks on all exceptions.)

And last, the big one: The **Debugger** window and its associated **Console**. The top portion of the window supported views for a stack trace and a variables display; the ubiquitous editor view took up the bottom portion. The toolbar had large buttons to control the flow of the debugging session. The separate Console window multiplexed text I/O with both the application and the `gdb` debugger.

Xcode 4 adapts its single Workspace window to debugging: It switches the Navigator area to the Debug navigator, which displays a stack trace for every thread in the target application. (Threading has been a part of the Cocoa application environment all along, and it has become common even in application code. It is time to make threads fully visible in debugger displays.) The Debug area, which by default slides up when you run an application, is split between a variables display and a console.

The big flow-control buttons are gone; there's no room for them in the toolbar. Instead, the strip at the top of the Debug area contains small buttons, like the ones in Xcode 3's in-editor debugger, to do the same thing. You can re-create the in-editor debugger by hiding the Debug area (middle segment of the toolbar's **View** control); the control strip remains at the bottom of the window, and when you hover over variables in the currently executing code, the same hierarchical tooltip appears to show you their values.

Browsers

Two browsers that drew on Xcode's capability to analyze and index your code are gone:

- ▶ The **Class Model** window, which provided an inheritance diagram for your project classes. It could be made to update itself as your code changed, but it was never editable (except to change the layout). If your inheritance tree was complex, it was a useful tool.

- ▶ Likewise the **Class Browser**, which listed classes your project referred to. It could be made hierarchical or flat, and classes could be made to show inherited methods as well as their own. The Class Browser is almost duplicated by the Symbol navigator, but the inherited-method feature is nowhere to be found in Xcode 4. Andy Lee's free AppKiDo documentation browsers (`http://homepage.mac.com/aglee/downloads/appkido.html`) supply the lack.

Source Control

Source Control (which Xcode 3 called SCM) felt like an add-on to Xcode 3—and it was. Xcode 4 integrates it into the basic workflow.

- ▶ When you create a project, Xcode offers to create a local Git repository for it. This is a cheap and easy way to get a panoply of features. You need only a basic understanding of version-control concepts to gain huge advantages.

- ▶ Comparing versions was done in a window that was obscure to access and didn't edit anything. Xcode 4's editor integrates comparison, logging, and "blame" into a major mode. The Version editor (third segment in the **Editor** control in the toolbar) lets you browse any two versions, even on different branches, directly. You can select the two versions using a Time Machine-like timeline.

- ▶ The comparison editor is ubiquitous. Before you commit a revision, a sheet appears that lets you browse all the files that will be committed to see the changes. The comparison view is a real editor—you can make last-minute changes before committing. When you merge branches or do a refactor, the comparison sheet shows you what changes will occur.

▶ Xcode 3 managed a fixed repertoire of repositories in the Preferences window. Because the only version-control systems it supports carry the full particulars of repositories in the working directories, Xcode 4 detects repos automatically. You can manage and browse your repositories in the **Repositories** panel of the Organizer.

▶ The Repositories browser, which displayed the branches and contents (by name only) of the known repositories, and allowed you to do operations like checking versions out, has gone into the much-more-capable Repositories organizer.

▶ Info windows for projects and files included an **SCM** tab that let you browse revisions that affected those files, check them out, and spawn windows (often just text editors) for viewing comparisons and blame. This is all incorporated into the Version editor in Xcode 4. The Repositories organizer gives you a consolidated view of the log for all revisions, as well as giving you direct access to every file in a revision.

▶ One simple operation—reverting a file to the last-committed revision—is provided through the Source Control section of the File inspector. However, this feature stopped working in Xcode 4.1, and it hadn't returned as of Xcode 4.3.

See Chapter 7 for the full story.

Interface Builder

One of the biggest differences in Xcode 4 is that Interface Builder is no longer a separate application; it is just one of the many editor modes in the single Workspace window. You should be glad about this. Tighter integration has many benefits, but the big feature—the wow feature—that comes of it is this:

You could always link outlets and actions by control-dragging between objects inside the XIB. Now you can control-drag from an XIB object into a class header's `@interface` and drop a new declaration for an outlet or action in that class. Xcode delves into the class's `@implementation` and writes assignment and deallocation code, and skeletons for the actions. See how in "Outlets" in Chapter 11, "Building a New View."

Interface Builder relied on floating palettes to provide an object library and the many inspectors needed to fully configure all the objects in a XIB. Xcode 4 doesn't do palettes. Where did everything go?

They all went into the Utility area at the right. The Utility area is divided into an inspector at the top and a library at the bottom. The inspector usually has only two tabs, for the selected file and for Quick Help. When Interface Builder is active, it adds at least four inspector tabs (Identity, Attributes, Size, and Connections), and two more (Bindings and View Effects) if the XIB is for a Mac application. See Figure 24.4.

FIGURE 24.4   For a Mac XIB, Interface Builder adds six inspector tabs to the File and Quick Help inspectors that are always there.

The separate window that represented the XIB file is gone, relieving a potential source of confusion. The XIB window displayed placeholder objects and top-level contents in the form of icons, a columnar browser, or a hierarchical outline. The browser view is gone. The new IB editor displays icons by default in a sidebar; they have no labels, but if you hover your mouse pointer over them, you will see tooltips that identify them. If you want detailed access to the XIB's contents, click the arrow button next to the bottom of the sidebar to expand it to an outline (called the "document structure area"). See Figure 24.5.

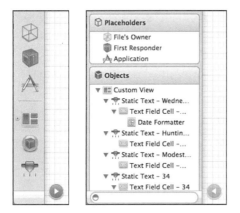

FIGURE 24.5   The arrowhead button next to the Interface Builder sidebar toggles the sidebar between the icon-only (left) and outline (right) views.

There is one big loss: IB no longer has a published interface for plug-ins. If you relied on a plug-in to configure your own objects for inclusion in a NIB, Interface Builder no longer loads it, and it refuses to load XIBs built with it. The only solution is to get a version-3 Interface Builder application and continue your work with it.

Other Changes

Many other things changed from version 3 to version 4:

- ▶ Xcode 3 was edging this way already, but now it's complete: The only distinction between what were Run and Debug is whether breakpoints are enabled.

- ▶ Shark has been removed from the developer tools. Instruments has expanded to do almost everything Shark did.

- ▶ The editor's "live issues" reporting eliminates the need to manually compile single files to check syntax; the **Build→Compile** (⌘K) command is gone. Errors don't always clear up when they are corrected. You need to issue **Product→Build** (⌘B) from time to time. Better still, run an analysis (**Product→Analyze** [⇧⌘B]); it catches more.

▶ Automatic Reference Counting (ARC), which makes it unnecessary (even illegal) to do your own memory management of Objective-C objects, is used in all project and target templates. This requires the `llvm` 3 compiler, which is the default. `llvm` 3 is necessary to get all the features of Xcode 4, such as live issues and Fix-It.

▶ The `gcc` compiler is no longer supported; Xcode converts existing projects to `llvm` 3. If you rely on `gcc` parsing behavior, a hybrid of a `gcc` front-end parser that feeds the `llvm` code generator is available as an option. Make the setting in the **Build Settings** tab of the Target editor, under "Compiler for C/C++/Objective-C."

▶ `llvm` is much faster than `gcc` and is smart enough that it can usually locate errors and warnings within a line, rather than flagging the whole line. When used for the **Analyze** action, it recognizes common errors (such as assignments in `if` statements, or tricky operator precedence) and even offers to fix the problems.

▶ CVS and Perforce are no longer supported for source control; the only options are Subversion and Git. If you are willing to do your version control through the command line or external applications, you can use any system you like.

▶ The Organizer's original purpose—managing directory trees, serving as a generalized text editor, and running `make` projects—is gone.

▶ In Xcode 3, you could drag a Core Data entity out of the Data Model editor and into a view in Interface Builder. IB would then offer to create a single, multiple, or master-detail interface for the entity. This isn't possible in Xcode 4.

▶ Earlier SDKs (more than one release behind for Mac OS X, anything earlier than the current iOS) are gone. Apple's position is that its operating systems are backward compatible, and all you need to do to produce a Leopard-compatible Mac application is to avoid post-10.5 API. There are two problems with this.

First, it's easy to let later API slip through, and without the ability to check your code against the earlier API, the first warning you have of the incompatibility may be when your users report crashes. Second, the `libcrypto` library in Mac OS X 10.5 was replaced in 10.6 with an incompatible version. Linking against the 10.6 SDK produces an app that crashes on 10.5 as it looks for a library that isn't there.

If this is a problem for you, see if you can convert to CommonCrypto or keep an installation of Xcode 3 in parallel with Xcode 4. Apple's recommendation is that you keep it on a separate 10.6 partition and reboot to use it. Users have found that if you have an existing Xcode 3 installation, it seems to work on 10.7; but there are no guarantees. If you didn't have Xcode 3 installed at the time you upgraded, you'll find that Xcode 3 will not install on a Lion system.

But if Xcode 3 is an option for you, don't worry about sharing work with users of Xcode 4. The project formats are forward compatible, even though 4-only features such as schemes and workspaces won't port back to 3.

Summary

Xcode 4 is radically different from its predecessor, and it can seem that few of the skills you won in Xcode 3 can carry over. The worst of it is that Xcode is a huge system, almost completely rewritten, and you can expect it to be buggy for at least another year.

But most of the changes fall into two categories: Things that have merely moved, and things that are better. There are still annoyances—the shift from the desktop model to the browser model takes a while to get used to, and Apple seems to have adhered to it to a greater degree than necessary—but most of what you know still applies; you just need to know where to look for it. I hope this chapter gave you a start.

## CHAPTER 25

Documentation in Xcode

The combined documentation for developer tools and the current versions of Mac OS X and iOS run to about 2GB, and Apple updates them continually. Xcode incorporates an extensive help and documentation system to give you quick access to the documents while you code and a browser for when you need to go into more depth. In this chapter, I'll show you how to make the most of the facilities Xcode provides and how you can add your own documentation.

Intrinsic Help

The first level of documentation is immediate and interactive: getting instructions on how to use Xcode features and descriptions for what you've selected in the editor. The emphasis is on getting you the information you need quickly.

The Quick Help Inspector

Quick Help is available to you in almost every editor. Simply expose the Utility area (right-hand segment of the **View** control) and select the Quick Help inspector (second tab).

> ▶ If you're editing source, and the editing cursor is in a symbol for which Apple has documentation, Quick Help will show you a summary of how a method (for instance) is invoked, a description of what it does, the types and purposes of its parameters, and what it returns. It will tell you the earliest version of the OS that supports it and offer you cross-references to overview documentation, related API, and the header

file in which the symbol is declared. The information is drawn from the docset corresponding to the SDK you use. See Figure 25.1, left.

Quick Help works on your own symbols, too, but all you get is a reference to the declaration—unless you provide documentation of your own. More on that later.

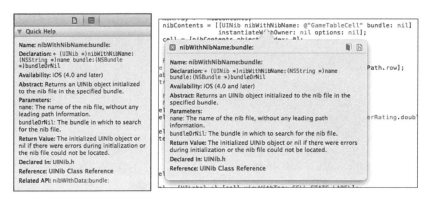

FIGURE 25.1   (left) When the Quick Help inspector is open and the text cursor is in any documented symbol, the inspector displays a summary of the symbol, parameters, and other information. It includes clickable cross-references. (right) If you hold down the Option key and click a documented symbol, Xcode displays a popover window with the same information. At the upper-right corner are buttons to jump to the full documentation or the header in which the symbol is declared.

▶ When you select an object in Interface Builder (IB), Quick Help provides documentation for the object's class.

▶ In the Project/Target editor's **Build Settings** tab, selecting a row fills Quick Help with what is usually the most complete documentation you can find of the setting. The description includes how the setting might get a default value, the build variable underlying the setting (see Appendix B, "Some Build Variables"), and the compiler flag, if any, the setting influences.

▶ In property list editors and the **Info** tab of the Target editor, if Xcode displays an English-language equivalent of a key in the editor, Quick Help will show you the underlying key.

The Quick Help Popover

Holding down the Option key and mousing into a symbol puts a dotted line under it and highlights it in blue. If you click, a popover appears with most of the content you'd see in the Quick Help inspector. See Figure 25.1, right. (You can do the same thing by selecting **Help→Quick Help for Selected Item, [^⌘?]**.)

The popover has a close (**x**) box in the upper-left corner to dismiss it; you can press the Escape key, or you can simply click away from it.

At the upper right are two buttons. The one that looks like a book opens the full documentation for that symbol in the Documentation organizer. The one that looks like a page with an "h" in it opens the header file in which the symbol is defined.

Option-double-clicking on a symbol brings up the Documentation organizer and initiates a search for the symbol. Unlike the book button in the popover, the search conforms to whatever search settings you had last time you searched, so if you don't see the results you expect, check to see whether the right document sets are selected. This is equivalent to selecting the symbol and issuing **Help→Search Documentation for Selected Text** [^⌥⌘/]).

The Quick Help popover is also available during code completion. When the completion pop-up displays, mouse over one of the choices. A **?** button appears at the right end of the row. Clicking it shows the Quick Help for that item. The completion pop-up remains open through the entire process.

Now is the time to mention command-clicking:

  ▶ Command-clicking a symbol opens the file in which the symbol is defined and highlights the definition. If there's more than one definition, a pop-up menu offers you the choice.

  ▶ As it does with many navigational gestures, command-*double*-clicking shows the declaration in a new window.

  ▶ Adding the Option key to a command-click shows the declaration in the assistant editor; remember that adding the Option key to any navigational gesture directs the result to the assistant editor.

NOTE

If you move your mouse pointer to a symbol and then depress the Command or Option key, you won't see the highlight, and the gesture won't work. Xcode starts tracking symbols only if the mouse pointer enters them with the modifier key already down.

Open Quickly

Most programmer's editors have some sort of open-quickly or open-selection command that enables you to select a filename and have the editor find and open the file named in the selection. Xcode's **File→Open Quickly**... (⇧⌘O) does the same. But that doesn't end it.

The Open Quickly dialog has a search field that does an incremental search of the names of the files, local and system, your project can access. All the possible matches are listed in a table, and when you select one, its location is shown in the path control below the table.

25

There's more: The search extends to symbols, not just filenames. Enter `componentsBrokenByLines`, and you see the match and its location in `SimpleCSVFile.m`. This is not a simple incremental match. Apple anticipated that you might want to look up a symbol or file whose name you don't quite remember; just enter the parts you do remember: Enter `compbbl`, and it finds (among others) `componentsBrokenByLines`. See Figure 25.2.

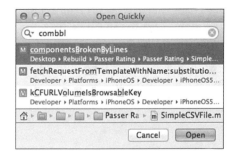

FIGURE 25.2   The Open Quickly dialog finds files and symbols accessible to your project based on an incremental search. You don't need to remember the whole name; any sequence you enter is matched against any sequence of characters in the name, consecutive or not.

Help

Like every Mac OS X application, Xcode has a help menu. The first item in it is not a menu item but an incremental search field. As you type, the contents of the menu are replaced with items in two sections:

▶ **Menu Items:** Lists every menu item that contains the text you typed. Mousing over the listed items opens the corresponding menu and places a pointer next to the item. Clicking a listed item has the same effect as selecting the item.

Some "hidden" items display, and some do not. "Alternate" items that appear only when you hold down a modifier key (open the **File** menu and press and release the Option key) can be found. You cannot find menu items that Xcode has removed—in particular, commands in the **Editor** menu that don't apply to the current editor.

▶ **Help Topics:** The results of searching the Developer Tools documentation set. Selecting one of these opens the Documentation organizer and shows the relevant article.

This is standard behavior for any completely implemented Mac OS X application.

The Quick Help and search items at the end of the menu have been covered. One of the remaining items, **Help→Documentation and API Reference** (⌥⌘?), simply opens the Organizer window and selects the Documentation organizer. The other two focus the Documentation organizer on two important articles in the Developer Tools documentation: The *Xcode User Guide*, which is Apple's introduction to the Xcode IDE, and the Xcode release notes.

> **NOTE**
>
> *Always* read Apple's release notes, which often contain essential information that never finds its way into the mainstream documentation. Unfortunately, Apple is not always diligent about putting current release notes for Xcode into the documentation.

Xcode How-To's

The contextual menus for many elements of the Organizer and Workspace windows include **Help** submenus. Selecting one of the help items opens the Documentation organizer on a brief how-to page for the selected feature. Many of these how-to's include videos showing how to perform common tasks.

The Documentation Organizer

Quick Help is good for focused reference, but you also need simply to read the documentation. To do this, use the Documentation organizer (**Window→Organizer [⇧⌘2]**, and select the **Documentation** tab). Like the Workspace window, the Documentation organizer has a navigator area at the left; **Editor→Hide/Show Navigator** toggles it. There are three tabs.

Browsing Documentation

The first tab reveals the Explore Documentation navigator. It contains a section for every documentation set you have loaded into Xcode. At the least, this includes the Developer Tools library and libraries for the current iOS and Mac OS X versions. As you go on, you accumulate more docsets.

Explore Documentation is an outline, nothing more. Clicking a row fills the documentation view with the corresponding article. When you click the disclosure triangle for a docset, you will see an alphabetical listing of the articles that make it up:

▶ API references are tagged with purple squares marked with a white "C."

▶ Guides and overviews are tagged with blue books.

▶ Sample code is shown with bright-blue Xcode project icons.

Each article can in turn be opened up into pages and sections. As usual, option-clicking a disclosure triangle fully opens or closes all the items under that row.

There is a jump bar at the top of the documentation view. The segments correspond to the hierarchy you see in the outline. There are forward and back buttons to page through your browsing history. Hold the mouse down on one, or select **Editor→History** to see a history menu.

At the left end of the jump bar is a related-item menu. If there is a PDF version of the document you view, selecting **Open PDF:** from the menu downloads and displays it. However, this doesn't do you much good: The viewer presents the whole page, which can be zoomed only through **Editor** menu commands for which there are no key equivalents, and you can't save the PDF.

> **NOTE**
>
> Apple is phasing PDF links out of Xcode docsets. If you want a usable PDF, search `developer.apple.com` for the document to find the PDF link.

Searching Documentation

The second tab is the Search Documentation navigator. The first time you see it, you find a search field, nothing else. When you type in it, Xcode performs an incremental search of your documentation sets, filling the navigator with matching items. These are divided into categories:

▸ **Reference** items jump you straight to the API references matching your search.

▸ **System Guides** are selected by a "fuzzier" full-text search. These are overview articles that relate to the terms you entered.

▸ **Tools Guides** are the same, but directed to developer-tools documentation. If you searched for **data model**, the System Guides category would show you articles about Core Data, and the Tools Guides would show instructions for the data-model editor.

▸ **Sample Code** lists example projects demonstrating techniques related to your search.

The default documentation search is probably not the best for your needs. If you look for a specific Cocoa Touch API, you may not want to match strings in the middle of symbols, you won't be interested in JavaScript interfaces, and Mac-only documents will only annoy you. This is when you click the magnifying-glass icon at the left of the search field and select **Show Find Options** in the resulting drop-down menu. See Figure 25.3.

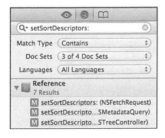

FIGURE 25.3   Select **Show Find Options** in the pop-up at the left end of the search field in the Search Documentation navigator to get better control over your documentation searches.

The options panel consists of three pop-up menus:

- ▶ **Match Type:** Lets you restrict matches to whole words (**Exact**) or prefixes, rather than allow embedded matches (**Contains**).

- ▶ **Doc Sets:** Contains the names of every documentation set you have. If no items are checked (or all), your search goes through all of them. Clicking a set includes or excludes it from searching. Here is where you'd shut Mac OS X documents out of your iOS search.

- ▶ **Languages:** Cocoa and system programming for Apple platforms entails APIs in many languages. This menu lets you select any combination among four: C, C++, JavaScript, and Objective-C.

Your selections, and the visibility of the options, will be maintained until you change them.

Bookmarks

The Documentation Bookmarks navigator is simple—simpler than it needs to be. When you select **Editor→Add Bookmark**, the title of the page you view is added to this list. When you click the item, Xcode brings you back to that page. Selecting a bookmark and pressing Delete removes the bookmark.

That's it. You can't rename a bookmark. There is no other information. The list is in the order in which you added the marks; you can't sort it.

Keeping Current

Xcode and Apple's documentation do not come out on the same schedule. They can't. Even if it were practical to halt one team while the other caught up to a release, the documents will still be extended and revised, and be ready for the public, at a much faster pace than a complex set of developer tools can.

When you first install Xcode, you don't have a complete local documentation library. What is packaged inside Xcode is a skeleton of a few hundred megabytes with minimal content, filled in with cross-references to Apple resources on the Web. The equivalent local library is an order of magnitude larger. Not including the full library makes downloading Xcode faster, and it frees Apple from providing an obsolete library (or having to rebuild the Xcode package every few weeks as the documentation is revised).

So the first thing you need to do when you install Xcode is to run it, need it or not. It immediately compares its local document set with what's on Apple's servers and commences a download of a gigabyte or more.

Documentation is provided in *documentation sets (docsets)*, essentially large websites plus the indexes that make Quick Help, the browsing outline, and full-text searching possible. Each docset is nearly self-contained, although it can have references out to the Web.

The top level of the Explore Documentation navigator lists each docset. You manage your

docsets with the **Documentation** tab of the **Downloads** panel of the Preferences window.
See Figure 25.4.

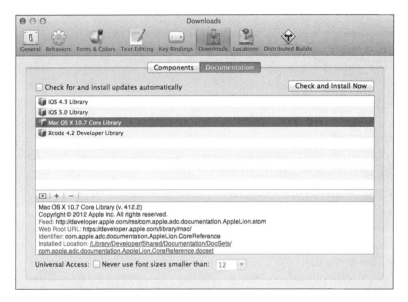

FIGURE 25.4   The **Documentation** tab of the **Downloads** panel of the Preferences window
lets you add, remove, and update your documentation sets. Clicking the expand button at the
bottom left of the table shows an information area that describes the selected docset.

The Documentation pane is dominated by a list of all documentation sets Xcode knows
about. If a set is known but not loaded, a **Get** button will appear next to its title. Click it,
and the button will gray out, and a gray Getting... notation will appear. There is an
"expand" button at the bottom-left corner of the listing. Clicking it opens an information
area, which shows the title, copyright, location, and update feed for the selected docset.

The documentation system uses RSS to monitor updates for documentation sets.
Checking the **Check for and install updates automatically** authorizes Xcode to do just
that; you can also click **Check and Install Now** to attempt updates immediately. At the
bottom, you can enforce a minimum displayed font size.

With the + button, you can specify a source or an RSS feed for a new documentation set.
The – button removes the selected set from the list.

The first time you download a particular docset—likely when you first run Xcode—you
will be asked for an administrator's login ID and password because downloaded docsets
are put in the privileged /Library/Developer/Documentation/DocSets directory. After you
authorize it, the privilege is permanent.

Because downloaded docsets are kept in /Library/Developer/Documentation/
DocSets, outside Xcode's directory, you can replace Xcode without duplicating or
redownloading the documentation.

The Activity area, in the middle of the toolbar, shows the progress of lengthy tasks. With
the small projects in this book, you've seen the progress bars flash in and out quickly. Big
downloads take longer, and this may be your first extended look at the Activity area.

There's room for only one progress bar in the area, but if more than one process is under
way, a circled number appears on the left side. Click it, and the Activity area expands to
display the progress of the active tasks. See Figure 25.5.

25

FIGURE 25.5   The Activity area in the middle of the Workspace window's toolbar (top) shows
the progress of one ongoing process. (bottom) Clicking the number button on the left expands it
to show the progress of all downloads.

NOTE

Docsets consist mainly of trees of HTML files, and you once could track down the root
of a document and view it with a web browser. That's becoming less and less practical
as Apple develops docsets to be applications that rely on support from Xcode's documentation system. Related to this, the HTML documents are downloaded files containing executable code (JavaScript). As such, Mac OS X flags them as "quarantine," and
interrupts you with a warning if you try to open them directly.

Generating Documentation

You are not restricted to Apple's documentation sets; you can create your own. Good
automatic documentation generators are available, and they can make the process of
indexing and installation easy. I'll be showing you Doxygen because it documents the
source of the iOS Passer Rating app.

Installing Doxygen

Doxygen is the most widely used general-purpose documentation generator in the world. Javadoc may have more users, but Doxygen covers more languages, including Objective-C. Download it from `http://www.doxygen.org/`; there is a build for Mac OS X, in the form of a `.dmg` disk image containing a single Mac application. Drag it into your `/Application` directory, and eject the disk image.

> **NOTE**
>
> It's important to what I'll be showing you that Doxygen be in the system `Applications` directory.

Doxygen can produce graphs—class diagrams, call trees, and include trees—to illustrate its documents. It has a simple graphics package of its own, but you can do more with the GraphViz package of graphical utilities. The Doxygen team recommends you get it from `http://www.ryandesign.com/graphviz/`. (You can find an excellent Mac/iOS application port of GraphViz at `http://www.pixelglow.com/graphviz/`, but for this purpose, you just need the command-line tools.) It's another `.dmg`; mount it and run the Installer package you find there.

You need the exact directory path to which the GraphViz executables were installed. It's inside `/usr/local`, but the next directory is named for the specific version of the package you installed. Do this: Open the Terminal application, and on the command line, type **cd /usr/local/graph**, and press the Tab key. The shell completes the name of the directory. Finish the line with **bin** and press Return. Then enter **pwd**. What the shell prints in response is the path you need.

What Doxygen Does

Doxygen scans your source code, particularly your header files, for declarations of classes, methods, functions, constants, and other symbols. It compiles them into an index and outputs documentation files. It can generate LaTeX, RTF, Microsoft help archives, man pages, and XML indexes; but you're interested in HTML.

A complex of web pages that organize the symbols you define would be interesting but not informative. What makes it into *documentation* are the specially formatted comments you add to your source. The markup is fairly inconspicuous and even informative for readers of the uninterpreted comments.

Here are some samples, from `SimpleCSVFile.h`:

```
///   \c NSError* \c userInfo dictionary key for the
///   line on which an error was detected. (\c NSNumber)
extern NSString * const      kCSVErrorLineKey;


. . .


/**
 Parser for simple CSV files.
```

SimpleCSVFile will open a file and attempt to extract
key-value data from it. It is expected that the first
line will include keys that identify the fields in the
data stream.

@warning This is not a general CSV parser.
In particular, it does not handle quotes, embedded commas,
or escaping.
*/

@interface SimpleCSVFile : NSObject {
}

. . .
/**
Parse the CSV file.
Loops through the lines of the input file, interpreting the
first line as unique keys for the data fields contained in
the remaining lines.

The keys and values for each line are gathered into an
NSDictionary, which is presented line-by-line to the
delegate object.

It is an error for the file to have a line with a different
number of fields than specified in the header line.

@param[out] error A pointer to an \c NSError object
                   pointer, or nil. If non-nil, and an
                   error occurs (signified by a return
                   value of \c NO), *error will describe
                   the problem.

@return   Whether parsing succeeded. If \c NO, and
           an \c NSError** parameter was supplied,
           \p *error will describe the problem.

@see   SimpleCSVDelegate
*/
- (BOOL) run: (NSError **) error;

/// The path to the CSV file.
/// Setting this property has no effect after run: is called.
@property(nonatomic, copy) NSString *   path;

Usually, Doxygen comments precede whatever they document. Block comments begin with an extra asterisk: /**. You can also use inline comments with an extra slash: ///. You can set up Doxygen to use the Javadoc convention of pulling out the first line of a comment as a summary to be shown in index tables.

Markup keywords begin with @ or \. Use the backslash for inline markup, like the \c that calls out the next word as monospaced "code." Xcode gives markup strings a distinctive color. A few of the available flags follow:

▶ `@param`: The first word is the parameter name; everything thereafter is a description. There can be more than one `@param` directive.

▶ `@return`: Describes the return value of a function/method.

▶ `@exception`: The first word is the name of an exception a function/method could raise; the rest is a description. There can be more than one `@exception`.

▶ `@see`: An external URL or an internal symbol that Doxygen can link to.

▶ `@warning`: Text that is presented with a red bar in the margin.

▶ `@todo`: Commentary on work yet to be done for the API.

▶ `@bug`: Commentary on a bug in the API.

▶ `@author`: The name, URL, or email address of the author of the annotated code.

▶ `@deprecated`: Flags and indexes an API as deprecated, with your notation.

▶ `@c`, `@p`: One word of "code" or "parameter" text that can be set in a monofont. Stretches of more than one word should be set out in the corresponding HTML markup.

▶ `@em`, `@e`, `@i`: One word to be set in italics.

▶ `@b`: One word to be set in boldface.

There are many more features and refinements than I can possibly present in this book. You can learn everything from the manual available on the Doxygen site (182 PDF pages for Doxygen 1.7.5).

The results are striking—well formatted and attractively presented. See the entry for
-[SimpleCSVFile run:] in Figure 25.6.

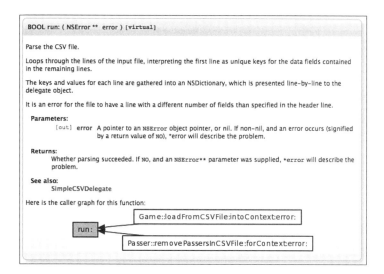

FIGURE 25.6   The Doxygen entry for -[SimpleCSVFile run:].

Configuring Doxygen: The Wizard

doxygen proper is a command-line tool that processes your source code under the direction of a configuration file. There are *many* options, and the Doxygen app for Mac OS X is mostly an editor for the configuration. Double-click the Doxygen icon to run it. What you see is a "wizard" window with a list of views on the left and a form on the right. See Figure 25.7.

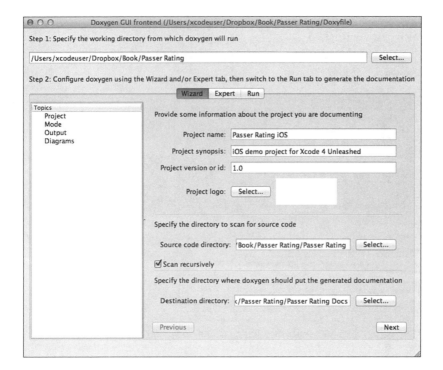

FIGURE 25.7   The Doxygen "wizard" window.

doxygen being a UNIX command-line tool, it needs a working directory. The first thing you do is set it, using the affordance at the top of the window. There's a text field there to enter the path directly, but use the **Select...** button to pick the `Passer Rating` project directory—that's the directory that contains the project file, not the one that contains the source.

Now fill out the configuration. You do this in two stages; the **Wizard** tab presents a simplified English-language interface that you can use for most of the setup. Then you round it out in the **Expert** tab, which is just a structured editor for the configuration file.

Project Panel

Here is the setup you'll do through the Project panel:

▶ Project name: `Passer Rating`.

▶ Project synopsis: Something brief to explain what Passer Rating is: `iOS demo project for Xcode 4 Unleashed`.

▶ Project version or id: 1.0.

▶ If you supply a logo image, it will render full-size on every page of the documentation. Be discreet.

- ▶ **Source code directory:** Doxygen works by going through your source files, parsing, and indexing them. Use **Select...** to choose the source directory within the project directory. Check **Scan recursively** to search subdirectories as well.

- ▶ **Destination directory:** This is where the generated documentation goes. Do *not* put it in the source directory; the version-control implications could be nightmarish. Click the **Select...** button, and in the select-file dialog, select the project directory, and click **New Folder**. Enter a name like `Passer Rating Docs`. Select that new directory and click **Choose**.

Mode Panel

The **Mode** panel tells Doxygen about the target files and how to interpret them.

- ▶ For the extraction mode, pick **All Entities**. Doxygen generates documentation for all methods, constants, functions, and so on, even if you haven't yet put documentation comments on them. In a production project, you might want to filter out things you've decided not to document, but for this demo, it will be fun to see what Doxygen can turn up.

- ▶ You are also asked to "optimize" for the language the project is written in. Objective-C is not an offer, but it's a radio group, so you have to pick one. Leave this option alone; you can take care of it in the **Expert** tab.

Output Panel

Doxygen can produce documents in any or all of five different formats. Check only **HTML, with navigation panel** and **With search function**. The **Change color...** button gives you hue, saturation, and value sliders to dress up the emitted pages; suit yourself.

Diagrams Panel

Select **Use dot tool from the GraphViz package**, and have fun. Check all the available graph types.

Configuring Doxygen: Expert Settings

If you want, you can go to the **Run** tab, run Doxygen, and have it show you the results. (But you haven't told it where to find GraphViz yet, so go back to the **Diagrams** panel and choose some other option.) But you can get better results if you use the **Expert** tab.

To serve a multitude of needs and tastes, Doxygen has a multitude of options. They are all documented in the manual you can download from the website. They are all in the **Expert** tab. You need touch only a few.

The expert listing labels each setting with the name it has in the key-value pairs in the configuration file. If you hover your mouse over a name, an explanation will appear in the text area at the bottom left. Each setting has an editor appropriate to its data type. Settings labeled in black haven't changed from their defaults; if you change one, it will be labeled in red.

Project Panel

Check JAVADOC_AUTOBRIEF to emulate Javadoc's feature in which the first sentence of a documentation block is harvested as a short description in summary tables. Otherwise, you'd need to call out brief descriptions with @brief.

In the **Mode** panel of the **Wizard** tab, you were forced to "optimize" the output to present API for a particular language, none of them Objective-C. You get to undo this by locating all the OPTIMIZE_OUTPUT_FOR... items and unchecking them.

Doxygen infers the language of a source file from its extension, so when it parses your .m files, it recognizes them as Objective-C. .h files remain ambiguous, which is the right thing for many projects. Relieve the ambiguity by adding a line to the EXTENSION_MAPPING table: Enter **h=Objective-C** in the text field, and click the + button.

HTML Panel

This panel controls the formatting the HTML Doxygen produces. This is where you set up Doxygen to index your documentation as an Xcode docset.

▶ GENERATE_DOCSET is the master setting for generating a docset. Check it.

▶ DOCSET_FEEDNAME sets a name for a grouping of documentation sets. The set you build now is for the iOS Passer Rating app, but it might be part of a suite of docsets for *Xcode 4 Unleashed*. Set it to **Xcode 4 Unleashed**.

▶ DOCSET_BUNDLE_ID is a unique identifier for this set; it sets the bundle identifier in the docset's Info.plist. You can use **com.wt9t.x4u.docs.ios**.

▶ DOCSET_PUBLISHER_ID, by contrast, uniquely identifies you as the source of this and other docsets. You can use **com.wt9t.x4u.docs**.

▶ DOCSET_PUBLISHER_NAME is your name as presented to humans. (I'm **Fritz Anderson**.)

Dot Panel

Here at last is where you use the path to the GraphViz tools I had you record from the Terminal a while back. Type it, beginning at **/usr** and ending at **/bin** (omit the tool name), in DOT_PATH.

Running Doxygen

You've been creating a reusable configuration file, and you should save it. Select **File→Save** (⌘S). The default name for the file is Doxyfile, and there's no reason to change it. I recommend placing it in the proposed working directory, which is the directory that contains Passer Rating.xcodeproj.

At last you are ready to produce some documents. Select the **Run** tab, and click **Run doxygen**. The text area fills with the run log, which is intimidatingly long. If you elected dot as the graphics generator, and a lot of graph types, some of the dot processing may take a minute.

The doxygen tool will not halt with formatting errors, nor even call them out conspicuously. Be sure at least to skim the log for error messages. The first run may take a couple of minutes, but doxygen has the grace not to regenerate graphs for structures that have not changed.

When processing is done, click **Show HTML output**. Your preferred web browser opens the root page of the generated documentation. This is the designated "main," or overview, page, and if you don't specify one, it will be blank except for a navigation bar at the top. Clicking in the bar shows you more: indexes of classes and their members, files and their contents, and to-dos and bugs. If you asked Doxygen for a client-side search interface, every page will include a search field that can do an incremental search of the docset.

> **NOTE**
>
> The contents of the `Passer Rating Docs` directory are all derived data. You should not add the directory to your version-control repository.

Installing a Docset

When you set `GENERATE_DOCSET`, Doxygen adds a `Makefile` that directs `make` to install the docset into `~/Library/Developer/Shared/Documentation/DocSets`, where Xcode can find it. In Terminal, set the working directory to the generated HTML directory, and run `make`:

```
$ # Assuming you're in the project directory:
$ cd Passer\ Rating\ Docs/html
$ make install
       .
       .
       .

Output from make
       .
       .
       .
$
```

> **NOTE**
>
> Xcode looks for documentation sets in `~/Library` first, then `/Library`, and then in its own package.

> **NOTE**
>
> Don't use `sudo` to run `make`. It's not necessary—you already have write privileges for your own `Library` directory—and you'd be creating directories and files owned by root, which you can't change or delete.

Quit and reopen Xcode; open the Documentation organizer. Your docset should show up
in the Explore Documentation outline. (It might be the *only* thing in the outline, but
switching to another organizer and going back should clean up the list.) The outline
traces through all the indexes in the set, and Quick Help in your source code work
(roughly). See Figure 25.8.

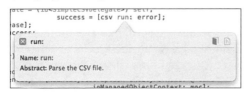

FIGURE 25.8   Installing Doxygen documentation as a document set activates limited Quick
Help for your symbols. The Book button in the upper-right corner jumps you to the full documentation.

Making Doxygen Part of Your Builds

You can add document generation to Xcode. The works of doxygen are all in a command-
line tool, which you can invoke from a "Run Script" build phase, or as a pre-action or
post-action for the Archive action in the Scheme editor. I'll show you how to do it as a
separate target that you can invoke when you want to.

Open the iOS Passer Rating project in Xcode, and select the project icon at the top of the
Project navigator so the Target editor is shown. Click the **Add Target** button at the
bottom of the editor; navigate the New Target assistant to **Other→Aggregate**. The aggregate target is meant to group other targets for a coordinated build, but it's an empty
target, which is what you want. Name it something like **Docset**.

With the Docset target selected, click the **Add Build Phase** button, and select **Add Run
Script**. The new phase is added; click the disclosure triangle to open it. The editor asks for
the **Shell** language for the script; leave it as **/bin/sh**.

Enter the following script:

```
# Set this to the installation location
#   for the Doxygen application:
DOXY_PATH=/Applications/Doxygen.app
# Set to the name of the documentation directory:
DOC_DIR_NAME="$PROJECT_NAME Docs"

LIBDEV_DIR="/Users/$USER/Library/Developer"
DOCSET_DIR="$LIBDEV_DIR/Shared/Documentation/DocSets/"

# Make the project directory (containing the .xcodeproj)
#   the current directory:
cd "$PROJECT_DIR"
# Invoke the doxygen command:
$DOXY_PATH/Contents/Resources/doxygen Doxyfile
```

```
# Go to the generated HTML document directory:
cd "$DOC_DIR_NAME"/html
#
Install the docset in "/Library:
make install

Create a temporary AppleScript that reloads the user docsets:
rm -f "$TEMP_DIR/loadDocSet.scpt"

echo "tell application \"Xcode\"" >> "$TEMP_DIR/loadDocSet.scpt"
echo "load documentation set with path \"$DOCSET_DIR\"" \
>> "$TEMP_DIR/loadDocSet.scpt"
echo "end tell" >> "$TEMP_DIR/loadDocSet.scpt"

# Run AppleScript:
osascript "$TEMP_DIR/loadDocSet.scpt"
```

The script inherits project and target build settings, such as PROJECT_NAME, as environment variables. See Appendix B for what's available.

NOTE

The ingenious AppleScript that reloads the docsets without restarting Xcode is adapted from Apple's article "Using Doxygen to Create Xcode Documentation Sets," which you can find in the Documentation organizer. Xcode responds to a few AppleScript commands, but the support, as I write this, is so spotty that I won't cover it.

Leave the rest of the editor alone.

Now, when you've added documentation comments to your code, you can switch the Scheme selector in the toolbar to **Docset**, issue **Project→Build** (⌘B), and have the docset built and loaded automatically. You can review the output of the doxygen tool in the Log navigator; see Chapter 26, "The Xcode Build System," for more.

OTHER DOCUMENTATION GENERATORS

Doxygen has the annoyance that its terminology and formatting aren't tailored to Objective-C; it's hard to minimize its C++ conventions. Other options are available that have the advantage of matching the style of Apple's own docs. Apple's HeaderDoc is supplied with the Xcode tools. It is simple to generate a suite of HTML documentation—all that's involved are a couple of command-line tools and customizing some template files. However, things rapidly become difficult when you try to generate a docset; you're left to hand-code some of the indexes. Search the tools documentation for HeaderDoc for more information. Apple-Doc, http://appledoc.gentlebytes.com/, is an open-source generator that produces docsets. It's not as mature as Doxygen, and although AppleDoc's narrower focus makes the configuration system less complex conceptually, the lack of a graphical editor hurts it.

Summary

This chapter took you on an in-depth tour of Xcode's documentation system. You saw how to use Quick Help to get on-the-spot guidance on API, Interface Builder objects, and build settings and how to quickly access the declarations of methods and other symbols in your code.

I showed you the Documentation organizer and how to navigate it, particularly the search options that can filter out the results you don't care about. You learned how to manage and update your document sets.

Finally, you saw that you aren't limited to what Apple gives you; there are tools that enable you to add your own documentation to the documentation system. I went into detail on the Doxygen automatic-documentation tool and how it can simplify the process of deriving attractive and useful documents from your code.

## CHAPTER 26

The Xcode Build System

If you're used to building software with UNIX tools such as make, odds are you don't quite trust IDEs such as Xcode. In a makefile, you can directly set compiler options, even file by file. You can designate build dependencies, so a change to a header file forces recompilations of the implementation files that depend on it—gcc and llvm even have a mode that generates the dependency trees.

At first glance, Xcode doesn't give you that control. It's "magic," and while you're proud to make magic for your users, you don't trust it for yourself.

This chapter aims to take some of the magic out of the Xcode build system. Even if you aren't a veteran of make-based projects, you'll gain a better understanding of what Xcode does for you and how you can control it.

A makefile is organized around a hierarchy of goals. Some goals, such as the frequently used clean or install targets, are abstract, but most are files. Associated with each goal is a list of other goals that are antecedents—dependencies—of that goal and a script for turning the antecedents into something that satisfies the goal. Most commonly, the antecedents are input files for the programs that the script runs to produce a target file. The genius of make comes from the rule that if any target is more recently modified than all of its antecedents, it is presumed to embody their current state, and it is not necessary to run the script to produce it again. The combination of a tree of dependencies and this pruning rule make make a powerful and efficient tool for automating such tasks as building software products.

The organizing unit of a makefile is the target-dependency-action group. But in the case of application development, this group is often stereotyped to the extent that you don't even have to specify it; make provides a default rule that looks like this:

```
%.o    :    %.c
    $(CC) -c $(CPPFLAGS) $(CFLAGS) -o $@ $<
```

So all the programmer need do is list all the constituent .o files in the project, and the built-in rule produces the .o files as needed. Often, the task of maintaining a makefile becomes less one of maintaining dependencies than one of keeping lists.

In the same way, Xcode makes dependency analysis a matter of list-keeping by taking advantage of the fact that projects are targeted at specific kinds of executable products, such as applications, libraries, tools, or plug-ins. Knowing how the build process ends, Xcode can do the right thing with the files that go into the project.

A file in an Xcode workspace belongs to three distinct lists:

Projects: A file appears once in the Project navigator for each project it belongs to. This has nothing to do with whether it has any effect on any product of a project. It might, for instance, be a document you're keeping handy for reference, or some notes you're taking. If you're working with a workspace, a file might be in the workspace without being in any project; the easiest way to do this is to make sure no project is selected (command-click to undo any selections) and select **File→Add Files to... (⌥⌘A)**.

Targets: A file may belong to zero or more *targets* in a project. A file is included in a target's file list because it is a part of that target's product, whether as a source file or as a resource to be copied literally into the product. When a file is added to a project, Xcode asks you which targets in the project should include the file. You can also add files to a target through the check boxes in the File inspector, or by dragging them into a build phase in the Target editor.

NOTE

A target is identified with the set of files that comprise it. There is no concept of including or excluding files from a single target on the basis of its being built with a Release or Debug configuration. If you need disjoint sets of files, make a separate target for each set; a file can belong to more than one target, and you can set preprocessor macros per-target.

Build Phases: What role a file plays in a target depends on what *phase* of the target the file belongs to. When a file is added to a target, Xcode assigns it to a build phase based on the type of the file: Files with llvm-compilable suffixes get assigned to the "Compile Sources" phase; libraries, to the "Link Binary with Libraries" phase; and most others to the "Copy Bundle Resources" phase. See Figure 26.1.

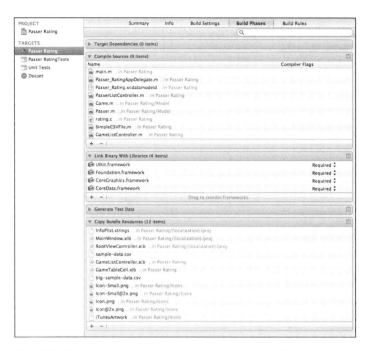

FIGURE 26.1   Build phases in a modest project. You gain access to build phases by selecting a project item in the Project navigator, clicking a target, and then the **Build Phases** tab in the Target editor. The phases are represented by tables that can be expanded to reveal the files that belong to them. One of the ways to add a file to a phase is to drag it into the phase's table.

Build phases are executed in the order in which they appear in the Target editor. You'd almost always want the "Compile Sources" phase to complete before the "Link Binary with Libraries" phase—that's the way they come—but you *can* drag them into any order you like.

> **NOTE**
>
> Xcode 3 and earlier did not guarantee the order in which the phases would execute—it scheduled them by the order of dependencies and its own necessities. This added an element of mystery to the building process that Xcode 4 has relieved.

When you create a target, either in the process of creating an Xcode project or by adding a target to an existing project, you specify the kind of product you want to produce, and you can't change it except by making another target. The target type forms one anchor—the endpoint—in the Xcode build system's dependency analysis: It tells the build system what the product's ultimate structure is—single file or package—and how to link the executable.

The other anchor of the build system is the set of build-phase members for the target. The "Compile Sources" build phase, along with the sources you add to it, yield object files, which are the inputs to the linkage phase implicit in your choice of target type. The various file-copying phases and the files you supply for them yield the copy commands needed to populate the auxiliary structure of an application.

What a makefile developer does with explicit dependencies and the default rules, Xcode does by inference: It determines how new files are to be processed into a product and how that processing is to be done. Even if you use the product of one target to build another, Xcode will detect the dependency and incorporate the build of the dependent target into the process for the composite target. All Xcode needs is for the two targets to be within the same workspace—they don't even need to be in the same project.

Xcode Build Variables

The action for the default make rule for .c files parameterizes almost the entire action. The command for the C compiler and the set of flags to pass are left to the makefile variables CC, CPPFLAGS, and CFLAGS. You set these flags at the head of the file to suitable values, and all the compilations in your build comply.

Xcode relies similarly on variables to organize build options but at a much finer granularity. There is one variable for each of the most common settings. For instance, the variable GCC_ENABLE_CPP_RTTI controls whether llvm's -fno-rtti will be added to suppress the generation of runtime type information in C++. This variable is set by a pop-up ("Enable C++ Runtime Types") in the **Build Variables** tab of the Target editor. See Figure 26.2.

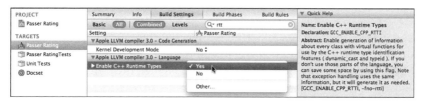

FIGURE 26.2   The list of settings in the **Build Settings** tab of the Target editor is extensive, but you can get it under control by typing something relevant to the setting in the search field. Typing **RTT** narrows the list down to a setting for C++ runtime type information, but also to a setting whose description merely refers to RTTI. The Quick Help inspector in the Utility area explains each setting, including the name of the associated build variable and the compiler flags it sets.

Let's take a good look at the **Build Settings** tab. Select a project in the Project navigator to fill the Editor area with the Project/Target editor; then select a target. Click the **Build Settings** tab. Right under the tab bar, you see two pairs of buttons: **Basic/All**, and **Combined/Levels**. **Basic** narrows the list down to a handful of essential elements; I'll get to the distinction between the combined and by-level presentations shortly. For now, the most straightforward presentation is **All** and **Combined**.

The list you see is a front end for most of the build variables Xcode maintains for this target. If you have the Utility area (right-hand segment in the **View** control) visible, and the Quick Help (second) inspector selected, you can see a description of any setting you select. In brackets, at the end of the description, are the name of the build variable the item controls and what compiler option, if any, it affects. Both the label and the description are searchable: The list in Figure 26.2 was narrowed down to two entries by typing **RTT** into the search field at the top of the list.

NOTE

It's common for closely crafted makefiles to customize the compiler flags for some of the source files. The Xcode build system allows for this. In the **Build Phase** tab, the table for the "Compile Sources" phase has a second column, "Compiler Flags." Double-click an entry in that column to get a popover editor for additional flags for that file. You won't get Quick Help for what you enter, but you can explore the **Build Settings** list to see what options are available. What you type will be added to the flags used in compiling the file—it's not possible to override the general settings, and it's not possible to make separate per-file settings for different configurations.

Settings Hierarchy

The "Combined" list of settings shown in the **Build Settings** tab is the authoritative list of what flags and directives will be applied in building the target. However, the Xcode build system provides richer control over those settings. What's in the combined list is a synthesis of settings that come from a hierarchy of up to six layers.

- BSD environment variables
- Xcode's own default values
- The current configuration set for the whole project
- The current configuration set for the current target
- Command-line arguments to the `xcodebuild` command-line tool, if you're using it
- Added per-file compiler options

Figure 26.3 illustrates how the hierarchy works.

26

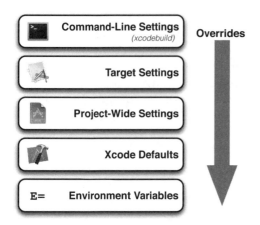

FIGURE 26.3   The hierarchy of build settings in Xcode and `xcodebuild`. A setting may be made at one or more of these layers, but the topmost setting in the hierarchy controls. Settings in higher layers may refer to settings from lower layers by the variable reference `$(inherited)`. The top layer, command-line settings, is present only in an `xcodebuild` invocation.

You deal most often with target and project settings; the others rarely arise. The project level allows you to set policies for every target in the project—things like the root SDK, or warnings you always want to see—so a change in one place affects all. You can still exempt a product from the general policy by putting an alternative setting into its target: The target setting overrides the project setting.

With this in mind, you can click the **Levels** button in the bar under the **Build Settings** tab (Figure 26.4). The Target editor now shows four columns for each setting, representing the default, project, and target values, and the net value that is actually effective for the target. You can edit only the middle two columns—target and project. The level that is responsible for the effective setting is highlighted in green.

PROJECT		Summary	Info	Build Settings	Build Phases	Build Rules	
📄 Passer Rating	Basic **All**	Combined	**Levels**		(Q▾		
TARGETS	Setting		↓ Resolved	↓ Passer Rating	📄 Passer Rating	⎙ iOS Default
🅰 **Passer Rating**	▼ Other C Flags		<Multiple values>		<Multiple values>	
📄 Passer RatingTests	Debug					
📄 Unit Tests	Release		–DNS_BLOCK_ASSE...		**–DNS_BLOCK_ASS...**	
◎ Docset	▼ Other C++ Flags		<Multiple values>			
	Debug					
	Release		~DNS_BLOCK_ASSE...			
	Precompile Prefix Header		Yes ⏷	Yes ⏷		No – $ ⏷
	Prefix Header		Passer Rating/Pas...	Passer Rating/Pas...		•
	Recognize Built-in Functions		Yes ⏷			Yes ⏷
	Recognize Pascal Strings		Yes ⏷			Yes ⏷
	Set Output File Subtype to ALL		No ⏷			No ⏷
	Short Enumeration Constants		No ⏷			No ⏷
	Use Standard System Header Directory...		Yes ⏷			Yes ⏷
	▼ Apple LLVM compiler 3.0 – Preprocessing					
	▼ Preprocessor Macros		<Multiple values>		<Multiple values>	
	Debug		DEBUG=1		**DEBUG=1**	
	Release					
	Preprocessor Macros Not Used In Preco...					

FIGURE 26.4   With the **Levels** view selected, the Target editor shows how each level of the settings hierarchy contributes to the settings that will be used to build the target. The chain proceeds from right to left, starting with Xcode's default for the project type at the right, through the project and target levels, and to the net setting on the left. You can edit the settings at the project or target level. The place where the operative value for a setting is selected is highlighted in green.

NOTE

The same **Build Settings** tab is available in the Project editor, but without the target-level column.

Each level that sets (not just inherits) a value is shown in bold with a green background. The distinction between setting and inheritance is important: If, for instance, you set a string setting to empty at the target level, the effective setting will be an empty string, *not* the setting inherited from the project; if you change the project setting, the effective setting, through the target, will still be blank—watch for that green box. Likewise, setting a value to be the same as the value to the right isn't an acceptance of the inherited value; it's just an override that happens to repeat the inherited value.

If you want to remove an override from the hierarchy, select the line for that setting, and press the Delete key. The setting won't go away—it just clears the value from the level (project or target) on which the editor operates. You see the effect when you see the current level's value lose its boldfacing, and the green box go down to the next-lower level. When you select a different row in the table, the cells that don't carry values will turn blank.

Editing Build Variables

The **Build Settings** table is intelligent about what values you can put into it.

▶ Some values—such as the multiple flags you can put into the "Other C Flags" setting—are logically lists. Xcode lets you edit the items individually, in a table to which you can add and remove rows.

▶ Some settings, such as Booleans or code-signing identities, are constrained to the few values that make sense for them. The **Value** column shows a pop-up menu with the possible values.

▶ Any value can be edited free-form—if you click in the value, and move the mouse pointer a little, you are given a text field.

▶ If you edit a value at the target level and want to supplement, rather than replace, the inherited value, include $(inherited) where you want the original setting to appear.

The **Build Settings** table is filtered for your consumption. Underlying the descriptions in the Setting column are the names of variables Xcode uses to specify the build; and the value column displays the settings as they *effectively* are, not as they *actually* are. You can see this when editing the text of variables whose value depends on the content of other variables: The "Architectures" setting may look like "Standard (armv6 armv7)" in the list, but if you edit it as text, you find it's $(ARCHS_STANDARD_32_BIT).

26

NOTE

If you've done shell scripting, you're used to delimiting environment variable names in braces: `${visual}`. Strings in parentheses are replaced by the output of the commands they contain. This is *not so* when you use Xcode build variables. Use parentheses to refer to them: `$(SDKROOT)`.

You can change the table to display the underlying variable names and values. The command **Show Setting Names** in the **Editor** menu reveals the names of the build variables; **Show Definitions** shows the raw text of the settings.

Configurations

So far, I've treated build settings as the product of a simple hierarchy of defaults and overrides. But build settings can be varied on another axis: A target may have different settings based on your purpose in building it, such as debugging, release, or distribution. You encapsulate these settings in *build configurations*, which you can select for each action in your product's scheme.

When it generates a new project for you, Xcode provides two configurations, Debug and Release, which it sets up with reasonable values for those two purposes. In general, the Debug configuration generates more debugging information, and turns off code optimization so your program executes line by line in the debugger, as you'd expect. Both Mac OS X and iOS run apps on two or more processor architectures, and the Debug configuration saves time by building the target for one architecture only.

Switching between configurations is easy: The **Info** tab for each action in the Scheme editor includes a **Build Configuration** pop-up that lets you choose the configuration you use for that action. You can make the switch and take an action in one step by holding down the Option key while invoking the action; the Scheme editor sheet drops down, and you can make your changes before proceeding.

If your target depends on other targets, even in other projects, those other targets will be built with the configuration you set at build time, as long as they have a configuration of the same name; otherwise they will be built in their default configurations.

Adjusting Configurations

The point of a build configuration is to have alternative settings for each purpose. This is where you get into conditional settings. As you've browsed the **Build Settings** tab, you've noticed that some settings have disclosure triangles next to them (Figure 26.5), and their values are tagged with a grayed-out "<Multiple values>." These settings have different values depending on which configuration is used. Click on the triangle, and the row opens to show subrows for each available configuration, and you can make your choices there.

Setting	Passer Rating
▼ Other C Flags	\<Multiple values\>
Debug	
Release	-DNS_BLOCK_ASSERTIONS=1
▶ Other C++ Flags	\<Multiple values\>
Precompile Prefix Header	Yes ⬍

FIGURE 26.5   When a setting has different values for different configurations, its value displays as "\<Multiple values\>," and Xcode displays a disclosure triangle for the row. Opening the triangle shows the configurations and their values.

If you hover the mouse pointer over a row for which there are no per-configuration settings, a temporary disclosure triangle appears. Opening that row again shows the values (identical until you change them) assigned to the setting for each configuration.

Figure 26.6 ties it all together: It shows how settings can percolate up from the defaults, through the project and target settings, and finally to the values that direct and condition the build process.

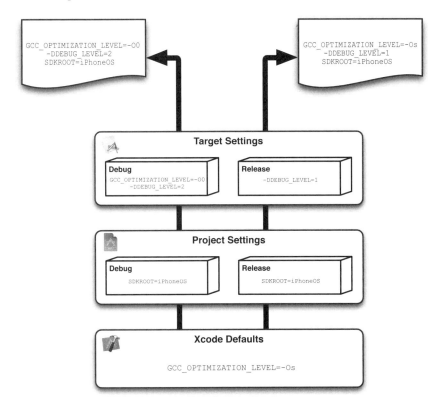

FIGURE 26.6   A complete example of the inheritance of build settings. By default, Xcode sets all compilations to optimize for size (bottom); that setting survives into Release builds, but for the Debug configuration, the target turns optimization off. The projcct sets the base SDK for all builds to iPhoneOS, meaning whatever iOS SDK is current (middle). The developer defines a DEBUG_LEVEL macro to different values depending on the configuration (top). The result is a set of build settings tailored to debugging (top left) and release (top right).

Adding Configurations

You can add configurations of your own. The **Info** tab of the Project editor includes the list of all the configurations available to the project. You start out with Debug and Release. To create your new configuration, click the + button; this pops up a menu offering to duplicate one of the existing configurations—it doesn't make sense to offer a new, empty configuration because the new configuration must include *some* settings. Make your selection, enter a name, and you're done.

Configuration Files

Configurations, too, come with disclosure triangles. Open one, and you see a list of the targets the project contains. This lets you select a configuration file that adjusts the settings for each target.

What's a configuration file? Here's the rationale: Say you have several projects. Perhaps you have policies for settings you must have for all of them, and the defaults supplied by Xcode aren't appropriate for you. If you just use the Project/Target editor, you need to make those settings by hand for each configuration in each project. If your requirements vary by target type, it gets that much worse.

Configuration (.xcconfig) files are the solution. These are text files that contain key-value pairs for any settings you want to enforce.

Creating a Configuration File

You start on an xcconfig file by selecting **File→New→File...** (⌘N), and finding "Configuration Settings File" in the Other part of the New File assistant. The assistant then puts you through the routine of naming and placing the file and assigning it to a project.

> **NOTE**
>
> An xcconfig file must be included in a project before the project can find and use it.

When you've done that, you find you have a text file that's empty but for a comment block with your name, copyright, and date at the top. What do you do now? Open the **Build Settings** tab in either a Project or Target editor. You can copy (**Edit→Copy** [⌘C]) rows from the editor, and paste them into the xcconfig, but there's a catch: You can't copy rows marked "<Multiple values>." You need to use the Shift or Command keys to cherry-pick the settings that interest you, and copy or drag them into the file. You can then edit the values to suit your requirements.

When that is done, you can return to the Project editor's Info tab, and use the pop-ups in the "Based on Configuration File" column to select the xcconfig file.

SDK- and Architecture-Specific Settings

Cocoa development often involves targeting different SDKs and processor architectures with different binaries. You may have ARMv7 assembly in your iOS app that isn't runnable on ARMv6 devices or the Simulator. You may want to use the Mac OS X 10.6 SDK for 32-bit builds, but 10.7 for 64 bits. The xcconfig format allows for these. For instance, the file may contain

```
(1) GCC_VERSION = com.apple.compilers.llvm.clang.1_0
(2) GCC_VERSION[sdk=iphonesimulator4.3][arch=*] =
             com.apple.compilers.llvmgcc42
(3) GCC_VERSION[sdk=iphoneos4.3][arch=armv6] = 4.2
```

1. Use clang (the version of the llvm compiler that incorporates a parser for Apple's coding conventions) for any builds, unless a condition overrides it.

2. If the build uses the iOS simulator SDK, use the gcc-fronted llvm compiler. (I broke the line for space; it should be all on one line.)

3. If the build is for iOS 4.3 on a device, *and* for the ARMv6 architecture, use gcc 4.2. (This insane configuration—Xcode 4 doesn't even come with gcc, and gcc is terrible at generating ARM code—is only an example.)

The matching to SDK and architecture is done by glob expression, which means that if you have to express a range of matches, like "any ios 5," you can match on iphoneos5*, as an override to an unconditional setting for other OSes.

26

> **NOTE**
>
> The graphical editor also allows you to set conditions. When you hover the mouse pointer over a configuration in a setting, a small **+** button appears; clicking it adds a condition row inside the configuration. The title of that row is a drop-down menu, in which you can select from the available conditions. Because Xcode arranges conditional settings *within* configurations, you have to duplicate conditions for each configuration.

Preprocessing xcconfig Files

As with C-family source files, you can insert the contents of one xcconfig file into another with an #include directive. That way, you can have a base configuration file containing settings common to all your targets and build configurations, and #include that in files that are specific to each of them.

This enables an interesting trick. Consider the following configuration file (call it common.xcconfig):

```
MY_LIBS_FOR_DEBUG   = -lmystuff_debug
MY_LIBS_FOR_RELEASE = -lmystuff
OTHER_LDFLAGS       = $(MY_LIBS_FOR_$(WHICH_LIB))
```

There may be a `Debugging.xcconfig` file that sets

```
WHICH_LIB = DEBUG
#include "common.xcconfig"
```

...and a `Release.xcconfig` file that contains

```
WHICH_LIB = RELEASE
#include "common.xcconfig"
```

The effect is that `OTHER_LDFLAGS` will be set to the value of `MY_LIBS_FOR_DEBUG` from `Debug.xcconfig`, and `MY_LIBS_FOR_RELEASE` from `Release.xcconfig`. In this simple case, it would have been easier just to set `OTHER_LDFLAGS` yourself, but quite sophisticated conditional configurations can be built up this way.

There are no header search paths for `xcconfig` files. If you `#include` a file, it has to be in the same directory.

The `xcodebuild` Tool

Sometimes there is no substitute for a command-line tool. The UNIX command line presents a well understood interface for scripting and controlling complex tools. Apple has provided a command-line interface to the Xcode build system through the `xcode-build` tool. Using `xcodebuild` is simple: Set the working directory to the directory containing an `.xcodeproj` project package, and invoke `xcodebuild`, specifying the project, target, configuration, and any build settings you want to set. If only one `.xcodeproj` package is in the directory, all these options can be defaulted by simply entering

```
$ xcodebuild
```

That command builds the first target in the current configuration of the only `.xcodeproj` package in the working directory. Apple's intention is that `xcodebuild` have the same role in a nightly build or routine-release script that `make` would have.

In building a target, specify one of five actions for `xcodebuild`:

- ▶ **build**, the default, builds the specified target out of `SRCROOT` into `SYMROOT`. This is the same as the **Build** command in the Xcode application.

- ▶ **clean** removes the product and any intermediate files from `SYMROOT`. This is the same as the **Clean** command in the Xcode application.

- ▶ **install** builds the specified target and installs it at `INSTALL_DIR` (usually `DSTROOT`). The Installation Preprocessing build variable is set. There is no direct equivalent to this action in Xcode because there is no way to elevate Xcode's privilege for setting ownership, permissions, and destination directory.

▶ **installsrc** copies the project directory to SRCROOT. In Project Builder, Xcode's ancestor, this action restricted itself to the project file package and the source files listed in it, but it now seems to do nothing a Finder copy or command-line cp wouldn't do.

▶ **archive** does the equivalent of the **Product→Archive** command in Xcode. You must specify the workspace and scheme for the build.

NOTE

Settings like SRCROOT can be set for a run of xcodebuild by including assignment pairs (SETTING=value) among the parameters.

If more than one project or workspace package is in the current directory, you must specify which you are interested in, with the respective -project or -workspace option, followed by the name of the package. Not specifying a target is the same as passing the name of the first target in the -target option; you can also specify -alltargets.

xcodebuild uses the configuration you specify in Scheme editor panel for the build action, unless you pass a -configuration flag in the command.

See man xcodebuild for full details.

If you have more than one set of developer tools installed, you need to be sure that the right xcodebuild is used. Conventional UNIX practice would be to manipulate $PATH, or establish symbolic links, but the xcode-select tool lets you make the switch on-the-fly. Use the -switch option to change the developer-tools directory (such as /Developer within Xcode.app) and -print-path to examine the current setting. xcode-select affects the version of xcodebuild that will be used, as well as agvtool, ibtool, opendiff, xcodeindex, and instruments. Other command-line tools, such as llvm, ld, or gdb, are still drawn from /usr/bin—but xcodebuild uses the versions of those tools in the selected developer directory. man xcode-select can tell you more.

Custom Build Rules

Xcode's build system can be extended to new file types and processing tools. The default rules in the build system match file extensions to product types and process any source files that are newer than the products. You can add a custom rule that instructs the build system to look for files whose names match a pattern and apply a command to such files. See Figure 26.7, top.

NOTE

Another way to extend the build system is by adding a "Run Script" build phase. You've already seen it in the "Some Test Data" section of Chapter 9, "An iOS Application: Model." "Run Script" phases allow a lot more flexibility in how to structure the action but sacrifice the build rule's applicability to every file of a given type.

Create a rule by clicking the **Add Build Rule** button at the bottom of the **Build Rules** editor. A row appears at the top of the table, containing an editor for your new rule. The **Process** pop-up menu allows you to select from some of the types of source files that Xcode knows about and includes a **Source files with names matching:** item for you to specify source files with a glob expression (like ***.lemon**).

The **Using** pop-up shows all Xcode's standard compilers, or you can select **Custom script:** to open an editor for your own script. See Figure 26.7, bottom. Don't worry about the size of this field; it grows vertically as you type. Remember that you can chain shell commands with the && operator.

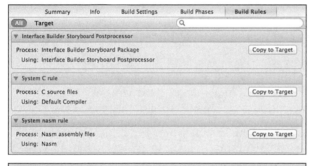

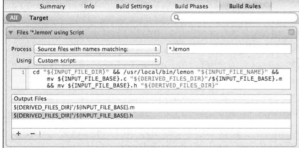

FIGURE 26.7   (top) The **Build Rules** tab of the Target editor lets you match up file types with the tools that process them for a build. When you first examine the list, it contains the default suite of actions for the standard file types. (bottom) Clicking the **Add Build Rule** button at the bottom of the editor adds a row to the table, in which you can specify a file type and the rule (possibly your own script) to process it.

You may use any build variable you like in the shell command. Additionally, some variables are specific to custom rule invocations:

▶ INPUT_FILE_PATH, the full path to the source file (/Users/xcodeuser/MyProject/grammar.lemon)

▶ INPUT_FILE_DIR, the directory containing the source file (/Users/xcodeuser/MyProject/)

▶ INPUT_FILE_NAME, the name of the source file (grammar.lemon)

▶ INPUT_FILE_BASE, the base, unsuffixed, name of the source file (grammar)

Apple recommends that intermediate files, such as the source files output by parser generators, be put into the directory named in the DERIVED_FILE_DIR variable.

> **NOTE**
>
> In this example, adding a .lemon file to the project won't do what you'd hope. The build rule recognizes the file as a source file, but Xcode doesn't: Simply adding the file puts it into a "Copy Bundle Resources" build phase. You must drag the file from the copy phase to the "Compile Sources" phase. After that, with the product file in the derived-sources directory, the product file compiles automatically.

You can't delete or edit the defaults that are initially in the rules list, but any rule you add overrides a corresponding rule that appears lower in the list. You can set priorities by dragging your rules higher or lower. You can't drag a rule down among the standard rules, but that doesn't matter: Why would you add a custom rule and then specify that the standard one should override it?

The Build Log

You set the build system into motion by selecting an action or by issuing the **Build** (⌘B) command, or one of its relatives, from the **Product** menu. (**Build** is just an alias for **Product→Build For→Build For Running**, [⇧⌘R].)

> **NOTE**
>
> After you memorize the keyboard equivalents for actions such as Run, Test, Profile, and Analyze, you can hold down the Shift key to do the corresponding build without going through with the action.

The result, if everything goes well, is a file or package embodying your product. If it doesn't, the now-familiar Issues navigator lists all the errors, warnings, and notes that turned up, and you can select an issue to jump to the place in your source that raised it.

But sometimes that isn't enough. You want to see how the build was done, right or wrong—perhaps you suspect that a step hadn't been taken. And if you run into an error in linkage or code signing, the Issues navigator is of limited help because there is no corresponding source file. That's where the Log navigator comes in.

The Log navigator (the seventh tab in the Navigator area) contains an item for each major event in the life of your project, such as actions, debugging sessions, or source-control commands—anything that could generate text logs from tools that handle the events.

Do a build, select the Log navigator, and click the top item, representing the results of the last action you took. What you see is a summary of the steps that went into the action. See Figure 26.8.

26

FIGURE 26.8   The log for a build can be filtered to narrow it to the items you want to focus on. If you select **All Messages** (not shown), you get a list of every action taken in the build, including the steps that succeeded. If you select **All Issues**, the list narrows down to errors, warnings, and analyzer notes. **Errors Only** limits the display to error messages only.

The buttons immediately below the tab bar offer the choices **All/Recent** and **All Messages/All Issues/Errors Only**. The latter group filters the list in order of importance: The all-messages setting lists everything that happened, good or not; the others eliminate the entries for successful steps and for steps that would not prevent the build from completing.

The **All** setting displays every step that contributed to the current state of the target. That's not the same as a list of what happened the last time you did a build: Your last build did not repeat compilations for source files that had not changed; the contributions for those files come from earlier builds. The **All** setting folds those older compilations into a complete history of the current target. If you want to restrict the list to what was done in the last build, select **Recent**.

A Simple Build Transcript

Now that you have the principles down, let's see how they reduce to the actual commands that build an application. Remember that the Xcode build system, built into the Xcode application, doesn't do any actual compiling or linking—any real building at all. That's done by llvm and the other command-line tools under the direction of the build system.

The process is not hidden. You can get a full transcript from the results Xcode displays when you select a build from the Log navigator. At first impression, it's just an abstract of what happened, but it's easy to go deeper.

First, you can see the underlying command for any step by clicking it in the log listing. At the right end of the entry, a small lines-of-text button appears. Click it, and the entry expands to show the corresponding command and any messages it generated. See Figure 26.9. You can open up all the entries by selecting **Editor→Expand All Transcripts**.

FIGURE 26.9   Clicking the lines-of-text button that appears when you select a log entry expands the entry to a complete transcript of the commands that went into that step of the build.

Perhaps that isn't overwhelming enough. Select **Copy Transcript for Shown Results**… **as Text** from the contextual menu or the **Editor** menu, and paste the results into an empty text file. Each step involves two or more commands, and the build system autogenerates *a lot* of compiler flags and search paths.

Let's go through the highlights of a simple build. It's for a Mac OS X application called "Cookie Maker," targeted for Lion on both 32- and 64-bit Intel processors in the Release configuration. I've broken long lines into series of indented lines; and dropped lines and path elements (replaced by "…") that would inflate the example without shedding any light. If you want to see the whole thing, try a build of your own.

Info.plist

```
ProcessInfoPlistFile ".../Cookie Maker.app/Contents/Info.plist"
    Cookie_Maker-Info.plist
cd "/Users/xcodeuser/MyProject/Cookie Maker"
builtin-infoPlistUtility Cookie_Maker-Info.plist
    -genpkginfo ".../Cookie Maker.app/Contents/PkgInfo"
    -expandbuildsettings -platform macosx
    -o ".../Cookie Maker.app/Contents/Info.plist"
```

The first thing to notice is that Xcode begins each step with a pseudo-command that specifies what the step is to do—in this case `ProcessInfoPlistFile`. What follows are the UNIX commands that do the work of the pseudo-command. Here, Xcode uses a private command, `builtin-infoPlistUtility`, to process the project's `Info.plist` file (for instance by substituting the values of build variables for the references in the source file), and copy the result into the `Contents` directory of the application package.

This is true to the nature of the Xcode build process, which is about more than compiling program code. It focuses on the full product, including creating the structure of the package. You usually don't have to think about such things.

26

Resources

```
CpResource English.lproj/Credits.rtf
    ".../Cookie Maker.app/Contents/Resources/English.lproj/Credits.rtf"
cd "/Users/xcodeuser/MyProject/Cookie Maker"
builtin-copy -exclude .DS_Store -exclude CVS -exclude .svn
    -exclude .git -strip-debug-symbols
    -resolve-src-symlinks
    "/Users/xcodeuser/MyProject/Cookie Maker/English.lproj/Credits.rtf"
    ".../Cookie Maker.app/Contents/Resources/English.lproj"


CopyStringsFile
    ".../Cookie Maker.app/Contents/.../InfoPlist.strings"
    English.lproj/InfoPlist.strings
cd "/Users/xcodeuser/MyProject/Cookie Maker"
builtin-copyStrings --validate --inputencoding utf-16
    --outputencoding UTF-16
    --outdir ".../Cookie Maker.app/Contents/Resources/English.lproj"
    -- English.lproj/InfoPlist.strings


CompileXIB English.lproj/MainMenu.xib
cd "/Users/xcodeuser/MyProject/Cookie Maker"
setenv XCODE_DEVELOPER_USR_PATH .../Developer/usr/bin/...
/Developer/usr/bin/ibtool --errors --warnings --notices
    --output-format human-readable-text
    --compile ".../Cookie Maker.app/Contents/.../MainMenu.nib"
    "/Users/xcodeuser/MyProject/Cookie Maker/English.lproj/MainMenu.xib"
    --sdk .../Developer/SDKs/MacOSX10.7.sdk
```

Xcode's CpResource pseudo-command invokes a private builtin-copy command, which can copy files and directories while filtering out noise content like debugging symbols and SCM directories.

CopyStringsFile is implemented by a private builtin-copyStrings tool that checks the integrity of .strings files, ensures they have the proper encoding, and moves them into place in the application package.

The builtin commands aren't actual command-line tools. They're simply placeholders for tasks that Xcode completes in the IDE's own code. These simple operations are the only ones that Xcode does not farm out to external tools.

Interface Builder XIBs, you remember, are merely source files for the NIBs that applications use to instantiate objects. The CompileXIB step, done through the ibtool command, takes care of the transformation. I don't show the DataModelCompile step, which feeds data-model files into momc to produce managed-object model .mom files for use in an application.

Precompiled Header

```
ProcessPCH .../Build/PrecompiledHeaders/.../Cookie_Maker_Prefix.pch.pth
    Cookie_Maker_Prefix.pch normal x86_64 objective-c
    com.apple.compilers.llvm.clang.1_0.compiler
cd "/Users/xcodeuser/MyProject/Cookie Maker"
setenv LANG en_US.US-ASCII
.../Developer/usr/bin/clang -x objective-c-header -arch x86_64
    -fmessage-length=0 -fdiagnostics-print-source-range-info
    ...
    -isysroot .../Developer/SDKs/MacOSX10.7.sdk
    -fasm-blocks -mmacosx-version-min=10.7 -gdwarf-2
    -fvisibility=hidden
...
    -c "/Users/xcodeuser/MyProject/Cookie Maker/Cookie_Maker_Prefix.pch"
    -o .../Build/PrecompiledHeaders/.../Cookie_Maker_Prefix.pch.pth
    -MMD -MT dependencies -MF ...Cookie_Maker_Prefix.pch.d
```

Now you get down to some real compiling. The target's precompiled header, on which all subsequent compilations depend, is built here. The ProcessPCH pseudo-command calls for reducing Cookie_Maker_Prefix.pch in your project to the precompiled Cookie_Maker_Prefix.pch.pth in the build-intermediates cache. This boils down to an invocation of the clang compiler as specified in the target build settings.

The clang Xcode uses for this step is not the /usr/bin/clang that a make-based build would typically use. The command name specifies that the compiler is to be found in Xcode's directory tree. The Xcode tool set is independent of the "system" tool set. Depending on the options you selected when you installed Xcode, you may not even have a compiler in /usr/bin.

```
ProcessPCH
    .../Build/PrecompiledHeaders/.../Cookie_Maker_Prefix.pch.pth
    Cookie_Maker_Prefix.pch normal i386 objective-c
    com.apple.compilers.llvm.clang.1_0.compiler
cd "/Users/xcodeuser/MyProject/Cookie Maker"
setenv LANG en_US.US-ASCII
.../Developer/usr/bin/clang -x objective-c-header -arch i386
```

You're building a precompiled header again. Didn't you just do that? You can see the difference on what is (in my edit) the third line of the pseudo-command and at the end of the first line of the clang invocation: The first build specified the target architecture as x86_64. This time, it's i386.

This is typical of Xcode builds that target more than one architecture: Code-generation commands are run separately for each. The build system links a separate executable for each and then uses the lipo command to merge them into one universal binary.

26

Compiling Source Files

```
CompileC ".../Cookie Maker.build/Objects-normal/x8 6_64/CMDocument.o"
    Classes/CMDocument.m normal x86_64 objective-c
    com.apple.compilers.llvm.clang.1_0.compiler
    cd "/Users/xcodeuser/MyProject/Cookie Maker"
setenv LANG en_US.US-ASCII
.../Developer/usr/bin/clang -x objective-c
    -arch x86_64 -fmessage-length=0
    -fdiagnostics-print-source-range-info
    -fdiagnostics-show-category=id
    ...
    -isysroot .../Developer/SDKs/MacOSX10.7.sdk
    -fasm-blocks -mmacosx-version-min=10.7 -gdwarf-2
    -fvisibility=hidden
    ...
    "-I.../Cookie Maker.build/DerivedSources/x86_64"
    "-I.../Cookie Maker.build/DerivedSources"
    -F.../Build/Products/Release
    -include .../Build/PrecompiledHeaders/.../Cookie_Maker_Prefix.pch
    -MMD -MT dependencies
    -MF ".../Cookie Maker.build/Objects-normal/x86_64/CMDocument.d"
    -c "/Users/xcodeuser/MyProject/Cookie Maker/Classes/CMDocument.m"
    -o ".../Cookie Maker.build/Objects-normal/x86_64/CMDocument.o"


...


CompileC ".../Cookie Maker.build/
    Objects-normal/i38 6/CMDocument.o" Classes/CMDocument.m
    normal i386 objective-c
    com.apple.compilers.llvm.clang.1_0.compiler
cd "/Users/xcodeuser/MyProject/Cookie Maker"
setenv LANG en_US.US-ASCII
.../Developer/usr/bin/clang -x objective-c
    -arch i386 -fmessage-length=0
    ...
    -c "/Users/xcodeuser/MyProject/Cookie Maker/Classes/CMDocument.m"
    -o ".../Cookie Maker.build/Objects-normal/i386/CMDocument.o"
```

This is the compilation of CMDocument.m, one of many source files in the project. The CompileC pseudo-command specifies the object file to be derived, the source file, that this is the "normal" (as opposed to the "debug" or "profile") variant, targeting 64-bit Intel, to be compiled as Objective-C by the clang compiler.

The build system elaborates this with the compiler switches specified in the build variables for this target and configuration. For instance:

- ▶ `-isysroot` specifies that the "system" include files and libraries are to be found in the Mac OS X 10.7 SDK directory, and not in "live" locations like `/System/Library/Frameworks` or `/usr/include`. The SDK setting specifies the *latest features* the product supports.

- ▶ `-mmacosx-version-min` shows that the *earliest system* the product can run on is Mac OS X 10.7.

- ▶ The various `-I` phrases direct `clang` to the directories containing header files for the application; and to a header-map (`.hmap`) file that lists the specific headers the build system knows about, which saves `clang` the trouble of scanning all the include directories for each file.

- ▶ Nonsystem frameworks are in the directory specified with the `-F` flag.

- ▶ `-include` directs `clang` to a file to be read before any other compilation is done. In this case this is the precompiled `Cookie_Maker_Prefix.pch` file.

- ▶ -c specifies the source file.

- ▶ -o specifies the resulting object file.

The `CompileC` step is repeated for `CMDocument.m`, this time for 32-bit Intel (`-arch i38 6`). In the real transcript, this step occurs much later: All the compiling and linking for one architecture is finished before any work is done on the next.

Linking

```
Ld ".../Cookie Maker.build/Objects-normal/x8 6_64/Cookie Maker"
    normal x86_64
cd "/Users/xcodeuser/MyProject/Cookie Maker"
setenv MACOSX_DEPLOYMENT_TARGET 10.7
.../Developer/usr/bin/clang -arch x86_64
    -isysroot .../Developer/SDKs/MacOSX10.7.sdk
    -L.../Build/Products/Release -F.../Build/Products/Release
    -filelist ".../x86_64/Cookie Maker.LinkFileList"
    -mmacosx-version-min=10.7 -framework Cocoa
    -o ".../Cookie Maker.build/Objects-normal/x8 6_64/Cookie Maker"
```

Now that all the source for an architecture has been compiled, it's time to link it into a single-architecture binary. The `Ld` pseudo-command specifies that a "normal" Intel binary is to be deposited into a holding directory named `x86_64/`. The flags, derived from the build settings for the target and configuration, are much the same as for the compilation step. The `-L` and `-F` flags identify the location of the target's libraries and frameworks, and `-filelist` indicates a file that lists the object (`.o`) files that contain the object code compiled from the target's source.

There's another `Ld` step, for the `i386` architecture, which differs mainly in the use of `i386` wherever `x86_64` had appeared.

26

Making a Universal Binary

```
CreateUniversalBinary "...Cookie Maker.app/Contents/MacOS/Cookie Maker"
    normal  "x86_64 i386"
cd "/Users/xcodeuser/MyProject/Cookie Maker"
/usr/bin/lipo -create ".../x86_64/Cookie Maker"
    ".../i386/Cookie Maker"
    -output "...Cookie Maker.app/Contents/MacOS/Cookie Maker"
```

The build system has segregated the compilation and linking of the product for each desired architecture; single-architecture binaries are now held in separate directories. This step uses the lipo (for "fat" binaries—get it?) tool to meld them into a single, universal binary. Mac OS X and iOS inspect universal binaries and select the code compiled for the architecture that best fits the machine.

Here lipo is told to create the fat Cookie Maker executable in the proper place in the Cookie Maker.app package, from architecture-specific files in the x86_64/ and i386/ holding directories.

Touch

```
Touch ".../Cookie Maker.app"
cd "/Users/xcodeuser/MyProject/Cookie Maker"
/usr/bin/touch -c ".../Cookie Maker.app"
```

Build systems determine whether action is needed by seeing whether the product is older than any of its constituents. In this case, the product is the Cookie Maker.app package directory. Unfortunately, all the changes Xcode has made *inside* the directory don't change the modification date of the directory. So the last step is to mark the application as new by applying the standard tool touch to the package directory.

Summary

This was an important chapter if you want to know how Xcode works. It explained how the build system built into Xcode takes the place of traditional makefiles and the effort needed to keep them current. It showed how a build is divided into phases that "contain" files to be worked on. Settings for compilers and other tools are an essential part of configuring a build, and you saw how Xcode organizes them by project, target, and configuration.

You saw how you can use the build system from a script, so your builds can be managed without having to trigger them manually from the IDE.

Finally, you examined the Log navigator, how to get a transcript of the commands that underlie the build process, and how to analyze a transcript.

## CHAPTER 27

Instruments

Instruments is a framework for software-measurement tools called...instruments. (Uppercase-I Instruments is the application, lowercase-i instruments are components of the Instruments application.) The analogy is to a multitrack recording deck. Instruments records activity into tracks (one per instrument), building the data on a timeline like audio on a tape.

You've seen Instruments before, in Chapter 14, "Measurement and Analysis," where it helped you track down some memory and performance bugs in the Passer Rating iPhone app. It deserves a closer look. I'll show you how to navigate the Instruments trace window, and how to choose instruments to fit your needs.

What Instruments Is

The focus on a timeline makes Instruments unique. Historically, profiling and debugging tools did one thing at a time. You had Shark (available with Xcode 2 and 3), which sampled a running application to collect aggregate statistics of where it spent its time. Shark had several modes for taking different statistics; if you wanted another mode, you ran Shark again. Shark's profile data was aggregated over the whole session; if you wanted to profile a particular piece of your application, there was a hot key for you to turn profiling on and off.

Separately, there was a profiling application called MallocDebug, which collected cumulative, statistical call trees for calls to `malloc` and `free`. The results were cumulative across a profiling session, so you'd know how the biggest, or most, allocations happened, but not when.

If you needed the distribution and history of *object* allocations, by class, there was an Object Alloc application. And if you wanted to know how the application was spending its time while it was making those allocations, you quit MallocDebug or Object Alloc and ran the target app again under Shark because the other apps did only one thing.

Instruments is different. It is comprehensive. There are instruments for most ways you'd want to analyze your code, and Instruments runs them *all at the same time*. The results are laid out by time, in parallel. Did clicking a **Compute** button result in Core Data fetches? Or had the fetches already been done earlier? Did other disk activity eat up bandwidth? In the application? Elsewhere in the system? Is the application leaking file descriptors, and if so, when, and in response to what? If you hand data off to another process, how does the recipient's memory usage change in response to the handoff, and how does it relate to the use of file descriptors in both the recipient and master applications?

Instruments can answer these questions. You can relate file descriptors to disk activity, and disk activity to Core Data events, with stack traces for every one of these because Instruments captures the data on a timeline, all in parallel, event by event. And you can target different instruments on different applications (or even the system as a whole) at the same time.

For events—such as individual allocations or system calls—Instruments keeps a complete record each time. For time profiling, Instruments does statistical sampling, but it keeps each sample. That means that even if you want an aggregate, *you get to pick the aggregate*.

Say the list of passers in Passer Rating for the iPhone stutters when you scroll it. With Shark, you'd have to start Passer Rating, get to where you'd be scrolling as quickly as you could, do the scrolling, and then kill it at once so your statistical sample wouldn't be polluted by whatever followed the part you were interested in. And you'd be too late because the CPU time soaked up by initialization would swamp the little spikes incurred by reloading the passer table cells.

In Instruments, by contrast, you don't have to worry about one part of the program polluting your statistics. You can select just the part of the timeline that has to do with scrolling, and you can see what your app was doing just then.

> **NOTE**
>
> Most of the power of Instruments lies in the analysis tools it provides after a recording is made, but don't ignore the advantage it provides in showing program state dynamically: If you can't see when a memory total or file I/O begins and settles down (for instance), you won't know when to stop the recording for analysis in the first place.

Running Instruments

In Chapter 14, you started Instruments from Xcode by issuing **Product→Profile** (⌘-I), or selecting the **Profile** variant of the large Action button at the left end of the Xcode toolbar. You could set the trace template you wanted in the Profile panel of the Scheme editor. With profiling integrated into the Xcode workflow, this is the most common way you use Instruments.

For specialized uses, you'll want to go beyond the few templates the Profile action gives you. Instruments can run and attach to applications independently, and you can set up any instruments you like for the trace.

You start Instruments by selecting **Xcode→Open Developer Tool→Instruments** in Xcode. Once it's launched, hold the mouse down on its icon in the Dock, and select **Options→Keep in Dock** from the menu.

When you start it, Instruments automatically opens a document (called a *trace document*) and displays a sheet offering you a choice of templates populated with instruments for common tasks. See Figure 27.1. I'll have a list of templates that Apple provides in "The Templates" section later in this chapter.

FIGURE 27.1   When you create a new trace document in Instruments, it shows you an empty document and a sheet for choosing among templates prepopulated with instruments for common tasks.

The Trace Document Window

The initial form of a trace document window is simple: A toolbar at the top and a stack of instruments in the view that dominates the window. After you record data into the document, the window becomes much richer. Let's go through Figure 27.2 and identify the components.

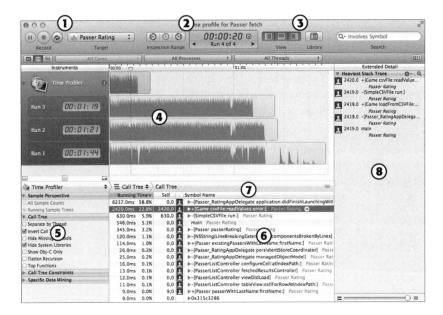

FIGURE 27.2   A typical Instruments window after data has been recorded. The Extended Detail area (at right) has also been exposed. The numbered parts are discussed in the text.

The Toolbar

The toolbar comes in three sections. The controls at left (1) control recording and the execution of the target applications. There is a **Pause** button for suspending and resuming data collection; a **Record/ Drive & Record/Stop** button to start and stop data collection; and a **Loop** button for running a recorded human-interface script repeatedly.

> **NOTE**
>
> When you start recording, you will often be asked for an administrator's password. The kind of deep monitoring many instruments do is a security breach, and the system makes you show you are authorized to do it.

The **Target** pop-up designates the process or executable that all instruments in the document will target, unless you specify a different target for individual instruments. The choices are:

▶ The top of the menu lets you choose the device Instruments is to focus on. It determines what processes and targets are available for tracing.

▶ **All Processes:** Data will be collected from all the processes, user and system, on the target device. For instance, the Core Data instruments (Mac only) can measure the Core Data activity of all processes. Not every instrument can span processes; if your document contains no instruments that can sample systemwide, this option will be disabled.

- ▶ **Attach to Process:** Data will be collected from a process that is already running; select it from the submenu. Some instruments require that their targets be launched from Instruments and cannot attach to running processes. If you use only nonattaching instruments, this option will be disabled.

- ▶ **Choose Target:** When you start recording, Instruments launches the selected application or tool and collects data from it. The submenu contains items for applications you've recorded previously and has a **Choose Target…** item to drop a browser sheet to choose a fresh application.

- ▶ **Instrument Specific:** Each instrument collects data from the target specified in the Target pop-up of its configuration inspector. The instruments in a trace document do not all have to collect data from the same target.

- ▶ **Edit Active Target:** Drops a sheet for editing the arguments and environment variables to pass to the target when it launches.

- ▶ **Options:** A submenu that directs standard I/O to Instruments or the device log; and for the iOS Simulator, selects the mode (iPhone or iPad) in which the simulator is to operate.

The **Target** pop-up is not selectable while Instruments is recording.

The center section (*2*) relates to time. The clock view in the center of the toolbar displays the total time period recorded in the document. If you click the clock-face icon to the right of the time display, the clock shows the position of the "playback head" in the time scale at the top of the Track area.

The clock view also controls which run of the document is displayed. Each time you click **Record**, a new recording, with a timeline of its own, is added to the document. The run now displayed is shown like "Run 1 of 2," and you can switch among them by clicking the arrowhead buttons to either side.

> **NOTE**
>
> You can also browse among runs by selecting **View→Run Browser (^Tab)**. The contents of the window will be replaced by a "cover flow" partial view of the traces in each run, along with particulars of when it was run, on what, and so on.

Most instruments display subsets of the data they collect if you select a time span within the recording. To do so, move the playback head to the beginning of the span, and click the left segment of the Inspection Range control (Figure 27.3); then move the head to the end of the span, and click the segment on the right. The selected span is highlighted, and the Display is restricted to data collected in the span. To clear the selection, click the segment in the middle.

FIGURE 27.3   The center section of a trace document's toolbar displays a clock and controls for selecting a span of time within a recording. The clock view shows the total time in the document (or if you click the icon at the right of the clock, the position of the "playback head") and the run displayed if there is more than one.

> **NOTE**
>
> Option-dragging across an interval in one of the traces will also set an inspection range.

The right section (3) provides convenient controls for display. **View** is the familiar three-segment control that hides and shows the Title/Options, Detail, and Extended Detail panes. **Library** shows and hides the Library window. The **Search** field filters the Detail area by symbols or libraries that match the keywords you enter.

The Track Area

The Track area (4) is the focus of the document window and the only component you see when a document is first opened. This is the area you drag new instruments into. Each instrument occupies its own row, with a configuration block on the left, and the instrument's track on the right.

The configuration block (see Figure 27.4) shows the instrument's name and icon. To the left is a disclosure triangle, so you can see the instrument's tracks for previous runs in the document. To the right is an inspector button (i) that reveals a configuration inspector for the instrument.

FIGURE 27.4   A stack of instrument tracks in a trace document. Each instrument has its own row, with a timeline extending to the right, calibrated in seconds. Clicking an instrument's Configuration button opens a inspector containing settings for the instrument. Some of these control the style of the graph and which of its data an instrument displays and can be changed at any time. The pop-up at the top of the inspector selects what process the instrument is to collect data from and must be set before recording begins.

The tracks to the right of the configuration blocks display the data collected by the instruments on a timeline. The configuration inspector controls what data is plotted, and how it displays.

NOTE

Most instruments also put a Configure button in the lower-right corner for more options on how the instrument collects data. The distinction between the main and configure sides of the block is not well defined, so be sure to check both. Further, the Options view in the Detail area can contain settings that affect what data is collected. Sometimes, you can't set these until after you record a trace; check, and be aware that you may have to prepare the options after a throwaway run.

At the top of the timeline is a ruler matching the data to the time at which is was collected. The scale of the track can be controlled by the slider below the configuration blocks. In the ruler you see a white triangle, the *playback head*. Drag the playback head and use the **Inspection Range** control to select intervals within the recording. As you drag the head across the track, many instruments label their tracks with the value of their data at that time.

NOTE

Shift-dragging across a track zooms it so that the span you select fills the width of the window.

The Detail Area

The Detail area (5 and 6) appears when a trace is run. **View→Detail** (⌘D), and the middle segment of the **View** control in the toolbar toggle the Detail area.

When you select an instrument in the Track view, the data for the instrument collection is shown in tabular form in the Table view of the Detail area. What's in the table varies among instruments. The Detail jump bar (7) controls which table displays. As you drill down into the data for a detail row, elements are added to the jump bar; click higher-level elements to return to the corresponding views.

The Options view (5) filters the table's contents; it may also have controls that configure an instrument or trigger an instrument's actions. The options vary by instrument and table type, but most instruments collect call trees and have a "Call Tree" section among the options. The call-tree display options are:

▶ **Separate by Thread:** Call trees are normally merged with no regard for which thread the calls occurred in. Separating the trees by thread can help you weed out calls in threads you aren't interested in.

27

▶ **Invert Call Tree:** The default (top-down) presentation of call trees starts at the runtime `start` function, branching out through the successive calls down to the leaf functions that are the events the instrument records. Checking this box inverts the trees, so they are bottom-up. For a Cocoa application, this often means that `objc_msgSend` (for instance) branches out to all its callers, those branch out to their callers, and so on.

▶ **Hide Missing Symbols:** Checking this box hides functions that don't have symbols associated with them. Most of the libraries in the system frameworks include symbols for their functions, and those can at least suggest what's going on. (And, of course, your code has symbols because you've made sure your "Debug Information Format" build setting is set to "DWARF with dSYM File"—it won't inflate the size of your code.)

▶ **Hide System Libraries:** This skips over functions in system libraries. Reading the names of the library calls may help you get an idea of what is going on, but if you're looking for code you can do something about, you don't want to see them. Using this option along with **Invert Call Tree** often tells an explicit story about what your code does. `objc_msgSend` is so ubiquitous in Cocoa code that finding it in a stack trace doesn't tell you much; paring the trees down to where all those calls came from tells you everything.

▶ **Show Obj-C Only:** Checking this narrows the list down to calls made from Objective-C methods, whether in system libraries or elsewhere. Another way to cut out the possible distraction of calls you don't care to see.

▶ **Flatten Recursion:** This lumps every call a function makes to itself into a single item. Recursive calls can run up the length of a call stack without being informative.

> **NOTE**
>
> Stack traces in the Extended Detail area reflect your settings of these filters.

You can also add call-tree constraints, such as minimum and maximum call counts. The idea is to prune (or focus on) calls that are not frequently made. Another constraint that may be available (for instance in the Time Profiler instrument) can filter call trees by the amount of time (minimum, maximum, or both) they took up in the course of the run.

The Extended Detail Area

The Extended Detail area (8) typically includes a stack trace when you select an item in the Detail area that carries stack information. When the selected item is part of a call tree, the Extended Detail area shows the "heaviest" stack, the one that accounts for the most of whatever the instrument keeps track of. Selecting a frame in the call stack highlights the corresponding call in the call-tree outline. Double-clicking a frame shows the corresponding source code in the Detail area, with banners showing where the instrument "hit" in the function, and what proportion of those function hits fell on which lines. Use the jump bar to back out of the listing display.

A stack trace in the Extended Detail area has an Action (gear) menu at the top. Most commands in this menu have to do with how the calls in the trace are formatted, but a couple are of particular interest. **Look Up API Documentation** acts like option-clicking on a symbol in Xcode: It opens a window showing the documentation for the selected method. **Trace Call Duration** creates a new instrument in the current document to record the stack trace whenever the function is called and how long it takes to execute.

As with Xcode's Debug navigator, the Extended Detail area has a slider at the bottom to condense the stack trace to "interesting" frames, generally defined as your functions, their callers, and the functions they call. Sliding the control all the way to the right gives you the full stack; to the left, just one (usually uninformative) call. If you don't see your code in the stack, be sure to check the slider to ensure it hasn't filtered out what you need to see.

The Library

Instruments get into a document either by being instantiated from a template or by being dragged in from the Library window.

The Library palette (**Window→Library**, ⌘L, or the **Library** toggle button in the toolbar) lists all the known instruments. Initially this is a repertoire of Apple-supplied tracks, but you can add your own. The palette lists all known instruments. Selecting one fills the pane below the list with a description (which has always been the same as the description in the list, but we can hope for the future). See Figure 27.5.

FIGURE 27.5   A scrolling list of available instruments dominates the Library palette. The selected instrument is described in the panel below. Selecting a category from the pop-up menu narrows the list down by task, and the search field at the bottom allows you to find an instrument from its name or description.

The Library gathers instruments into groups; these are initially hidden but can be seen if you select **Show Group Banners** from the **Action** (gear) pop-up at the lower-left corner of the palette. The action menu also enables you to create groups of your own. The pop-up at the top of the palette narrows the list down by group, and the search field at the bottom enables you to filter the list by searching for text in the names and descriptions.

Instrument Configuration

Configuration inspectors vary by instrument, but some elements are used frequently.

There is a **Target** pop-up that initially points to the document's default target (set with the **Target** menu in the toolbar). If no default target has been selected, or if the **Target** menu has been set to **Instrument Specific**, the instrument's **Target** is active. You can select from processes already running, applications that Instruments had sampled before, a new application or tool of your choice, or with many instruments, the system as a whole.

The ability to set a target for each instrument is important: It allows you to examine the behavior of an application and other processes with which it communicates simultaneously.

In the **Track Display** section, there are three controls: A **Style** pop-up, a **Type** pop-up, and a **Zoom** slider.

The usual **Style** menu selects among graphing styles for the numeric data the instrument records. These may include the following:

- ▶ **Line Graph:** The track displays as a colored line connecting each datum in the series. You can choose the color in the list of the available series.

- ▶ **Filled Line Graph:** The same as **Line**, but the area under the line is colored.

- ▶ **Point Graph:** Each datum displays as a discrete symbol in the track. You can choose the symbols in the list of available series in the inspector.

- ▶ **Block Graph:** A bar graph, showing each datum as a colored rectangle. In instruments that record events, the block is as wide as the time to the next event.

- ▶ **Peak Graph:** Shows the data collected by an instrument that records events (such as the Core Data instruments) as a vertical line at each event. Every time something happens, the graph shows a blip.

NOTE

Most instruments record events, not quantities that vary over time. The data displayed may not even be a continuous variable but may be a mere tag, like the ID of a thread or a file descriptor. The Peak style is the most suitable style for event recordings. Such displays are still useful because they give you a landmark for examining the matching data in the other tracks.

The **Type** menu offers two choices for instruments that can record more than one data series. **Overlay** displays all series on a single graph. The displayed data probably overlaps, but in point and line displays, this probably doesn't matter, and filled displays are translucent, so the two series don't obscure each other. **Stacked** displays each series in separate strips, one above the other.

Zoom increases the height of the instrument's track. This is especially handy in stacked displays, so you can view multiple traces without squishing them into illegibility. The slider clicks to integer multiples of the standard track height, from 1 to 10 units.

You can change the **Track Display** settings even after the instrument has collected its data. You can find a shortcut for the **Zoom** slider in the **View** menu, as **Increase Deck Size** (⌘+) and **Decrease Deck Size** (⌘-).

For instruments that can collect more than one series, a **Statistics to Graph** section shows a check box for each available series, with a pop-up to select the shape of points for a Point Graph, plus a color well.

Recording

There is more than one way to start recording in Instruments. The most obvious is to create a trace document and click the **Record** button on the toolbar. Recording starts, the target application comes to the front, you perform your test, switch back to Instruments, and click the same button, now labeled **Stop**.

The first time you record into a document that contains a User Interface instrument (Mac targets only), the recording button is labeled **Record**, as usual. When the UI track contains events, the recording button is labeled **Drive & Record**. When you click it, no new events are recorded into the UI track; instead the events already there are *replayed* so you can reproduce your tests.

If you want to record a fresh User Interface track, open the configuration inspector (with the **i** button in the instrument's label) and select **Capture** from the **Action** pop-up. The recording button reverts to **Record**.

A second way to record is through the Quick Start feature (Mac targets only), which allows you to start recording with a systemwide hot-key combination. To set a hot key, open the Instruments Preferences window and select the **Quick Start** tab. This tab includes a table listing every system- and user-supplied template. Double-click in the column next to the template you choose, and press the desired hot-key combination. The combination must include at least two modifier keys (such as Command, Shift, and so on).

With the hot key set, move the mouse over a window belonging to the application you want to target; then press the key combination. Instruments launches if it is not running already, opens a new trace document behind your application with the template you selected, targets it on your application, and starts recording. To stop, make sure your mouse is over one of the target's windows, and press the key combination again (or switch to Instruments and click **Stop**).

The requirement to point the mouse at one of the target's windows allows you to start simultaneous traces on more than one application.

If you select **Quick Start Headless** in the **Quick Start** tab, the trace document will not be visible until you switch to Instruments. To remove a hot key, select the template in the **Quick Start** table, and press the Delete key.

The third way to record is through the Mini Instruments window. Selecting **View→Mini Instruments** hides all of Instruments' windows and substitutes a floating heads-up window (see Figure 27.6) listing all the open trace documents.

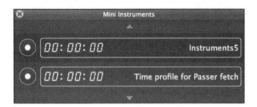

FIGURE 27.6   The Mini Instruments heads-up window. It lists each open trace document next to a clock and a recording button. Scroll through the list using the arrowheads at top and bottom.

The window lists all the trace documents that were open when you switched to Mini mode; scroll through by clicking the up or down arrowheads above and below the list. At the left of each item is a button for starting (round icon) or stopping (square icon) recording and a clock to show how long recording has been going on. Stopping and restarting a recording adds a new run to the document.

As with Quick Start keys, Mini Instruments has the advantages that it's convenient to start recording in the middle of an application's run (handy if you are recording a User Interface track that you want to loop) and that you can control recording without switching out of the target application (which can also impair a UI recording).

You can return to the full display of Instruments by clicking the Close (**x**) button in the upper-left corner of the Mini Instruments window.

While a trace runs, Instruments analyzes the data it collects, building up profiles and tables. Often it has to refer back to earlier data (like matching memory events to blocks and updating living-versus-transient counts) to keep the analysis current. Computers are fast, but the process takes resources away from the target application and can force Instruments to skip data points. You can prevent this by deferring analysis until the trace stops. **File→Record Options…** (⌥⌘R) sets parameters for tracing, like delaying data collection until a fixed time after launching the application or limiting collection to a fixed period. See Figure 27.7. The option you're interested in is the **Deferred Mode** check box. While it's checked, Instruments grays-out the trace window until the run ends.

Saving and Reopening

Like any other Macintosh document, a trace document can be saved. The document contains its instruments and all the data they've collected. There can be a lot of data, so expect a trace document to be large—tens of megabytes are not uncommon. Trace documents generally respond well to ZIP archiving.

It's likely that you will need a uniform layout of instruments that isn't included in the default templates provided by Apple. You can easily create templates of your own, which appear in the template sheet presented when you create a new trace document. Configure a document as you want it, and select **File→Save as Template...**.

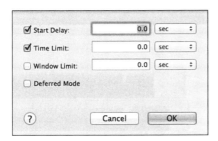

FIGURE 27.7   **File→Record Options...** (⌥⌘R) produces a sheet in which you can restrict the scope of an Instruments tracing session and improve the efficiency of the trace by deferring analysis until after the trace is done.

The ensuing save-file sheet is the standard one, focused on the directory in which Instruments looks for your templates, `~/Library/Application Support/Instruments/Templates`. The name you give your file will be the label shown in the template-choice sheet. At the lower left of the sheet is a well into which you can drag an icon (for instance, if your template is for testing your application, you'd want to drop your application's icon file here), or you can hold the mouse button over the well to choose Apple-provided icons from a pop-up. The panel provides a text area for the description to be shown in the template-choice sheet.

▶ The document's suite of instruments, and their configurations, will be saved in the template.

▶ The template includes the default and instrument-specific targets you set.

▶ If you include a prerecorded User Interface track, the contents will be saved. This way you can produce uniform test documents simply by creating a new trace document and selecting the template.

As you'd expect, you can reopen a trace document by double-clicking it in the Finder, or through the **File→Open...** (⌘O) command. All the data is as it was when the document was saved. Clicking **Record** (⌘R) adds a new run to the document.

27

> **NOTE**
>
> There are three ways to run traces without having to launch Instruments. With the `instruments` command-line tool, you can select the target application and either a template or an existing trace document to capture the trace data. The `DTPerformanceSession` framework allows you to initiate traces from your source code, without having to bother with the Instruments app's template and document infrastructure. And `iprofiler` provides the same lightweight profiling service from the command line. See `man instruments`, `man iprofiler`, and the `DTPerformanceSession` documentation for details.

The Instruments

Here are the built-in instruments as of the time this book was written. Not all instruments appear in the Library window—instruments such as Core Animation may be available only through file templates. Start with the grouping used in the Library window (select **Show Group Banners** from the **Action** (gear) pop-up at the bottom left), and extend the groups from there.

> **NOTE**
>
> Apple is free to add or remove built-in instruments or to change their capabilities. This can't be a definitive list. For the latest information, search for the *Instruments User Guide* in the Developer Tools Reference in the Xcode Documentation window. Alas, the only documentation some instruments have is the description in the Library palette.

Most Mac and iOS Simulator instruments are DTrace-based (see the section on "Custom Instruments," later). DTrace automatically records thread ID and a stack trace, and implicitly the stack depth, at the time of an event. Every numeric-valued property of the event is eligible for graphing in the instrument's track, which accounts for the odd offer of "Thread ID" for plotting in such instruments.

All instruments can target any single process, or all processes on the system, unless the description says otherwise. The Instruments library puts some instruments in more than one group; I'll generally list them in the first group in which they appear, but if an iOS-only instrument appears in the "iOS" group, it is listed there.

Core Data

These instruments monitor significant events in an application's use of Core Data. Unfortunately, they are all Mac-only.

Core Data Cache Misses: A faulted Core Data object may already be in memory; it may be held in its `NSPersistentStoreCoordinator`'s cache. If, however, you fire a fault on an object that *isn't* in the cache (a "cache miss"), you've come into an expensive operation, as the object has to be freshly read from the database. You want to minimize the effect of cache faults by preloading the objects when it doesn't impair user experience.

This instrument shows where cache misses happen. It records the thread ID and stack trace of each miss, and how much time was taken to satisfy the miss, for objects and relationships.

Core Data Faults: Core Data objects can be expensive both in terms of memory and of the time it takes to load them into memory. Often, an `NSManagedObject` or a to-many relationship is given to you as a *fault*, a kind of IOU that will be paid off in actual data when you reference data in the object.

This instrument captures every firing (payoff) of an object or relationship fault. It can display the thread ID and stack depth of the fault, as well as how long it took to satisfy object and relationship faults.

Core Data Fetches: Captures the thread ID and stack trace of every fetch operation under Core Data, along with the number of objects fetched and how long it took to complete the fetch.

Core Data Saves: At each save operation in Core Data, records the thread ID, stack trace, and how long the save took.

Custom Instruments

Sudden Termination (Mac only): Simulates the Lion feature of directly killing apps that volunteer that they'd be safe to kill. This instrument flags all your file-system activity that happens while you've signaled the system that a sudden kill would be okay. If you're actively reading and writing files, it may not be a good idea to subject yourself to termination without notice.

Cocoa Layout (Mac only): Under autolayout, observes changes to `NSLayoutConstraint` objects—when they are created, added to windows, and removed. This template is one part of the workflow for debugging issues with Cocoa Layout. Run your app under Instruments with this template. In `gdb`, determine a layout constraint that is incorrect, and note the object's address. Use the search field in Instruments to filter out all but that one constraint. Looking at the constraint descriptions over time, determine the point at which things went awry. The backtrace for that change should help you debug your code.

Dispatch

Dispatch (Mac only): Records Grand Central Dispatch events, the status of queues, and the duration of dispatched tasks.

File System

Directory I/O (Mac only): Records every event of system calls affecting directories, such as creation, moving, mounting, unmounting, renaming, and linking. The data includes thread ID, stack trace, call, path to the file directory affected, and the destination path.

File Activity (Mac only): Records every call to `open`, `close`, `fstat`, `open$UNIX2003`, and `close$UNIX2003`. The instrument captures the thread ID, the call stack, the call, the file descriptor, and the path.

File Attributes (Mac only): For every event of changing the owner, group, or access mode of a file (chown, chgrp, chmod) this instrument records thread ID, a stack trace, the called function, the file descriptor number, the group and user IDs, the mode flags, and the path to the file affected.

File Locks (Mac only): Records the thread ID, stack trace, function, option flags, and path for every call to the flock system function.

I/O Activity (iOS only): Combines the functionality of all the Mac-only instruments in this category into one comprehensive instrument for iOS. By default, it collects only how long each call lasted, but click the Configure button to see what else is available.

Garbage Collection

Garbage Collection (Mac only): Measures across the beginning and end of the scavenge phase of garbage collection. It records whether the reclamation was generational and how long scavenging took. It also records the number of objects and bytes reclaimed.

Graphics

Core Animation (iOS): Collects statistics for the current state of OpenGL, including wait times for callers, counts of surfaces and textures, and how full video RAM is, as it relates to your app's use of the high-level Core Animation framework.

OpenGL ES Analyzer (iOS): Analyzes your app's usage of OpenGL ES, flagging stalls and other errors, yielding a ranked table of problems and suggestions on how to avoid them.

OpenGL Driver (Mac) **and OpenGL ES Driver** (iOS): Collects the same statistics as the Core Animation instrument, at the lower level of OpenGL/OpenGL ES.

Input/Output

Reads/Writes: reads and writes to file descriptors. Each event includes the thread ID, the name of the function being called, a stack trace, the descriptor and path of the file, and the number of bytes read or written.

Master Tracks

User Interface (Mac only): On first run, records mouse and keyboard events as you use your Mac OS X application. After that, when you start a trace, the events are played back so you can have a uniform baseline for your program as you make adjustments.

Memory

Allocations (iOS and Mac): Collects a comprehensive history of every block of memory allocated during the run of the trace. Every event is tagged with the block address and the current stack trace. Configuration options let you track Cocoa reference-counting events and create "zombie" objects. You learned how to use it in Chapter 14.

Leaks (iOS and Mac): Tracks the allocation and deallocation of objects in an application to detect the objects' being allocated and then lost—in other words, memory leaks. Leaks does not rely simply on balancing allocations and deallocations; it periodically sweeps your program's heap to detect blocks that are not referenced by active memory. If the Allocations instrument is set to monitor zombies, Leaks won't record because zombie objects, which are never deallocated, are all leaked. For an extensive example, see Chapter 14.

Object Graph (Mac only): Garbage collection, if you have it enabled in your Mac OS X application, is not a panacea for memory management. Entire trees of objects will be collected and returned to the heap (eventually), but that requires that the collector thread see no references to any part of a tree in global or stack memory. If you forget to clear a reference out, the objects stay alive, and you have something that's as bad as a leak. The Object Graph instrument shows you what object trees are alive and how they're anchored.

Shared Memory (Mac only): Records an event when shared memory is opened or unlinked. The event includes calling thread ID and an executable, stack trace, function (shm_open/shm_unlink) and parameters (name of the shared memory object, flags, and mode_t). Selecting an event in the Detail table puts a stack trace into the Extended Detail pane.

VM Tracker (iOS and Mac): Takes a "snapshot" of the virtual-memory zones associated with your application, recording the size of each zone, and whether it is shared, or private. The trace shows total usage, but the real story is in the "dirty" trace: The VM system can share things like system libraries across applications from a single chunk of physical RAM; and memory that the app hasn't written to is "clean"—the system can simulate that memory as zeroes, without taking up any actual RAM. As soon as your app writes to memory, those addresses become dirty and must consume precious physical memory.

Don't bother with VM Tracker on the iOS Simulator; at the virtual-memory level, it's a Mac application, with no relation to how memory would be used on an iOS device.

By default, you have to click a **Snapshot Now** button in the Options view to collect heap data. You can check **Automatic Snapshotting** if you want to collect data periodically.

System

Activity Monitor (iOS and Mac): An analog to the UNIX top command with the option to focus on only one process. This instrument is too varied to explain fully here, but its features should be easy to understand if you explore its configuration inspector. It collects 31 summary statistics on a running process, including thread counts, physical memory usage, virtual memory activity, network usage, disk operations, and percentages of CPU load. Remember that you can have more than one Activity Monitor instrument running, targeting different applications or the system as a whole.

CPU Monitor (iOS and Mac): The Activity Monitor with % Total Load, % User Load, and % System Load selected.

Counters (Mac only): Tracks events affecting the hardware diagnostic counters built into each core of the CPU.

Disk Monitor (iOS and Mac): The Activity Monitor with Disk Read/Write Operations Per Second and Disk Bytes Read/Written Per second checked.

Memory Monitor (iOS and Mac): The Activity Monitor with Physical Memory Used/Free, Virtual Memory Size, and Page Ins/Outs checked.

Network Activity Monitor (iOS and Mac): The Activity Monitor with four of eight network statistics active: Network Packets/Bytes In/Out Per Second. It omits the absolute numbers of packets and bytes transmitted.

Process (Mac only): Records thread ID, stack trace, process ID, exit status, and executable path for each start (execve) and end (exit) event in a process.

Sampler (iOS and Mac): Periodically samples the target application at fixed intervals (1 ms by default, but you can set it in the inspector), and records a stack trace each time. This instrument has been superseded by Time Profiler, except in cases, like measuring graphics performance, when it is essential to minimize the effect of CPU sampling on other measurements.

Spin Monitor (Mac only): Focuses on one Mac OS X application, or all, and logs stack traces when they become unresponsive. An application is "unresponsive" when it has spent more than a few seconds without attempting to collect a human-interface event. This is when the multicolored spinning "beachball" cursor occurs.

This is a serious fault in an application, but you can't often reproduce spins. Spin Monitor sleeps most of the time, taking up few resources until a spin activates it.

Time Profiler (iOS and Mac): Periodically samples the target application at fixed intervals (1 ms by default, but you can set it in the inspector), and records a stack trace each time. You can then get a statistical picture of what parts of your application are taking up the most time. This is an essential tool, doing what most people mean when they speak of profiling an application. Chapter 14 demonstrated the use of Time Profiler.

When Time Profiler is in a trace document, a bar is added above the Trace area that lets you refine the profile: The segment control at the left provides an overview trace (middle), or it can divide the trace among CPU cores (left) or by thread (right). A series of pop-up menus lets you restrict the trace by processor core, process, and thread; and to color-code by user and kernel load. A pop-up at the right end of the bar shows the colors used in the chart.

iOS Energy Instruments

These instruments for iOS performance don't rely on Instruments to run the trace because running them only when the device is tethered to a Mac would be counterproductive. When you designate a device for development, Xcode (or Instruments) installs a daemon on the device that can log activity that influences power drain.

You can analyze the logs when the device is plugged into Instruments again. Open Instruments and select **File→Import Energy Diagnostics from Device**.

By default, logging is off and must be turned on with the Settings app. The daemon can be turned off with the **Developer** panel in Settings or by an untethered reboot. If the battery runs out entirely, the daemon won't restart.

Bluetooth, GPS, and **WiFi:** Log when the respective radios are on.

CPU Activity: A compact version of Activity Monitor, showing the total load on the CPU, with breakouts for the foreground app, audio, and graphics.

Display Brightness: Records the on/off state and brightness setting of the device's backlight. Ambient-light adjustments don't get logged.

Energy Usage: Overall power drain on a scale of 20. When the device is plugged or unplugged to a power source, the event is flagged.

Network Activity: Logs overall network usage in terms of bit and packet rates.

Sleep/Wake: Logs whether the device is asleep, along with sleep-transition states.

Threads/Locks

JavaThread (Mac only): A unique instrument, in that it does not display its trace as a vertical graph. Instead, the trace is a stack of bars, extending horizontally through time, that represent the threads in a Java application. A bar appears when a thread starts. It is colored green while it runs; yellow while it waits; and red while it is blocked. The bar disappears when the thread halts. A sample is taken whenever such thread events occur; the Detail table shows the time of day at which the sample was taken, and the number of threads existing at that time.

Thread States (Mac only): Represents each thread in the target application by a block, colored to indicate the state of the thread—running, waiting, suspended, and so on—at each moment. Open the configuration block (i) to see the color code. See Figure 27.8.

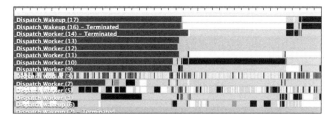

FIGURE 27.8   The Thread States instrument shows the state of every thread in a process as a stack of color-coded bars.

UI Automation

Automation (iOS only): Executes a JavaScript script that exercises the UI of an iOS application on a device or the iOS Simulator. Add other instruments to the trace document to produce a package that can reproduce a test and record the performance of your app as you develop it. You configure the instrument in the Options view of the Detail area. The most important part is the Scripts section, where the **Add** drop-down menu allows you to **Import...** a .js file to the track, or **Create...** one in an editor within the Detail area.

UI Automation comes with an extensive class tree; consult the "Instruments User Guide" and the "UIAutomation Reference Collection" for details.

User Interface

Carbon Events (Mac only): Monitors events returned from WaitNextEvent. Carbon Events records an event at every return from WaitNextEvent. It captures a the thread ID, stack trace, the event code, and a string (like "Key Down") that characterizes the event.

Cocoa Events (Mac only): Records the event objects dispatched through every call to -[NSApplication sendEvent:]. It captures the thread ID, stack trace, the event code, and a string (like "Left Mouse Down") that characterizes the event.

Instruments Available to iOS

The listing above mixed the instruments that are available to all platorms. For reference, here are the instruments that are specifically available to iOS:

▶ **Activity Monitor**

▶ **Allocations**

▶ **Bluetooth**

▶ **Core Animation**

▶ **CPU Activity**

▶ **CPU Monitor**

▶ **Disk Monitor**

▶ **Display Brightness**

▶ **Energy Usage**

▶ **GPS**

▶ **I/O Activity**

▶ **Leaks**

▶ **Memory Monitor**

▶ **Network Activity**

▶ **Network Activity Monitor**

▶ **OpenGL ES Driver**

▶ **Sampler**

▶ **Scheduling**

- ▶ Sleep/Wake
- ▶ System Calls
- ▶ VM Operations
- ▶ VM Tracker
- ▶ WiFi

Custom Instruments

Many of the instruments included in Instruments consist of code specially written for the task, but most involve no compiled code at all. They are made from editable templates: You can examine these instruments—this may be the only way to get authoritative details on what an instrument does—and you can create instruments of your own.

Let's see what a scripted instrument looks like. Create a trace document from the File Activity template, select the **Reads/Writes** instrument and then **Instrument→Edit 'Reads/Writes' Instrument** (or simply double-click the instrument's label). An editing sheet (see Figure 27.9) appears, with fields for the instrument's name, category, and description, and a long scrolling list of *probes*, handlers for events the instrument is meant to capture.

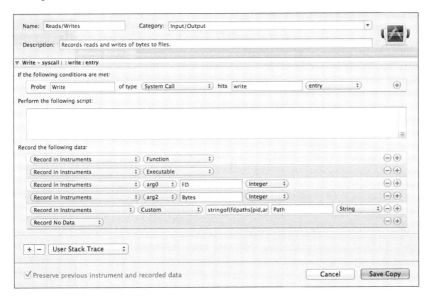

FIGURE 27.9   The Edit Instrument sheet for the Reads/Writes instrument. The sheet is dominated by an editable list of events the instrument is to capture. The portion that specifies how to record entries to the system `write` function is shown here.

Refer to Figure 27.9 to see the event list scrolled to the condition called **Write**, in the domain **System Call**, for the symbol `write`. It triggers when `write` is entered. Next comes

the text of a script to be executed when the probe is triggered. Instruments uses the
DTrace kernel facility, which has its own scripting language; for instance, this event might
put the time at which the event occurred into a thread variable of the probe so that a
write-exit probe could calculate the duration of the call and record it. In this case, the
scripting text is blank.

Then comes a series of items specifying what information is to be kept for the trace graph
or for the Detail view. In the case of Reads/Writes, this is:

▶ The name of the function.

▶ The name of the executable.

▶ The first argument (the file descriptor), which is an integer to be labeled "FD."

▶ A string, to be labeled "Path," calculated from an expression in the DTrace language:
  A file path, derived from the file descriptor within the executable.

▶ The third argument (the size of the write), which is an integer to be labeled "Bytes."

At the bottom of the edit sheet is a drop-down menu that controls whether the instrument records a stack trace for its events, and whether it is a user-, system-, or Java-space
stack.

Integer-valued records are included in the configuration inspector's list of **Statistics to
Graph** and are eligible to display in the instrument's trace. This accounts for the odd
presence of "tid" (the thread ID, which is automatically captured in every case) in the list
of available plots you see if you click the **Configure** button in the instrument-configura-
tion block.

The customization sheet is a front end for the scripting language for the kernel-provided
DTrace tool; only kernel-level code is capable of detecting call events in every process. The
section "Creating Custom Instruments with DTrace" in the *Instruments User Guide* offers
enough of an introduction to the language to get you started on your own instruments.

To make your own instrument, start with **Instrument→Build New Instrument**... (⌘B).
An instrument editing sheet drops from the front trace document, and you can proceed
from there.

If visiting `http://wikis.sun.com/display/DTrace/Documentation` has made you a DTrace
expert, you may find it more convenient, or more flexible, to write your scripts directly,
without going through the customization sheet. Select **File→DTrace Script Export**... to
save a script covering every instrument in the current document, and **File→DTrace Data
Import**... to load a custom script in. You can export DTrace scripts only from documents
that contain DTrace instruments exclusively.

The stack trace in the Extended Detail view provides another way to create a custom
instrument. Select one of the function frames in the listing and then **Trace Call Duration**
from the stack trace's **Action** (gear) menu. Instruments adds a custom instrument to the
current document that triggers on entry and exit to record how long it took to execute
the function.

The Templates

When you create a new Instruments document, a sheet drops down offering a choice among templates, preconfigured sets of instruments for common tasks. Click the configuration of your choice, and press one of the buttons at the bottom of the sheet:

▶ **Open an Existing File**… abandons the new document and presents a standard get-file dialog for opening an old one. This is simply a convenience, equivalent to canceling the sheet and performing **File→Open…** (⌘O).

▶ **Cancel** closes the untitled document without saving.

▶ **Record** does a lot of work. It creates the document and populates it with the selected template's instruments. Then it starts recording. When a trace document doesn't have a default target application—as a newly instantiated document would not—Instruments has to associate an application with each instrument in the document. A variant on the standard open-file dialog appears, allowing you to pick the target application or tool, and to specify arguments and environment variables. You can specify one target for all the instruments by checking the **Apply to All Instruments** box. When all the targets are set, Instruments launches them and starts recording.

▶ **Choose** creates the document and populates it with the instruments for the selected template.

NOTE

The Profile panel of Xcode's Scheme editor lets you choose from a few templates to use when you launch your application for profiling. Summon the Profile scheme editor by holding down the Option key while issuing the Profile action.

27

The version of Instruments I'm using came with more than two dozen templates, sorted by platform and purpose. That number is likely to grow as new requirements and new combinations come together to create new tools. Here is a sample—browse the New Document assistant and instantiate a few templates yourself to see what's available to you.

For Both Mac and iOS

Blank: This is straightforward; it's a trace document with no instruments attached, ready to receive your choices. Pick the instruments you want from the Library palette, and drag them into the Trace area.

Activity Monitor: Just the Activity Monitor instrument; think of it as a logging version of the top command-line utility.

Allocations: The Allocations and VM Tracker instruments. This is one of the templates you used in Chapter 14.

Leaks: Uses the Allocations and Leaks instruments to capture a history of your object allocations and track down objects that still take up memory even though no other objects refer to them. You saw this one in Chapter 14, too.

Here is how Apple describes the **System Trace** template: "Provides comprehensive information about system behavior by showing when threads are scheduled, and showing all their transitions from user into system code via either system calls or memory operations."

I can't offer my own comment because on my system, System Trace crashes Instruments when it tries to analyze its data. The template uses the Scheduling, System Calls, and VM Operations instruments. It collects data in deferred mode, so as not to harm system performance.

Time Profiler is just the Time Profiler instrument, which was covered in the first part of Chapter 14.

Zombies (Mac and iOS Simulator *only*) contains the Allocations instrument with **Enable NSZombie** detection checked. You saw something similar in Chapter 14.

iOS Only

Automation: Consists of the Automation instrument, to drive an iOS device through JavaScript. You are expected to add other instruments to meet your specific needs to track performance.

Core Animation: Contains the Core Animation and Sampler instruments. Sampler is a bit lighter-weight than Time Profiler, which is important if you are to get a read on graphics performance without interference from the profiler.

Energy Diagnostics: Encompasses all the instruments for analyzing energy-usage logs from an iOS device. This template isn't meant to drive or live-sample the device; it just processes what the device recorded in regular use.

Network Connections: Uses the instrument of the same name (which is not available in the library) to analyze your app's use of IP network connections.

OpenGL ES Analysis: Combines the OpenGL ES Analyzer, which gives detailed diagnostics—and suggestions—on OpenGL performance, with OpenGL Driver.

OpenGL ES Driver: Collects OpenGL performance statistics with the instrument of the same name, and matches the stats to the sampled stack traces from the lightweight Sampler instrument.

System Usage: Provides a complete picture of your app's file system activity through the I/O Activity instrument.

Mac Only

Cocoa Layout: Contains the Cocoa Layout instrument.

Core Data: Combines the Core Data Fetches, Cache Misses, and Saves instruments.

Counters: Includes the Counters instrument.

Dispatch: Contains the Dispatch instrument.

File Activity: Gives a complete picture of your application's use of the file system. It uses File Activity, Reads/Writes, File Attributes, and Directory I/O.

GC Monitor: Contains Object Graph, Allocations, and Garbage Collection, a suite that should give you a picture of how garbage collection is affecting your performance, and help you track down object trees that persist because of uncleared references.

Multicore: Gives you a track on Grand Central Dispatch with the Thread States and Dispatch instruments.

Sudden Termination: Contains the Sudden Termination and Activity Monitor instruments.

UI Recorder: Starts you with just the User Interface instrument, to record and play back user events for a consistently reproducible test case. You add other tracks as needed to measure what you want.

Summary

Instruments is a big topic, and I've taken you through most of it. You started with a tour of the trace document window and moved on to populating it from the Library window. You learned general principles of how to configure an instrument track.

You saw the various ways to start and stop recordings, including human-interface recordings that can be played back to generate repeatable tests for your applications. You walked through a partial inventory of the instruments and document templates Apple supplies, and how to create your own. As your needs and expertise progress, you'll want to consult the *Instruments User Guide* in Xcode's Documentation browser.

27

CHAPTER 28

Snippets

IN THIS CHAPTER

▶ Learning tricks

▶ Avoiding traps

*X*code 4 Unleashed relies mostly on narrative to take you on a tour of using Xcode for Cocoa development. I tried to cover as much as I could in the first three parts, and I mopped up the remaining big topics in the fourth. That leaves some small topics—tricks and traps—that didn't fit anywhere else.

Tricks

First, some advice on techniques that can make your life with Xcode easier. I've mentioned some of them before, but they're worth repeating.

General

▶ The **Editor** menu is extremely variable—it adjusts to the type of file in the active editor. If you're sure there's a feature for doing what you want, but can't find it by typing in the field at the top of the **Help** menu, be sure to bring up a related file, and click in it to adjust the **Editor** menu.

▶ In a complex project, an object in a XIB may take part, as provider or recipient, in dozens of outlets, actions, and bindings, each with its own context-limited editor. You don't have to click through all the editors; select the object, select the Connection (sixth) inspector, and all the connections will be there in one place.

▶ Not every useful preference in Xcode is accessible through the Preferences window; some must be set through the `defaults` command-line tool. Look for the article "Xcode User Default Reference" in the Documentation organizer. Treat this document carefully, though; the copy was written for Xcode 3.1.

When in doubt, apply

```
defaults read com.apple.xcode preferenceName
```

to keys to make sure they exist, or at least to capture the current values in case you need to back out.

▶ Some build settings are read-only, reflecting the state of the set or derived values from other settings. Some settings exist but don't have a graphical interface; there are more settings than there are entries in the Target editor's **Build Settings** tab. Appendix B, "Some Build Variables," provides a summary. You can use any of the settings as variables to build up values for the **Build Settings** tab or Info.plist, and you can set the "unlisted" but writable ones if you need to by clicking **Add Build Setting** at the bottom of the Target editor and choosing **Add User-Defined Setting**.

Build settings are also available to "Run Script" phases as environment variables.

▶ You may find some user-defined items at the bottom of the **Build Settings** table. This is how Xcode preserves settings it doesn't recognize. What it recognizes depends on the context: If, for instance, you have a project that doesn't have any compilable files, Xcode won't load its list of compiler options, and those options display as user-defined.

Older projects are another source of unrecognized settings. Some options are no longer supported in Xcode 4. When you open a project, Xcode may even offer to "modernize" your project by removing them. What you do about this is up to you. Usually, it's a good idea, but if you share the project file with others who are building for older versions of Mac OS X (such as before 10.5), you'll want to preserve those settings for their benefit.

One setting that bears repeating is $(inherited). Targets inherit build settings from the project, which in turn inherits settings from Xcode's defaults. Sometimes you want to add to, not replace, an inherited setting. Use $(inherited) to include the inherited value in your setting.

▶ You've seen Xcode's offer to incorporate directories as "folder references" when you add files to a project. The Project navigator shows two different kinds of folder icon: What you've seen throughout this book are "group" folders. Basically, these are simply organizational tools, a way to group files you've decided are related. Each file in a group is itself a member of the project.

But sometimes, adding a folder to a project means adding the folder itself. Suppose that you were building an educational program about presidents of the United States and wanted the Resources directory of the application to include a subdirectory containing a picture of each president. Your intention is that the application include that directory and whatever it may contain—as new administrations or replacement portraits come in—and not the particular files.

In such a case, when you add the portrait folder, you check **Create folder references for any added folders** in the add-files sheet. The folder you dragged in appears in the list in the same blue color as folders in the Finder, not in the yellow of Xcode's file-grouping folders. The folder reference can then be dragged into the "Copy Bundle Resources" build phase; the folder and its contents, whatever they might be at build time, will be copied into the product's Resources directory.

▶ Chapter 4, "Active Debugging," mentioned how Mac OS X usually supersedes the default debugger-control keys for hardware control. You aren't stuck with Xcode's choices. The **Key Bindings** panel of the Preferences window lists all the editor functions and application commands, and allows you to set or change the key equivalents for any of them. The default set can't be changed, but click the + button to create a customizable copy.

The **Conflicts** button in the key table's header is particularly useful. It shows you all the Xcode assignments that are superseded by the system or by other key assignments in Xcode.

▶ I've made much of the fact that the Project navigator is not a directory or file-system tool; it reflects the way you want to structure the project, and not the placement of files in the file system's directories. This isn't *quite* true.

If an Xcode project's file references were arbitrary, they'd have to be absolute paths. That would mean that all the files would be identified by a path that ran through your home directory. Suppose you were sharing the project with another developer. The project and its files would be in *her* directory, and the reference to your home directory would be wrong.

The solution would seem to be to keep the path relative to the project file—and indeed that is one of the options. It is not, however, the option Xcode uses by default. The default is **Relative to Group**, as shown in the **Location** pop-up in the File inspector. There are other choices, such as relative-to-build-products, relative to the developer directory, and, yes, absolute path. If you have defined source trees, you can make the path relative to one of those, too.

But what does "relative to group" mean? If you click on a group folder, you'll see in the File inspector that groups, too, have paths (which can, in turn, be absolute or relative). Groups still aren't directories: More than one group can refer to the same file directory, and not all members of a group need to be in the same place.

Putting a file-system location on a group has the advantage that you can have two directories in your file system, containing files that have the same names. Maybe the one contains live classes, and the other "mocks" for testing. Switching between the two would then be a simple matter of changing the path of the corresponding group.

If the group's directory does not enclose a file in the group, that file's path will be stored as project-relative.

28

▶ Renaming is another file-management service the Project navigator provides. It uses the same gestures as in the Finder. To rename a file or group, click once to select it and then again a second later. The item becomes editable. Or select the item and press Return.

If the project is under version control, Xcode will do the necessary work to ensure the change is noted in the repository.

The Jump Bar

The jump bar appears at the top of every editor view, gives you a sequence of pop-ups for navigating the hierarchy of your project. Clicking a segment gives you a menu of the groups and files at the corresponding level, and the groups have submenus, so you can navigate down to files in one operation. It's not a complete replacement for the Project navigator, but if you have an idea of where things are (or have a good group hierarchy), you can sometimes do without the navigator. If the file on display has indexable parts, such as methods in an .m file or objects in a XIB, the bar continues down to those.

▶ If you hold down the Command key when you select a segment of the jump bar, the menu sorts alphabetically. There is no way to make alphabetic sorting permanent.

▶ As with any method of cross-file navigation, if you hold down the Option key while selecting from the jump bar, the selected file will be put in the assistant editor.

▶ At the left end of the jump bar is a drop-down menu marked by eight small rectangles. This is the Related Items menu. Xcode fills this menu with categories for almost anything you could imagine that would be related to the file on display— recently edited and unsaved files; counterparts (headers and implementation files); parents, siblings, and children in the class tree; files that are included by this file, and files it includes; owned XIB files, or classes referenced in a XIB file; and derived (preprocessed or disassembled) text.

Don't confuse the Related Items menu with the automatic settings available at the root of the jump bar in the assistant editor. Related Items is attached to every editor pane and is a simple selector for files; when you use it, the pane focuses on the selected file, and it won't switch automatically.

Code Folding Ribbon

When I had you abate some Xcode features in Chapter 2, "Kicking the Tires," you went to the **Text Editing** panel of the Preferences window and turned off **Show: Code Folding Ribbon**. The feature is useful, but "noisy"—with the ribbon visible, mousing into the left margin of the editor puts transient highlights in the content.

Many text editors implement folding: You click a control, usually in the margin, or use a menu command or key equivalent, and the editor collapses the selected block of text. A possibly long stretch of code is elided to a single line, and you can see the higher-level structure of a function.

The code-folding ribbon does the same thing: Turning it on adds a stripe between the gutter and the text areas of the editor. The deeper the text next to the ribbon is nested, the darker the ribbon gets. When you mouse into the ribbon, Xcode highlights the text to show the extent of the code block containing that line. Clicking the ribbon collapses that block. See Figure 28.1.

```
88      - (void)configureView
89      {
90          NSString *      fieldName;
91          NSString *      strValue;
92          NSNumber *      numValue;
93
94          //  Set all the string labels
95          for (NSString * prop
96              in [GameListController stringProperties]) {
97              NSString    *value = [self.passer valueForKey: prop];
98              fieldName = [prop stringByAppendingString: @"Label"];
99              [[self valueForKey: fieldName] setText: value];
100         }
101
102         //  Set all the integer labels
103         for (NSString * prop
```

```
88      - (void)configureView
89      {
90          NSString *      fieldName;
91          NSString *      strValue;
92          NSNumber *      numValue;
93
94          //  Set all the string labels
95          for (NSString * prop
96              in [GameListController stringProperties]) {…}
101
102         //  Set all the integer labels
103         for (NSString * prop
104             in [GameListController integerProperties]) {
105             numValue = [self.passer valueForKey: prop];
106
107             fieldName = [prop stringByAppendingString: @"Label"];
```

FIGURE 28.1   When enabled in the **Text Editing** panel of the Preferences window, the code-folding ribbon appears as a strip at the left margin of the editor views. It shows progressively darker bands for each level of nesting in the code. Hovering the mouse pointer over the ribbon (top) highlights the lines at that level of nesting (or deeper). Clicking the ribbon reduces the nested block to a single line, marked with a disclosure triangle in the ribbon and a yellow ellipsis bubble in place of the folded code.

Double-clicking the ellipsis bubble or clicking the disclosure triangle in the ribbon expands the text. You can find menu commands for code folding and their key equivalents, in the submenu at **Editor→Code Folding**.

The Assistant Editor

You've done a lot with the assistant editor, but let me cover the basics all in one place: The assistant editor is shown when you click the middle segment of the **Editor** control in the Workspace window's toolbar. It also appears when you navigate to a file while holding down the Option key.

▶ The wow feature of the assistant editor is that it can track the file displayed in the primary editor and show a counterpart, such as the .h file for an .m or a .c. The options for autofilling the assistant editor go beyond counterparts: You can direct the assistant to related files in the class hierarchy, XIBs, files that include or are included by the primary editor, and processed content, such as assembly and preprocessed code. For categories that have more than one file, such as includes, the jump bar picks up a switch panel—a number between two arrowheads—at the right end. Click the arrowheads to navigate through the category.

▶ You can modify the option-key gesture that puts a destination file into the assistant pane. The **General** panel of the Preferences window enables you to customize how Xcode responds to navigational gestures:

  ▶ Simple click navigation can go to the primary editor (the big one on the left) or whatever editor you're using at the moment.

  ▶ Adding the Option key can send the selected file to the assistant editor, an additional assistant pane, a new tab, or a new window.

  ▶ Double-clicking can direct the file to a new window or a new tab.

  ▶ Further, if you navigate with the Option and Shift keys, Xcode offers you a heads-up display offering you a graphical picker for placing the file in an existing or new view. See Figure 28.2.

FIGURE 28.2   The Navigation Chooser appears when you select a file with the Option and Shift keys depressed. It is a graphical browser that lets you choose where the file is displayed. Double-click one of the offered spaces to put the file there. The menu equivalent is **Navigate→Open In...** (⌥⌘<).

▶ You can have more than one assistant view; there's a + button at the top-right corner of the view to add another. The x button next to it, of course, closes the pane.

▶ You aren't stuck with the side-by-side arrangement of the primary and assistant editors. The **View→Assistant Editor** submenu offers you a choice of dividing the primary and assistant areas vertically or horizontally; or cascading all editors in coequal rows or columns.

Interface Builder

▶ You can keep IBAction and IBOutlet declarations out of your controllers' public interfaces by declaring them in class extensions (private interface declarations that look like @interface *className* ()). Interface Builder discovers these and allows you to link to them.

Instruments and Debugging

▶ One big tip: Apple keeps two technical notes, "Mac OS X Debugging Magic (TN2124)," and "iOS Debugging Magic (TN2239)," continually updated with the latest techniques for making debugging easier. Search for **Debugging Magic** in the Documentation organizer.

▶ The breakpoints I've had you set in this book have all been simple, unconditional breakpoints. These are useful instruments, but blunt. If you're looking for a particular condition in your program, you have the choice of pumping the **Continue** button until the condition is met (and hoping you don't press **Continue** again out of habit), or of inserting logging and if statements and conditions that you can break on when the program itself detects the condition. The latter can involve so much infrastructure, such as static counters, that the debugging apparatus itself becomes a debuggable problem.

Xcode enables you to handle such things in the debugger instead of your code. Right-click a breakpoint, either the marker next to your code or the entry in the Breakpoint navigator, and select **Edit Breakpoint** in the resulting contextual menu. A popover window appears, attached to the breakpoint. See Figure 28.3.

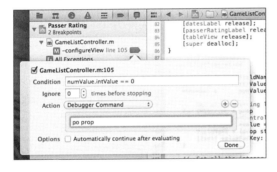

FIGURE 28.3   Right-clicking a breakpoint and selecting **Edit Breakpoint** reveals a popover that enables you to set conditions and actions.

With the popover, you can set a C-language condition that must be met before the breakpoint fires, a count of hits that must accumulate before it fires, a series of debugger commands to execute when it fires, and whether execution should continue after the commands instead of halting the program. The breakpoint in Figure 28.3 hits only if numValue.intValue is zero. If it does, it will print the description of the prop object and pauses.

▶ Apple's guess is that every programmer on a team is interested in his own section of code and is not in the breakpoints others set to debug their sections. Breakpoints are therefore kept at the most-personal level: in the Workspace if there is one, in per-user settings if not. You can drag breakpoints in the Breakpoint navigator between the projects in a Workspace and use the contextual menu to "share" them, changing their visibility from per user to global.

28

▶ You've probably found that when you click the **Continue** button in the Debugger, and the application you're debugging reaches its run loop, the application comes to the foreground, only to hit a breakpoint and bring Xcode back. This can be distracting, so the **Product** menu has a **Debug Workflow** submenu that lets you select **Standard Windowing** (the behavior just described), or keeping either the app or Xcode front at all times. The same menu lets you force assembly listings in the debugger for when you need to examine instruction and don't want to switch to the assembly view each time.

▶ The Leaks and Allocations instruments take care of most memory problems but not all of them. Sometimes, unused objects persist in memory, but because they have residual references, they aren't visible as leaks. Allocations has a button in its options area titled **Mark Heap**. Get your application started up and stable, and click **Mark Heap**. Then do something that consumes memory but *should* return it to its original state—such as opening a document, editing it, and closing it. Do it repeatedly. Mark the heap again.

The heapshot-analysis table shows you all the objects that were created, but not deallocated, at the end of the process. Not all will be leftovers—objects can legitimately accumulate in caches—but you should satisfy yourself that they are what they should be.

Apple engineer Bill Bumgarner has an excellent tutorial on this. Search the Web for his name and "heapshot."

▶ When you debug or test an iOS application, you often want to start your app's data with a known state. Getting to that state may take many minutes' effort, and doing so repeatedly would be a tedious time-waster. Xcode can help you. Plug in your device that has your app installed and in the state you want to preserve. In the source list of the Devices organizer, select **Applications**, and find your app. The lower part of the panel shows the complete data directories in the app sandbox. See Figure 28.4.

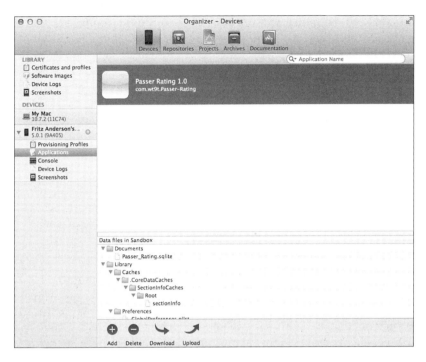

FIGURE 28.4   Selecting your application in the Devices organizer shows the contents of the app's data directories. Using the buttons at the bottom of the page, you can export the data to an archive on your Mac and restore it from an archive.

The **Download** button at the bottom of the panel lets you save the complete data to an archive package (`.xcappdata`). The **Upload** button restores an archive to the application sandbox.

You can start your debugging session with saved application data by going to the **Options** tab of the **Run** panel of the Scheme editor and selecting the archive file from the **Application Data** pop-up. If you go to the **Test** panel, each test target in the **Info** tab has a pop-up in the Test Application column to select the initial data for all tests.

Building

▶ This is not an Xcode tip but something every programmer should take to heart: Compiler warnings are there for a reason. `llvm` is getting better and better at catching common programming errors and violations of the coding conventions on which Cocoa relies. Many of the questions raised on support forums (see Appendix D, "Resources") arise from novices' ignoring warnings. Fix every warning. Then run the analyzer (**Product→Analyze [⇧⌘B]**) and fix those, too.

▶ Xcode assumes that products built with the Run action (or **Product→Build** [⌘B], which is a synonym for **Build for Running**) are debugging articles and not fit for release to other users; and Archive builds, which are fit for release, are comparatively rare. Xcode therefore does not take much trouble to make build product files easy to find. For archive builds, open the Archives organizer, select the archive, and click **Share…**; one of the options is to export an `.app` bundle. For run builds, do the build, find the product in the Products group in the Project navigator, and choose **Show in Finder** in the contextual menu.

▶ The philosophy behind the Run action is that you should be running and debugging your application as close to immediately as possible. Therefore Xcode takes some shortcuts. One of them is that it doesn't build your application from scratch. It generates only the elements that have to change, and inserts them into the previous copy of the app. If you remove a resource file from your "Copy Bundle Resources" build phase, the file will still be a part of your debugging article. If you need the file to be gone, you'll have to **Product→Clean** (⇧⌘K) to force a fresh rebuild.

▶ In Chapter 26, "The Xcode Build System," I said there is no way to change the set of files in a target, so if you have debug and release versions of a file, you can't switch between them in the Debug and Release configurations of your target. As applied to libraries, this isn't strictly true. The trick is to take the library *out* of the Link Binary With Libraries file, and instead pass the name of the desired library in the Other Linker Flags (OTHER_LDFLAGS) build setting.

In the **Build** Settings tab of the Target editor, search for **other** to find the setting. Open the disclosure triangle next to it, double-click the value for the Debug configuration, and click the + button to add an item to the list. Add the library (suppose it's named `libmyname_debug.a`) by typing **-lmyname_debug** into the new row. Do the same, for the release version of the library, in the Release item.

> **NOTE**
>
> Chapter 26 shows you an even cleverer way to do the same thing with `xcconfig` files.

▶ The linker has strong opinions on what libraries it should link into an executable. In particular, for Mac OS X builds, it *always* links dynamic libraries (`.dylib`) in preference to static libraries (`.a`). You can override this by making sure the full path to the `.a` appears in the link command line. Just add the full path to the library, including the suffix and the `lib` prefix, to the "Other Linker Flags" (OTHER_LDFLAGS) build setting. You can reduce the dependency on the file paths on your machine, by using the BUILT_PRODUCTS_DIR build variable instead of the directory path.

▶ The optimization-setting flag for `llvm` goes in a progression from `-O0` (none at all) to `-O3` (everything). The temptation, when driving for the sleekest, whizziest application, is to turn the knob up fully and let the optimizer fly. And yet the standard Release setting for optimization in Xcode is `-Os`—optimize for *size*. What's going on?

The problem is that -O3 optimization can dramatically increase the size of the generated code: llvm autonomously converts function calls to in-line code so that the content of those functions repeat, perhaps many times, throughout the application. It turns counted for loops into *n* iterations of the loop body, one after the other, because it's quicker to run straight through four copies of the same code than to keep a counter, test it against four, and conditionally branch.

All these optimizations are ingenious, but they can be short-sighted. Modern processors are much faster than the main memory buses that serve them; waiting for data or program instructions to load can stall a processor for a substantial portion of time. Therefore, fast cache memory is put between the processor and RAM to make the instruction stream available at a pace that keeps up with the CPU. But cache sizes are limited. An application that has been doubled in size by unrolling and inlining everywhere can overrun the cache and hit RAM to fetch instructions at least twice as often. In the usual case, "faster" code runs slower than smaller code. Keep the Release configuration at -Os.

▶ The default features of Xcode's build and analysis actions only scratch the surface of what llvm and the clang analyzer can do for you. Compiler options and in-line attribute directives enable you to fine-tune the analysis and assist in optimizing your code. Look up the complete manuals at http://clang.llvm.org/docs/UsersManual.html and http://clanganalyzer.llvm.org/annotations.html.

Managing Schemes

Product→**Manage Schemes**… brings down an editor sheet for creating, hiding, and deleting schemes. (The same can be found by clicking **Manage Schemes**… at the bottom of the Scheme Editor.)

Left to itself, Xcode creates a scheme—a collection of actions and dependencies surrounding the Run, Test, Profile, Analyze, and Archive build actions—for each target you create. The Manage Schemes editor enables you to take charge of this process. You can turn off autocreation, and add and delete schemes.

Schemes are stored in projects or workspaces. Usually, a scheme is associated with a particular user—what you want for a build environment in the course of your work. The Manage Schemes editor (Figure 28.5) lets you pick what project a scheme is to be kept in and enables you to "share" it so that your scheme can be visible to every user of the project. You then have your choice between a "company" scheme that provides a standard operating environment for a project, while still having the choice of a scheme with your own scripts for your own needs.

You can also export schemes to .xcscheme XML files and import them.

28

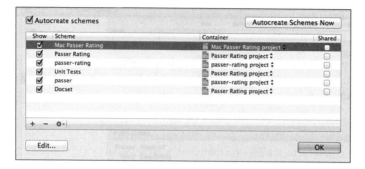

FIGURE 28.5   The Manage Schemes editor lets you take manual control of creating and deleting schemes, rather than leaving it to Xcode to match schemes one-to-one with targets.

Traps

Development is hard. Therefore Xcode is hard, both because it has to do a lot and because any application that has to do a lot is subject to bugs and annoyances. Here are a few things to watch out for:

▶ When you remove an IBOutlet from your source, llvm reacts immediately, flagging errors and warnings on all references in your project—*except* for outlet connections in your XIBs. As soon as you change an outlet (or an IBAction), audit the related objects in Interface Builder (IB). Most of these are in File's Owner; select it and look in the Connection (sixth) inspector for orphaned connections.

▶ Related: The Search navigator can find text in your project, and it can also turn up Core Data attributes. It cannot search XIBs, so if you're looking for bindings, outlets, or actions, you're stuck with examining the Connection inspector in IB.

▶ In the name of simplicity, Xcode presents a bare search field for Find, Project Search, and Documentation search. There are options to be had. The magnifying-glass icon at the left end of the search field anchors a drop-down menu, and the first item is **Show Find Options**. You get options for case-sensitivity and part-, prefix-, or whole-word matching. For text searches, you can search against a regular expression; documentation searches can be filtered by SDK and applicable programming language.

In the project and documentation searches, when you open the options panel, it stays open. Not so for the in-file Find bar: It goes away when you switch away from a file, even though the settings you made persist in later searches, with nothing to show what those settings are.

▶ You may be looking for a replace-all-in-selection action in the editor Find bar. There is none. In Xcode 3, the feature could be found by holding down the Option key—the **Replace** button would be relabeled **In Selection**. I don't know whether the feature will ever come back, but if you're looking for it, that's what you can try.

▶ If you instantiate an iOS template, the VALID_ARCHS setting is armv7 only. All iOS devices currently sold use processors with the ARMv7 architecture, but the original iPhone and the iPhone 3G (and the contemporary iPod Touches) ran ARMv6, which doesn't recognize ARMv7 instructions. If you want to target the earlier devices, remember to add armv6 to both VALID_ARCHS and ARCHS. Be sure to review "Required Device Capabilities" (UlRequiredDeviceCapabilities) in Info.plist (or the **Info** tab of the Target editor) to make sure that armv7 is not required.

▶ Xcode's source-control system is aggressive. If it finds Subversion or Git support directories in your project tree, it will initiate adds, deletions, and renames on your repository when you do those things in the Project navigator. Worse, if it goes through too many iterations of changes (maybe your source tree is in rapid flux as you try and abandon new files), it can get confused by the resulting tangle of history. There is no way to prevent this; you can only hope for bug fixes, or at least for a switch that stops it from trying to manage versions. You can palliate the situation by switching to the command line periodically and manually restoring the version-control state to what you want.

▶ One big gap in Xcode's version-control support is *tags*. When your work comes to a significant milestone—such as a version release—you need to mark the revision with a name that allows you to return the project to that point. All version-control systems allow for this. Xcode won't set, display, or revert to tags. You must go to the command line and use the git tag or svn cp subcommands.

▶ If you look in the AppleScript Editor application for the Xcode dictionary, you'll see what purports to be an extensive scripting interface that you could use, for instance, to create and configure Xcode projects programmatically. Experiment, if you'd like—some of the commands perform as promised. As of Xcode 4.2, most do not.

If you're interested in generating Xcode projects, look up the Generate Your Projects (Gyp) and cmake projects, as well as Jetbrains' AppCode IDE.

▶ One of the files that are automatically generated when you instantiate a bundle (including application) target is a precursor file for Info.plist, named *target name*-Info.plist. By misadventure, this file might find its way into the target's "Copy Bundle Resources" build phase. That would put the file into the built product, which is a mistake. It's a *source* file, and its product, Info.plist, will be built and inserted into the product automatically.

▶ As I write this, Xcode could not handle having a project open in more than one workspace at a time. Xcode often prevents your trying (though not necessarily telling you why the option fails), but in many cases it allows it and then behaves erratically.

28

▶ Objective-C being a dynamic language, the compiler allows any object to receive any message. Implementations may be completely unrelated; all the compiler has to do is load the receiver, the selector, and the parameters onto the stack and call for the message to be dispatched.

This works well, but the ideal breaks down with the return value: It might be an integer, a float, a pointer, or a `struct`, and depending on the processor architecture, those results may be stored in completely different locations. The compiler must generate the instructions to take the result from the correct place.

Things are still fine if all methods with a given signature return the same result type; as long as the compiler has seen some declaration of the method, it can proceed. Even if the compiler has seen declarations of different return types, it can still do the right thing if the receiving object's class is known.

Where it breaks down is when the receiver is declared to be `id` or `Class` and so provides no indication of what methods it implements or how they return. The compiler's default behavior in that circumstance is to *silently guess*. This is an abundant source of obscure bugs. If you set "Strict Selector Matching" in the build settings, the compiler will still guess, but it will also warn. Then you can go back and use a cast or a typed object pointer to guide the compiler to the correct return type.

▶ Objective-C's dynamism can bite you in another way: A static library (`libname.a`) can include class implementations. Objective-C code might refer to classes only by name. The linker doesn't see those as code-symbol references—they're just strings. If the linker is set to strip "unreferenced" objects out of libraries when it links an application, the dynamic references will fail. The same problem arises when a library contains categories that add to classes that are already present in the application.

Force the linker to include all the contents of all `.a` archives by including `-all_load` in the "Other Linker Flags" (`OTHER_LDFLAGS`) build setting. If you want to be more selective, put `-force_load` *path*/*to*/*libName*.a in the setting for each library you want to force.

It would be more practical to have the linker select Objective-C static libraries automatically for this treatment. There is an `-ObjC` flag for exactly this purpose, but historically the 64-bit linker ignored this flag. It may be worthwhile to try the `-ObjC` flag first to see if Apple has fixed it.

▶ If you're used to UNIX or Linux development, you're accustomed to global macros such as `NDEBUG` and `DEBUG`, and expect them to be set for you automatically.

If the argument to the standard C `assert()` macro is zero, it halts the program. If `NDEBUG` is set, `assert()` does nothing, so you can publish code that might still exhibit the bug you put in the assertion for, but at least it won't crash.

The `NS_BLOCK_ASSERTIONS` macro does the same with Cocoa's `NSAssert` family of assertion macros.

Many developers like to define a DEBUG macro to guard logging and assertion code. It's not a standard macro, but it's very common.

Xcode's project templates define DEBUG=1 for the Debug configuration; NDEBUG and NS_BLOCK_ASSERTIONS are never set. An easy way to cut down on the size of your released code is to open the **Build Settings** tab in the Target editor and double-click the value for the Release version of the Preprocessor Macros setting. You get a table to enter the definitions; click the + button to add lines. Set NDEBUG and NS_BLOCK_ASSERTIONS, and don't set DEBUG. Remember to include $(inherited) to preserve definitions made at other levels.

> **NOTE**
>
> Don't prefix the symbols you put in "Preprocessor Macros" with -D, even though that's what would go into the clang command line; the setting does that automatically.

▶ HFS+, the recommended file system for Mac OS X, is case-preserving—files will get names in the same case as you provide—but is not case-sensitive: Xcode.txt, XCODE.TXT, and xcode.txt all refer to the same file. Most other UNIX variants are case-sensitive, so if you import code, be on the lookout for the assumption that the following two lines refer to different files:

```
#include "polishShoes.h"
#include "PolishShoes.h"
```

By the same token, make sure that your code uses filenames with consistent letter casing. Even if you don't expect to port your work, HFS+ isn't the only file system a Macintosh application sees and a case-sensitive version of HFS+ does exist. On iOS, the file system is case-sensitive.

28

PART V
Appendixes

IN THIS PART

Objective-C

Xcode is built for Cocoa development, and Cocoa development is not language-neutral. Cocoa doesn't work without Objective-C. C++ is an object-oriented language, but that isn't enough; it can't do the dynamic dispatch that Cocoa relies on, and there are no Cocoa bindings for C++. Apple tried supporting Cocoa-in-Java in early versions of Mac OS X, but the match wasn't perfect, it was hard to maintain, and nobody used it.

NOTE

If you're writing for Mac OS X, Cocoa isn't absolutely Objective-C. There are bindings to Cocoa—through bridges to the Objective-C runtime—for Ruby and Python, which are also dynamically dispatched languages. But even those frameworks depend on your ability to read and understand Objective-C. Both frameworks are included in Mac OS X; you can find documentation at `/Developer/Documentation/Python/PyObjC` (subject to relocation in XCode 4.3) and `http://www.macruby.org/`. For iOS, you're out of luck.

This book focuses on the workflow of iOS and Mac OS X programming rather than on specific programming techniques. A full treatment of the Objective-C language would take up too much space. You can find a good tutorial and reference on Objective-C in the ADC Reference Library; search for "Introduction to the Objective-C Programming Language." However, you see a lot of Objective-C in this book, so a reading knowledge can help.

The Basics

The first thing to know about Objective-C is that it is a proper superset of C. Unlike with C++, any legal C program is legal Objective-C. Basic Objective-C is only a small addition. It adds some language-specific directives, which are identified by being prefixed with the @ sign. It introduces only one new expression type, the *message invocation*. A message invocation is delimited by brackets, begins with an object pointer, and continues with the name of a message and the message's parameters. For example, [foo retain] sends the retain message to the object pointed to by foo. A more complex invocation might be

```
NSSize      unitSize = { 1.0, 1.0 };
unitSize =  [myView convertSize: unitSize
                    fromView: nil];
```

Here, an NSSize struct is sent, along with nil, in the message convertSize:fromView: to myView. The returned value, another NSSize struct, is assigned to unitSize. Parameters to messages are interspersed with the message name, which usually documents each parameter. The colons, indicating the need for a parameter, are a part of the message name; aMessage and aMessage: would be two different messages. (These are not "labeled parameters." The order matters.)

The variable at the beginning of a message invocation is an object pointer. There are no static or stack-based objects in Objective-C. Objective-C adds a type, id, for a generic pointer to an object (like a void * that can accept messages), or you can get some compile-time type checking by specifying an explicit type pointer, like such as NSView * or Passer *.

Classes are objects and can have methods. Class methods are declared and defined with a leading "+," whereas instance methods are declared and defined with a leading "–." It's common to refer to methods by a plus or minus to indicate their domain, followed by the class and signature in brackets, such as -[NSView convertSize:fromView:] or +[NSObject alloc].

Method invocation is not as tightly bound to types in Objective-C as member-function calls are in C++. The same message can be sent to objects in different classes even if they have no common ancestor; the only thing that matters is the message selector (its name). It has been common in Objective-C programs to establish "informal protocols," groups of methods that objects can implement to participate in the workings of a package.

There are also *formal* protocols, declared in blocks beginning with the @protocol directive. If a class is declared to implement a protocol (by following the @interface declaration with the protocol name in angle brackets), the compiler will check to see that it defines all the required methods. If an object variable is declared to implement a protocol (for instance, id <NSCoding> obj says you don't care what class obj belongs to so long as it implements <NSCoding>), the compiler will check (at compile-time only) to see that anything assigned to it implements that protocol and will accept sending the protocol's messages to that object without warning.

Objective-C 2.0 made protocols more flexible, and most of the informal protocols in earlier SDKs have been converted to formal ones. The iOS SDKs use formal protocols exclusively.

A Class Interface

Objective-C source-code files are identified by the .m suffix. Typically, you write one implementation (.m) file for each class, accompanied by a header (.h) file declaring the public interface of that class. A class implementation must be preceded by the matching interface; code that uses the class must also be preceded by the interface.

Here's the interface for a simple class:

```
#import <Cocoa/Cocoa.h>                          // 1

@class  Citation;                                // 2

@interface DataPoint : NSObject <NSCoding>  {    // 3
    double          x;                           // 4
    double          y;
    NSString *      comment;
    Citation *      whereFrom;
}

- (id) initWithX: (double) xValue
           Y: (double) yValue;                   // 5

+ (DataPoint *) dataPointWithX: (double) xVal
                          Y: (double) yVal;      // 6

@property(assign) double    x;                   // 7
@property(assign) double    y;
@property(copy) NSString *  comment;
@property(retain) Citation * whereFrom;
@property(readonly) double   distanceFromZero;

@end                                             // 8
```

This is how you read the class interface:

1. Before the interface, you #import the umbrella header for the Cocoa framework, so the compiler knows about Cocoa classes and methods. Objective-C code typically uses #import instead of #include because #import prevents a file from being re-read if it's been parsed already. Most C libraries do the same thing by guarding the contents of header files with #ifndef / #define / #endif, but #import prevents the file from even being read. #import was standard in Objective-C from the beginning and has been an extension in the gcc compiler for many years.

2. The class you're about to declare makes reference to objects of the Citation class. This is a forward declaration of that class—an explanation that the symbol Citation refers to an Objective-C class, without worrying about any of the details. That way, the compiler knows all it needs to parse this interface: Citation is a class, and Citation * is a pointer to an object.

3. This begins the interface. It names the class (DataPoint) and says it is a specialization of NSObject. It also promises that DataPoint implements the NSCoding protocol. Objective-C classes may inherit from only one superclass, but the limitation is mostly relieved by protocols and dynamic method dispatch.

4. The instance variables (*ivars*) are listed between a pair of braces. Notionally (until recently, literally), an object is just a C struct with a couple of hidden fields added. The instance variables are just fields in the struct, and the declarations are no different from what they'd be in a C program. DataPoint carries pointers to an NSString and a Citation. Objective-C objects are always allocated in the memory heap and are *never* declared statically. A special case is id, which is a pointer to an object whose class you are indifferent to; it's the object equivalent to a void pointer.

5. This declares an *instance method*; you can tell because it begins with a "–". Its return value is id; its name is initWithX:Y:, and the parameters after the colons are both double-precision floating-point numbers.

6. And this is a *class method*, which you can identify by the "+." It's much the same as initWithX:Y:, but it promises its return value is a pointer to a DataPoint.

7. @property directives are new to Objective-C 2.0. They declare key-value coding accessors that enable you to get and set properties with a convenient dot notation. In the simplest form, the compiler can automatically back these up with functions that set and return the instance variables of the same name according to the options set out in the parentheses. I'll get to properties in the section on Objective-C 2.0 later in this appendix.

8. @end closes out the @interface. Don't forget this.

Properties and methods can be declared in any order—and even mixed.

A Class Implementation

Now go through the outline of the implementation of this DataPoint class:

```
#import "DataPoint.h"                          // 1
#import "Citation.h"

@implementation DataPoint                      // 2

@synthesize x;                                 // 3
@synthesize y;
@synthesize comment;
```

```objc
@synthesize whereFrom;
@dynamic distanceFromZero;

- (id) initWithX: (double) xValue                // 4
            Y: (double) yValue
{
    if (self = [super init]) {
        x = xValue;
        y = yValue;
        comment = [@"<none>" copy];
    }

    return self;
}


+ (DataPoint *) dataPointWithX: (double) xVal
                          Y: (double) yVal
{
    return [[[self alloc] initWithX: xVal Y: yVal]
            autorelease];
}
- (void) dealloc                                 // 5
{
    [comment release];
    [whereFrom release];
    [super dealloc];
}

- (double) distanceFromZero                       // 6
{
    return sqrt(self.x * self.x + self.y * self.y);
}

- (void) encodeWithCoder: (NSCoder *) aCoder     // 7
{
    // ...
}

- (id) initWithCoder: (NSCoder *) aCoder
{
    if (self = [super init]) {
        // ...
    }
    return self;
}

@end                                             // 8
```

1. #import the headers for DataPoint and Citation. An @implementation without an @interface is illegal; and now that you use Citation (though not in this skeleton code), the compiler must know the details from its interface.

2. @implementation begins the code for the class. Method code must be inside an @implementation that associates it with a class.

3. These directives tell the compiler to write code to implement the @propertys declared in the interface. @synthesize asks for a simple getter and setter for the instance variable of the same name. @dynamic promises that the property will be implemented elsewhere—in this case, right in the implementation.

4. These are the definitions of the methods declared in the interface. They're regular C functions, except for two things: The method header is in the notation for an Objective-C method, and some of the code uses the [object message: param] notation for invoking methods. In dataPointWithX:Y:, the messages go three deep. Notice the [super init] call in initWithX:Y:; you invoke your superclass's implementation of a method by sending the message to super.

5. It's not strictly a feature of Objective-C, but the dealloc method deserves special mention. Every class descended from NSObject, unless it is to run exclusively under garbage collection, *must* implement a dealloc method to release any objects the instance owns and then call [super dealloc]. (Automatic Reference Counting may eliminate dealloc entirely.)

6. You made a @property declaration for a read-only property named distanceFromZero, but there's no instance variable of that name. In the @implementation block, you said it was @dynamic. Here you provide the promised implementation in the form of a method of that name. The property was declared readonly; if it were read-write, you'd also need to provide a setDistanceFromZero: method.

7. The @interface for DataPoint said it implemented the NSCoding protocol. If the compiler got to the end of the @implementation block without seeing definitions for the non-@optional methods in NSCoding, it would warn you.

8. As with the @interface block, @implementation blocks must have an @end.

Objective-C 2.0 and Cocoa

If all you want right now is to skim the sample code in this book, you can stop right now. You know enough to puzzle out the rest. If you want to stay on, I'll cover how Apple added to the Objective-C language to support some Cocoa-only design patterns. I'll start with the patterns, and move on to how the language grew to accommodate them.

The first iteration of Objective-C, from the mid-1980s, was like C: a simple language with no semantics tied to any particular library. You could write (minimally functional) programs in either language, without using the standard libraries that came with them.

Objective-C 2.0 is a language for writing Cocoa programs. It has many features that support Cocoa technologies and need the Cocoa framework to work. The most prominent of these are Key-Value Coding (KVC) and memory management.

Key-Value Coding

Apple holds a patent on KVC. Objects in Objective-C have *attributes* (*properties* is a better name but let me avoid the confusion with @property). Attributes are data that the object at least notionally holds and can receive. They can be data the object literally holds, in instance variables, or data that reflects the object's state but isn't backed by data in memory, like DataPoint's distanceFromZero.

Key-Value Coding is a protocol, implemented in NSObject, that provides access to attributes in a way that is indifferent to how the attributes are implemented. Users of a KVC-compliant object can take advantage of two methods:

- valueForKey: Returns the value of an attribute of the object named by a string passed as the argument. Nonobject values are wrapped in the equivalent Cocoa objects.

- setValue:forKey: Sets the value (again, nonobjects should be passed in a Cocoa wrapper) for a named attribute.

An example: You have an application with two classes, BaseMap and Bus, and an NSManagedObject entity called BusStop.

- BaseMap keeps the geographic bounds of a map in a CGRect struct.

- Bus has two instance variables, named _longitude and _latitude. They are NSStrings. There are no methods or @property declarations that have those names. It happens that NSString has a method, doubleValue, that parses a string into a double precision floating-point number.

- The BusStop entity has two attributes, also named longitude and latitude. You can set up the managed-object model so those attributes are NSNumbers. There is no BusStop class; bus stops are represented as NSManagedObject objects. NSNumber also implements a doubleValue method for unwrapping a double value.

You want BaseMap to have a single method that tells you whether a bus or a stop is on the map. It can be written

```
- (BOOL) includesLocationOf: (id) anObject
{
   CGPoint           coords;
   coords.x = [[anObject valueForKey:  @"longitude"] doubleValue];
   coords.y = [[anObject valueForKey:  @"latitude"] doubleValue];
   return CGRectContainsPoint(geoBounds, coords);
}
```

Look at what happened here: anObject could be a Bus object, or an NSManagedObject. They both have a latitude and a longitude in some sense, but they are kept in different ways, one in struct fields and the other in columns in an SQLite database. The valueForKey: method finds them both.

How does KVC find an attribute named longitude?

1. If there's a method named getLongitude, longitude, or isLongitude (a name that makes more sense for Boolean attributes), it's used. setValue:forKey: would use a method named setLongitude:. If you @synthesize a property, or if it's a Core Data attribute, you get longitude and setLongitude: automatically.

2. If there's an instance variable named _longitude, _isLongitude, longitude, or isLongitude, it uses that directly.

NOTE

This is a gross simplification. It doesn't cover the application of valueForKey: to container classes such as NSArray and NSSet.

NOTE

The NIB-loading mechanism hooks the loaded objects to the owning object's IBOutlets using KVC (or in Mac OS X, something like it). If you have an NSTextField referenced through a temperature instance variable, and a setTemperature: method to set a property of your model, the NIB loader will use setTemperature: in an attempt to link up the text field, and the instance variable remains nil.

Memory Management

Cocoa manages memory in one of two ways. Garbage collection (GC) takes care of reclaiming the memory used by unused objects automatically, but it is available on Mac OS X only, and is falling into disfavor even there. It uses a dedicated thread to periodically sweep memory for unreferenced object trees and reclaims them. The process is not constant, so unreclaimed memory can build up, even though the GC thread runs practically continually. On a Mac, with processor cores and RAM to spare, and the ability to swap large idle objects out to disk, the limitations of GC are not an urgent consideration.

iOS devices can't spare the processor time, the power, or the RAM, and they can't swap memory. iOS will never have garbage collection.

Most memory management in Cocoa is done through reference counting.

Under classic reference counting, you acquire and release memory for your objects by an "ownership" model: Every object that wants a persistent reference to another object takes ownership of it. You take ownership either by creating it through a method whose name begins with `alloc`, `copy`, `mutableCopy`, or `new`, or by sending it `retain`. You relinquish ownership by sending it `release` or `autorelease`. When the last owner relinquishes ownership, the object is sent `dealloc`, it chains further `releases` to the objects it holds, and its memory is freed.

`autorelease` doesn't immediately release the object; instead, it hands ownership to a broker object (an autorelease pool) that schedules it for release later, typically in the application run loop after all your code has returned to the Cocoa code that called it. This has the effect that you can receive ephemeral references to objects without worrying about releasing them.

Veterans of C++ assume that `dealloc` is a destructor. Like a destructor, it returns memory to the heap; but unlike a destructor, it must not be relied upon to release other resources such as file descriptors or network connections. Memory management in Cocoa is effectively an asynchronous task. You cannot rely on any object's being deallocated promptly, or at all. Cocoa may retain references to your objects that you don't know about, and when your application exits, it "deallocates" objects by returning the entire heap to the system without resort to `dealloc`. If you have nonmemory resources you need to release, the thing to do is to provide a "close" method to release them, identify when you are done with them, and then use the close method.

It's easy to release an object not enough (leaking the object and soaking up memory) or too much (causing crashes or subtler bugs when other "owners" try to access invalidated objects). Apple found that the great majority of application crashes came from reference-counting errors.

Attribute Accessors and Memory Management

Consider accessors—getters and setters—for object instance variables. Getters are straightforward; just return the value of the variable:

```
- (NSString *) comment
{
    return comment;
}
```

Setters are trickier and depend on how you need to manage them. Here are some classical implementations of getters, so you can see what has to be done:

```
- (void) setComment: (NSString *) newComment
{
```

```
    if (comment != newComment) {
        [comment release];
        comment = [newComment copy];
    }
}

- (void) setCitation: (Citation *) newCitation
{
    if (citation != newCitation) {
        [citation release];
        citation = [newCitation retain];
    }
}

- (void) setX: (double) newX
{
    x = newX;
}
```

setComment: *copies* the new comment string because it might be an instance of the subclass NSMutableString, which the owner could change later and thus change the content of DataPoint's comment. DataPoint doesn't want the comment to change, so it keeps a copy of its own. The comment is an *attribute* of the object.

For setCitation:, on the other hand, DataPoint wants to keep an ongoing relation to a particular Citation object. It adds its ownership to the object pointer and puts it into an instance variable. The citation instance variable keeps a *relationship* of the object.

A double isn't an object. It's a scalar attribute, and setX: can just assign it to the instance variable.

Here you have setters for three different instance variables. If you used the KVC method setValue:forKey: (remembering to wrap the value for x in an NSNumber) to set them, they'd look identical. But they represent different strategies for assuming the value. Things get more complicated if you worry about threading: If setCitation: gets preempted between the release and the retain, other threads may see a DataPoint with a citation instance variable pointing off into freed memory. You must set locks on both the setter and the getter.

Properties

In recent years, Apple developers have said, "Who are we kidding? People are using this language to write Cocoa applications, so why don't we add features that make Cocoa programming easier?" Objective-C 2.0 introduced *properties*. You use an object's properties by appending a dot and the property name to the object variable:

```
// Assume DataPoint:
// - defines and synthesizes properties x and y
```

```
// - does not define getter or setter methods for x and y

DataPoint *        point = [DataPoint dataPointWithX: 1.0 Y: 2.0];

NSLog(@"point x = %f y = %f", point.x, point.y);
// point x=1.0 y=2.0

point.x = 12.5;
NSLog(@"point x = %f y = %f", point.x, point.y);
// point x = 12.5 y = 2.0
```

Naïvely, properties should simply assign into instance variables and return the contents. For a scalar value such as DataPoint's x and y, that's the right thing to do. It's the *wrong* thing to do in the case of comment and citation, which are object pointers and must be retained or copied as necessary.

Well, properties are just semantic sugar for KVC attributes, so you could define the methods comment, setComment:, citation, and setCitation:, and everything will work fine. But one of the goals of having properties is to cut down on the repetitive code you need to write. Look back at those object setters, and realize that if DataPoint had a dozen object references, it would need a dozen setter methods, identical but for the names of the attributes.

So when you declare a property, you can ask the compiler to write the accessor methods for you, by putting @synthesize directives in the @implementation block.

> **NOTE**
>
> If you compile exclusively for 64-bit architectures, or for iOS, there's a third option: You can make @property declarations, @synthesize them, and provide neither instance variables nor accessor methods. The "modern" runtime library will create the instance variables for you.

You've seen there's more than one strategy for setters, so you can control which ones to use by putting specifiers into the declaration, such as @property (nonatomic, copy) NSString * comment;. Here is a simplified list of the options:

▶ readwrite/readonly: If a property is readwrite (the default), @synthesize provides both a getter and a setter. If it's read-only, there will be no setter, and attempts to assign into the property result in a compiler error.

▶ assign/retain/copy: The generated setter sets the instance variable by simple assignment, by retaining the object or by copying it.

It's different under Automatic Reference Counting (ARC): An accessor for an object is either strong (roughly, retain) or weak (roughly assign but with the advantage that when a weakly held object is deallocated, the property is automatically set to nil). You can still ask for copy.

▶ `atomic`/`nonatomic`: An atomic getter and setter guards access to the property so that neither accessor starts while the other is in process. That's the default; you must specify `nonatomic` if you're not worried about threading issues. Nonatomic accessors are a bit faster.

If you declare a property in a class's interface, its implementation must include a `@synthesize` directive to construct the accessors, or `@dynamic` to promise that the accessors will be provided elsewhere (such as by Core Data), or actual implementations of the accessors. You can declare a property that isn't backed by an instance variable; just provide a getter and (if `readwrite`) a setter.

Properties are an Objective-C 2.0 feature that is tightly tied to Cocoa. They make Cocoa memory management and key-value coding compliance much easier to do by making them part of the language. If you use properties, you are tied to Cocoa.

In principle, you don't need to use properties. Billions of lines of Cocoa programs exist that antedate properties, and they still work (or at least work no worse than they did). The Mac OS X SDKs are being slowly converted to replace declared accessors with properties; and the iOS SDKs, which don't have to worry about legacy code, use properties whenever possible. But properties are still just a cover for getter and setter methods. If you want to write `[uiView setFrame:]` instead of `uiView.frame =`, you can.

Conversely, if a class *doesn't* declare a property, but does have accessor methods, the compiler will let you use the dot notation. `NSString` declares `doubleValue` only as an accessor method, but it's perfectly legal to write `aString.doubleValue`.

Automatic Reference Counting

Properties make reference counting much safer, but they don't nearly cure the dangers. Not every object reference gets gated through a property access—some are held by local variables, and some are made directly to instance variables. So how to abate how error-prone reference counting is? One of the early fruits of the `llvm` compiler project was the Clang front-end parser. Clang knows the Cocoa memory conventions, and it can determine whether the retains and releases balance out in any one method. Because it can reason about all the possible execution paths through a method, it can catch edge cases in which one combination of conditions would result in an under- or over-release. Clang/llvm 1.0 was available as a stand-alone tool for checking Cocoa memory management in 2009, and Clang/llvm 2.0 was incorporated into Xcode 3.2 and 4.0 as an analysis tool.

With version 3.0, Apple was confident enough in `llvm` to graduate it from mere error-checking: If the compiler is smart enough to catch every instance of an object's needing to live or be released, why shouldn't the compiler do all the preserving and releasing?

With Xcode 4.2, Apple introduced Automatic Reference Counting (ARC), which does exactly that. Set the build setting Objective-C Automatic Reference Counting to YES, and the compiler generates the necessary memory-management calls for you, and better than you could do it yourself. Not only are `retains`, `releases`, and `autoreleases` unnecessary, they are illegal.

All Cocoa project and target templates have ARC turned on by default. If you have legacy code, you can select **Edit→Refactor→Convert to Objective-C ARC**.... The refactoring engine shows you its proposed changes; you can approve them, and you're ready to compile and test.

> **NOTE**
>
> Although ARC handles memory management for Cocoa, it does nothing for other kinds of objects: The Core Foundation C libraries have a number of data types that are identical to their Cocoa counterparts, but ARC won't reach them; you must call `CFRetain` and `CFRelease`. If you manage memory with the `malloc` family from the C standard library (including C++ objects), you must do it yourself. llvm 3 provides various "bridging" casts to manage the border between Cocoa and Core Foundation memory management. It's a big and subtle subject; look up "Transitioning to ARC Release Notes" in the Documentation organizer for the details.

ARC requires some runtime support, which is built into Mac OS X 10.7 and iOS 5. It is also available in 10.6 and 4.3, with the limitation that zeroing weak references are not possible.

Fast Enumeration

Another feature added by Objective-C 2.0 is *fast enumeration*. Cocoa has a number of container classes, such as NSArray, NSDictionary, NSSet, and their mutable variants. Sooner or later you'll want to go through the contained objects. The original Objective-C had no knowledge of library classes, so Cocoa had a class, NSEnumerator, that would encapsulate your progress in stepping through the container:

```
NSArray *       anArray /* ... */;
NSEnumerator *  iter = [anArray objectEnumerator];
id              current;
while (current = [iter nextObject]) {
    NSNumber *  lon = [current valueForKey: @"longitude"];
    /* ... */
}
```

There were two problems with this: It's verbose, and it involves a method dispatch to advance the NSEnumerator, and probably more as the enumerator accesses the NSArray to locate the next object. Apple engineers must have had another who-are-we-kidding moment: If Objective-C could exploit how NSArray accesses its objects internally, iterating it becomes much easier and faster.

So the same loop now looks like this:

```
NSArray *       anArray = /* ... */;
for (BusStop * current in anArray) {
    NSNumber *  lon = [current valueForKey: ("longitude")];
    /* ... */
}
```

This is another departure from the C language—though it doesn't make pure-C code incompatible. It adds a for...in statement that takes a loop variable and a pointer to an object that implements the NSFastEnumeration protocol. Implementing NSFastEnumeration properly is a bit of a trick, but Apple provides the interface for doing it. In all likelihood, you'll be content to use it on the Cocoa containers.

Foundation Data Types

My coverage of Cocoa is limited, but Foundation, a subframework of Cocoa, provides data types that most people would think of as being a part of a language, such as arrays and strings. Here is an overview of the most important classes:

▶ **NSString** represents a string of (notionally) 16-bit Unicode characters. The most common expression of an NSString in Objective-C is the built-in NSString literal: @"a string". The class provides formatted initializers (akin to sprintf()), conversions to numeric types, substring extraction, and more.

▶ **NSData** encapsulates an uninterpreted block of bytes. NSData can be constructed from a memory buffer (making a copy or not), the contents of a file (memory-mapped or not), or data found at a URL. There are methods to access the contents of the buffer and extract ranges from it. Many, many methods in Cocoa either take or yield buffers in the form of NSData.

▶ **NSArray** is an ordered sequence of objects. You typically construct one with -initWithObjects:, passing it a nil-terminated list of the contents. You can index into it, and step through it with NSFastEnumeration. You can't put a nil into an NSArray; use +[NSNull null] (guaranteed to be a singleton, so you can just compare the object pointers) instead. The contents of an NSArray do not have to be of the same type.

▶ **NSDictionary**, in its most common use, stores and retrieves objects based on NSString keys. You initialize it with a list of objects and their keys, and send it objectForKey: to get an object back. NSFastEnumeration steps through the keys. Foundation uses NSDictionary as a structured container in preference to C structs custom-made for a given purpose. Again, use +[NSNull null] to store a nil.

▶ **NSDate** represents a point in time, notionally in seconds from the UNIX epoch, unrelated to a calendar or time zone; NSDateFormatter and NSCalendar take care of presentational issues like that. Foundation expresses timeouts and timestamps as NSDates.

▶ **NSNumber** contains a numeric value, whether float, integer, or (via the NSDecimalNumber subclass) fixed-point. It has methods for extracting its value into scalar primitives such as float or int. If you want to save a number in a Foundation collection, first convert it to NSNumber. NSNumberFormatter takes care of getting an NSNumber into and out of human-readable form.

▶ **NSValue** is the superclass of NSNumber. It's a way to wrap ordinary pointers and C structs (such as points, ranges, and rectangles) so that they can be stored in containers and passed between methods that expect objects.

▶ **NSSet** is an *unordered* container of objects. It guarantees that no object is stored twice and can report quickly whether it contains a particular object. It can't contain a nil. It implements NSFastEnumeration, though not as efficiently as NSArray. Core Data exposes to-many relationships as NSSets. Don't automatically reach for NSArray for a collection that doesn't need a natural order; NSSet can often serve you better.

Most of these classes have mutable subclasses—NSMutableString, NSMutableArray, and so on—that enable you to make changes to an object in-place, without having to create a new object to reflect the change, and without any worries about buffer overruns. Remember that these subclasses inherit their superclasses' methods, so if you're looking for the prefix of an NSMutableString, look to NSString for substringToIndex:. Be aware that when you copy one of these objects, the copy method returns an *immutable* object, and mutableCopy returns a *mutable* one, regardless of whether the original was mutable.

All of them are toll-free bridged with Core Foundation, Apple's C library for safe and correct fundamental data types. You can use pointers to these objects interchangeably with their CF equivalents—an NSMutableString pointer and a CFMutableStringRef, for instance. Core Foundation has the advantage of being much more flexible; the collection types, for instance, can tolerate nonobject values, including NULLs. But remember: ARC requires you to use the __bridge family of pointer qualifiers when you exchange bridged objects with Core Foundation. Much of Core Foundation (called CFLite) is open source.

Many of these classes have initializers and factory methods that pull the objects directly from files and URLs; -[NSString initWithContentsOfURL:encoding:error:] is an example. Other methods write them to files. These methods are synchronous and could lock your application up for a noticeable amount of time, resulting in the spinning "beachball" cursor on Mac OS X, and possibly a forced quit in an iOS app. The asynchronous URL-loading classes in Foundation are a better bet for production code.

Another common feature of these basic classes (other than NSValue, NSSet, and NSDecimalNumber) is that they are directly representable in property lists. See Chapter 23, "Property Lists."

The C++ Standard Template Library provides many templates for conceptually similar data types, but those templates demand, or make promises of, specific implementations. Foundation, by contrast, exposes only abstract superclasses that describe the behavior of the data and leaves implementation to subclasses that are never identified to you. An NSMutableString, for instance, may internally be a simple array of ASCII bytes, of 16-bit Unicode code points, of UTF-8 bytes, or a tree of substring arrays to make local edits easier. The implementation may *change* over the object's lifetime. Foundation has, over its quarter-century of development, been optimized to the point that a single mutable object can, over a large range of sizes, exhibit better performance than a data type committed to a single strategy.

Dynamic Dispatch

I mentioned dynamic method dispatch earlier. When you code a method call, the Objective-C compiler does not link the call to any specific code or class. The dispatch to the method's implementation is done at run time. Briefly, the method's name—its *selector*—is a string that indexes into the object's table of method implementations. If an implementation is in the table, it's run. If not, there are a few strategies for seeing whether the call can be forwarded or improvised. If everything fails, an exception is raised.

One thing this allows is "duck typing" (if it quacks like a duck...): If the object can handle the call, it doesn't matter what class it belongs to. Two objects need not share a superclass that declares a doubleValue method to respond to a doubleValue call.

Consider IBAction methods, which respond to control actions. In Interface Builder, you give a button a target—the object that is meant to respond to a click—and an action—the selector of the target's handler. Responders are free to have any number of handler methods, with any names they like; because the button keeps the selector, it can use it to fire the handler. Notionally

```
- (void) mouseButtonReleased
{
    [self.target performSelector: self.actionSelector
                      withObject: self
                      afterDelay: 0.0];
}
```

A number of methods take a selector name (a SEL), naked of any implementing class. You use the @selector directive to construct the constant:

```
@selector(performSelector:withObject:afterDelay:).
```

If you specify a class for an object variable, the Objective-C compiler will warn you if the class is not known to declare a method you use. The warning is advisory because you don't need to declare any methods, and methods are subject to definition or resolution at run time. However, it is good practice to clear those warnings up. First, it puts you on the way to making sure you do have implementations for the methods you use (thus saving the run time error). Second, when the compiler doesn't have a declaration for a method, it guesses that its parameters and return value are all of type id. If any of those are not objects, you risk distortion from type conversions; and on some architectures, return values will appear in different register or memory locations depending on the actual type.

Veterans of strongly typed languages such as C++ have two main objections. First, that putting off the discovery that an object doesn't implement a method until run time is hard to debug and reduces confidence that a program is correct. In my experience, the bug is rare, and with a decent debugger it's easy to characterize. No experienced Cocoa developer would purchase machine-assured "correctness" at the cost of Cocoa's dynamism and abstraction.

Second, it is inefficient. At the limit, yes it is. You would not do image convolutions or audio processing in Objective-C. A profile would show the processor spending most of its time in method dispatch. C and C++ (or FORTRAN) are the only way to go for performance-critical regions of code; but bear in mind that Objective-C is C, and Objective-C++ is C++. Cocoa is not a high-performance computing framework. It is, however, a framework for running a human interface and handling high-level network tasks. Both involve more idle time than not. That it takes a microsecond to respond to a mouse click instead of tens of nanoseconds doesn't matter. That the framework provides an elegant and maintainable way to provide the response does matter.

Objective-C++

There is a lot of useful C++ code out there, and it's true that the tightly defined implementation strategy of that language can produce code that runs much faster. Further, you may have to deal with data formats and logic that you want to share for compatibility (or sharing effort) with other platforms. For many tasks, C++ is the right choice.

But, if you want to put that functionality into a Mac OS X or iOS program, you must write Objective-C. How to square the circle?

Objective-C++ bears the same relation to C++ as Objective-C does to C: It is a proper superset of the language. Objective-C++ objects can have C++ objects as instance variables, and those will be constructed and destructed as automatically as though they were declared in scope.

Xcode compilers will recognize a file as Objective-C++ if its name has the suffix `.mm`. That would include any C++ file that uses Objective-C directives or works with Objective-C methods. It would include any Objective-C file that uses C++ keywords, objects, or functions.

Summary

This appendix is meant as a quick introduction to the Objective-C programming language. This book teaches how to use the Xcode tools, so programming languages and techniques are outside my brief. If I've given you enough to see what the sample code is trying to do, so you can see how Xcode adapts itself to your work, I've done my job.

But Xcode, Cocoa, and Objective-C are symbionts: Cocoa depends on the features of Objective-C; Objective-C is evolving to support Cocoa; and Xcode is designed to make it easier to use both. The second part of this appendix explored how the language has expanded to take some headaches out of Cocoa programming.

To go much further than this Summary, enter `Objective-C Programming Language` in the search field of the Documentation organizer, and select the title that matches it. It's readable and authoritative.

Some Build Variables

This appendix offers a brief list of the major build variables that control the Xcode build system. Build variables determine compiler flags, search paths, installation behavior, and essential information such as product names. You can find a comprehensive explanation of Xcode's build variables in the Documentation organizer by searching for the title string **Build Setting Reference** in the Developer Tools Reference documentation set.

You can see all the build variables available to "Run Script" build phases by creating a phase that consists of only one command such as echo and then checking **Show environment variables in build log.** You will find more than 250 variables. Here's a list of the more useful ones. For purposes of example, assume that user xcodeuser is making a debug build of a Mac OS X application named MyApp out of a project named MyProject; the project uses the 10.7 SDK and Xcode 4.2. (The /Developer directory was still available to 4.2; see the Xcode 4.3 release notes for the new structure. One of the functions of these build settings is to hide the location of the development environment behind abstract variables.) See Figure B.1.

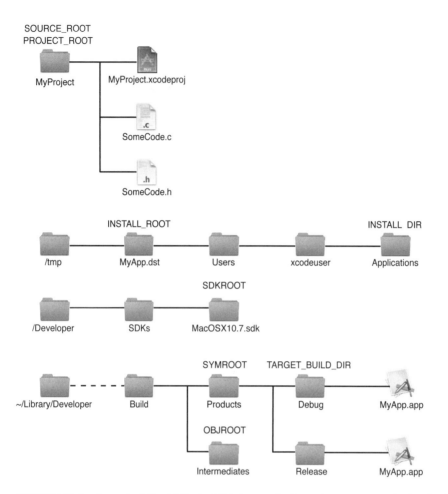

FIGURE B.1   Layout of the MyProject/MyApp project used as an example for the build variables listed here.

Some of these settings have no corresponding interface in the **Build Settings** tabs of the Target or Project editor. You can set these—if they are not read-only—by selecting **Add User-Defined Setting** from the **Add Build Setting** button at the bottom of the Target editor. Xcode will add a new line to the list, and you can enter the setting's name in the Setting column, and the value under the level you want to set it at. Boolean values are kept as YES and NO.

The authoritative name for a build variable is its setting name—the name of the actual build variable, as visible in environment variables and substitutable into other settings and Info.plist expansions. You can find the corresponding entries in a **Build Settings** tab by typing the setting name into the tab's search field.

NOTE

Settings can be made conditional according to what processor architecture the product is built for or what SDK is used. See Chapter 26, "The Xcode Build System," for details.

The **Build Settings** tab can display setting names instead of the descriptive "setting titles." The **Show Setting Names/Show Setting Titles** item in the Editor menu toggles between the "real" names and the descriptive titles.

Similarly, you can control how setting values display. A setting may be defined in terms of another setting, as when you specify an installation directory by $(HOME)/Applications. By default, Xcode displays embedded build variables by expanding them. The **Show Definitions/Show Values** item in the **Editor** menu changes the display so that variable references are shown either literally or as-interpreted.

Useful Build Variables

With no further ado, here is a list of selected build variables grouped by general function and then by a rough general-to-specific order within those groups.

Environment

These are read-only variables that you can use in scripts or to build up other build settings.

- ▶ PROJECT: The name of the Xcode project, without extension. (MyProject)

- ▶ OS: The operating system on which the product is *built*. It is always MACOS. (MACOS)

- ▶ PLATFORM_NAME: The name of the target platform, macosx, iphonesimulator, or iphoneos. (macosx)

- ▶ HOME: The path to your home directory.

- ▶ USER: The username of the person doing the build. There is a corresponding UID variable for the numeric user ID.

- ▶ GROUP: The group name of the person doing the build. There is a corresponding GID variable for the numeric group ID.

- ▶ DEVELOPER_DIR: The directory you chose for the Xcode installation. The DEVELOPER_ variables are important because they make your scripts portable if you have installed more than one version of Xcode, and for developers who did not install Xcode in the root /Developer directory. Many of the DEVELOPER_ paths have parallel PLATFORM settings because the tool and frameworks sets may vary depending on whether you develop for Mac OS X or iOS. (/Developer)

- ▶ DEVELOPER_APPLICATIONS_DIR: The folder inside DEVELOPER_DIR containing Xcode and the other developer applications. (/Developer/Applications)

▶ DEVELOPER_BIN_DIR: The folder inside DEVELOPER_DIR containing the BSD tools, such as clang, that Xcode uses. If you write scripts that execute development tools such as clang or yacc directly, use this path *instead* of /usr/bin. The tools in this directory are the versions that correspond to the version of Xcode you use. (/Developer/usr/bin)

▶ DEVELOPER_FRAMEWORKS_DIR: The folder inside DEVELOPER_DIR that contains development frameworks, such as for unit tests. There's also a QUOTED variant that you can use in confidence that a shell interpreter won't mangle it. (/Developer/Library/Frameworks)

▶ DEVELOPER_LIBRARY_DIR: The folder inside DEVELOPER_DIR containing files (templates, plug-ins, and so on) that support the developer tools. (/Developer/Library)

▶ DEVELOPER_SDK_DIR: The folder inside DEVELOPER_DIR that contains software development kits. (/Developer/SDKs)

▶ DEVELOPER_TOOLS_DIR: Contains BSD tools, such as SetFile, that are specific to Mac OS X development and would not be expected to be in /usr/bin. (/Developer/Tools)

▶ DEVELOPER_USR_DIR: The folder inside DEVELOPER_DIR that you should use as a prefix for the standard include, sbin, share, and other directories you'd ordinarily look for in the root /usr directory. (/Developer/usr)

▶ NATIVE_ARCH: The architecture on which the current build takes place. This is the same as CURRENT_ARCH and (if the target is Mac OS X) NATIVE_ARCH_ACTUAL. You can't actually use CURRENT_ARCH in a script—"Run Script" build phases are run only once per build, so the value you see for CURRENT_ARCH is only one of the architectures that will actually be built. If your script must hit every architecture targeted, have it iterate through ARCHS. (x86_64)

▶ NATIVE_ARCH_32_BIT and NATIVE_ARCH_64_BIT: These are like NATIVE_ARCH but refer to the 32-bit and 64-bit variants of the native architecture. On an iOS build, these settings are moot, and Xcode reports them as being for Intel processors. (i386 and x86_64)

▶ MAC_OS_X_VERSION_ACTUAL: A four-digit number designating the version of Mac OS X on which the build is being done. The first two digits are 10, the third is 7, and the last is the minor version. This value will be in trouble if 10.7 reaches a minor version above 9, as 10.4 did. (1070)

▶ MAC_OS_X_VERSION_MAJOR: A four-digit number that is the same as MAC_OS_X_VERSION_ACTUAL, but with the last digit set to zero. (1070)

▶ MAC_OS_X_VERSION_MINOR: A four-digit number that designates the current OS version, omitting the leading 10. In Xcode 4.1 and up, the first two digits are always 07; the second two are the minor version, safe through Mac OS X version 10.7.99. (0700)

▶ XCODE_VERSION_ACTUAL (0420), XCODE_VERSION_MAJOR (0400), XCODE_VERSION_MINOR (0420): This is the same version information as in the MAC_OS_X_VERSION settings, but for Xcode.

Build Targets

▶ ACTION: The task the build system carries out, corresponding to the action parameter for xcodebuild. There is no setting corresponding to the Xcode action (Run, Test, Profile, Analyze, or Archive) that instigates the build. (build)

▶ CONFIGURATION: The name of the selected build configuration. (Debug)

▶ PACKAGE_TYPE: The kind of product to be built is identified by a UIT. This isn't easy to figure out *a priori* for use in your scripts. The thing to do is to add a "Run Script" build phase in your project one time to echo the value of this setting, so you know what to test for. Related is PRODUCT_TYPE, which identifies nonpackage products such as .dylib or .a. (com.apple.package-type.wrapper.application)

▶ PRODUCT_NAME: The name of the thing the current target builds. Target templates default this setting to be the same as the name of the target, but you can change this. PRODUCT_NAME does not include any prefix (such as lib) or suffix (such as .app or .dylib) that would be used in the actual name of the product's file or bundle. (MyApp)

▶ TARGET_NAME: The name of the active target. The target usually has the same name as the product, but this is not necessarily the case. For instance, a separate target for running unit tests might yield the same product as the project's principal target but have another name, such as MyApp (testing). (MyApp)

▶ PROJECT_NAME: The name of the project file without the .xcodeproj extension. (MyProject)

▶ EXECUTABLE_NAME: The name of the product's executable binary file including any prefixes or suffixes made necessary by its file type. This defaults to the EXECUTABLE_PREFIX, plus PRODUCT_NAME, plus EXECUTABLE_EXTENSION, but you could change this. (Although it's hard to imagine why you would.) (MyApp)

▶ EXECUTABLE_PREFIX: The prefix needed for the product's filename to conform to the product type. If this were a static library target, for instance, this variable would be lib.

▶ EXECUTABLE_EXTENSION: The suffix needed for the product's filename to conform to the product type. If this were a static library target, this variable would be .a.

▶ WRAPPER_NAME: If the product being built takes the form of a bundle (such as an application or a framework), this is the full name of the bundle directory. This is the PRODUCT_NAME plus the WRAPPER_SUFFIX. (MyApp.app).

▶ `MACH_O_TYPE`: Set to `mh_execute`, `mh_dylib`, `mh_bundle`, `staticlib`, or `mh_object`, as the case may be, to indicate what role the executable binary product plays. This is immutable—it's set when you create a new project or target and is what the build system uses to determine how to generate the final product. (`mh_execute`)

Source Locations

▶ `PROJECT_DIR`: The directory that contains the project file. (`/Users/xcodeuser/MyProject`)

▶ `PROJECT_FILE_PATH`: The full path to the project file. (`/Users/xcodeuser/MyProject/MyProject.xcodeproj`)

▶ `SDKROOT`: The root of the tree in which to search for system headers and libraries; this is simple for Mac OS X SDKs but gets more involved after you get into the platform and OS options in the iOS SDK. (`/Developer/SDKs/MacOSX10.7.sdk`)

▶ `SOURCE_ROOT` (previously `SRCROOT`): The folder containing the source code for the project, usually the project document's directory. (`/Users/xcodeuser/MyProject`)

Destination Locations

These are the directories to which object files, derived files, and products are directed in the course of a build. Many of these are somewhere in the "derived data" directory for your project. You can set that directory using the **File→Project Settings…** command, in the **Build** tab, but typically you use the default directory, deep within the `Library` folder of your home directory. The path to the default directory goes deep and involves a unique identifier string, so it's not practical to spell out in this list. If you see a path beginning with `/Users/xcodeuser/Library`, you can take it that it's the derived-data directory.

The whole idea of the derived-data directory is to locate in one place all the files—there are many, and they are large—that Xcode generates in managing and building your projects. These files are derived in that they contain only information that follows from your source files and settings. They can be reconstructed completely from the contents of your project. *You do not want to put derived files in your project directory tree* if you intend to share it or put it under revision control. If you must put the derived directory in your project directory, make sure to give it a name you can match in the ignored-files patterns in your Subversion or Git configurations.

If you want to inspect the derived-data directory, open the Projects organizer. Find your project in the list on the left, and see the panel at the top of the detail view. The full path to the directory will be shown (middle-truncated if the window is too narrow). Next to it is a small arrow button that shows the directory in the Finder.

▶ `OBJROOT`: The folder containing, perhaps indirectly, the intermediate products, such as object files, of the build. Unless you override the location for intermediate files, this folder will be buried deep in your user `Library` directory. (`/Users/xcodeuser/Library/Developer/...Build/Intermediates`)

▸ SYMROOT: The container for folders that receive symbol-rich, meaning not-yet-stripped, versions of the product. This, too, is buried in your own Library directory. (/Users/xcodeuser/Library/Developer/...Build/Products)

▸ DSTROOT: The directory into which the product is "installed." This is usually in the /tmp tree, and the project makes and populates subdirectories in DSTROOT as though it were the root of your file system. It is relevant only in install builds, which are available only through xcodebuild. This made more sense back in the days when Project Builder was a veneer on make because makefile projects typically have install targets to distribute the product across the file system. Nowadays, DSTROOT is useful only if you build and test system or kernel software. (/tmp/MyApp.dst)

▸ BUILT_PRODUCTS_DIR: The full path to the directory that receives either every product of the project or, if the products are scattered, symbolic links to every product. A script can therefore depend on reaching all the products through this path. By default $(SYMROOT)/$(CONFIGURATION) and therefore deep within your Library directory. CONFIGURATION_BUILD_DIR is a synonym. (/Users/xcodeuser/Library/Developer/...Build/Products/Debug)

▸ TARGET_BUILD_DIR: The directory into which the product of the *current* target is built. It is the installation location, in an install build; otherwise, it is the CONFIGURATION subdirectory of the SYMROOT directory (/Users/xcodeuser/Library/Developer/...Build/Products/Debug)

▸ DERIVED_FILE_DIR: The directory that receives intermediate source files generated in the course of a build, such as the sources generated by the bison parser generator. This variable is paralleled by DERIVED_FILES_DIR and DERIVED_SOURCES_DIR. If you have a more general need for a place to put a temporary file, consult the Xcode documentation for PROJECT_TEMP_DIR or TARGET_TEMP_DIR. (/Users/xcodeuser/Library/Developer/...MyApp.build/DerivedSources)

▸ OBJECT_FILE_DIR: The directory containing subdirectories, one per architecture, containing compiled object files. It's in the derived-data folder, which by default is deep within your Library directory. (/Users/xcodeuser/Library/Developer/...MyApp.build/Objects)

Bundle Locations

▸ SHALLOW_BUNDLE: If this is YES, the other settings in this section are moot because the product bundle is like an iOS application—all the files, except for localizations, are immediately inside the bundle directory, without the Mac OS X bundle structure.

▸ CONTENTS_FOLDER_PATH: The path within the target build directory that contains the structural directories of a bundle product (MyApp.app/Contents)

▶ EXECUTABLE_FOLDER_PATH: The path in a bundle target in the target build directory into which the product's executable file is to be built. Not to be confused with EXECUTABLES_FOLDER_PATH, which points to a directory for "additional binary files," named Executables, in the Contents directory. (MyApp.app/Contents/MacOS)

▶ EXECUTABLE_PATH: The path within TARGET_BUILD_DIR to the executable binary. (MyApp.app/Contents/MacOS/MyApp)

▶ FRAMEWORKS_FOLDER_PATH: The path in a bundle target in the target build directory that contains frameworks used by the product. There are variables for other possible bundle directories; see the Xcode documentation for more. (MyApp.app/Contents/Frameworks)

▶ UNLOCALIZED_RESOURCES_FOLDER_PATH: The directory within a bundle product in the target build directory that receives file resources (MyApp.app/Contents/Resources)

Compiler Settings

There are many, many possible compiler settings; I'll mention a comparative few. Most of these carry the GCC_ prefix, even though from Xcode 4.2 on, you'll probably use clang. This is to keep compatibility with older projects.

▶ ARCHS: The architectures, as a space-separated list, for which the product is to be built. (x86_64)

▶ ARCHS_STANDARD_32_64_BIT, ARCHS_STANDARD_32_BIT, and ARCHS_STANDARD_64_BIT: These provide an à la carte selection of architectures that answers to the indicated register widths. (x86_64 i386, i386, and x86_64)

▶ VALID_ARCHS: The possible values that could go into the ARCHS list. The list encompasses all the architectures for which Xcode *can* build. If an architecture appears in ARCHS but not in VALID_ARCHS, it won't be built. (i386 x86_64)

▶ GCC_VERSION: The compiler version to use. When the compiler actually was gcc, this was the gcc version number, like 4.2. With clang, it's a string that indicates version 1.0 regardless of the actual version. (com.apple.compilers.llvm.clang.1_0)

▶ GCC_PREPROCESSOR_DEFINITIONS: A space-separated list of symbols to be #defined in all compilations. Items of the form *symbol=value* assign values to the symbols. Symbols defined in this way are incorporated in precompiled headers. Related is GCC_PREPROCESSOR_DEFINITIONS_NOT_USED_IN_PRECOMPS, which specifies symbols defined in every compilation but not incorporated in precompiled headers. This enables you to share precompiled headers between build configurations with variants in global definitions taken as options in the respective configurations.

▶ GCC_ENABLE_OBJC_GC: This variable controls whether the project compiles Objective-C source with support for garbage collection.

▶ If it is Unsupported, no garbage collection will be done, and no special compiler flag will be set.

▶ If Required, garbage collection will be used, and anything that links with the compiled code is expected to use garbage collection. The compiler is passed the flag -fobjc_gc_only.

▶ If Supported, the code does not use garbage collection itself, but can link with GC binaries. This is useful only if you write a single library to link with both environments. The compiler is passed the flag -fobjc_gc.

▶ CLANG_ENABLE_OBJC_ARC: Whether Automatic Reference Counting is enabled. (NO)

▶ GCC_TREAT_WARNINGS_AS_ERRORS: It's good practice to treat a build as failed even if the only issues were warnings, not errors: Even if an executable binary could be generated, it won't be. This flag isn't set by default, but maybe it should be; in most cases, warnings point out logical mistakes that you need to debug anyway. (NO)

▶ OTHER_CFLAGS: The catchall variable that receives compiler options that do not have their own build variables for C compilation. It's easy to put in this variable an option that contradicts a setting made in the **Build Settings** tab, with unpredictable results. Therefore, it's a good idea to type a flag into the search field, to see whether a direct setting is available. There is also an OTHER_CPLUSPLUSFLAGS variable. For linker flags, the equivalent is OTHER_LDFLAGS. (empty)

▶ WARNING_FLAGS: A string of options setting warning options for all compilations. Apple tries to provide fine-grained control of warnings through check boxes in the settings table, so look to be sure that there isn't a check box for your warning before putting it into this variable. The build-variable prefix for those settings is GCC_WARN. The equivalent for the linker is WARNING_LDFLAGS. (empty)

Search Paths

▶ HEADER_SEARCH_PATHS: A space-delimited list of paths to directories in which the compiler should search for headers, in addition to standard locations such as /usr/include. If you add your own paths, carry the default paths through by putting $(inherited) at the beginning or end of your list. If the headers in question are in frameworks, set FRAMEWORK_SEARCH_PATHS instead. SDKROOT is prepended to the paths of system headers and frameworks.
(/Users/xcodeuser/Library/...Debug/include)

▶ LIBRARY_SEARCH_PATHS: A space-delimited list of paths to directories in which the compiler should search for libraries. If set, SDKROOT is prepended to the paths of system libraries. Developers sometimes are given libraries in production and debug forms, as binaries, with no source; they'd like to use one version of the library in Debug builds and the other in Release builds. A solution is to put the two library versions in separate directories and specify different LIBRARY_SEARCH_PATHSs for the two build configurations. ((/Users/xcodeuser/Library/...Products/Debug))

▶ MACOSX_DEPLOYMENT_TARGET: The minimum version of Mac OS X on which the product can run; symbols in the SDK from later versions of the OS are weak-linked. There is also an IPHONEOS_DEPLOYMENT_TARGET. (10.7)

Deployment

▶ DEPLOYMENT_POSTPROCESSING: Indicates whether the build system is to strip symbols from the product, install it to INSTALL_DIR, and set its ownership and permissions (if YES). The install build action sets this option, or you could set it yourself in one of your configurations. (NO)

▶ INSTALL_PATH: The intended directory that would receive the installed product. (/Users/xcodeuser/Applications)

▶ INSTALL_ROOT: The path to prepend to the INSTALL_PATH to hold the installation tree—install builds do not, by default, install directly to the "live" installation destinations. (/tmp/MyApp.dst)

▶ INSTALL_DIR: The full path of the directory to receive the product. Obtained by concatenating $(iNSTALL_ROOT)/$(lNSTALL_PATH). (/tmp/MyApp.dst/Users/xcodeuser/Applications)

▶ INSTALL_OWNER: The owner of the MyApp.app product when installation is done. (xcodeuser)

▶ INSTALL_GROUP: The group for the MyApp.app product when installation is done. (xcodeuser)

▶ INSTALL_MODE_FLAG: The permissions for the installed MyApp.app product. (u+w, go-w,a+rX)

▶ REMOVE_CVS_FROM_RESOURCES and REMOVE_SVN_FRØM_RESOURCES: The CVS and Subversion SCM systems work by populating every directory in a working copy with directories for their own record-keeping. You do not want these in your distributed product. If these settings are YES, they won't be. That's the default, and the **Build** tab won't offer you the option, so if you want to be eccentric, you need to add the settings. (YES by default)

Info.plist

▶ INFOPLIST_FILE: The name of the file that is the *source* for the bundle's Info.plist file, if the product of this target is a bundle. This should not be Info.plist because a project with more than one target must generate more than one Info.plist file. (MyApp-Info.plist)

- ▶ INFOPLIST_PREPROCESS: If YES, preprocesses the INFOPLIST_FILE, using a C-style preprocessor. You can specify a prefix file with INFOPLIST_PREFIX_HEADER and set symbols with INFOPLIST_PREPROCESSOR_DEFINITIONS. (NO)

- ▶ INFOPLIST_EXPAND_BUILD_SETTINGS: Controls whether build settings should be expanded in the generated Info.plist. This allows you, for instance to fill the CFBundleExecutable key with $(EXECUTABLE_NAME), and be assured that if you ever change the name of the product, Info.plist will always be in sync. (YES)

- ▶ INFOPLIST_OUTPUT_FORMAT: Your choice of the possible file formats for the Info.plist property-list file. This is binary if you want the binary format; same-as-input if you want to preserve the existing format; anything else gets you an XML plist. (same-as-input)

- ▶ STRINGS_FILE_OUTPUT_ENCODING: .strings files map symbolic strings (usually English-language names) to strings that would be used for display in a particular language. If you do localization, you have a .strings file for every language and region you support. But every application has an Info-Plist.strings file to localize copyright notices, application names, and the like. By default, these are encoded as UTF-16, but so many tools generate UTF-8 that that's an option, too. (UTF-16, by default)

Source Trees

A source tree provides a particular kind of build variable, a path to a directory or to the root directory of a tree with a known structure. The path can be a location to receive build results or provide access to a system of libraries and headers. When used to build source paths, a source tree provides a reliable shorthand for packages that do not belong in the directory tree of any one project.

For example, I use the eSellerate libraries in some of my projects. I define a source tree for the eSellerate libraries by opening the Preferences window, selecting the **Source Trees** tab of the **Locations** panel, and clicking the + button to add an entry. I chose **ESELLERATE_DIR** for the setting name and **eSellerate Directory** for the display name, and typed the full pathname for the root of the eSellerate SDK into the path column.

Now, when I add a file reference to my project, I can use the File inspector in the Utility area to set **Location** to **Relative to eSellerate Directory**. Regardless of who copies or clones my project, as long as they have defined an ESELLERATE_DIR source tree, the project can find that file in their copy of that directory. I don't have to care about the details of the path, and I especially don't have to set up double-dot relative directory references.

Search trees are global—they span projects—but are per-user.

Project and Target Templates

Cocoa development is insupportable without Xcode's templates. Xcode provides templates for more than 30 products, plus variants. When you instantiate one, you are set up with skeleton implementations of the classes you need for that product and the settings you need for building it.

The overall course of instantiating a project template is more-or-less uniform:

1. Ask for a new project by selecting **File→New→Project...** (⇧⌘ N). An empty Workspace window appears and drops a New Project assistant.

2. Select the type of the main product of the project (or at least the first product you want to work on): The list at the left of the assistant is divided into two parts (iOS and Mac OS X), which include categories for the targets. When you select a category, the main view fills with icons representing the templates in that category; clicking one of them gives you a description of the template. Click **Next** when you've made your choice. See Figure C.1.

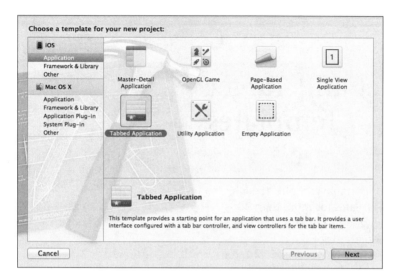

FIGURE C.1   The New Project assistant presents categories of products for iOS and Mac OS X. Selecting one gives you an array of product types and a description of each. Click **Next** to choose the selected template.

3. Set some options for the project's product. At the least, this can include a field for the **Product Name**. There are two other common options because most targets produce bundles that should uniquely identify themselves in their Info.plists:

   ▶ **Company Identifier:** This should be a reverse-domain-format string that identifies you, to make the bundle identifier unique.

   ▶ **Bundle Identifier:** This isn't editable. It concatenates your company identifier and the product name, altered so it conforms to the RFC format covering domain names.

4. In templates that generate code for more than one class, you are offered a **Class Prefix**, a short string it prepends to the generated class names. You should supply at least three uppercase letters.

5. Fill in other options, as needed by the product type. These often determine what skeleton code goes into the source files the template starts you out with. In any template that might remotely involve Objective-C, you are given the option **Use Automatic Reference Counting** (ARC). If you develop for iOS 5 or Mac OS X 10.7 (or can tolerate the lack of zeroing weak references in 4.3 and 10.6.8), there is no reason not to check this option.

   Click **Next**.

6. Use the select-file sheet that appears to choose the directory into which Xcode places the project directory. A check box lets you create a local Git repository for the project.

Those are the basics. These are the details.

iOS Project Templates

The iOS part of the list has three categories.

Application

▶ **Master-Detail Application:** This creates an application that navigates a hierarchy with a series of tables headed by a navigation controller to manage the stack. Eventually, you'll end the hierarchy in a "detail view" for displaying or editing specific information. On the iPhone, this would be a full-screen view, but for the iPad, the template gives you a UlSplitViewController to put master and detail into separate parts of the display.

The template offers you many options:

   ▶ **Device Family** to target the app at iPhone, iPad, or both ("Universal").

   ▶ **Use Storyboard** to base the app on a Storyboard full-application layout, rather than a series of XIBs.

   ▶ **Use Core Data** to add a data-model file to the project; add initialization of the Core Data stack to the application delegate; and add NSFetchedResultsController support to the root table view.

   ▶ **Use Automatic Reference Counting**.

   ▶ **Include Unit Tests** to add a testing target to the project. This will be an *application* test suite, and it will be incorporated into the app's build scheme for the Test action. You cannot remove the added target from the application scheme.

▶ **OpenGL Game:** This sets you up with an OpenGL ES view and an application timer to direct animation in the view. You have the options to include Storyboard, ARC, and application unit tests.

▶ **Page-Based Application:** The main view of the application is set up to use a UlPageViewController so the user can swipe across views with a page-turning animation. This is new in iOS 5. The options are **Device Family**, **Use Automatic Reference Counting**, and **Include Unit Tests**.

▶ **Single View Application**: For apps that don't do any navigation. This has the same options as the Master-Detail Application but doesn't offer Core Data.

▶ **Tabbed Application**: This is for an application that has a `UITabBar` at the bottom and a `UITabBarController` to switch among independent view controllers. The template starts you with two view controllers and a XIB for each. What it doesn't give you is the customary `MainWindow.xib` file; instead it sets up the tab controller and its items in the application delegate. This feels odd, but the alternative, as done before Xcode 4.2, was to create the tab controller in the XIB, and it was nearly impossible to get the hierarchy and the cross-NIB references right.

As with the Single View Application, this template does not offer Core Data. Given that at least one of your controllers is apt to involve a master-detail interface, you may want to add it back. The easiest way to do this is to instantiate a template for a throwaway project, copy the construction of the Core Data stack out of the application delegate, and paste the methods into your own app delegate.

▶ **Utility Application**: A utility application presents simple information, with no navigation at all; think of a clock or some other desk accessory that the user brings up, glances at, and puts away. Utility applications have a second view that flips over to configure the main view. This template gives you two view controllers, a toolbar with an **Info** button to switch between them, and a flip animation. You can add Storyboard, Core Data, ARC, and unit tests.

▶ **Empty Application**: This is just what it says. There is no XIB (the window is initialized in the application delegate) and no view controller. This is the only iOS application template that doesn't start you with a runnable app. Storyboard is not an option, but Core Data, ARC, and unit testing are.

Framework & Library

iOS does not permit developers to load any kind of executable (except for script files that have not been downloaded from an external source): No plug-ins, no dynamic libraries. So there is only one kind of product in this category—**Cocoa Touch Static Library**. This takes a product name and names the product `libproductname.a`. You can add a unit-testing target, and ARC is an option.

Other

This category contains the **Empty** template. The only thing in the project directory is the project file. There are no build configurations, no build settings, and no targets. After you add a target, the project picks up the settings and configurations from the target, and it behaves as a normal project. There are no options other than the project name.

Mac OS X Project Templates

On iOS, you can build applications and static libraries, and that's it. Mac OS X is a more open system. Not only can you build applications, you also can build dynamic libraries and frameworks, kernel extensions, and plug-ins for a great variety of system services. This means there are a lot more templates.

Application

▶ **Cocoa Application:** Sets you up for any application using the Cocoa application framework with Objective-C. Carbon is no longer available. There are a slew of options:

    ▶ You can select one **App Store Category** from a pop-up; if you need more (you are entitled to three), edit `Info.plist` directly.

    ▶ Check **Create Document-Based Application** to have Xcode set up an `NSDocument` subclass and initialize your `Info.plist` to register the document type with Launch Services. If you don't check this box, the template will generate an application delegate class instead. In either case, the *Class Prefix* you set is prepended to the class name.

    ▶ After you call for a document, you must fill in the **Document Extension** for the file type.

    ▶ Regardless of whether you have a document type, you can ask to **Use Core Data**; if you have a document, it is made a subclass of `NSPersistentDocument`; otherwise the template puts code in the application delegate to set up the Core Data stack.

    ▶ Checking **Include Unit Tests** attaches an application test suite to the application target.

    ▶ If you check **Use Core Data**, you have the option to **Include Spotlight Importer**. The added target implements an indexing plug-in for the systemwide Spotlight search utility. The setup for that target is fairly complex (you need two UUIDs), and the template takes care of most of it, but you need to edit it for your own keys, entities, and properties. The target includes a read-me file that tells you what you need to do. You get both a `GetMetadataForFile` function to tag entire document files and a Spotlight-importer class to separately index individual items in a document.

▶ **Cocoa-AppleScript Application:** A number of languages, such as Lua, Perl, Python, and Ruby have been "bridged" to Cocoa; you can write real Mac OS X applications almost exclusively in those languages. Those are external projects you can find on the Web; Apple includes a project template for its own scripting language, AppleScript. Instantiating this template gets you XIBs for the main menu and for a document class. The document is backed not by an Objective-C `.m` file but by an `.applescript` script.

It's an interesting concept, but there are limitations. Having complete support for all of Cocoa in AppleScript is good, but if you like the near-English syntax of the language, you won't have much benefit from it because all of the Cocoa interface is function calls with the same names as the Objective-C interfaces. This is not a royal road to Cocoa programming: You need to learn as much API as if you were writing Objective-C, in a language that doesn't completely match up.

Xcode does not have a file template for new `.applescript` files; you must use the AppleScript Editor application to extend the app. This is probably for the best—why should Xcode duplicate a dedicated editor?—but take it as a sign that it's an awkward fit.

▶ **Command Line Tool**: You met this template in Chapter 2, "Kicking the Tires." It produces a BSD program you can execute from the command line. There are six variations, depending on the base library you intend to use:

   ▶ **C**: The standard C libraries.

   ▶ **C++**: The standard C++ libraries.

   ▶ **Core Data:** The Core Data and Foundation frameworks; this is an especially attractive option if you want to build a Core Data database with preloaded records.

   ▶ **Core Foundation:** The Core Foundation framework, which provides safe data types through a C interface.

   ▶ **Core Services:** Core Foundation and Core Services, a framework that works with Apple Events, the CFNetwork higher-level networking package, and Launch Services.

   ▶ **Foundation:** The Foundation framework, which gives you safe data types, high-level networking, and many other services with an Objective-C interface.

Framework & Library

Because nearly every component of Mac OS X, from applications down to the kernel, can load external code, you can build many kinds of libraries, frameworks, and plug-ins. The next six categories encompass most of the specialties.

▶ **Cocoa Framework:** A framework is a structured bundle that combines a dynamic library with the headers you need to develop with it and the resources it needs to run.

▶ **Cocoa Library:** By contrast, a Cocoa library is just a single file encompassing Objective-C classes and their associated code. You have the choice of a dynamic library or a static one.

▶ **Bundle:** This is the most general template for a multiple-file library. It has an `Info.plist` file, a `Resource` directory, and presumably, some executable code (although the template doesn't give you any starter source files). You choose whether the bundle links with Cocoa or Core Foundation, the C library that provides essentially the same services as Cocoa Foundation. Most of the other templates for plug-ins and services are specializations of a generic bundle. If your application has a plug-in architecture, this is where you start.

▶ **XPC Service:** XPC is new in Mac OS X Lion. The idea is that applications would be more secure and less crash-prone if they could parcel their work out to separate processes. For instance, if Passer Rating could download passer statistics from the Net, it could leave the downloading to a process that would be privileged to access the network but not the UI or the file system. The worst an attacker could do is crash the download process; Passer Rating and the user's files could continue unscathed. The XPC framework provides lightweight interprocess communications for a few primitive data types and collections and makes it easy to dispatch code when traffic comes through the connection.

▶ **C/C++ Library:** This is a vanilla BSD library, written in C or C++. When you name the product `LibraryName`, the actual product is named `libLibraryName.a` or `.dylib`. You can choose between a dynamic library or a static one.

▶ **STL C++ Library:** A BSD library that uses the Standard Template Library under C++. You have two choices: **Dynamic** and **Standard Dynamic**. The only difference is that dynamic libraries hide all symbols unless they are specifically exported; standard-dynamic libraries export everything that isn't declared `private extern`.

Application Plug-in

▶ **Automator Action:** Automator is Apple's graphical scripting language for chaining AppleScripts, application services, and command-line scripts. The elements are "action tiles." This target produces your choice of the three types. It includes a XIB that can convert the Automator GUI to parameters for the action.

▶ **Address Book Action Plug-in:** The Apple Address Book application attaches commands to address-card fields (such as **Map this Address** for street addresses); you can write a plug-in that inserts commands of your own. This can include a simple window, if you want. Choose Objective-C or C.

▶ **Installer Plug-in:** Installation packages for Apple's Installer can enhance the process, to a limited extent, by inserting custom views into the installer workflow. You get a subclass of `InstallerPane` and a `.plist` to show where your panes should appear in the installation order.

▶ **Quartz Composer Plug-in:** Quartz Composer (QC) is a graphical scripting language for combining dynamic effects on images and video. Use **Xcode→Open Developer Tool→More Developer Tools**, download and install the graphics tools, and open Quartz Composer to see what's possible. When you have a processing workflow saved as a composition, you can incorporate it into your applications. The elements of the QC language are called "patches"—they specify inputs, outputs, and carry a description of what they do. This template lets you create binary-level patches of your own.

System Plug-in

These plug-ins produce bundles, so they take a product name and a company identifier. They contain skeleton code to guide you to the essential elements you must provide for the specific purpose of each.

▶ **Generic C++ Plug-in:** Sets up a C bundle interface for a C++ service.

▶ **Generic Kernel Extension:** KEXTs are code that can be loaded dynamically into the Derwin kernel. Don't use this template for drivers; use IOKit instead.

▶ **Image Unit Plug-in:** Core Image does in Objective-C what Quartz Composer does in compositions. Use this template to produce a distributable filter for images.

▶ **IOKit Driver:** Produces a kernel-level driver for I/O devices; it links against the IOKit library, which gives lightweight access to memory services and operation queues in C++.

▶ **Preference Pane:** Produces a pane for inclusion in the System Preferences application.

▶ **Quick Look Plug-in:** The service that renders the contents of a file in the Finder, in open-file sheets, and in Mail and other client applications. Use this template to write a lightweight renderer for your documents.

▶ **Screen Saver:** Produces a graphics program and a configuration panel for a screen saver.

▶ **Spotlight Importer:** Produces a plug-in that the system's indexer can use to extract metadata from your documents. You can ask for a Spotlight-importer target when you create a Cocoa application.

▶ **Sync Schema:** A sync schema bundle lets you provide code for the Mac OS X facility that synchronizes application data through MobileMe. With the demise of MobileMe, the framework is deprecated in Lion, but it's there for backward compatibility during the phase-out.

Other

▶ **Empty:** As with its counterpart in iOS, this project has nothing in it. You bring it to life by adding targets.

▶ **External Build System:** This project style brings you back to the early days of Project Builder when the NeXTStep IDE relied on make for a build system. You get project search, simple syntax coloring, and light indexing. The rest is up to make. The **Info** tab of the Target editor lets you specify the path to the build tool and its command-line arguments. If you check **Pass build settings in environment**, whatever you put in the **Build Settings** tab appears in your makefile as environment variables.

By default the arguments for make consist of $(ACTION). This is *not* the build action you select in the Product menu; this corresponds to the actions you can pass to xcodebuild. See Chapter 26, "The Xcode Build System," for details.

Target Templates

After you start a project, you can add products by clicking the **Add Target** button in the Project editor. Again, you'll be presented with a sheet to select the template and another to name it and select some options.

One difference is that you get a choice among the open projects to receive the target. This may not make sense to you: The **Add Target** button was in the editor for a particular project, and the configuration sheet comes down from that project's window; what's to choose? Remember the window might be a workspace, containing many projects; you have to choose.

A bigger difference is that you won't be offered a pick-file sheet for placing the target on-disk; the target's files go into the project directory.

Other than that, target templates are the same as project templates: same repertoire, same options. There is one more template, however. It's in the Other category of both the iOS and Mac OS X parts.

The **Aggregate** target exists solely to gather other targets into one dependency. When you build an aggregate, you build each of the targets in its Target Dependencies list. You'd do this if you were packaging several different products into an overall deliverable, such as the components of an installer package. In Chapter 25, "Documentation in Xcode," I show you how to use an Aggregate target to produce an application and its source documentation in one step.

iOS File Templates

Once you have a target going, you'll want to add files to it. There are only a handful of file types—text, XIBs, .storyboards, .xcdatamodels—and you can simply take empty versions of each and build what you want from there. But it's easier if you allow Xcode to instantiate a template that points you in the right direction.

As always, you pick the template from the New File assistant, fill in any options Xcode may offer you, and name and place the new file(s).

Cocoa Touch

These templates create the .m and .h files that define an Objective-C class.

  ▶ **Objective-C class:** If you want to create an Objective-C class, you'll want it to be a subclass of something else. (If it's your idea of fun, you could create your own root class, but most people regret it.) The options panel gives you a text field to name the new class and a combo box to fill in the superclass you want. (It offers

NSObject, UIViewController, UITableViewController, UlTableViewCell, and UIView.) If you enter any other class, you get the NSObject template with your choice filled in; the other provide skeleton code specialized for those classes.

If you choose one of the view-controller classes, Xcode will give you the option of creating a matching XIB, and indicating whether the target UI is for iPhone or iPad.

▶ **Objective-C category:** Use this template to extend an existing class without subclassing it. Name the category, and specify the class on which the category is to be placed; the default is NSObject. You get .h and .m files, with the base name *className+categoryName*.

▶ **Objective-C protocol:** Produces a header file with a @protocol declaration. The new protocol promises to implement <NSObject>.

▶ **Objective-C test case class:** You're given a choice between an application test and a logic test, but truth be told, there isn't much difference between the two templates: In one, the boilerplate test looks for the application delegate, and in the other, it tests whether integer addition works. You get proper inheritance from SenTestCase and a skeletal test method.

C and C++

These are dirt-simple templates. They #include iostream or stdio.h as the case may be, and they have comment-header blocks. That's it. Creating a .c or .cpp file doesn't even create the counterpart header file. The choices are:

▶ **Header File**

▶ **C File**

▶ **C++ File User Interface**

These are XIBs (and a storyboard) to start you on user-interface elements. They are not accompanied by any corresponding UIKit class declaration; to get one, approach the problem from the other end, and use the Objective-C class template. The only option for these templates is whether you target the iPhone or iPad family.

Be aware that the view-creating XIBs are tied to the family you choose. The root object of the XIB is the size of the device's screen, and you can't resize it. If you want to create a subview in its own XIB, use the **Empty** template, and drag a generic UlView in.

▶ **Storyboard:** Starts a storyboard package for an iOS 5 application.

▶ **View:** Creates a XIB for a view that is the size of the window for your chosen device. The view can be resized vertically to accommodate tabs and toolbars, but otherwise its dimensions are rigid.

▶ **Empty:** The XIB contains nothing at all.

▶ **Window:** A full-screen `UIWindow`. There's not much you can do with it until you drag a `UIView` into it. Dragging more than one view into the top level of a `UlWindow` doesn't work.

▶ **Application:** This is the same as the Window template, but it includes an object linked to the `UIApplication` as a delegate.

Core Data

These are two specialized documents for Core Data, plus a service that converts Core Data entities into Objective-C classes.

▶ **Data Model:** An `.xcdatamodel` is a file that Xcode compiles into a managed-object model (`.mom`) to organize Core Data databases in an application. You started working on data models in Chapter 9, "An iOS Application: Model."

▶ **Mapping Model:** As applications evolve, so do their data models. Porting data from older databases to new schemas is a vexed question. Core Data provides for "mapping models" to help automate the transition. This template asks for the original, source data model and the current, destination model and starts you on a mapping model to convert from the one to the other.

▶ **NSManagedObject subclass:** You used this template in Chapter 9, too. The template asks you to select a data model and entities within that model; it produces the `.h` and `.m` files to wrap those entities in Objective-C classes. Alternatively, you could focus Xcode's editor on a data model, and select **Editor→Create NSManagedObject Subclass**....

Resource

These are files that will be copied, whole and untouched (as you have edited them), into the product bundle.

▶ **GPX File:** You can use waypoints and paths encoded in GPS Exchange Format files to simulate Location Services interactions in the iOS simulator. This template gives you the outline of the XML code with a waypoint set in Cupertino.

▶ **Settings Bundle:** This isn't just one file. This template lays out a bundle directory describing a panel for the Settings app and linking the controls in that panel to your application's preferences.

▶ **Property List:** You worked with this template in Chapter 23, "Property Lists." It's an empty property list file.

▶ **RTF File:** A rich-text file in the commonly understood `.rtf` format. Mac OS X supports RTF natively, but iOS has no native rich-text file format.

▶ **Strings File:** You saw .strings files in Chapter 20, "Localization and Autolayout." .strings files map lists of strings to their versions in another language, so you can localize resources at run time or for translating resources.

Other

These files don't fit in any of the other categories.

▶ **Empty:** Just a blank file.

▶ **Assembly File:** For assembly source. It contains only a comment-header block.

▶ **Configuration Settings File:** This is the .xcconfig file you learned about in Chapter 26. It is blank.

▶ **Resource Rules:** Resource rules tell the codesign utility what elements in your application bundle are to be sealed when the app is signed. You will probably never use this. It may be more useful to Mac OS X applications, but strangely, the template isn't listed on the Mac side.

▶ **Shell Script:** An .sh file, headed with #!/bin/sh and a comment-header block. The rest is up to you.

Mac OS X File Templates

At the file level, the demands of Mac OS X's Cocoa are not that different from those of Cocoa Touch; there is a lot of overlap in the two template sets. I'll cover what's unique, and refer you to the iOS entries for the rest.

Cocoa

▶ **Objective-C class:** As with its iOS counterpart, this template gives you .h and .m files for the class you name, with special handling for certain superclasses (NSDocument, NSView, NSViewController, and NSWindowController). Unlike with the iOS variants, you won't get a matching XIB.

▶ **Objective-C category: Objective-C protocol**, and **Objective-C test case class** are the same as in iOS.

C and C++

These are the same three templates as in the iOS section.

User Interface

These are XIBs, filled out for common tasks in Mac OS X development:

▶ **Application:** This is equivalent to the `MainMenu.xib` file you'd get if you instantiated a Cocoa application template. You get a menu bar and a window. File's Owner is set to the `NSApplication`. You do not get an object to serve as an application delegate.

▶ **Main Menu:** A menu bar, prefilled with the standard menu items. File's owner is the `NSApplication`.

▶ **Window:** A document-style Cocoa window. There is no File's Owner.

▶ **View:** An empty, generic, `NSView`.

▶ **Empty:** It speaks for itself.

Core Data

These are the same templates as in iOS.

Resource

Here you have the same **Property List**, **Rich Text File**, and **Strings File** templates.

Other

There's an **Exports File** for providing the linker with a list of symbols you want to be visible between libraries and applications. Otherwise, the **Empty**, **Assembly File**, **Configuration Settings File**, and **Shell Script** templates are familiar to you.

The File Template Library

There is another way to add files to a project. Use the **View** control in the toolbar to expose the Utility area on the right. Choose the first tab in the lower panel to show the File Template library. The templates in the list parallel the ones you find in the New File assistant. There are no sections, but you can restrict the list to iOS or Mac OS X templates by selecting from the pop-up menu at the top of the library. You can further narrow the list by typing in the search field at the bottom. See Figure C.2.

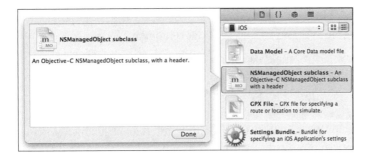

FIGURE C.2   The File Template library is the first tab in the Library pane in the lower part of the Utility area. The pop-up at the top of the library lets you narrow the list by platform, and the search field at the bottom filters the contents by their names and descriptions. Clicking an item and waiting a few seconds makes a pop-over window appear with a description of the template.

You instantiate a template by dragging it from the library into the Project navigator. As with the New File templates in the assistant, the templates usually don't stop at one file: If you drag in the UIViewController subclass template into your project, and respond to the put-file sheet to name and place the file, you'll get the header and implementation files, plus the matching XIB. What you won't get are the configuration options: To use the same example, the new XIB contains an iPhone view; if you want an iPad view, you need to delete the iPhone view from the XIB and insert a fresh one, and manually resize it to 768 x 1004.

Unlike with the Code Snippet library, you cannot add to the File Template library.

Summary

This appendix took you on a tour of the project, target, and file templates Xcode offers you. There is a lot to remember in Cocoa development, and it makes it much easier if you can have files installed for you with reminders of the points you have to hit. You also spent a moment or two on the File Template library, which makes file templates convenient—but at a price in flexibility.

Code snippets are a kind of template, at the subfile level; read all about them in the "Code Completion and Snippets" section of Chapter 11, "Building a New View."

APPENDIX D

Resources

IN THIS APPENDIX

▶ Finding references and tutorials

▶ Getting support

▶ Finding additional tools

I've tried to make this book thorough, but it isn't comprehensive. Xcode is too large and subtle a system to cover exhaustively, and Apple constantly updates it. Further, your needs as a Cocoa programmer go beyond simply using the tools. This appendix is a brief reference to resources you can use to go further and keep current.

Books

Before the iOS gold rush, there were few books about Cocoa and Xcode, and they were mostly quite good. Now, there are a lot more, and there is more...diversity. This time around, I'll offer a few of the better titles:

▶ Buck, Erik, *Cocoa Design Patterns* (2009). Cocoa conforms to a few fundamental patterns, and when you have those down, you've gone a long way toward understanding most of iOS and Mac OS X programming. Erik Buck's book is the best survey available.

▶ Hillegass, Aaron, *Cocoa Programming for Mac OS X*, Fourth Edition (2011), and *More Cocoa Programming for Mac OS X: The Big Nerd Ranch Guide* (2011). *Cocoa Programming* has started more developers on Mac OS X than any other book. You can't go wrong with it.

▶ Hillegass, Aaron, *iOS Programming: The Big Nerd Ranch Guide* (2011). Not interested in Mac OS X? Start here.

▶ Hillegass, Aaron, *Objective-C Programming: The Big Nerd Ranch Guide* (2011). Aaron takes you from C to Objective-C in his only beginner-level book.

▶ Kochan, Stephen, *Programming in Objective-C 2.0*, Fourth Edition (2011). The leading book about Objective-C, but remember that Cocoa is a subject that is orders of magnitude bigger than Objective-C. Make sure your library covers everything you want to know.

▶ Lee, Graham, *Test-Driven iOS Development* (2011). Test early, test every day: Lee's book shows you how.

▶ Neuberg, Matt, *Programming iOS 5: Fundamentals of iPhone, iPad, and iPod Touch Development* (2012). Matt Neuberg offers an exhaustive (1,000+ pages) introduction to all aspects of iOS programming.

On the Net

Do you have a question? Use Google or whatever search engine you prefer. Somebody has probably asked your question before and gotten a satisfactory answer. Even if you intend to ask on a public forum or list, search first. Apple's documentation is on the Web, and the search engines' indices are still better than the one in the Documentation organizer.

Then, if you can't find a good answer, ask. If you can say you've made a diligent attempt to find the answer, the people who can help you will be satisfied that you've done your homework and are worth helping.

If you take Eric Raymond's "How to Ask Questions the Smart Way," `http://catb.org/~esr/faqs/smart-questions.html`, to heart, you won't go far wrong.

Forums

Earlier editions of this book praised mailing lists (and mailing-list archives) and even USENET groups—I'll get to them. Time has moved on. People have become comfortable getting and keeping their knowledge in-the-cloud. Lists that carried more than a hundred messages a day a few years ago now tick along with 20 or fewer. If you want to ask a question, a Web forum may be the better bet.

▶ The Apple Developer Forums are now the main resource for finding solutions to Mac OS X and iOS problems. There are drawbacks, however: You can't get access to the Mac or iOS forums unless you are a paid member of the respective developer programs. Back when the only channels for discussion were public mailing lists, it was impossible to get help on nondisclosed subjects. During the long prerelease period of the iPhone SDK, if you were stumped, the only place to take your troubles was the Apple bug reporter. This had to stop. Apple set up the Web forums to solve the problem, but the trade-off is that you must accept the nondisclosure agreements, and you have to pay.

By the time the iPhone drought ended, people were committed to the forum; Apple never started any iOS-specific mailing lists. The developer forums are the place to go, particularly for iOS questions.

Another trade-off: The search facilities are horrible. The indexer is not customized to the subject of the forums, so if you look for a symbol declared in one of the Apple frameworks, the search engine may suggest you actually meant some technical term from veterinary medicine. If you search in a particular subforum, the initial results will be from that subforum, but if you try to refine the search, it will be applied to everything—iOS, Mac, current, archived, all. And because it is closed to the public, forum content isn't visible to the much better public search engines.

`http://devforums.apple.com/`

▶ Stack Overflow, `http://stackoverflow.com/`, provides an excellent exchange for technical questions of all kinds, Cocoa included. Little chat, a whole lot of solutions. With the Apple forums excluded from web search engines, you will find the best search results lead here.

Mailing Lists

Apple hosts dozens of lists on all aspects of developing for Mac OS X. You can find the full roster at `http://www.lists.apple.com/mailman/listinfo2`. Remember that like all technical mailing lists, these are restricted to questions and solutions for specific problems. Apple engineers read these lists in their spare time, and they are not required to answer postings; they cannot accept bug reports or feature requests. Take those to `http://bugreport.apple.com/`.

These four lists can probably be the most help to you:

▶ **xcode-users**: This list covers Xcode and the other Apple developer tools. It does not deal with programming questions; if you want to ask about what to do with Xcode, rather than how to use it, you'll be better off asking in `cocoa-dev` or `macosx-dev`. `http://www.lists.apple.com/mailman/listinfo2/xcode-users/`

▶ **cocoa-dev**: For questions about the Cocoa frameworks for both Mac OS X and iOS. `http://www.lists.apple.com/mailman/listinfo2/cocoa-dev/`

▶ **macosx-dev**: A list hosted by the Omni Group (makers of OmniOutliner, OmniGraffle, and other great Mac and iOS apps) to support Mac OS X development, regardless of technology. It is fully as useful as the Apple lists. `http://www.omni-group.com/mailman/listinfo/macosx-dev`

▶ **objc-language**: Handles questions about the Objective-C programming language. Questions about Cocoa programming are *not* on-topic here. `http://www.lists.apple.com/mailman/listinfo2/objc-language/`

The `lists.apple.com` website carries archives for each Apple mailing list, but for `xcode-users`, `cocoa-dev`, and Omni Group's `macosx-dev`, CocoaBuilder, `http://www.cocoabuilder.com/`, is the way to go. One crucial advantage is that it can sort search results by date or relevancy and aggregate messages by thread; the Apple site can't. The Cocoa archives go back to 2004; Xcode, 2005.

Developer Technical Support

One resource is in a class by itself. As part of your $99 developer-program membership, you get two incidents with Apple Developer Technical Support (DTS). (You can get more in 5- or 10-packs at about $50 per incident.) If you have a critical question that needs the right answer immediately, forums and mailing lists aren't the way to go. The people who know the right answer aren't required to be there, aren't required to answer, and are not allowed the free time to research your problem.

If you file a DTS incident, you will be assigned an engineer who will respond within 3 business days. He has access to OS source code and to the engineers who wrote it. He (usually) can come up with a solution to your problem that will work even if Apple revises the OS under you.

DTS isn't a gatekeeper for insider techniques. Net of bureaucratic lag, almost everything that has an answer will eventually have a public answer. What you're getting is an engineer with good communications skills, and enough of a knowledge base to respond to your particular problem.

Sites and Blogs

▶ The first place on the Web to go is `http://developer.apple.com/`, the site for Apple Developer Programs. It has everything you can find in Xcode's documentation packages, plus more articles, downloadable examples, business resources, screencasts, and a portal to the iOS, Mac OS X, and Safari developer pages. A good strategy for getting official (public) information from Apple is to do a Google search restricted to `site:developer.apple.com`.

If you browse to the iOS or Mac OS X documentation pages on your iPad, you will find that Apple has formatted them to look *almost* like a native iPad browser, with a split master-detail interface. And it *almost* works—as I write this, it was easy to get the navigation list out of sync with the page on display and be locked into a dead end.

▶ If you find a bug in Apple software, or need a feature, go to `http://bugreport.apple.com`. (You must register with Apple as a developer, but the free program is fine.) Be sure to file a complete report (Apple has guidelines for you), and if you're looking for a new feature, be sure to make a concrete case for how it would improve your product or workflow. `http://developer.apple.com/faq/bugreporting.html` will bring you up to speed on the details.

▶ `http://www.cocoadev.com/` is a wiki encompassing tutorials, references, and links to communities. It's oriented to Mac OS X. As with most wikis, there is a lot of information that hasn't been groomed in quite a while, but it could orient you well enough that you can find your way into the Apple documentation.

▶ Cocoa Literature, `http://cocoalit.com/`, aggregates Cocoa (iOS and Mac OS X) development posts throughout the web.

▶ Mike Ash's Friday Q&A blog covers iOS and Mac OS X topics in depth and breadth. The blog (updated, as you might expect, nearly every week) is at `http://www.mikeash.com/pyblog/`. You can buy it in ebook form from the links at `http://www.mikeash.com/book.html`. Send him money; he deserves it.

▶ `http://www.friday.com/bbum/category/science/technology/apple/mac-os-x/` is the Mac OS X portion of Apple engineer Bill Bumgarner's web log, providing accessible insights on Apple technologies, especially Objective-C, garbage collection, and debugging.

▶ `http://www.wilshipley.com/blog/labels/code.html` is the coding portion of Wil Shipley's web log. You should especially read his "Pimp My Code" series, critical reviews of coding practices based on a deep knowledge of Cocoa design.

▶ Cocoa Samurai, `http://cocoasamurai.blogspot.com/`, is Colin Wheeler's blog of extended articles on intermediate-to-advanced topics in Cocoa development. Look for his series of charts for Xcode keyboard shortcuts; the source, a Pages file, is on GitHub at `https://github.com/Machx/Xcode-Keyboard-Shortcuts`. Donate, if you can.

Face-to-Face

Sitting down with a more experienced developer, and asking how you can accomplish what you want to do, can do more to get you on your way, and faster, than any book (except this one). There are user groups all over the world where you can get help and share your experiences; and there are classes you can take to get up to speed.

Meetings

▶ CocoaHeads, `http://cocoaheads.org/`, is an international federation of user groups for Cocoa programmers. It meets every month in more than 100 cities worldwide.

▶ NSCoder Night, `http://nscodernight.com/`, is a less formal user group, where Cocoa programmers gather as often as weekly in pubs and coffee houses to share experiences and code. The site mentions meetings in nearly 60 cities around the world. Organizing one of your own should be easy; there's a wiki to publicize the location and times.

Classes

Any number of companies and educational institutions can teach you Cocoa programming. I'll mention two good ones, one pricey, one free, but check with your local college; you may be pleasantly surprised.

▶ Stanford University, CS 193, Developing Apps for iOS, `http://www.stanford.edu/class/cs193p/cgi-bin/drupal/`. This is a 25-part lecture series from a course taught by the Computer Science department at Stanford University. It's available free-of-charge through iTunes U—look for the link at the bottom of the front page of the iTunes Store.

▶ Big Nerd Ranch, `http://bignerdranch.com/`, Aaron Hillegass's training company, provides week-long boot camps on Mac OS X, iOS, Cocoa, Rails, Android, and OpenGL, at locations in North America and Europe. Your fee (starting at $3,500) includes lodging, meals, and transportation to and from the airport.

Other Software

The Xcode tools aren't everything. There are things they can't do, and there are things they don't do well. This section examines some tools that can make your life easier. There's more to consider: You can use any number of productivity tools to organize your efforts and provide resources for your apps. (I recommend a good, lean bitmapped-graphics editor, for instance.) I can only survey a few programming tools.

Prices are U.S. dollar equivalents as of late 2011, rounded to the nearest dollar.

Text Editors

The Xcode editor is a machine for producing Cocoa source code. It is crafted to a specific ideal of how a text editor should work. Maybe you don't share that ideal; maybe you need more direct access to text formats for which Xcode interposes a higher-level editor; maybe you need your own tools to customize your work environment.

Even if you're happy with Xcode for most tasks, as a committed Cocoa programmer you'll probably use one or more of these editors as well.

► *BBEdit*, from Bare Bones Software, is particularly good with large files and HTML. It can open anything. Its support for AppleScript, UNIX scripting, and "clipping" macros makes it readily extensible. This book was written in LaTeX with BBEdit. It is available from Bare Bones directly, and from the Mac App Store, but beware: Apple restricts the functionality of App Store releases, and it doesn't allow developers to warn customers about it. The App Store version does not include a suite of command-line tools that let you do edits, comparisons, and searches from scripts; go to Bare Bones's website for an add-on that supplies them. And the App Store version does not allow you to read or save files that you do not own—a must if you need to edit system configuration files; there is no fix for that, other than to buy from Bare Bones directly. `http://www.barebones.com/products/bbedit/` ($50)

> **NOTE**
>
> I should disclose that I am rewriting one of the chapters in the BBEdit manual. I had been a happy user of BBEdit for more than a decade before the subject was broached.

► Bare Bones provides a capable "light" version of BBEdit, *TextWrangler*. What you'll miss are BBEdit's extensive tools for Web development, text completion, version-control support, built-in shell worksheet, and ponies. `http://www.barebones.com/products/textwrangler/` (Free)

► *emacs* and *vi* are supplied with every standard installation of Mac OS X. If you have any background in the UNIX command line, you probably know how to use one of these and have nothing but contempt for the other.

There are Mac (or X Window) variants of both. Check Xemacs, `www.xemacs.org`; and Vico ($40 in the Mac App Store), an editor with vi key bindings that can use TextMate language bundles.

▶ *SubEthaEdit* is a clean editor that permits workgroups to work on a file simultaneously, with all participants contributing and seeing each others' changes in real time. Syntax coloring is available for all commonly-used languages. `http://www.codingmonkeys.de/` ($40)

▶ *TextMate*, from MacroMates, is a text editor with a huge capacity for customization. Syntax coloring and powerful keyboard shortcuts are available for dozens of languages and applications. The long-awaited TextMate 2 is now moving toward release. TextMate has an active user community, and many developers whose products consume formatted text provide free TextMate extension bundles. I use TextMate for all my Rails projects. `http://macromates.com/` ($56)

Accessories

There are many, many supplemental tools for Cocoa developers—check the "Developer Tools" category in the Mac App Store for scores of choices. Here are a few of the most useful:

▶ *Accessorizer*, by Kevin Callahan, started as a simple utility for converting instance-variable declarations in Objective-C classes into getter and setter methods. Well, with Objective-C 2.0, and synthesized ivars for @propertys, that problem is solved, isn't it?

Not so fast. There is still a lot of boilerplate code you must write in a Cocoa application, and Accessorizer can write much of it for you: For instance, if you have array properties, the code to make it a key-value-coding to-many relationship is maddening. Accessorizer can give you skeletons (and usable implementations) for all the methods you need. There's more: `http://www.kevincallahan.org/software/accessorizer.html`, or through the Mac App Store. ($5)

▶ *AppKiDo* and *AppKiDo-for-iPhone*. Documentation for Cocoa is getting better every day, but the format of the documents for the core API hasn't changed in 10 years. Navigation up and down the inheritance tree isn't practical—not all the links are there. Finding a method or class by a part of its name isn't practical—a search in the Documentation organizer can also turn up hundreds of matches in the overview documents. Even finding out what methods a class implements isn't practical—the class references document only the methods a class introduces, not the methods it inherits. AppKiDo provides the solution in a simple browser that shows the class tree and parses the Mac or iOS docset by section and method. One click of the mouse shows you all the methods a class implements.

AppKiDo isn't Apple software, and Apple has no obligation to keep the docsets compatible with AppKiDo's parsing methods, or to warn when they are changing. Apple breaks AppKiDo about once a year, so be prepared to spend a painful week or two waiting for the app to catch up. `http://homepage.mac.com/aglee/downloads/appkido.html` (Free)

▶ *mogenerator*, `http://rentzsch.github.com/mogenerator/`. You saw how Xcode's Data Model editor could take you directly from an entity in the model diagram to a roughed-in implementation for a custom subclass of `NSManagedObject`. What could be better? Well, think a moment: Time has passed. You are wiser. You want to amend your model and regenerate your classes to match, but... you added instance variables and methods of your own. Remember the makeover of the data model in Chapter 17, "Starting a Mac OS X Application." Repeating the class generation will wipe them out.

You can do it by hand. Or at the start, you could have pointed the `mogenerator` command-line tool at your data model and let it produce a fully implemented managed-object class, which `mogenerator` can regenerate as needed, and a subclass of that, to hold your customizations. No more tears. (Free)

Index

Symbols

A

planning, Model-View-Controller (MVC) design pattern, 87-90

provisioning. *See* provisioning

speed, measuring, 173-182

ARC (Automatic Reference Counting), 146, 195-196, 466-467

Mac OS X applications, 246-248

in Xcode 4, 367

archive action (xcodebuild), 401

ARCHS build variable, 480

ARCHS_STANDARD_32_64_BIT build variable, 480

ARCHS_STANDARD_32_BIT build variable, 480

ARCHS_STANDARD_64_BIT build variable, 480

Ash, Mike, 502

assemblers, 55

assembly code, 46, 48

Assembly File template, 496

assertions, SenTestingKit, 168

equality tests, 169

exceptions, 169-170

simple tests, 169

assistant editor, 355-356, 441-442

Assistant Editor command (View menu), 356

ATSApplicationFontsPath key (Info.plist), 316

Attach to Process command (Product menu), 332

attribute accessors, memory management, 463-464

attributes

in KVC (Key-Value Coding), 461

for Passer Rating project, 100-102

autolayout, 292-296

horizontal spacing, 297-300

vertical spacing, 297

automatic code completion, 139-141

Automatic Device Provisioning (ADP), 223-225

Automatic Reference Counting (ARC), 146, 195-196, 466-467

Mac OS X applications, 246-248

in Xcode 4, 367

Automation instrument, 429

Automation instrument template, 434

Automator Action template, 491

Autoresizing, 255-257

B

Bare Bones Software, 504

BBEdit, 504

behavior keys (Info.plist), 322

behaviors, 362-363

Behaviors panel, 40-42

Big Nerd Ranch, 503

binary files, creating universal binaries, 410

binary property lists, 348-349

bindings, 253

Game popover, 269-273

Game table, 268-269

Passer table, 266-268

running, 260-263

Team table, 260

Blame view, 81-82

Blank instrument template, 433

blogs, 502-503

Bluetooth instrument, 429

bookmarks, documentation, 375

books, 499-500

branching, 82-84

breakpoints, 36-37, 443

Breakpoints button, 36

Breakpoints editor, equivalent in Xcode 4, 363

Breakpoints navigator (Xcode 4), 363

browser (Xcode 4), 353-355, 364

browsing documentation, 373-374

Buck, Erik, 499

build action (xcodebuild), 400

Build command (Product menu), 30, 118

build configurations, 396

adding, 398

adjusting, 396-397

build errors, 28-30

build logs, 403-404

Build New Instrument command (Instrument menu), 432

build phases, 58, 390-391

Build Phases tab (Target editor), 49

build process

build configurations, 396-398

build logs, 403-404

build phases, 390-391

Build Settings, 393-395, 438

build transcript example. *See* build transcript example

build variables. *See* build variables

configuration files (.xcconfig), 398-400

custom build rules, 401-403

explained, 389-392

makefiles, 389-390

targets, 390

in Xcode 4, 358

xcodebuild tool, 400-401

Build Results window, equivalent in Xcode 4, 363

Build Settings, 393-395, 438

J–K

How can we make this index more useful? Email us at indexes@samspublishing.com

How can we make this index more useful? Email us at indexes@samspublishing.com

How can we make this index more useful? Email us at indexes@samspublishing.com

X–Z

.xcconfig files, **398**
  creating, 398
  preprocessing, 399-400
  SDK- and architecture-specific settings, 399
.xcdatamodel file, **99**
Xcode 4, **353**
  behaviors, 362-363
  browsers, 353-355, 364
  build process, 358
  desktop, 353-355
  editors
    assistant editor, 355-356
    Editor control, 355
    multiple editors, 356-358
  filtering files/symbols in, 360
  groups and files, 358-360
  Interface Builder, 365-366
  miscellaneous changes in, 366-367
  Source Control, 364-365
  special-purpose editors, 362-364
  Utility area, 365
  Workspace window, 354
  Xcode 3 Info windows, equivalents in,
    360-362
Xcode how-to's, **373**
xcode-users mailing list, **501**
XCODE-VERSION-ACTUAL build variable, **477**
XCODE_VERSION_MINOR build variable, **477**
XCODE_VERSION_MAJOR build variable, **477**
xcodebuild tool, **400-401**
XIB files, **96, 128-129**
  localization
    autolayout, 292-300
    translating view strings, 291
XPC Service template, **491**

zombies, **149, 189-193**
Zombies instrument template, **434**
Zoom menu (instrument configuration), **421**

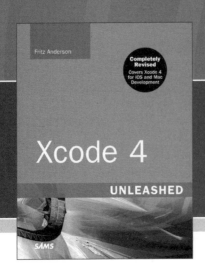

FREE
Online Edition

Safari®
Books Online

Your purchase of *Xcode 4 Unleashed* includes access to a free online edition for 45 days through the **Safari Books Online** subscription service. Nearly every Sams Publishing book is available online through **Safari Books Online**, along with thousands of books and videos from publishers such as Addison-Wesley Professional, Cisco Press, Exam Cram, IBM Press, O'Reilly Media, Prentice Hall, Que, and VMware Press.

Safari Books Online is a digital library providing searchable, on-demand access to thousands of technology, digital media, and professional development books and videos from leading publishers. With one monthly or yearly subscription price, you get unlimited access to learning tools and information on topics including mobile app and software development, tips and tricks on using your favorite gadgets, networking, project management, graphic design, and much more.

Activate your FREE Online Edition at
informit.com/safarifree

STEP 1:   Enter the coupon code: TMYREAA.

STEP 2:   New Safari users, complete the brief registration form.
Safari subscribers, just log in.

If you have difficulty registering on Safari or accessing the online edition,
please e-mail customer-service@safaribooksonline.com